MW01383521

The Second Coming of Paisley

Irish Studies
James MacKillop, *Series Editor*

Other titles in Irish Studies

Collaborative Dubliners: Joyce in Dialogue
Vicki Mahaffey, ed.

Dance Lessons: A Novel
Áine Greaney

Gender and Medicine in Ireland, 1700–1950
Margaret Preston and Margaret Ó hÓgartaigh, eds.

Ireland in Focus: Film, Photography, and Popular Culture
Eoin Flannery and Michael Griffin, eds.

The Irish Bridget: Irish Immigrant Women in Domestic Service in America, 1840–1930
Margaret Lynch-Brennan

Making Ireland Irish: Tourism and National Identity since the Irish Civil War
Eric G. E. Zuelow

Memory Ireland, Volume 1: *History and Modernity*
Oona Frawley, ed.

Memory Ireland, Volume 2: *Diaspora and Memory Practices*
Oona Frawley, ed.

Of Irish Descent: Origin Stories, Genealogy, and the Politics of Belonging
Catherine Nash

Suburban Affiliations: Social Relations in the Greater Dublin Area
Mary P. Corcoran, Jane Gray, and Michel Peillon

The Second Coming of Paisley

Militant Fundamentalism and Ulster Politics

Richard Lawrence Jordan

SYRACUSE UNIVERSITY PRESS

First Edition 2013
13 14 15 16 17 18 6 5 4 3 2 1

∞ The paper used in this publication meets the minimum requirements of the American National Standard for Information Sciences—Permanence of Paper for Printed Library Materials, ANSI Z39.48-1992.

For a listing of books published and distributed by Syracuse University Press, visit our website at SyracuseUniversityPress.syr.edu.

ISBN: 978-0-8156-3313-6

Library of Congress Cataloging-in-Publication Data
Available upon request from the publisher.

Manufactured in the United States of America

Contents

PART THREE

The Second Coming: *Paisley and Amillennial Politics*

The World of Academia

The acknowledgments for this book are intentionally short. Graduate schools—this work is derived from my dissertation at Louisiana State University, Baton Rouge—are notorious for those who help students and those who do not. That said, Meredith Veldman, my dissertation adviser, James Rogers of St. Thomas University and *New Hibernia Review*, Irene Whelan of Manhattanville College, New York, and James MacKillop of the Syracuse Press deserve special notice.

Moreover, as younger scholars conduct research, a love–hate relationship develops with the library/archival world: there are many librarians/archivists whose competency can be questioned, but there are also stars within the arcane world of catalogued and stored knowledge, and their help greatly added to the insights contained within this book. Without Stephen Gregory, who at the time of writing was the librarian of the Union Theological College in Belfast; Kenneth Henke from the Special Collections at Princeton Theological Seminary; Grace Mullen of Westminster Theological Seminary; and Patrick Robbins (as well as his staff of graduate students—the boys), who directs the Fundamentalism File at Bob Jones University, the thesis developed within this book would have been less innovative.

Abbreviations

ACCC	American Council of Christian Churches
BCPCC	British Council of Protestant Christian Churches
CDU	Campaign for Democracy in Ulster
CSJ	Campaign for Social Justice
DCAC	Derry Citizens' Action Committee
DHAC	Derry Housing Action Committee
DUP (UDUP)	(Ulster) Democratic Unionist Party
ECONI	Evangelical Contribution on Northern Ireland
EPS	Evangelical Protestant Society
FCC	Federal Council of Churches of Christ in America
HUAC	House Un-American Activities Committee
IBPFM	Independent Board for Presbyterian Foreign Missions
ICCC	International Council of Christian Churches
ICR	Irish Christian Relief
IRA	Irish Republican Army
IRS	US Internal Revenue Service
MFSA	Methodist Federation for Social Action
MP	member of Parliament
NCC	National Council of Churches of Christ in America
NICRA	Northern Ireland Civil Rights Association

NILP	Northern Ireland Labour Party
NUP	National Union of Protestants
PUP	Protestant Unionist Party
RUC	Royal Ulster Constabulary
SDLP	Social Democratic and Labour Party
UCDC	Ulster Constitution Defence Committee
UDA	Ulster Defense Association
UPA	Ulster Protestant Action
UPI	United Press International
UPV	Ulster Protestant Volunteers
UUP	Ulster Unionist Party
UVF	Ulster Volunteer Force
WCC	World Council of Churches

PART ONE

The Old Testament

The Background to Paisleyism

Introduction

On 4 October 1969, an enthusiastic crowd watched the Reverend Ian Paisley christen the new Martyrs Memorial Free Presbyterian Church in East Belfast, Northern Ireland. The approximately seven thousand Christians in attendance either were members of the new church or belonged to Northern Ireland's twenty-nine Free Presbyterian congregations or were supporters of the Reverend Paisley who attended other Protestant denominations. The new church, the largest in the British Isles, illustrated the growth that the Free Presbyterian Church of Ulster had enjoyed since 1951, when Free Presbyterianism began as a single congregation, as well as the growing religious and political influence Paisley exerted over the province's Protestant community.[1] The appearance of non–Free Presbyterians was important—they represented the support within Ulster Protestantism for the Calvinist and evangelical Christianity Paisley espoused and for the preacher's Unionist and Loyalist politics.[2]

A small number of attendees were not Irish, and their presence was more significant. Two British Baptists—the Reverends Brian Green of London and Jack Glass from Glasgow, Scotland—represented the influence and fellowship that Paisley held within Great Britain's small community of fundamentalist preachers. Arguably more important was the appearance of two leaders of America's militant fundamentalist community—the Reverend Carl McIntire of Collingswood, New Jersey, and Dr. Robert "Bob" Reynolds Jones Jr. from Greenville, South Carolina. Paisley and his four visiting allies symbolized the well-established and international bond of militant fundamentalist religiosity that converged in Ulster—Bob Jones's father preached in Belfast in 1934; McIntire had met Paisley when visiting Ireland in 1951; and Glass and Green had first come to Northern Ireland in the early 1960s. All five ministers of this transatlantic brotherhood shared three tenets: an adherence to traditional Calvinism; a belligerent rejection of Christian modernism, liberalism, and ecumenism; as well as an hostility toward the Roman Catholic Church. Moreover, these militants argued for complete separation from Christians who did not share their theology; for them, this "apostate" group included moderate fundamentalists and "New Evangelicals" as well as clerics and theologians who argued for a liberal version of Christian theology and joined ecumenical groups such as the World Council of Churches.[3]

Calvinism constituted a central tenet within militant fundamentalism in contrast to the theology of many moderate fundamentalists and evangelicals who took an Arminian position toward salvation. Although the theology John Calvin developed is well known, it is appropriate to note that the five basic points of Calvinism are: the total depravity of man; unconditional election; perseverance of the saints; irresistible grace; and limited atonement where Jesus Christ's crucifixion saves only those God elected (or predestination). Arminians accept the first four tenets but argue that personal decision can influence the work of the Holy Ghost, and humans make a conscious choice to accept or refuse Jesus Christ as their savior. Most militant fundamentalists adhered to a moderate understanding of God's election—the unconverted have an invitation to Christ through scripture and the work of the Holy Ghost—in contrast to conservative Calvinists, who proclaimed a traditional or "hyper"-Calvinist view of predestination: to conservatives, election comes only through God's grace and the Atonement. However, the moderate position that many militants accepted allows for revival and evangelization of the gospel.[4] Paisley and the British and American militants were also premillennialists who believed the Second Coming of Christ to be imminent and urged a Christian revival in preparation. Premillennials asserted that the duty of a "true" Christian is to save souls; Christ's return would begin the millennium, or one-thousand-year reign of God's Kingdom on Earth, and would be preceded by a series of signs—great apostasy in Christian churches, natural disasters and wars, the appearance of the Antichrist, the conversion of most Jews to Christianity and their return to Israel, and the tribulation of true believers to heaven. A vital component to premillennial eschatology requires "true Christians to expose liberalism and modernism and the work of the devil on Earth while eagerly awaiting Christ's kingdom; the combination will induce the End Times. In order to hasten the Second Coming, militant fundamentalists were charged by God to fight apostate organizations.[5]

Premillennial eschatology stood in contrast to the postmillennialism that liberals and modernists argued—human endeavors (a social gospel) would bring about the righteous, Christian world of the millennium, after which Christ would return, and the tribulation would take place. Both pre- and postmillennials argued that their version of the Second Coming called for revival of the Christian church—to prepare and lead Christians toward salvation. Before Christ could return, the gospel had to be preached to all nations—thus the importance of international fellowship. Militants employed revivalism not to convert the entire world to the Kingdom of God or to promote a social gospel, but to prepare the "Elect" for heaven. Although God's grace alone would save the Elect, the Holy Ghost can work through evangelists to bring them closer to God. Thus, militants saw themselves as God's chosen messengers to the Elect and only the Elect; they did not associate with Christians they believed to be apostate. This eschatology, combined with their Calvinist theology, influenced their political and religious views.[6]

The five militant preachers who gathered in East Belfast in October 1969 not only represented the internationalism of the fight against heterodoxy but exemplified the historical, cultural, and theological relationships between British, Irish, and American Protestantism. From the sixteenth century, several centuries of emigration—which began in Scotland, passed through Northern Ireland, and ended in North America—built a transatlantic connection. The plantation of Scottish and English Calvinism into the American colonies established a Reformed basis for American Protestantism, and the revivalism born in the British Isles helped evangelism to become the core of American religiosity and national culture. Therefore, revivalism created a theological bridge spanning England, Scotland, Northern Ireland, and North America. Revivalism not only helped to embed English and Scottish Calvinism into the American colonies but also shaped the fundamentalism that Americans formulated in the late nineteenth century, which traveled back to Northern Ireland in the 1920s.[7]

The presence of Irish, American, and British militants in Belfast that Sunday in 1969 testified not only to Martyrs Memorial's position as the bastion of militant fundamentalism in Ireland, but also to the church's locus as the springboard for militant fundamentalist politics in Ulster. The new church represented the theological relationship between Paisley, McIntire, and the Bob Jones family and was the nexus for three and a half centuries of Irish, British, and American political and religious controversies. All five clergymen personified the transatlantic political and Protestant tradition that opposed Christian liberalism and modernism and that in the twentieth century crusaded against civil rights, communism, and the Roman Catholic Church. They argued in favor of a political and Knoxian form of Calvinism and agreed that religious leaders could enter the political arena if the state failed to protect "Bible Protestantism."[8]

The Importance of Militant Fundamentalism

The opening of Martyrs Memorial marked a crossroad between the radical evangelicalism that defined Paisley's early career and the new political activism that shaped the following four decades. Employing memories of the Reformation and perceived visions of Roman Catholic repression, Paisley's sermons routinely referred to Martin Luther, the theologies of John Calvin and John Knox, and the cultural and theological connections between Calvinist Scotland, Protestant Ireland, and fundamentalist America. In the late 1940s and into the 1950s, Paisley took these images, his Calvinism and revivalism, and formulated them into a crusade against what he viewed as apostasy in Irish Protestant churches.[9] In the 1960s, he carried this religious crusade into the political arena when he opposed the ecumenical dialogue between the Church of England and the Roman Catholic Church, attacked Prime Minister Terence O'Neill's Northern Ireland government, and confronted the Catholic civil rights movement. These separate but related campaigns helped to form the movement dubbed "Paisleyism," Northern Ireland's indigenous militant fundamentalism. Paisley protested the Anglican attendance at the Second Vatican Council and every meeting between the Anglican leadership, the British royalty, and the Vatican, and he contested O'Neill's efforts to modernize Northern Ireland's economy, which required a rapprochement with Ulster's Catholic community. He attacked the discussions between Canterbury and Rome as treason, denounced "O'Neillism"[10] as a political form of ecumenism, and "exposed" civil rights as both a Roman Catholic and Communist front. The Paisley crusade against O'Neillism and Catholic civil rights was a major factor inciting the spiral of Catholic–Protestant communal tension, which exploded into sectarian violence, the deployment of the British army onto the streets of Ulster, and the imposition of British political and social policy over Northern Ireland. Paisley's denunciation of High Church Anglicanism during the 1960s was political as well as theological. However, it was not until the spring of 1969 that Paisley focused less on promoting premillennial fundamentalism and attacking Protestant apostasy and more toward building a political career that included a constituted political party and seats in the provincial, British, and European parliaments. By April 1970, Paisley had moved from opposition to the Unionist administration and Catholic civil rights and instead into the promotion of Loyalist politics.[11]

A fundamentalist background was important in the development of Paisleyism. Fundamentalism arose during the nineteenth and early twentieth centuries out of the theological and cultural differences alienating traditional, small-town America from the rising power and new morality of the urban, industrializing United States. To fundamentalists, traditional Protestantism meant a literal interpretation of the Bible as the sole and inerrant Word of God, a premillennial expectation of the Second Coming of Jesus Christ, and an adherence to revivalism and evangelicalism. Objecting to liberal and modernist theology as well as to the new culture developing within urban America, fundamentalism defended the conservative tenets of American Protestant churches and the Protestant basis of American society.[12]

In the 1920s, William Patterson (W. P.) Nicholson introduced US-style fundamentalism to a wide segment of the Protestant community in Northern Ireland. Nicholson's crusades took place during the contentious years that saw the partition of Ireland and the founding of the Northern Ireland statelet as a devolved province of the United Kingdom.

The formation of a Protestant state in Ulster caused substantial violence between the Catholic and Protestant communities, and fundamentalism accordingly became associated with sectarianism. Nicholson's fundamentalism also inspired more Ulster Protestants to question the liberalism and modernism popular among Ulster's clergy and academics, especially within the Presbyterian Church in Ireland. For example, in the 1920s Presbyterian fundamentalists instigated a major heresy trial in the Presbyterian General Assembly and joined with the Baptists and independents to separate from mainstream denominations.[13]

The Irish Evangelical Church was one such separating body. Its evangelical activities during the 1930s and 1940s encouraged a cross-section of Northern Ireland's fundamentalist community to withdraw from Protestant churches. The new church's founding clerics had connections to Princeton Theological Seminary and J. Gresham Machen, who was an important mentor to the Reverend Carl McIntire before they experienced their own falling out. Prior to the Second World War, Ulster separatists had few outlets to expand their community, and so they worked together to oppose liberalism and modernism. After 1945, the growth of Protestant gospel halls and small independent congregations gave fundamentalists a wider community and more opportunity to evangelize. The new conditions enabled militants to organize a larger fellowship as well as to question other fundamentalists with whom they disagreed on theological grounds.[14]

Paisley's transformation from a predominately religious crusader into a full-fledged politician was influenced, of course, by Northern Ireland's unique history and sectarian relationships. However, his crusade would have developed in a different manner if American militant fundamentalism had not been injected into his theology, his style of protest, and his self-image as a "martyr" and "prophet." To militant fundamentalists, Paisley became a martyr when he was put in jail in 1966 and a prophet in the 1970s after he made political proclamations that proved true (for instance, he prophesized direct rule). Starting in the 1950s, Paisley copied McIntire's style of public protest as well as his propensity to vehemently attack anyone who failed to follow his lead. McIntire's targets included fellow fundamentalists whom he perceived as weak in their opposition to Christian ecumenism and liberalism, Christian clergymen suspected of Communist and socialist sympathies, and even the US government, whose Cold War policies struck McIntire as passive and treasonous as well as an attack on Bible Protestantism.[15]

In the mid-1960s, a growing relationship with American militant fundamentalists enabled Paisley to visit the United States, trips that changed Northern Irish history. From April 1965 through the spring of 1968, Paisley made annual speaking tours of the United States and witnessed the social changes that the American civil rights movement, supported by effective federal government action, was imposing on American society. He spoke during the volatile period when the American South was forced to eliminate segregation in public facilities, to integrate schools, and to grant African Americans the right to vote. During the week in April 1968 that James Earl Ray assassinated Martin Luther King Jr. in Memphis and intense racial violence exploded in American cities, Paisley was attending the annual Bob Jones Bible Conference. It is no coincidence that when the Northern Ireland civil rights movement hit the streets of Ulster four months later, Paisley led the most vigorous counterdemonstrations. The defiance toward Catholic civil rights marked the newest and most radical element within Paisleyism.[16]

After twelve months of contentious civil rights marches and Paisleyite counterdemonstrations, sectarian street fighting erupted in Londonderry, Belfast, and other major cities in Northern Ireland. The violence resulted in the deployment of British army units on the streets of Ulster and Westminster's direct involvement in provincial security and communal affairs.[17] In the fall of 1969, the political situation in Northern Ireland and the deterioration of communal relations enhanced the significance of the opening of Martyrs Memorial Church and redirected Paisley's crusade toward a stronger involvement in the political process.[18] As British army operations grew and sectarian street fighting continued, and as the new Irish Republican Army (IRA) campaign unfolded, Paisley and his militant supporters were increasingly convinced that the policies of both the Unionist and British governments were incapable of maintaining public order. Moreover, Paisley believed that British efforts to mediate the Catholic–Protestant political division in Ulster threatened to increase Catholic political and ecumenical power and would lead to unification with the Republic of Ireland. The prospects of a united Ireland convinced him to mobilize supporters for political actions that took on the aura of a Protestant revival: "The irrevocable damage done . . . must not continue—you the electorate can play your role in delivering Ulster from the fate that our enemies have in store for us. The Loyalist motto—For God and Ulster—is most explicit; our faith is in God to maintain us, personally and rationally. Cast your vote for the Loyalist cause, and by so doing contribute to the Deliverance of Ulster."[19]

But combining religion and politics compromised Paisley's premillennial theology, moving it toward an amillennial position. Amillennialism is the traditional position the majority of Christian churches have professed since Christ's crucifixion and was the dominate view until the mid–nineteenth century. Amillennialism contradicts both post- and premillennial eschatology and argues that the Christian church has been in the millennium since Christ's time on earth, although this age is coming to an end. The Second Coming will not be preceded by a tribulation of Christians; the world will not be converted to Christianity before Christ comes; and God's Kingdom on Earth will not be established. Amillennials further assert that the world consists of both good and evil, which will continue to coexist until the Second Coming—when Christ appears, the Antichrist will be defeated, and a final judgment will occur. All "true" Christians will ascend to heaven afterward. Amillennials accepted the need for revival and evangelization, but the Elect do not have to be converted or a social gospel promoted.[20] Beginning in the 1970s, no longer was the primary focus of Paisley's crusade to prepare the Elect for Christ's return and therefore to demand that the Northern Irish government and Protestant churches follow God's commandments. Instead, he focused on constitutional politics to better protect God's Elect and to fight evil in the forms of Catholic civil rights, the unification of Ireland, and secular politics. His political agenda included four primary concerns: the organization of a new Northern Ireland government, the political relationship between the province and Westminster, the British government's efforts to bring Catholic political parties and the Republic of Ireland into the local political settlement, and the campaign against IRA violence. Another indication of Paisley's move toward amillennial politics was prophetic and at the time did not seem contradictory to his premillennial religiosity: in the early 1970s, Paisley and his supporters began considering a future with him as the political leader of the Ulster Protestant community.[21]

As Paisley became increasingly involved in the political process, he took on the public persona of an amillennial politician who would compromise his theology for political gain. If he had adopted political amillennialism during the 1950s and 1960s, it would not have been possible for him to develop into Northern Ireland's leading militant fundamentalist, to attack Irish fundamentalists who did not follow separatism, or to develop the bond with Carl McIntire and Bob Jones University and with militants throughout the British Isles. But the chain of events that transpired during the 1960s made the transition possible in the following decade: Paisley would not have moved toward amillennial politics if sectarian street fighting had not broken out in August 1969 and the British army deployed onto the street of Ulster.

Without the onset of civil rights activism and O'Neillism, Paisley's campaigns would have remained religious in focus and the advent of Free Presbyterianism would have been a minor historical incident that linked the Calvinism and revivalism of the British Isles with the militant fundamentalism that emerged in North America.[22] Moreover, without the influence of American militant fundamentalism, there would have been no Paisleyism. Even more important, it is possible to argue that the communal fighting would not have taken place if Paisley had chosen to ignore the Northern Ireland civil rights movement and that civil rights activism would have been less radical if "Paisleyite" activities had not made it difficult for Terence O'Neill to implement political and economic reforms. Without Paisleyism, it is safe to say, the "Troubles" would have unfolded very differently—if they unfolded at all.

From 1969 on, Paisley embarked on a political career during which he slowly and steadily betrayed his premillennial, militant fundamentalism. He formed the Ulster Democratic Unionist Party (DUP) in September 1971 and devoted more attention to political negotiations and campaigning and less to his crusade against Protestant apostasy. His attacks on the British government, the Ulster Unionist Party (UUP), and the Catholic

Church took on a secular and political tone. Throughout the extensive negotiations and political campaigns during the following two decades, Paisley and the DUP took a hard-line stance: they would not negotiate with Sinn Fein, refused to allow moderate Catholic politicians to sit as equals in a power-sharing government, and rejected a role for the Republic of Ireland in the Northern Ireland government. In the late 1990s, however, Paisley began to moderate. Furthermore, when the Democratic Unionist Party accepted a power-sharing agreement with the Social Democratic and Labour Party and agreed to consider an executive that included Sinn Fein, Paisley compromised the DUP's past political principles. In May 2007, the conversion to amillennial politics was complete when Paisley agreed to become Northern Ireland's first minister, and the DUP formed an administration with Sinn Fein as its junior partner.[23]

Paisley paid a high price for his political actions: he was "asked" to step down as the moderator of the Free Presbyterian Church, ending a fifty-six-year career as the church's only moderator, and he resigned as first minister and leader of the DUP. By May 2008, he had turned his back on all three positions.[24] Paisley's conversion to amillennial politics and his willingness to compromise with what he formerly condemned as "evil" are ironic: there is no doubt that the crusading preacher of the 1950s and 1960s would have vehemently opposed First Minister Paisley of 2007. Furthermore, not all Free Presbyterians and Democratic Unionists shared Paisley's new millenarian view. Many Free Presbyterians in Ulster felt betrayed and asserted that they would retain their adherence to the Paisleyite premillennial and militant fundamentalism that their former leader had discarded, and a militant fringe within the DUP argued for separation and a new political party to assert traditional Paisleyism.[25]

A Brief Historiography of Paisleyism

The Northern Ireland Troubles have been one of the most extensively studied conflicts in modern history. In early historiography, historians described Ulster's sectarian strife as economic class warfare and viewed the communal divide as a racial, multinational, and ethnic conflict between two competing cultures; the religious divide was considered largely cultural and theology therefore inconsequential.[26] Political historians asserted that Northern Ireland's system of pseudo-democracy drove the sectarian struggle: Northern Ireland contained two competing communities that employed their own nationalist myths for their own political aspirations. According to this theory, Paisleyism and Unionist dissent were a reaction to Terence O'Neill's policies. Only after O'Neill could not introduce meaningful reforms did the civil rights movement begin direct-action protests. When Paisley counterdemonstrated, the civil rights movement exploded into violence.[27]

Sociologists developed a deprivation theory: as the education of Catholics increased following the Second World War, they better comprehended their disadvantages in relation to the Protestant community and were more willing to consider violence in an attempt to end discrimination. Because the Catholic middle class generally shunned radical activism until the late 1960s, it was working-class activists who led the radicalization of the civil rights movement. The Protestant working class also suffered a sense of deprivation in relation to the Protestant middle and upper classes. An understanding of this economic gap inspired Protestant working-class extremists to form paramilitary organizations and to follow Paisley in an attempt to protect their percentage of Protestant privileges.[28]

Although Marxist historians further asserted that the deprivation of the working class created the civil rights movement, they also argued that the British and Northern Ireland governments manipulated the economic and social condition of the Protestant and Catholic working classes in order to maintain power. The British government supported the policies of the UUP to benefit British capitalists. In addition, Unionist policies were designed to deter the Protestant and Catholic working classes from uniting and threatening the Protestant ascendancy's political control of the Northern Ireland state.[29] But as the violence expanded in the 1970s, historians began to look at the Troubles as an internal conflict over political power, contradicting the core Marxist theory.[30]

During the initial years of sectarian violence, scholars generally presented the conflict in secular terms. In these accounts, Paisley appeared as a religious oddity and only one of numerous antagonists. Paisley had a role, but he appeared as the voice of a militant Protestant fringe that simply acerbated the core tension between British imperialism and Irish

Catholic nationalism. In the 1980s, however, historians began a broader analysis of Paisley's role. Several biographies examined Paisley's career and tried both to explain the meaning behind his religious crusade and to assess his effect on the civil rights movement. Ed Moloney, Andy Pollak, and Patrick Marrinan argued that Paisley's religious bigotry instigated communal violence, whereas Clifford Smyth added a position more sympathetic to Paisley, contending that Paisley articulated the Protestant community's anxiety. Steve Bruce, then a sociologist at Queen's University in Belfast, took a more sophisticated look at Paisleyism as the legitimate voice of a substantial segment of the Protestant community. He argued that although Paisleyism might appear bigoted to Catholics, Paisley's religious and political outlook developed out of a sincere concern to defend Bible Protestantism and the political union between Northern Ireland and Great Britain.[31]

These studies noted but did not explain fully Paisley's relationship with American militant fundamentalism. For example, Bruce examined Paisley's alliance with militant fundamentalists in America, but only with Bob Jones University.[32] A number of scholars, including Owen Dudley Edwards, briefly noted the Paisley–McIntire fellowship but presented this relationship as essentially peripheral to Paisley's activities and crusade in Northern Ireland. Only Martha Abele MacIver's 1984 dissertation on the influence of John Knox and John Calvin on Paisley's politics looked at the Bob Jones connection in more depth and linked Paisley with McIntire. MacIver argued that Paisley, the Jones family, and McIntire shared the same apocalyptic worldview, adhered to traditional Calvinism, and saw the Roman Catholic Church as the enemy of Protestant freedom. Moreover, F. Eugene Scott wrote a brief article on the political preaching tradition in Ulster and illustrated that Paisley's belligerent style followed a strategy established in the 1950s by Carl McIntire and Billy James Hargis, the Tulsa, Oklahoma–based anti-Communist crusader—a combination of American revivalism, confrontation, and political evangelism.[33]

As the Northern Ireland peace process progressed from the Sunningdale Agreement of 1973 through the Republican hunger strikes of 1980 and to the Anglo-Irish and Belfast Agreements and the paramilitary cease-fires that transpired over the following three decades, a substantial historiography of Northern Ireland politics emerged. Historians have produced a large library on the more important subjects, such as Unionist political relationships, the transformation of the Republican movement and Loyalist paramilitaries in the peace process, and the multifaceted relationship between the British and Dublin governments, on the one hand, and the Northern Ireland political parties, on the other. The politico Ian Paisley and the DUP have been portrayed as increasingly important participants. Even newer studies reflecting on the peace process have analyzed the end game of a long-running communal conflict but have minimized the theological aspect to Paisley's political activities. Paisley has been described as having a split personality—a powerful minister with an increasing appetite for political action.[34]

Only in the 1990s did the focus of the scholarship on Paisley shift from his religious activities of the 1950s and 1960s to his political career and leadership of the DUP. The transformation enabled more recent works to take a closer look at his move from a premillennial crusader to an amillennial politician. Gladys Ganiel has more recently produced valuable research connecting Ulster evangelicalism, the Free Presbyterian Church, and DUP politics as well as showing how the DUP adapted its ideology to political realities, such as homosexual rights.[35] Ed Moloney has expanded his earlier work with Andy Pollak to include a discussion of Paisley's deteriorating relationship with the Free Presbyterian Church in Ulster. Using privileged information from Free Presbyterian proceedings, Moloney briefly explores the reasons that Paisley compromised his earlier militancy in order to accept power sharing with Sinn Fein. Moloney does not attribute the reversal to a changed theology but cites Paisley's egotism, his desire to join the British establishment, and a long-term political plan. Although Steve Bruce and Patrick Mitchel contend that Paisley's political ascent might have compromised his theology, they do not adequately explain the connection between American militants and Paisley's militant fundamentalist crusade and political career.[36]

With the exception of Bruce and MacIver, earlier historians and sociologists who studied Northern Ireland limited their sources to those available in the British Isles: government records, parliamentary debates, and local media—both the secular press and the Free Presbyterian periodicals

The Revivalist and *The Protestant Telegraph*—were important sources, and interviews with Free Presbyterians were a consistent source of information. Paisley's published sermons articulated his religious views, and the DUP manifestos explained the party's platform. These writers, however, made little use of the American sources intimately connecting Paisley to American militant fundamentalists. For instance, the archives of Bob Jones University, the publications of the International Council of Christian Churches (an international fellowship in which Paisley and the Free Presbyterian Church were members until the mid-1970s), the *Christian Beacon* (the mouthpiece of Carl McIntire's Bible Presbyterian Church), and numerous other militant fundamentalist newspapers, such as the *Western Voice* published by Dr. Harvey Springer in Colorado and covering Paisley's activities in the late 1960s, were largely, although not entirely, ignored. Moreover, newly available resources—such as the Carl McIntire Collection held at Princeton Theological Seminary, which includes the correspondence between Carl McIntire, Paisley, and other Ulster fundamentalists during the 1950s—have not been researched until this study.[37]

1

The Transatlantic Background to Fundamentalism

When the Reverend Ian Paisley preached his first sermon to Martyrs Memorial Free Presbyterian Church, his message painted an image of the long transatlantic history of Calvinism, revivalism, and Bible Protestantism. He derived much of his Christian faith from the connection between British and North American culture and religiosity that had begun with the Puritan emigration and culminated in American militant fundamentalism. Paisley's religiosity betrayed his western Scottish and militant Ulster Protestant heritage. His immediate family came from a Scottish lineage that included the evangelical Church of Ireland and the Orange Order (the Loyal Orange Institution or, later, Grand Orange Lodge of Ireland) and that for generations had resided in County Tyrone in a contentious area evenly divided between Catholic and Protestant. The family's religious and political traditions inspired Paisley's father to join the Ulster Volunteer Force in 1912, to adopt staunch Loyalism and Unionism, and to develop an antagonism toward the Catholic Church.[1]

Paisley's family history supplemented his theology: James Kyle Paisley, Ian's father, a preacher who espoused an anti-Catholic, antimodernist, and antiliberal message, pushed his son toward theological militancy. Kyle Paisley's parents' devout Protestantism had influenced their son to become "saved" at age seventeen while attending a gospel campaign held in the Omagh YMCA. After this experience, the young man believed that he was divinely destined for the Lord's work. Within months of his conversion, Kyle Paisley joined the Baptist Church and took to itinerant preaching, organizing house meetings and open-air prayer sessions until called to lead a small, independent group that met in the Omagh Orange Hall in Grangemore. His ministry quickly expanded, and he began preaching to a wide range of Ulster's Protestants, including Independents, Baptists, Presbyterians, and Congregationalists. Kyle Paisley's tent-meeting ministry and his willingness to preach to diverse but conservative churches indicate an early path toward revivalism and nondenominationalism separatism.[2]

In October 1918, Kyle Paisley became the pastor of a small Baptist congregation in Armagh, whose members embraced the new fundamentalist doctrine. The twelve-member church espoused biblical infallibility and the divinity of Christ as well as the Reformed doctrines of salvation through God's grace and God's covenant with the righteous. Over the next decade, Kyle Paisley built the congregation to fifty-four members, and his Armagh ministry served as a stepping-stone. In May 1928, he moved to the larger Hill Street Baptist Church in Ballymena, a city that lay in the heart of Ulster's "Bible Belt."[3]

The elder Paisley did not agree with the entire doctrine that the Baptist Union of Great Britain and Ireland professed, and within five years he broke with it over what he saw as a tolerance for modernism. English Baptists, in communion with their conservative Irish brethren, were extremely active in adopting ecumenical ideas, and there were concerns that the Baptist Missionary Society supported liberal missionaries. Like many evangelicals in Ulster, Kyle Paisley was influenced by the fundamentalism of W. P. Nicholson, a position that drove him to withdraw from the Baptist Union.[4] Copying Nicholson, he preached a strong, uncompromising message against ecumenism and liberalism—a message that was not universally popular within his congregation. Not every member of his church accepted the decision to leave the Baptist Union or his attacks on several church congregants he charged with immorality. One member owned the land under a pub, and another reputedly had numerous affairs with local women. Refusing to heed a demand from the Baptist Union to repudiate his accusations, Kyle Paisley led a minority into a new independent fundamentalist church, the Waveney Road Tabernacle.[5] The new congregation drew up a Reformed and premillennial statement of faith adopted from the confession written by the famed nineteenth-century evangelical preacher Charles Haddon Spurgeon:

> We the undersigned, banded together in fraternal union, observing with growing pain and sorrow the loosening hold of many upon the truths of Revelation, are constrained to avow our firmest belief in the verbal inspiration of all Holy Scripture as originally given. To us, the Bible does not merely contain the Word of God, but is the Word of God. From beginning to end, we accept it, believe it, and continue to preach it. . . . We hold and maintain the truths generally known as "the doctrines of grace." The electing love of God the Father, the propitiatory and substitutionary sacrifice of His Son, Jesus Christ, regeneration by the Holy Ghost, the imputation of Christ's righteousness, the justification of the sinner (once for all) by faith, his walk in newness of life and growth in grace by the active indwelling of the Holy Ghost, and the priestly intercession of our Lord Jesus, as also the hopeless perdition of all who reject the Saviour. . . . Our hope is the personal pre-millennial return of the Lord Jesus in glory.[6]

Spurgeon had opposed hyper-Calvinism and had asserted a religiosity that allowed evangelizing to the unconverted; through evangelicalization, the Holy Ghost would lead the Elect to their salvation. Spurgeon's willingness to attack Christian leaders he thought liberal or modernist and his willingness to withdraw from the Baptist Union of Ireland and accept censure for his convictions inspired Kyle Paisley and his congregation. Spurgeon had called for separation from apostates—individuals and denominations—but not from like-minded Christians who remained in their denominations. In a tribute to his parents written nearly fifty years later, Ian Paisley reminisced that during his boyhood the Spurgeon name was revered in the Paisley household; Ian's older brother had even been christened Harold Spurgeon Paisley.[7]

The new separatist and Baptist church in Ballymena issued its covenant with God, employing the legacies of the Israelites, the Reformation, and Scottish Calvinism: "As God providentially raised up Elijah, we believe He is now calling out a faithful remnant to maintain a testimony, free from compromise against every opposition of the enemy. To maintain a Testimony, to the super nationalism of modernism, and the deception of fanaticism, and the formality of a dead and defunct orthodoxy."[8] With this declaration and covenant, the Waveney Road church committed itself to a militant and fundamentalist religiosity. Kyle Paisley had chosen a separatist path that few Irish Baptist ministers followed, although many were fundamentalists in the American tradition. He in turn inspired his son to the same course, passing the transatlantic legacy of Calvinist, revivalist, and anti-Catholic militant fundamentalism to a new generation.[9]

Revivalism

The regeneration of Calvinist religiosity in American and Ulster militant fundamentalist separatism began in western Scotland. During the early seventeenth century, revivals broke out that became an integral part of Scottish devotion. Over the next 150 years, Scottish revivalism and Calvinism were exported through Ulster and into the American colonies. During the eighteenth and nineteenth centuries, revivalism in North America combined with New World culture and politics to form an indigenous Calvinism that combined traditional Reformed tenets, evangelicalism, and American republicanism. It was these religious and political fundamentals that American militants repatriated to Northern Ireland and that Kyle Paisley and his Waveney Road congregation adopted. The metamorphosis resulted from several interlocking but different courses. The first was based on Scottish revivalism and theological controversies over subscription and the means to salvation, and the second was founded on the political and economic completion within the British Isles. Taken together, these parallel strands profoundly affected the political and theological atmosphere in Ireland and North America and in both regions established a tradition that combined politics with evangelical preaching. In Northern Ireland, a Protestant statelet and Ulster Protestantism's evangelical identity developed, and in North America revivalism and Presbyterian theological differences spurred development of American evangelicalism and North American fundamentalism. At the heart of this transatlantic process stood the revival tradition pioneered in western Scotland.

Ulster Scot immigrants introduced American Presbyterianism to the Scottish tradition of revivalism. It is necessary to look at Ulster revivalism because it was a defining characteristic of the religious observance of the Ulster Scot laity and had an impact on colonial Presbyterianism. Leigh Eric Schmidt has shown that the origins of American revivalism can be traced to the sacramental season and the "holy fairs" of western Scotland that were transplanted in Ulster in the early seventeenth century.[10] Communal festivals could last for days, and these sacramental fairs were based around the medieval religiosity that made the Eucharist the central element of Calvinist, post-Reformation spirituality.[11] In 1625, the first Ulster revival broke out at Six-Mile-Water, a small village in County Antrim near Belfast, when James Glendinning preached to his flock regarding their sinful nature. The participation of local and Scottish-born pastors was vital to the spread and success of the revival, and within eight years experiential Christianity spread across Ulster. Revivalism was popular among the laity and attracted younger, itinerant Presbyterian ministers. The emotionalism inherent to a revival created a "born-again" experience and the personal relationship with God the laity desired. The Irish Presbyterian and Anglican hierarchies and representatives of the English Crown opposed the Six-Mile-Water Revival, however, and the revival ended when Charles I restricted the movement of Presbyterian preachers. A tradition of revivalism and enthusiasm had nonetheless been established within Ulster Presbyterianism, yet in spite of its popularity the Irish Presbyterian Church would not adopt it into official church practice.[12]

In the 1660s, itinerant preachers, or "conventiclers," reappeared in western Scotland, where they spoke to large outdoor gatherings. Many went to Ulster as traveling missionaries, where they conducted smaller, private meetings—introducing a new cycle of revivalism. These conventicles were in essence a continuation of the revivals that took place three decades earlier. Conventiclers showed an acute militancy in their public confrontations with secular authority, which caused many Presbyterian ministers and presbyteries in Ulster to disapprove of their methods. But once again the laity supported the emotional meetings, helping to further this tradition that combined radicalism and revivalist Presbyterianism. Through their confrontational style and the theology they espoused, conventiclers can be seen as the forerunners of the political preachers of the nineteenth and twentieth centuries, most notably the Reverends Henry Cooke and Ian Paisley.[13]

Ulster revivalism developed amid the Scottish theological controversies of the seventeenth and eighteenth centuries. The laity's piety and many ministers' conservatism enabled the Synod of Ulster to maintain an orthodox Calvinist theology, but in the 1700s official tolerance for a new and liberal view of subscription to the Westminster Confession of Faith threatened this unity. The divisive issues that the Ulster Synod faced originated in the Scottish General Assembly. The Universities of Glasgow and Edinburgh employed professors who accepted the enlightened argument that unjust monarchs (not necessarily ungodly) could be overthrown—in contradiction to Knoxian Calvinism. Moreover, Unitarian ideas were openly expressed and dispensed alongside the lectures on enlightened philosophy. To these innovators, belief in the Trinity and reverence for the Westminster Confession were matters of individual conscience. However, the new ideas upset the Presbyterian masses and much of the church leadership, both of whom maintained traditional Reformed ideals. The Scottish Church responded with a test of conscience or subscription to the Confession. Those who refused to profess their Calvinism publicly became "Non-Subscribers" and moved to secede from the assembly. Because Presbyterian ministers in Ulster were trained in Scotland, these controversies were exported to Ireland.[14]

In Ulster, Non-Subscribers were expelled from the Synod of Ulster and in 1720 organized themselves into the Presbytery of Antrim. Two subsequent Non-Subscribing presbyteries were formed in Armagh and Belfast. Many Non-Subscribers were adherents to the new ideals of the "New Light," a phrase coined in the 1720s. New Lighters were liberal on subscription and believed that through revival the Holy Ghost helped to prepare the Elect for salvation; the Westminster Confession of Faith was man made and not scriptural, and subscription was undemocratic and a matter of private judgment. They still professed the Calvinist doctrine of Election, but they believed that Christians could prepare themselves for God's grace. Old Light Presbyterians argued for a strict definition of predestination—salvation came only to the Elect, and human effort could not affect His decision—and for an uncompromising subscription to the Westminster Confession of Faith.[15]

A second separatist movement withdrew from the Scottish Kirk in the early eighteenth century. These "Seceders" were upset that the church allowed wealthy congregants to select ministerial candidates and to provide the majority of their support, both of which were contrary to Presbyterian practice. The local elite appointed ministers who accepted a liberal interpretation of the Doctrine of Grace. In 1745, Seceder missionaries were welcomed in Ireland because of their hell-fire and revivalist preaching as well as their opposition to New Light Presbyterianism. Within a year, the first Seceder congregation in Ulster was formed at Lylehill. Many Ulster Presbyterians accepted the populist, emotional, and itinerant preaching.[16] Andrew Holmes argues that a substantial element within Ulster's Old Light and Seceder communities accepted the revivalism and acquiesced to the moderate viewpoint that God's grace and Christ's atonement, guided by the Holy Spirit, were available to the Elect. Over the next two centuries, this religiosity enabled a wide spectrum of the faithful within Irish and American Presbyterianism to declare themselves evangelicals in the 1800s. Patrick Griffin, however, asserts that until the nineteenth century there was a limit to the popularity of itinerant and populist preaching. Revivals attracted only a minority of adherents in Ulster, and until the 1798 Rebellion and the Act of Union, Irish Presbyterians were concerned mainly with theological arguments. As a consequence, the popularity of revivalism and New Light in Ulster is not as important as their export to North America and their adoption by American colonists.[17]

In the late 1600s, Ireland witnessed a human and theological exodus to the American colonies. A majority of the Irishmen who emigrated were Presbyterians who objected to the laws that restrained dissent in Ireland and to the economic restrictions that hindered Irish prosperity. Irish wool could only be exported to England, and there were limitations on the shipping of Irish livestock. A series of crop failures and outbreaks of cattle disease accelerated the exodus to the American colonies. At first, small groups of Ulster Scot Presbyterians departed for North America in the late seventeenth century, but by 1718 thousands were setting sail. Driven out by high rents and excessive tithes, slumping linen sales, poor harvests, and high corn costs, these emigrants were enticed by America's free land and the low taxes in the colonies.[18]

Between 1718 and 1776, approximately one hundred thousand Ulstermen went to North America, the majority to the Pennsylvania and New York frontiers. In regions such as the Susquehanna Valley, Ulster Scots lived a life of isolation, hard work, and poverty and maintained their Christian traditions despite a shortage of Presbyterian ministers. Forced into dangerous, Indian-populated areas by the colony's ruling Quakers, Congregationalists, and Anglicans, the Presbyterians in the New World sought to impose Scottish Calvinism and discipline as a means to maintain order and to assert their Scottish and Ulster heritages. Two significant traditions they hung onto were revivalism and subscription to the Westminster Confession.[19]

Irish Non-Subscribers and Seceders transplanted revivalism and theological divisions into colonial Presbyterianism. Revivalism and itinerant preaching upset church unity in the American colonies, although both were popular among younger Ulstermen and those who migrated to America. Because Presbyterians were most numerous in the middle colonies, and because Philadelphia was America's largest and most important city, the first colonial presbytery was formed in the City of Brotherly Love. By 1716, enough churches existed that two additional presbyteries, Long Island (New York) and New Castle (Delaware), were founded, and the Synod of Philadelphia was formed. But theological differences divided the new synod. Wary of Deism, the Philadelphia Presbytery demanded that its clergy publicly subscribe to the Westminster Confession of Faith. Some ministers, however, argued that the confession should not rival scripture in importance and demanded that it be voluntary and private. To reconcile these differences, a public profession was demanded, but the manner and style were left to personal conscience.[20]

Despite these efforts at reconciliation and compromise, the Philadelphia Synod continued to face divisive issues. A new influx of itinerant New Light preachers from Ireland and Scotland called for revival. The itinerant New Lighters did not use the standard Presbyterian method of preaching, where consecutive biblical verses were examined until a chapter was finished; they instead spoke as the spirit moved them. Furthermore, itinerant preachers did not seek permission from the local pastor when entering a new area, thus violating denominational protocol. These practices were well suited to frontier revivalism. Wary of New Light theology and alarmed by the growth of Deism in the colonies, Old Light ministers in the Philadelphia Synod demanded a strict subscription to the Westminster Confession and the preaching of traditional Reformed doctrine. To maintain denominational unity, the synod agreed to further compromise: although subscription became the synod's official policy, enforcement was left up to the individual presbyteries.[21]

In the 1720s, William Tennett led the American New Light movement and crusaded for emotional preaching. Tennett, an Irishman, established a private seminary in Neshaminy, Pennsylvania, to train ministers willing to profess a more moral and enthusiastic ministry. In the early eighteenth century, Tennett's school—which critics called the "Log College"—was the only Presbyterian institute of higher learning in North America. Log College ministers espoused a fire-and-brimstone form of preaching, warning sinners of God's wrath and arguing that regeneration came through stages. During one sermon, Tennett preached from Deuteronomy 29; two and a half centuries later the Reverend Ian Paisley used the same emotional preaching style and scriptural authority to profess his militant fundamentalist argument. Through their support for itinerancy, the New Lighters and the Log College prepared the laity for the Great Awakenings of the 1730s and early 1740s and for the important preaching tour of the Englishman George Whitefield. Arriving in Philadelphia in November 1739, Whitefield drew large crowds and was instrumental in increasing the popularity of emotional piety among the laity. The Awakenings and revivalist fervor, however, further divided colonial Presbyterianism: Old Lights wanted a more traditional observance, whereas New Lights accepted the need for revival. By the mid-1700s, New Light and revivalism became the majority opinion among the laity, and those congregations adhering to Old Light Presbyterianism witnessed a deep decline in membership.[22]

A few differences separated the American church from the Ulster church and would affect political activism in the subsequent centuries. Irish Presbyterian ministers received the *regium donum,* a stipend that the Irish administration paid to Presbyterian ministers, and thus were not financially dependent on the congregation, as were American ministers. Perhaps that is the reason American Presbyterianism officially supported revivalism and became what Marilyn Westerkamp describes as a denomination of the laity—in which the congregation influenced church theology and practices as much as the clergy did.[23] In the late eighteenth century, however, the most significant point of difference between Ulstermen and Americans was the question of political involvement. Whereas Ulster Scots in America were a major driving force behind the colonial rebellion, the same was not true in Ireland. Many Irish Presbyterians supported the revolution, but the number fell as the American revolutionaries aligned with Catholic France.[24] As Ireland drifted toward rebellion, however, the Synod of Ulster took a stronger interest in British and Irish politics. In contrast, the new General Assembly of the Presbyterian Church in the new country moved toward an apolitical stance and backed the First Amendment of the US Constitution. American Presbyterians supported the separation of church and state and religious tolerance, and the American church rarely intervened in politics. For instance, the General Assembly revised its interpretation of the Westminster Confession to fit the new US Constitution, and civil magistrates could no longer confer with any Presbyterian authority for advice.[25]

Adopting apolitics made it easier for American Presbyterianism to concentrate on religious matters, such as expanding its membership, spreading the gospel, and opening new congregations during the American move westward. The constant migration and the sparse population of the new territories, however, made it difficult for Presbyterians to provide an adequate supply of educated ministers and to build sufficient churches, which enabled smaller and vibrant denominations to form many of the new congregations: Presbyterians faced a particular challenge from the growth of the Methodist and Baptist churches, two organizations well adapted to frontier expansion. Methodists and Baptists attracted Independents indifferent to organized religion and open to the revivalist argument that a conversion experience was available to anyone. Facing a substantial loss in church membership, the Presbyterian General Assembly and the Congregational Union (the descendants of New England Puritans) agreed to the Plan of Union, a system designed to help establish new churches where members of both denominations could worship.[26]

The expansion westward coincided with a recurrence of revivalism, most notably the Cane Ridge Revival that began in Kentucky in August 1801. Both Mark Noll and Eric Leigh Schmidt argue that these gatherings resembled the Scottish and Irish evangelistic gatherings of the previous two centuries. Schmidt further asserts that on the American frontier Scottish and Ulster Scot sacramentalism and revivalism were transformed into camp meetings, from which Cane Ridge emerged.[27] The revivalism on the frontier spread throughout the Southeast and into western New York during the 1820s, and the American propensity for individual piety inspired new denominations in rural areas. The Disciples of Christ wanted a devotion based on the New Testament, whereas the Cumberland Presbyterian Church—founded in 1810 from congregations and ministers expelled from the Kentucky Synod for their revivalist tendencies—argued for a liberal form of subscription and a more Arminian conception of election. Cumberland Presbyterianism accepted a predestination that showed God's love for all humanity and that conformed more easily to the conditions of the frontier than did traditional Presbyterianism. Cumberland questioned the traditional or hyper-Calvinism of transatlantic Presbyterianism. Many Presbyterians on the frontier accepted the more liberal and independent view of predestination, and, moreover, the new sect better employed the less-educated clergy of rural areas and made salvation available to a wider section of the church.[28]

In the early 1800s, revivalism increased in importance and popularity, but at the same time it compromised Calvinist theology. Beginning in 1824 with small meetings, Charles G. Finney's preaching sparked revivals—the Second Great Awakening—during which he argued that Christians had to act for salvation, thus contradicting the Calvinist tenet of the total depravity of humanity. Finney professed an emotional, semi-Arminian message, where believers could influence conversion and hasten the Second Coming: moral business practices, slave emancipation, and a just society would quicken Christ's return. Finney challenged the traditional Calvinism of Old Light Presbyterianism, arguing that human inability, not depravity, limited the atonement and helping to further unite revivalism and moderate Calvinism. Finney's theology maintained a traditional Calvinist foundation, however, and argued for a confluence of emotionalism and election, ensuring some conservative support.[29]

Dwight L. Moody continued Finney's revivalist legacy that opposed hyper-Calvinism. Born in 1837 in Northfield, Massachusetts, Moody moved to Chicago, where he established a street-preaching ministry. He opened his own Sunday school and took part in missionary work among Union soldiers during the Civil War. It was not in the United States, however, but in Scotland and England that Moody made his name. He became a transatlantic "prophet" during a series of revivals that began in the late 1860s. He drew large crowds by employing innovative techniques, such as Ira Sankey's gospel singing and harmonium playing, and by preaching in a forceful, charismatic style. Moody was successful because his theology, which blended the Calvinistic doctrine of Election and an individual choice for Christ, appealed to middle-class British and Irish evangelicals. Although his fame ensured that his subsequent revivals in America were well attended, his real success came through the support he received from a wide spectrum of American denominations. Moody's revivalism helped to form the new bond emerging among the evangelicals in America's diverse churches.[30] Finney and Moody continued the transatlantic cycle of revivalism, which merged Scottish and Ulster religiosity into American culture and which was exported back to the British Isles. Moreover, Finney and Moody's revivalism and evangelicalism, in conjunction with their adherence to predestination and a traditional interpretation of scripture, would reappear in the twentieth century as essential tenets in militant fundamentalist theology.[31]

The Fundamentals

In spite of the enthusiasm generated through revivalism, in the 1830s American Presbyterianism divided over this issue as well as over church authority, financial support for independent missionary and educational agencies, and abolition. The New Light–Old Light controversy reemerged as a battle pitting a liberal New School theology against Old School conservatism.[32] Old School Presbyterians insisted that the General Assembly employ sanctions to maintain the basic tenets of Calvinism. The liberal New England theology espoused by Nathaniel Taylor—the first professor of the new Yale Divinity School—brought the divisions out into the open. New Schoolers supported Taylor's form of Pelagianism, which argued that original sin did not taint human nature; humans committed sins only when they were acts of free will. Moreover, Christians could—with the help of the Holy Spirit—employ reason to find salvation, and an individual could escape damnation with a conversion experience and a sin-free lifestyle. New School revivalism harmonized well with Taylor's argument, but the Old School focus on divine sovereignty, the Election of the saved, and total depravity clashed sharply with Taylor's theology. In 1837, Presbyterians split into two denominations after New School ministers were expelled from the General Assembly.[33]

Two years later New and Old School Presbyterians in the North agreed to a compromise: northern Presbyterianism reaffirmed the authority of the Westminster Confession, while accepting that New Schoolers did not have to make a public affirmation of faith. The compromise on sanctions would be important in future schisms because it would be difficult for conservatives to enforce church doctrine. The Old School contingent in the North and the South effectively abandoned sanctions as the means to assert church authority, and the reunited church consented to the New Light theology of experiential conversion.[34] The influence of revivalism and evangelicalism temporarily deterred the growth of religious indifference and sects such as Deism and Unitarianism, and liberal and "enthusiastic" Presbyterians were less inclined to adopt modernist ideas. But this agreement on evangelism did not prevent future splits within both the northern and southern denominations, nor would it block the introduction of ecumenical activity and modernist ideas. Potentially divisive issues such as interdenominational unity, missionary work, and support for the Social Gospel were left for future generations to work out.[35]

During the ensuing decades, the United States witnessed a social transformation that was intimately connected to religious issues. Industrialization, urbanization, and immigration altered the rural and Protestant culture of the United States, most dramatically with the massive immigration of Irish Catholics. Small-town Americans were alarmed by the growing urban populations and the economic and cultural power of the large cities. The rise of the city came at the same time that biblical criticism and theological modernism fragmented America's major Protestant denominations. Thus, theological differences paralleled demographic changes.

An influx of Germanic biblical scholarship shook the foundation of Protestant denominations. Higher criticism arrived in the United States in the early nineteenth century, creating minor controversies, but it was in the 1870s that conflict with traditionalists erupted into open battle. Protestant academics who studied in Germany brought home a critical evaluation of the Bible that questioned the authorship and dating of various biblical texts and employed the historical method to reexamine the life of Jesus Christ. However, higher criticism by itself did not shake the traditional, evangelical beliefs held by many Americans. New School revivalism had already weakened American orthodoxy as it sought to accommodate evangelical ideals with urban secularization in an attempt to promote moral reform and interdenominational cooperation. Such ideals made defending biblical infallibility difficult, and German-trained academics such as Charles Briggs found a receptive audience for the new critical methods. Although these academic ideas were generally contained within northern seminaries and scholarly journals, they faced intense opposition from both conservative and liberal theologians. By the end of the nineteenth century, however, the higher-critical method was firmly rooted in academic theology.[36]

The controversy over higher criticism overlapped with the upheavals associated with Charles Darwin's theories of evolution and natural selection. Darwin's *Origin of Species* deepened the Protestant "crisis of faith" that connected the liberal Christianity of the early nineteenth century with the modernist Christianity of the late 1800s. Liberal Christians argued that human ability could build the Kingdom of God on Earth and believed in interdenominational cooperation while respecting the authority of the Bible. Darwinism and German biblical criticism, which questioned scripture, further eroded belief in orthodox Christianity, and evangelical fervor in the United States dropped after the Civil War. Until the mid-1870s, however, Americans either ignored or accommodated to

Darwinism, on the one hand, or rejected evolution and natural selection as unproven, on the other.[37]

Many Christians argued that Darwinism posed no threat to their beliefs; evolution bore witness to the divine plan for humanity. They interpreted evolution to mean improvement and asserted that through Christian action human beings could better both themselves and their world—a human-created revival of the church. Henry Ward Beecher, the brother of Harriet Beecher Stowe, is an example of a liberal preacher who believed that science and human efforts to improve morality would compel the Kingdom of God. The combination of an optimistic embrace of evolutionary theory with higher-critical readings of the Bible helped to produce a new evangelicalism and the Social Gospel. The new evangelicals attempted to dispense their message through interdenominational cooperation, old-fashioned preaching, and pamphlets. They also found direct action, such as home visitations and urban missions, effective. Many liberals thought American capitalism and idleness were evil; society could be saved through human collective action. The concept that Christian activists from various denominations could work together to intervene in the social order came to fruition in the early twentieth century. In 1909, liberals representing America's major churches created the Federal Council of Churches of Christ in America (FCC) as an ecumenical organization to proselytize the Social Gospel.[38]

The dispute among conservative, liberal, and modernist Christians was centered within universities and seminaries; liberals and modernists increasingly controlled the larger theological schools, especially in the northern states. Theological heterodoxy within American seminaries caused a great uneasiness among conservative Calvinists, who perceived that a considerable number of young clerics were turning from traditional theology. Many theological students were New Schoolers and opposed these orthodox tenets and ultra-Calvinist doctrine, such as double predestination. For American Presbyterianism, however, Princeton Theological Seminary became the main battlefield for the conservative–modernist conflict. In the denomination's oldest institution, Old School academics rose to the defense of traditional Calvinism and several times charged modernist colleagues with heresy.[39]

The contest between the conservative and liberal-modernist interpretations of Christianity became entangled in the argument over eschatology. In Britain, conservatives responded to liberal Christianity with dispensational premillennialism, an innovation developed by John Nelson Darby and exported to North America. Dispensationalist ideas were not new, but Darby organized them into an updated, coherent system. Dispensationalism—based in a Calvinist context—argues that God divides history into seven eras, or dispensations, each with a different plan of salvation. In the nineteenth century, Christianity had progressed to the sixth era or church age, during which Christians were to prepare for the Second Coming of Christ, the seventh and final era.[40]

In the 1830s, Darby split from the Church of Ireland and helped to found the Plymouth Brethren movement as a separatist movement within the British Isles; the sect sought to purify the Anglican churches with Independent congregations, open membership, and no trained clergy. Darby's preaching and Dispensationalism appealed to both Baptist and Presbyterian Calvinists, exemplifying these groups' shared theological worldview. As a consequence, Dispensationalism became popular in the United States owing to John Nelson Darby's seven missionary trips to North America and to the prophetic and Bible conferences begun in 1876 in Niagara, New York. Associates of Dwight L. Moody, who were Calvinist Presbyterians and Baptists and premillennial Dispensationalists, founded these meetings, a yearly event known as the Niagara Bible Conference and held until 1901, as well as the International Prophecy Conference held every decade until the First World War. Dispensationalism became an important component within fundamentalist theology.[41]

The Dispensationalist movement was rooted in millennialism and traced its legacy to England's religious and political battles during the seventeenth century. Understanding the politicoreligious background to millenarian belief is vital comprehending its reception in North America. Puritans, who believed that Stuart despotism, the monarchy's cavorting with Catholicism, and the Thirty Years' War signaled the imminent return of Christ, brought millenarian ideas to the American colonies. Stuart policies and Anglican bishops were threatening to return England to the Antichrist, and Puritan preachers, such as Jonathan Edwards and

Cotton Mather, preached about the Second Coming. Paul Boyer argues that England's colonization of North America took place in an eschatological context. As the call for revival grew in the colonies, many Americans believed that millennialism and the experiential conversion experience were intimately connected, and after the American Revolution both ideas were enthusiastically accepted on the frontier. The millennial movement was especially strong among Calvinists, Independents, and separatists, who believed that the End Times were imminent. Millennials argued that Roman Catholic tyranny, Protestant apostasy, and the ideals inspired by the Enlightenment and the French Revolution were hastening Christ's return to earth, as revealed in the Book of Revelation.[42]

After the American Civil War, the millenarian movement grew and became embroiled in the debates over the Social Gospel, the authority of the Bible, and the compatibility of science and orthodoxy. During the nineteenth century, millenarians divided over the Second Coming and the conception of Christ's Kingdom on Earth. From the American Revolution through the 1860s, postmillennialism overcame the amillennial view and became the prevalent position. The belief in human progress drove the Social Gospel and missionary fervor and dominated America's Protestant seminaries and many clerics' eschatological view. However, owing to the devastation that Civil War inflicted on the United States, many revivalists and New School Presbyterians adopted a premillennial position that had also gained acceptance among many conservatives. The growing urbanization and anti-intellectualism prompted a more pessimistic outlook for humanity. Moreover, conservative Calvinists disliked the Christian progressives, who united in an interdenominational effort to better social conditions.[43]

Although both post- and premillennials accepted the need to proselytize the gospel, postmillennials sought to spread a social gospel, whereas premillennials acted to prepare the Elect for tribulation. Mission work was accordingly a vital sacrament to premillennial Dispensationalists as well as to liberal postmillennials. In the 1880s, D. L. Moody helped to found the summer Bible conferences held in Northfield, Massachusetts, which followed the legacy of the annual Niagara Bible Conferences, as well as the Chicago Bible Institute to train students for overseas missionary work.[44]

Moody's Bible conferences and the Chicago college helped create a pool of premillenarian activists for the battles of the early twentieth century that pitted fundamentalists against modernists and proponents of the Social Gospel. George Marsden argues that it was within these evangelical Bible conferences, Bible studies, and Bible schools that fundamentalism was nourished. Hence, a combination of theological conservatism, premillennial pessimism, and the revivalist anti-intellectualism taught in conservative Bible colleges coalesced around prophetic Bible conferences to foment fundamentalism.[45]

The trauma and upheaval of the 1910s—the First World War, labor violence, and social changes—pushed modernism and traditional Protestantism into direct confrontation. Many Americans perceived that public life in urban areas appeared increasingly risqué and that personal morals were on the decline. A growing fear of Catholic and Jewish immigration and of communism also marked American politics and culture. Fundamentalists and conservatives blamed the onset of the world war, German atrocities, and the social strife of the late 1910s on Germanic biblical criticism, atheism, secularization, and Social Darwinism. The trauma of the First World War reinvigorated premillennials and conservatives alike; the war and the social and cultural changes of its aftermath seemed to be an omen of the End Times and an attack on the traditional Calvinist religiosity inherent to the conservative American way of life. At the center of this struggle stood the conflict between traditional Christianity and modernism.[46]

In response, evangelicals—premillennialists, revivalists, and conservatives—united in a nondenominational effort to save orthodox Christianity and to prepare for the Second Coming. The coalition's first efforts predated the First World War: in 1910, the first of a twelve-volume series of articles containing conservative and millenarian ideas was published, and three million copies were mass-mailed throughout the United States. *The Fundamentals* shaped the basic tenets of conservative and premillennialist ideas into a coherent theological system. These basics included the affirmation of Jesus Christ's virgin birth, divine nature, bodily resurrection, and Second Coming; the doctrine of Christ's death as blood atonement for the sin of humanity; the belief in eternal salvation through faith in the grace of God; the depravity of man; and the inerrancy and divine inspiration of scripture. With a defined theology, fundamentalists began to organize as a movement. In late May 1919, William Bell Riley, pastor of the First Baptist Church in Minneapolis, Minnesota, formed the World Christian Fundamentals Association as an interdenominational and premillennial organization to fight modernism within Protestant denominations.[47]

After the First World War, the new fundamentalist alliance continued its attack on modernism. Fearing the growth and influence of the fundamentalist movement, liberal clerics counterattacked during denominational meetings and from their pulpits. Harry Emerson Fosdick summed up their concern in May 1922 when he preached his famous sermon "Shall the Fundamentalists Win?" to the First Presbyterian Church in New York City. Considered the most influential American preacher of the period owing to his radio broadcasts, Fosdick, a Baptist but also an associate pastor at the church, brought the controversy into the public arena. He argued that liberals were tolerant because they were willing to compromise to reconcile the divisions between the various Protestant churches, whereas fundamentalists were intolerant because they maintained a rigid and old-fashioned theology. The sermon was published within three major Christian journals and distributed as a pamphlet that was mailed to thousands of American clergymen. Fosdick's message resonated with the modernists of the Presbyterian Church in the U.S.A., who generally kept a low public profile and their modernist theology out of their Sunday sermons. The publicity given to the sermon necessitated a conservative rebuttal; Clarence Edward Macartney of the Arch Street Presbyterian Church in Philadelphia fired the first shot and in "Shall Unbelief Win?" argued that liberalism was a stepping-stone to atheism.[48]

The fundamentalist–modernist battle increasingly centered on evolution. William Jennings Bryan best expressed the conservative and fundamentalist position. When he gave the James Sprunt lectures at the Union Theological Seminary in Richmond, Virginia, in October 1921, he argued for biblical inerrancy and against Darwinism and evolution.[49] Bryan, who came out of the Cumberland Presbyterian tradition, was a populist layman from rural Illinois, a two-term Congressman, and a three-time candidate for president. He was not a Dispensationalist, however, or a premillennialist.

He originally advocated the Social Gospel, belonged to the FCC, and tacitly accepted evolution until the devastation of the First World War changed his perspective. Bryan withdrew from the Federal Council and argued that evolutionary science not only threatened Christian tenets, but also human progress. According to Edward Larson, Bryan asserted that Darwinism led to the militarism that caused the First World War. But the issue that shocked Bryan and conservative Christians into action was the teaching of evolution in American universities and high schools.[50]

The fundamentalist–modernist debate over evolution came to a head during the Scopes trial. The antievolution position was ridiculed within the American press, causing support for fundamentalism to decline. As fundamentalist fervor ebbed, the theology lost much of its moderate, conservative, and middle-class support. Although historians have been divided on its impact, the Scopes trial was important to the survival of fundamentalism and how American Protestants came to view the theological concept. George Marsden and Joel Carpenter argue that the trial painted fundamentalism as an ignorant and rural concept to many moderate Christians. However, Edward Larson has shown that the trial did not universally discredit fundamentalism, that many moderate Christians disliked Clarence Darrow's hostile atheism, and that only later, during the 1930s, did the national press portray the trial as an evolutionist victory.[51]

After the Scopes trial, the fundamentalist movement suffered schism and further defeat. A split between conservatives and Bible literalists developed, and fundamentalists lost the important theological battles they fought with liberals and modernists within Protestant denominations.[52] But as fundamentalism lost the respect of seminary-educated clerics within the larger denominations, it grew in strength among the evangelical clerics and the laity of America's Protestant churches. New summer Bible conferences were organized, fundamentalist radio programs flourished, and new Bible colleges were founded. For instance, after Bob Jones Sr. opened his first college in Lynn Haven, Florida, in 1927, he used radio to promote his new school. By the late 1930s, there were more than four hundred evangelical radio broadcasts in the United States. Not only did fundamentalism survive within every American Protestant denomination, but after the 1920s it became more dynamic and influential. Carpenter further asserts that the survival of American fundamentalism can be credited to the development of two competing branches, one evangelical and inclusive, the other militant and separatist.[53]

After the embarrassing setback of the Scopes trial, fundamentalists divided into several interlocking groups: conservatives and separatists.[54] Conservative evangelicals attacked clerics and academics who professed a literal fundamentalist doctrine not based on traditional Calvinism, whereas conservatives and fundamentalists who remained within their churches took a position against their brethren who argued for separatism. Militant separatists took the theological stance that the Bible forbade fundamentalists to have fellowship with apostates and that a true Christian church must expel such recreants. If expulsion proved impossible, then true Christians must separate into their own churches. It was these separatists who became militant fundamentalists during the 1930s; militant fundamentalism became a grassroots movement of independent churches and preachers. Decentralized organizations of like-minded militants formed in the 1930s, most notably the Union of Regular Baptist Churches of Ontario and Quebec, the General Association of Regular Baptist Churches, and the Independent Fundamental Churches of America. In addition, the emergence of fundamentalist preachers with a nationwide popularity—William Bell Riley; J. Frank Norris of Fort Worth, Texas; John Roach Straton of New York; and Mark Matthews of Seattle, among the most important—gave the movement organization and direction. In 1937, a more militant and confrontational leadership emerged when the Reverend Carl McIntire and his Bible Presbyterian Church began a crusade against Protestant apostasy, the Roman Catholic Church, and communism.[55]

2

The Twentieth-Century Reformation

The Gospel of Militant Fundamentalism

In the 1930s, the concerns of the American fundamentalist community transcended theology and refocused on politics and social mores. Within militant fundamentalism, national and international politics and a defense of American capitalism rivaled the defense of Bible Protestantism. Whereas communism had worried militants during the interwar period, the onset of the Cold War created a morbid fear of the Soviet Union and the expanding ecumenical movement that militants believed appeased communism.[1] A coalition of Christian "patriots," fundamentalist associations, and independent preachers led the American response. The most vocal voice that arose was that of the Reverend Carl McIntire of Collingswood, New Jersey. McIntire's crusade began as a defense of fundamentalist Protestantism against ecumenism, Christian liberalism, and the Roman Catholic Church, but after the Second World War it took on an ideological component that was unique to North America. From the 1940s on, McIntire crusaded against what he perceived as the weakness of American foreign policy toward the Soviet Union and the People's Republic of China. He also campaigned against Communist infiltration of the US government and military as well as the "Red" subversion of Protestant churches.[2] To understand McIntire's crusade, it is necessary to examine the factors that drove McIntire to split from both mainstream Presbyterianism and conservative fundamentalists who had left the Presbyterian Church and to assert his views publicly. To comprehend how McIntire and American militant fundamentalism influenced Paisley's ministry, it is accordingly essential to analyze McIntire's early career, his style of protest, and the developing relationship between McIntire and Paisley. Through McIntire's international network, Paisley gained valuable friendships, which were important in shaping the Ulsterman's theological and political ideals and to raising his stature in the British Isles.

The Presbyterian Schism

Although most American denominations experienced the fundamentalist controversy, it hit Presbyterianism the hardest. As previously mentioned, the Princeton Theological Seminary took the lead in the mid–nineteenth century in defending traditional conservative Presbyterianism, although some professors held a view on creation and biblical inerrancy that differed from the Westminster Confession. Princeton's conservatives were influenced by James McCosh, recruited from the Free Church of Scotland in 1868 to be the institution's president. McCosh brought with him Scottish commonsense rationalism, which argued that science and scripture could be reconciled through reason and philosophy. Moreover, the Scotsman saw a need to compromise with orthodox Calvinism as a means to combat Darwinism and biblical criticism. The imported philosophy established a conservative base at Princeton in contrast to Presbyterianism's other, more liberal seminaries. To militant fundamentalists, proponents of Germanic higher biblical criticism and modernism increasingly corrupted these institutions, all of which were located in the American North. The most important Presbyterian college infected was the Union Theological Seminary in Manhattan, maintained by the liberal Presbytery of New York.[3]

During the last two decades of the nineteenth century, the conflict within the Presbyterian Church in the U.S.A. erupted into open battles. There were a number of heresy trials, the most important being that of Dr. Charles Briggs, the professor of biblical theology at Union Theological. Brought to trial in 1891 for asserting modernist concepts,[4] Briggs attacked Princetonian Old School Presbyterianism as a new version of medieval Scholasticism and as a doctrine that contradicted Calvinism. He articulated his theological ideas in three books published in the 1880s: *Biblical Study: Its Principles, Methods, and History,* a history of higher criticism; *American Presbyterianism: Its Origin and Early History,* which argued against church authority (specifically the use of church authority to sanction modernists) and the concept of subscription; and *Whither? A Theological Question for Our Times,* which called for a modernist revision of Presbyterianism that accepted evolution and promoted ecumenism. Throughout his works, Briggs argued that liberals and the New Theology were the true defenders of the Bible and the Westminster Confession.[5] Briggs also allowed a series on higher criticism to be published in the *Presbyterian Review,* a periodical he coedited. After he outlined his views during his Inaugural Address to the Union Theological Seminary in 1891, conservatives could no longer remain quiet. At the General Assembly in Detroit the same year, a vote to remove Briggs from his professorship passed. At first, the New York Presbytery refused to bring Briggs to trial, but during the 1892 General Assembly conservatives forced it to do so. When Briggs was suspended from the ministry during the 1893 General Assembly, Union Theological Seminary officially separated itself from the Presbyterian Church in the U.S.A.[6]

Presbyterian conservatives condemned several other professors during the 1890s: Harry Preserved Smith, an Old Testament professor at Lane Seminary, and Arthur Cushman McGiffert, the church history professor at Union Theological, were tried for heresy, and James Woodrow, the uncle of future president Woodrow Wilson and teacher at Columbia Seminary in South Carolina, came under attack for teaching evolution and the compatibility of the Bible and science. All three were supported by their schools, although only Smith managed to retain his position. These cases illustrated the division between liberal Presbyterian academics and conservative ministers within the Presbyterian Church. Because modernist professors had support within liberal presbyteries—such as New York and Augusta, Georgia—conservatives were compelled during the 1890s to make a stand against the public displays of modernism. Conservatives issued the "Portland Deliverance"—their statement against higher criticism—and many Presbyterians who denied the literal truth of the Bible and the Confession were asked to leave the church. Liberals and modernists were not silenced, however, and worked quietly within seminaries and church bodies to press their theological views.[7]

Liberal influence slowly gained in strength within mainstream Presbyterianism. In order to maintain denominational unity, the Presbyterian Church in the U.S.A. revised the Westminster Confession in 1903 to state that all infants and adults, except those who knowingly continued to commit sin, could obtain salvation. But the Presbyterian General Assembly also adopted the "Five Essential Points" in 1910, which confirmed the basic and supernatural tenets of fundamentalist theology[8] and stated that the church officially retained its basic conservatism. The affirmation of the Five Essential Points contained a demand pointed at Harry Emerson Fosdick: the First Presbyterian Church in New York City was ordered to preach conservative Presbyterian theology. However, the Five Points accommodated liberals because it did not demand strict subscription and thus inspired new liberal defiance. Modernists mounted a new attack against conservative Presbyterianism: eighty-five commissioners at the General Assembly protested the action against Fosdick, and the New York Presbytery refused to condemn him. Then, in June 1923, the New York Presbytery defied the General Assembly and licensed two ministers who openly denied the doctrine of the virgin birth. Because the assembly would not affirm denominational authority, hope for any rapprochement between liberals and conservatives was dashed. Although the Five Points were reaffirmed, the election for moderator put William Jennings Bryan up against Charles F. Wishart, the president of the College of Wooster, who embraced evolutionary science. Wishart narrowly won, but in a conciliatory move that aimed to maintain denominational peace the General Assembly appointed Bryan to chair the Committee of Home Missions.[9]

To promote denominational unity and to defend liberal and modernist ministers, 149 liberal Presbyterian ministers met in upstate New York at the Auburn Seminary in December 1923 to draft a resolution denouncing the Five Essential Points as unconstitutional. *An Affirmation Designed to Safeguard the Unity and Liberty of the Presbyterian Church in the United States of America* argued that although most signers held the church's traditional doctrine, Presbyterians were entitled to interpret scripture in their own way. Referred to as the "Auburn Affirmation," this nonbinding statement effectively voided the Five Points, allowing liberal-minded

Presbyterians to consider them guidelines. The Presbyterian Church had clearly split into two factions.[10]

Conservatives and fundamentalists held mass meetings in New York and Pittsburgh to defend the fundamentalist viewpoint and to attack modernism, and at first they appeared successful. The 1924 General Assembly elected the conservative Clarence Macartney as moderator and Bryan as vice moderator and appointed conservatives to head each assembly committee. An internal split between conservatives and fundamentalists, however, made it impossible for fundamentalists to influence the General Assembly. Although conservatives wanted to maintain a mandatory belief in predestination and subscription to the Westminster Confession and supported a literal interpretation of the Bible, they did not want a schism and would not acquiesce to the outright condemnation of Presbyterian modernists. Hence, no action was taken against either the Auburn Affirmation or the New York Presbytery. Although a conservative was again elected moderator in 1925, moderate conservatives backed down from a threat to separate from the General Assembly when liberals and modernists warned that they would leave the denomination. According to Joel Carpenter, it was hard for fundamentalists to oppose Presbyterian modernists because of the church's tradition of loose discipline, the denomination's history of tolerating opposing ideas, and the wavering support from many conservatives. As a consequence, conservatives and fundamentalists lost control of the assembly. At the 1927 General Assembly, the Five Essential Points were declared nonbinding, and the assembly revoked its right to hear heresy trials, thus eliminating the use of sanctions to enforce orthodoxy.[11]

Two years later liberal theologians took over the direction of the Princeton Theological Seminary. Princeton had been administered through two boards, one answerable to the Presbyterian General Assembly and one made up of independent trustees who controlled the seminary's property. In 1929, however, the school's administration was reorganized so that the seminary would have a single assembly-appointed board. Not all Princetonian academics accepted the change. J. Gresham Machen, a New Testament professor at the seminary, took up the conservative counterattack, uniting with Presbyterian fundamentalists. Over the previous half-century,

Princeton's faculty had been slowly splitting between Old School conservatives, such as Machen, who wanted to teach only orthodox theology, and those who were more tolerant in their Christianity. Machen was not a strict fundamentalist, but a theological conservative who believed that traditional Calvinism could redeem modern culture. He also thought that the battle against modernism was an academic struggle that should be fought within seminaries and universities. Machen initially asserted that fundamentalist piety was an Arminian threat to the Westminster Confession, but in *Christianity and Liberalism* he allied with fundamentalism against liberals and modernists. He argued that modernism was not Christianity, but a new religion. Upset that two members of the new Princeton Theological Seminary board had signed the Auburn Affirmation and were not disciplined, Machen and three other faculty members resigned from the seminary in June 1929. The following fall, Machen, with the help of twenty-nine current and former students, formed the Westminster Theological Seminary. The new institution placed itself under the Presbytery of Philadelphia, one of Presbyterianism's most conservative presbyteries, and Westminster remained within the Presbyterian Church.[12]

Machen also began an attack against modernist foreign missionaries, singling out those working in China in particular. In 1927, eight presbyteries of the Presbyterian Church in China united with Congregationalists, Methodists, and Baptists to form the Church of Christ in China. The new church allowed its missionaries to promote Buddhist and Confucian principles as a means to explain Christian tenets to the Chinese, a measure that Dr. Robert E. Speer, the senior secretary of the Presbyterian Board of Foreign Missions and the moderator of the General Assembly, supported. In 1933, Machen sponsored an overture to the assembly attacking the "Layman's Inquiry," an interdenominational report arguing for new missionary churches based on this syncretic approach. Speer refused to condemn the report. When the overture was defeated, in June 1933 Machen helped found and was elected president of the Independent Board for Presbyterian Foreign Missions (IBPFM).[13] Independent of the Presbyterian Church, the new mission board supported conservative and fundamentalist missionaries and solicited funds within Presbyterian churches. The 1934 General Assembly declared that the Independent Board was contrary to Presbyterian principles and charged that those who remained active in the organization violated their ordination and membership vows. After Machen refused to repudiate the IBPFM, the judicial commission of the New Brunswick Presbytery brought him to trial in October 1935. The General Assembly convicted him of insubordination and the violation of church peace and suspended him from the ministry. After the assembly denied his appeal in June 1936, Machen helped to establish the fundamentalist Presbyterian Church of America (thus making a formal break with the Presbyterian Church in the U.S.A.).[14]

Throughout the controversy, Presbyterian fundamentalists backed the conservative leader, Machen. Of all his supporters, the most important was Carl McIntire, one of the students who followed him to the Westminster Seminary. The young cleric adamantly backed Machen in his stance against modernism among missionaries. For example, McIntire presented his own overture to the West Jersey Presbytery against modernist foreign missionaries and issued an extensive pamphlet that attacked Speer for his failure to eradicate "apostates" among Asian missionaries. The charges against Speer were ironic considering that he had contributed to volume 3 of *The Fundamentals,* his article "Foreign Missions or World-Wide Evangelism" asserting that missions were vital to the belief in the Christian God. Speer also argued that different cultures "are not free to hold contradictory conceptions of the same God," thus criticizing modernist interpretations of Christian tenets.[15]

Ordained by the General Assembly, McIntire was accepted as the pastor of the Collingswood (New Jersey) Presbyterian Church following a brief stint in Atlantic City. Elected to the IBPFM in April 1934, he became the new board's most vocal advocate, despite remaining a minister and commissioner to the assembly's own mission agency.[16] He induced the Woman's Missionary Society of his Collingswood congregation to question the modernism within the assembly's Board of Foreign Missions. According to McIntire, the denomination's Women's Committee recommended that missionaries use Arian pamphlets that questioned Christ's divinity. These modernist tracts also argued that, contrary to scripture, Jesus loved human life and accordingly was reluctant to ascend to heaven. The Board of Foreign Missions denied it had approved the pamphlets, but

McIntire argued that the board was responsible for the work and for its subcommittees' theological position.[17]

The Presbytery of West Jersey suspended McIntire in June 1936 for making abusive speeches against opponents and charged him with failure to maintain denominational peace, violation of ordination vows, and insubordination. A Presbyterian court of appeals eventually withdrew McIntire's credentials as a minister, the only Presbyterian minister during this period to suffer that fate. In response and in defense of their pastor, the congregation of the Collingswood Presbyterian Church voted overwhelmingly to withdraw from the General Assembly.[18]

The Bible Presbyterian Church

The Collingswood Church joined with Machen, J. Oliver Buswell, who was the president of Wheaton College in Illinois,[19] and a group of fundamentalist Presbyterian ministers to form the Presbyterian Church of America. At a meeting in Syracuse, New York, Machen united with conservative and fundamentalist allies to separate officially from the Presbyterian Church in the U.S.A. One week later the new Knox Presbyterian Church in Philadelphia became the first of many fundamentalist and Presbyterian congregations to join the new church, and within another two months nine Presbyterian Church of America presbyteries were established throughout the United States.[20]

The harmonious relationship between Machen and McIntire did not last long. The two allies disagreed over theology, church independence, and issues of personal morality. As an Old School conservative, Machen was not committed to premillennialism. He staffed the Westminster Theological Seminary with conservative professors who adhered to the original Westminster Confession of Faith and professed amillennialism. The school instituted a network of Calvinists who did not accept the Social Gospel or liberal and modernist Christianity.[21] Machen also did not believe in Dispensationalism and did not support the Scofield Reference Bible based on that theology. McIntire, in contrast, accepted the more Arminian confession as amended by the General Assembly in 1903 and ardently embraced the Scofield Bible and premillennialism. He professed a more liberal (or less hyper) view on predestination and believed that the

Holy Ghost helped the Elect to understand their predetermination. McIntire also took exception to Machen's leniency on moral issues: Machen would not dismiss Westminster students and faculty who smoked, danced, or drank, nor would the General Assembly of the Presbyterian Church of America condemn such behavior. It was Machen's view on separation, however, that drove the sharpest wedge between him and McIntire. Although Machen would not have fellowship with modernists who denied the Trinity or the authority of scripture, he did not believe in a complete separation from Christians who were not strict fundamentalists.[22]

The division of the Presbyterian Church of America between Machen's Old School Presbyterianism and McIntire's militant fundamentalism played itself out on two battlefields: the struggle for control of the IBPFM and the struggle to make appointments to the Westminster Theological Seminary. Machen insisted that the new seminary officially support the IBPFM, a move that violated the missionary agency's independence. But McIntire, who wanted the board to retain its independent authority, won the battle. In the fall of 1936, fundamentalists took control of the IBPFM and ousted Machen from its presidency.

Machen died on 1 January 1937, but his passing did not heal the fundamentalist–conservative division. After the Presbyterian Church of America declined to elect the militant fundamentalist candidate, Reverend Milo Fisher Jamison, as moderator, McIntire and his congregation withdrew from the new denomination. Fourteen church ministers followed, and the remaining members regrouped as the Orthodox Presbyterian Church. McIntire's party met in Philadelphia to found the Bible Presbyterian Synod and set up its own seminary, Faith Theological.[23] McIntire's confrontation with Machen showed that he was willing to wage battle with not only the modernism within mainstream Presbyterianism, but also conservatives and fundamentalists who did not follow his moral viewpoints or separatism. Because of these actions and his ouster from the General Assembly, McIntire's reputation as a militant maverick grew, and militant fundamentalism had a self-professed martyr.[24]

On 1 January 1938, when Paisley was barely ten years old, McIntire began spreading his separatist gospel to the Christian masses in America. With the formation of the Bible Presbyterian Church, he obtained a safe pulpit to preach his brand of theology, and with Faith Theological Seminary he created a base to train like-minded ministers and missionaries. Moreover, he put into place the tools necessary to take advantage of mass media. In 1936, he started the *Christian Beacon,* an eight-page weekly containing articles outlining the Bible Presbyterians' theological, political, and cultural viewpoints. The small newspaper also had articles from the American and international press critical of McIntire's ministry and his church, but they were usually refuted by pro-McIntire pieces, editorials, and letters and were included to illustrate the threat to militant fundamentalism and to support McIntire's self-professed martyrdom. Shortly thereafter, McIntire founded the Christian Beacon Press to publish his writings and took to the airwaves on WPEN, a Philadelphia-based radio station.[25]

Although the use of the news media and radio marked the beginning of McIntire's nationwide crusade against modernism, he needed to gain control over his own church property. After his suspension from the Presbyterian Church in the U.S.A. in July 1936, McIntire still remained in his ministerial position, but he served a church to which the mainstream denomination had legal title. Under Presbyterian rules, a congregation selects and dismisses the minister they want to serve their church, but they do so under the guidance of the local presbytery and regional synod and select from a list that the presbytery approves.[26] Having been so elected and never removed by his flock, who viewed McIntire's suspension as illegal, McIntire remained as the pastor of the Collingswood church—despite having joined the Presbyterian Church of America and then the Bible Presbyterian Synod. Preaching out of the Collingswood Presbyterian Church gave McIntire a pulpit and a congregation, but the Presbyterian Church in the U.S.A. still owned the actual church building and the land on which it stood.[27]

To remove McIntire, the Presbyterian General Assembly chose to work from within his church body. Immediately after his suspension, five dissident members filed a court action asking for McIntire's removal and for the church's property to revert back to the Presbyterian Church in the U.S.A. The Bible Presbyterians answered the suit and countered that the real issue was an attack on their militant fundamentalist theology and McIntire's leadership, not property rights. They also argued that the congregation itself owned the church property. The court disagreed and ordered McIntire to vacate the church. McIntire appealed and remained as Collingswood's minister for two more years while the case dragged through the appeals process. When the court issued a final decision in March 1938, one thousand supporters of McIntire witnessed as the presiding judge gave McIntire two weeks to leave his pulpit. Supported by the overwhelming majority of his church, McIntire began preaching several blocks away in a tent until a newer, bigger structure was built.[28]

In a style that other militant fundamentalists and Ian Paisley would emulate, McIntire used the legal trouble to further his ministry. He made sure his eviction became national news. The Sunday after he left Collingswood Presbyterian for the final time, he arranged for a small contingent of newspapermen to witness his weekly sermon, preached in his tent. The service, which also was the groundbreaking ceremony for his new church, drew 1,200 worshippers, in contrast to the concurrent attendance at his former church, where 200 heard Dr. Frederick W. Loetcher of Princeton Theological Seminary lead a subdued meeting. A short time later and to great personal fanfare and substantial press coverage, McIntire and his congregation moved into the new Bible Presbyterian Church of Collingswood, New Jersey.[29]

The Fellowship of Militant Fundamentalists

From this humble beginning, McIntire emerged as a substantial figure within the American militant fundamentalist community and the head of his own denomination. With a secure operating base, he focused on the core issue of his crusade: modernism within the Presbyterian Church and the ecumenical organizations that supported the despised theology. He chose as his first targets the FCC and an organization whose existence was still in the discussion stage, the World Council of Churches (WCC). The FCC was founded to propagate the Social Gospel and to promote ecumenism. It wanted a campaign to spread its message throughout the world, although the impending crisis in Europe and Asia, the rise of totalitarianism, and the expectation of war made it difficult to advance plans for an alternate organization. Militant fundamentalists intensely disliked the Federal Council. Although premillennialists and fundamentalists supported social action, to them a social gospel had to support the regenerating work of Christ, to help to hasten the Second Coming, and not to betray Christ's atonement. To militants, liberals endorsed social programs in a way that transcended Calvinist tenets. Equally galling was the FCC's control over the religious broadcasting that major networks provided free of charge to Protestant, Catholic, and Jewish groups; the FCC had demanded and won the right to represent all Protestant denominations on the airwaves. Conservative and militant fundamentalists argued that this was unfair and that the Federal Council represented only the liberal and modernist viewpoints, not the entire spectrum of Protestantism. To militants, the FCC's broadcast monopoly demonstrated rising liberal and modernist influence within Protestant churches and within the American government.[30]

McIntire and his militant fundamentalist allies within the Bible Presbyterian Church, Westminster Theological Seminary, and the IBPFM decided to form their own organization to counter the FCC. During a September 1941 meeting at the National Bible Institute in New York, a small group of independent fundamentalists joined McIntire and the Bible Protestants to form the American Council of Christian Churches (ACCC), electing McIntire as its first president. The organization sought to advance a four-point agenda: to proclaim what they considered to be proper Christian theology and biblical separatism; to attack modernism; to expose Communist influence within Protestant churches; and to form a fellowship for Christian churches "true" to biblical Protestantism.[31] The new militant council did not expand quickly; only the Bible Protestant Church of Camden, New Jersey—a city just two miles from Collingswood—initially joined the new organization. The Bible Protestant Church—originally a small Methodist Protestant denomination—was separatist, having split from the Eastern Conference of the Methodist Protestant Church in 1939 when the conference proposed to unite with the Methodist Episcopal Church, the forerunner of the modern United Methodist Church. To McIntire, the addition of Methodist fundamentalists, despite their Arminian leanings, was important. Methodism was America's largest Protestant denomination and therefore, next to American Presbyterianism, the nation's most apostate group.[32]

The combination of Wesleyan and Calvinist churches made the ACCC an organization theologically more diverse than Bible Presbyterianism and the Faith Theological Seminary as well as less ultra-Calvinist. Although the ACCC sought new members, its membership criteria were separatist, restricting its expansion. It did not allow denominations to join that belonged to the FCC, although independent congregations and individuals within these churches could join if they publicly repudiated the FCC.[33] The small independent churches and the heads of several Bible colleges that joined the new group included five important fundamentalists—the presidents of Shelton College, the Moody Bible Institute, and the Philadelphia School of the Bible, J. Oliver Buswell, Dr. William Houghton, and Reverend J. Davis Adams, respectively—as well as the pastor of St. Paul's Lutheran Church in Camden, New Jersey, and a member of the New York State Gideons.[34] The sponsoring committee for the new organization included Bob Jones Sr., the founder of Bob Jones College. The American Council provided important publicity for McIntire, enabling him to attract new converts to his separatist network.[35] In the early 1950s, it remained small but accepted the membership of thirteen denominations and organizations, the two most notable being Baptist fundamentalists: Thomas Todhunter (T. T.) Shields and the Union of Regular Baptist Churches of Ontario and Quebec as well as the Independent Bible Baptist Missions, organized by Harvey H. Springer, a Colorado evangelist. The strict separation espoused by the new council limited its size: to separatists, it was more important to maintain a small and separate but correct, fundamentalist fellowship of those they considered to be God's Elect.[36]

McIntire understood that his separatist movement needed a recognizable moniker, and so Bible Presbyterians promoted their crusade as the Twentieth Century Reformation Movement. To articulate his ideas, the Christian Beacon Press published McIntire's *Twentieth Century Reformation* in 1944, which argued that militant fundamentalism was in essence a reform movement and the best defense for the American version of free government and capitalism. Two years later McIntire wrote *Author of Liberty* to blame the onset of the Cold War and the threat of communism on both America's failure to maintain true Christianity and the Roman Catholic Church's "totalitarianism." McIntire attacked what he saw as the socialist trend within the federal government and the leftist and liberal campaign against America's Protestant heritage. He viewed the progressive income tax, the Fair Employment Practices Code, and closed trade shops not only as threats to Christian liberty and devotion—because, in his view, they deprived the individual of self-esteem and responsibility—but also as incitements to class and racial hatred because they created envy.[37]

During the second half of the 1940s, as the Cold War polarized the world, a corresponding theological divide developed in American and European churches, with modernists and militant fundamentalists on opposing poles and conservative Christians attempting to mediate the differences. The multiple threats of ecumenism, modernism, and communism, on the one hand, and acquiescence from conservatives, on the other, appeared to militant fundamentalists as elements within a single conspiracy. To militants, the same battle played itself out within American foreign and domestic policies as well as within American Protestantism. McIntire perceived communism to be infiltrating both the American government and America's churches. For instance, in October 1946, he attacked the FCC for its criticism of America's contentious foreign policy toward the Soviet Union. The FCC had declared American policy intolerant and "contrary to the basic principles of the Christian faith." To McIntire, the FCC's actions amounted to political and theological treason. Thus, the divide separating McIntire's militant fundamentalism from both conservative and liberal Christians had political and economic implications as well as theological connotations.[38]

The dual threats of the Cold War and Christian modernism enabled McIntire to rally a network of militant fundamentalists and secular Christian "patriots" to his Twentieth Century Reformation. To press McIntire's position, the ACCC passed a resolution at its seventh annual convention in October 1948 calling for a showdown with the Soviets. The ACCC asserted that because the United States alone had the nuclear bomb, America must launch a first strike before the Soviet Union developed its own. McIntire declared: "It is a betrayal of Christian principles and common decency for us to sit up and permit such a revolutionary force to gain advantage for the enslavement of the world." He called for war with the Soviets: "We call upon the representatives of the freedom-loving nations for a complete and frank showdown with Russia. . . . For us to have the atomic bomb, and in the name of false morality born of a perverted sense of self-respect and pacifist propaganda, to await the hour when Russia has her bombs to precipitate an atomic war, is the height of insanity and will, when the fateful hour comes, be a just punishment upon us."[39]

McIntire's statement, couched in premillennial and eschatological rhetoric, constituted an appeal to the US government to hasten the Battle of Armageddon, which follows the events outlined in the Book of Revelation. McIntire and the ACCC connected the betrayal of Christian principles that such appeasement permitted with Satan's strategy to penetrate Christian churches using modernism. McIntire's message was political as well as theological.[40]

In 1948, McIntire and the ACCC attacked the appointment of John Foster Dulles as secretary of state. The council argued that Dulles was a Soviet appeaser, an adherent to the Social Gospel—in other words, a Communist sympathizer and a socialist—and a supporter of both the FCC and the WCC. Militants were outraged that Dulles, a Presbyterian elder, had been defense council for Harry Emerson Fosdick in 1924 and two decades later became vice president of the WCC International Affairs Commission.[41] McIntire and the ACCC also attacked the appointment of an American ambassador to the Vatican. When President Harry S. Truman nominated General Mark W. Clark for the post, McIntire charged that this act was a betrayal of America's Protestant heritage. It did not matter that Franklin Delano Roosevelt had already broken tradition and appointed a special representative to the Vatican in the 1940s. Truman withdrew Clark's nomination, but his action was only in part owing to the militant fundamentalist opposition. A wide spectrum of moderate and liberal Protestant opinion—including the FCC, the National Association of Evangelicals, and smaller organizations such as Protestants and Other Americans United for Separation of Church and State and the National Sunday School Association—also argued against the move. To all concerned, Truman's decision violated the American tradition of separation of church and state; the US government should not have diplomatic ties with any church, especially the Roman Catholic Church.[42]

The campaign against the ambassador to the Vatican involved both moderate and militant fundamentalists. They campaigned in two different ways, however: the moderate National Association of Evangelicals called for associated churches to hold a vigil against the appointment, whereas the militant ACCC sent McIntire, the Reverend Harvey Springer, and approximately five hundred clergymen to Washington, DC, with a fifty-thousand-signature petition. During the accompanying protest, which blocked the entrance to a Senate Foreign Relations Committee hearing, McIntire restated the perceived connection between communism and Catholicism when he declared: "Communism is an enemy, we are all against, but we have another enemy too, older, shrewder. It is Roman Catholicism and its bid for world power. In the United States it is Spellmanism [referring to the New York cardinal Francis Spellman]."[43]

When the WCC formed in Amsterdam in September 1948, McIntire and his militant fundamentalist allies preempted the move. McIntire was once again one step ahead of the modernists. In the previous week, he had created his own global organization, the International Council of Christian Churches (ICCC). Its purpose was to promote a worldwide fellowship of militant fundamentalist churches to attack the Roman Catholic Church and to confront the WCC for its socialist and ecumenical agenda. According to McIntire, the WCC aimed to unite all Protestant churches under the auspices of Rome and to promote socialist policies. The founding members of the ICCC illustrated its international appeal: McIntire (as president); the Canadian T. T. Shields; J. J. van der Schuit, a theological professor from the Netherlands; and the Reverend Chia Yu Ming, the moderator of the Presbyterian Church of Christ in China (Nanking). In order to broaden the appeal of his international council, McIntire made an important concession to militant eschatology: members could profess amillennialism as well as premillennialism. McIntire's wider attitude toward the Second Coming seemed insignificant in 1948 but established a precedent for future allies, such as the Reverend Ian Paisley.[44]

McIntire and the ICCC found much to attack in the WCC. The WCC published one report condemning the excesses of both communism *and* capitalism as incompatible with Christianity and another promoting the United Nations as an avenue for world peace. The ICCC viewed the WCC reports as endorsements for socialism, for a one-world government, and for a united church under Roman Catholic leadership. To the ICCC, all three "ideals" were omens of the Second Coming of Jesus Christ. Militant fundamentalists had to contest apostasy and the work of the devil in order to hasten the new millennium.[45]

The next target for McIntire and the ACCC became the National Council of Churches of Christ in America (NCC), which the Federal Council of Churches of Christ, twenty-five Protestant churches, and four Eastern Orthodox denominations formed in Cleveland, Ohio, in late December 1950. Like the FCC, the NCC's stated goal was to further the Social Gospel and to promote ecumenism. Not only did McIntire and his allies picket the NCC's founding convention, but McIntire attended with a press pass. The militant was proud when Charles P. Taft of the National Lay Committee denounced him from the stage; far from being offended, McIntire saw the resulting notoriety as vindication of his antiecumenical and anti-Communist campaigns and further proof of his self-professed martyrdom. In the *Christian Beacon*, he boasted of the dislike modernists showed him and attacked the National Council's modernist, pacifist, and socialist leanings.[46]

What galled McIntire and the militant fundamentalists the most, however, was the new Bible that the NCC sponsored and published in 1952. The result of fifteen years of work by thirty-two liberal, modernist, and orthodox biblical scholars, the Revised Standard Version was intended to modernize the language of the King James Version and clarify the theological message. Fundamentalists attacked the Revised Version with numerous "Back to the Bible" rallies and several new Bible burnings in large cities.[47] They denounced the new Bible translation for what they perceived as Unitarian, modernist, ecumenical, and Communist leanings. McIntire argued that the new translation minimized the prophetic references to Jesus Christ in important Old Testament passages.[48] For instance, in Isaiah 7:14 no longer had a virgin conceived the son of God, but Christ was the offspring of an ordinary young woman.[49] Passages from the New Testament were revised as well: Romans 9:5 was altered from "Whose are the fathers, and of whom as concerning the flesh Christ came, who is overall, God blessed forever. Amen" to "To them belong the patriarchs, and of their race, according to the flesh, is the Christ. God who is over all be blessed forever. Amen." Militant fundamentalists believed that with the change the Revised Standard Version compromised Christ's divinity. These differences might seem subtle, but to militants the nuances were designed to question basic Christian tenets, to undermine the fundamentalist faith in biblical inerrancy, and to promote a liberal and modernist interpretation among the new Bible's readers. More galling was the success of the new Bible; within eight weeks, it sold more than one and a half million copies.[50]

The attacks on the Revised Standard Bible took on an anti-Semitic and vicious tone. On 5 December 1948, William Denton, an English-born evangelist who broadcasted out of Akron, Ohio, criticized the new translation as a conspiracy among Jewish Marxists to defile the white race.[51] In the face of the outrage his comments generated, the ACCC defended Denton, charging that the denunciation of him was Communist inspired. In his *Defender* magazine, Gerald B. Winrod, a Nazi sympathizer and anti-Semite,[52] asserted that Jewish scholars were behind the new translations and that Jews controlled the NCC. Despite his open anti-Semitism, Winrod received militant fundamentalist support when he opened the Defender Seminary in Puerto Rico in 1954; several years later he granted an honorary doctorate to Billy James Hargis, a new ally of Carl McIntire. There is no evidence that McIntire and Hargis were anti-Semites, but the fact that the ACCC openly worked with such men raised questions within mainstream Protestantism regarding the organization's motivation and moral values.[53]

During this period, McIntire organized a global network in an attempt to rival the WCC's. In the late 1940s, for example, he and the ICCC made an effort to reach out to East Asian fundamentalists. In December 1949, McIntire led sixteen militant fundamentalists, including T. T. Shields, to Bangkok to protest the East Asian Christian Conference that the WCC and the International Missionary Council had set up. McIntire asserted that his group went to Thailand to "inform the national churches of Southeast Asia of the departure from the Bible by the World Council, to expose the leadership in Asia for its support of communism, and to keep the World Council from the consolidation of this part of the world."[54] He blasted the conference and its leader, Asian WCC president Dr. T. C. Chao of China, as an advocate for communism, charging: "[Chao] welcomed Communists in China as liberators and accepted a post on the People's Consultative Council to advise the Reds."[55] The seven-point resolution that the conference adopted supported Chao's Communist appeasement and called for Asian Christians to

> distinguish between social revolution, which seeks justice, and the totalitarian ideology which interprets and perverts it. Churches [in East Asia] should take the initiative in bridging the gap between church and organized labor in town and village. . . . The revolution in China, though led by Communists, may not yet have manifested fully the evil consequences of the moral relativism integral to communism, and the churches' task in China may be specifically to seek to provide a moral and religious foundation for the new sense of social freedom and economic justice among the people.[56]

Militant fundamentalists regarded the resolution as a call for a Communist China, and it vindicated the past efforts of militants to expose modernism among Chinese missionaries. In response, McIntire vowed to organize his own Conference of Christian Churches in Asia.[57]

A Second Plenary Congress of the ICCC was held in Geneva, Switzerland, in 1950, the Third Congress four years later in Philadelphia, and the Fourth Congress in Petropolis, Brazil, in 1958. Philadelphia had been chosen when the ICCC could not find an adequate facility in Evanston, Illinois, to confront the WCC meeting being held in that city that year. Even the Orthodox Presbyterian Church—the denomination J. Gresham Machen had helped to found—joined the International Council, although it withdrew after a few years because the ICCC accepted denominations that professed Dispensationalism and did not adhere to strict versions of the Reformed faith (for instance, fundamentalist Methodists). McIntire was the official president of the ACCC for only one year, but he remained in control of the ICCC for several decades and maintained the organization's headquarters at his Collingswood, New Jersey, church. In this manner, he retained more power over his international fellowship than he did over its American counterpart.[58]

During the 1950s, McIntire cooperated not only with militant fundamentalists, but with secular forces, such as Senator Joseph R. McCarthy of Wisconsin. McCarthy headed the Permanent Subcommittee on Investigations of the House Un-American Activities Committee (HUAC).[59] The relationship that developed between militant fundamentalists and McCarthy created a strong link between the secular American right-wing and their religious counterparts; militant fundamentalists avidly collaborated with both McCarthy and the HUAC, despite McCarthy's Catholicism. McIntire's willingness to overlook McCarthy's Catholicism—and thus to compromise militant fundamentalist theology and separatism—showed his political pragmatism. Two decades later Paisley copied this political amillennialism.[60] However, militant fundamentalists and right-wing politicians had overlapping but different priorities. McCarthy and militant fundamentalists mutually attacked numerous Christian and secular groups and leaders, including the United Nations, the NCC, the WCC, Secretary of State George C. Marshall, and the Voice of America. But McCarthy and the HUAC were concerned primarily with Communist subversion of the US government. Other groups, such as churches, were secondary. In contrast, McIntire and fellow militant fundamentalists were preoccupied with Communist infiltration of Protestant churches and placed politics in a subsidiary role. But when McCarthy and other right-wing politicians charged that Communists were infiltrating Christian churches, their assertions vindicated McIntire and his fellow militant fundamentalists in the eyes of a substantial segment of the American public.[61]

Although the majority of Americans still considered McIntire and other militant fundamentalists to be extremists, cooperation with Congressmen and congressional committees gave militants a degree of respectability. In late November 1948, Chairman J. Parnell Thomas of New Jersey and the HUAC published five pamphlets, with titles such as *100 Things You Should Know about Communism and Religion,* all claiming that Communists had made deep inroads into American churches and religious groups. Two churchmen, the Reverends Claude C. Williams and Eliot White, were denounced as outright Communists. Williams, a Cumberland Presbyterian, made a career supporting black automobile workers in Detroit and civil rights in the South and was defrocked for unorthodox theology. From his pulpit at Grace Episcopal Church in New York, Eliot White argued for a socialist America. The YMCA, the Methodist Federation for Social Action (MFSA), the *Protestant Digest* magazine, and the Epworth League—a defunct Methodist group—were named as Communist-front groups. The Thomas Committee charged that "the Communist Party of the United States assigns members to join organizations, in order to take control where possible, and in any case to influence thought and action toward Communist ends."[62]

In July 1952, the HUAC conducted another series of hearings in New York City on the penetration of communism into American Protestant churches. The committee heard former Communists testify to the collaboration between modernist Protestant leaders—especially the Methodist ones—and Communist front groups that was directed from Moscow. Because the committee's report did not receive extensive coverage in the secular press, militant fundamentalists claimed that the media and churches conspired to cover up the situation. The same year, the Methodist General Conference passed a resolution denouncing the MFSA, demanding that it drop the moniker *Methodist*. McIntire, the ACCC, and the International Council unsurprisingly praised the governmental report.[63]

McCarthy relied to a great extent on information, "evidence," provided by militant fundamentalists, but the relationship was mutually beneficial. McIntire and his allies joined with Christian laymen to provide source material for McCarthy, and militant fundamentalists used the HUAC's reports and hearings to support their attacks on Christian leaders.[64] It was important for militant Christians that McCarthy's style of attack involved innuendo and guilt by association while not offering hard facts. By publicly making charges and then withdrawing them when asked to provide proof, McCarthy could condemn a victim and refuse to provide a forum to respond, citing senatorial privilege. When the charges were directed at Protestant targets and the secular press routinely printed the charges, militant fundamentalism benefited.[65]

At times, McCarthy used religious imagery to support his political accusations. Warren L. Vinz argues not only that McCarthy reiterated what McIntire and his allies had already charged and often made religious references in his speeches, but that McCarthy's secular charges paralleled the premillennial view of the Second Coming. According to Vinz, McCarthy made frequent allusions to God and politicoreligious references: the Soviet Union was the evil exposed in Revelation; Armageddon was coming; the United Nations represented futile and humanly efforts. He alluded to atheistic communism and asserted that John Foster Dulles equated the Sermon on the Mount with an endorsement for communism. To McCarthy, a struggle with the Soviet Union was inevitable, and liberal humanist efforts, such as the United Nations, which favored the Eastern bloc, supported the Communist advance.[66]

The link between McCarthy, the HUAC, and militant fundamentalists was manifest in a group of ultraconservative writers and Christian laymen—most notably J. B. Matthews, Edgar C. Bundy, John T. Flynn, and Verne F. Kaub. This diverse group specialized in exposing the Communist infiltration of churches and the government. As a young man, Matthews, the son of a Methodist fundamentalist minister from Kentucky, had become a Methodist missionary to Malaya and originally advocated the Social Gospel, racial equality, and pacifism. In the 1930s, he chaired the American League Against War and Fascism—a group that included the American Communist Party—until he turned to the right and joined the Dies Committee (the forerunner of the HUAC) in August 1938. Matthews became disillusioned after he supported the Consumers Union during a contentious strike by its employees and the Left denounced him. He became the star witness for the Dies Committee as well as its research director. After the Second World War, he worked for the ACCC and wrote anti-Communist articles for various newspapers and periodicals, most notably the *American Mercury.*[67]

Hired by William Randolph Hearst as a specialist on communism, Matthews convinced Hearst, a powerful newspaper publisher, to support McCarthy and subsequently was hired as a researcher for the senator's Permanent Subcommittee on Investigations. Matthews became a direct link between the HUAC and militant fundamentalists. An outcry of opposition was heard from moderates, however, after McCarthy appointed Matthews to be executive staff director of the Subcommittee on Investigations. A larger uproar broke out when Matthews's article "Reds and Our Churches" appeared in the July 1953 edition of the *American Mercury,* forcing his resignation. The article was written to support Representative Harold H. Velde of Illinois, who had announced his own investigation into Communist clergymen. Matthews asserted that seven thousand American clergymen were Communist Party members or sympathizers, that HUAC had the names of 471 Protestant pacifists, and that "the largest single group supporting the communist apparatus in the United States today is composed of Protestant clergymen."[68] The ACCC petitioned President Eisenhower to reinstate Matthews, but under pressure from the NCC and a cross-section of Christian groups—including the Southern Baptist Conference and the FCC—the president refused to intervene. Militant fundamentalist support continued, however, and McIntire and Matthews maintained a relationship until Matthews's death in 1966.[69]

Major Edgar C. Bundy, a retired air force intelligence officer and ordained Southern Baptist minister, also became a close associate of McIntire's. Bundy joined the National Laymen's Council of the Church League of America, a group founded in March 1937 as a private intelligence office to sell information about any person or organization suspected of communism, socialism, or civil libertarianism. Anyone could purchase Church League reports, and it was provided free of charge to interested parties within the US government.[70] In the 1950s, Bundy disseminated militant information through the *News and Views* monthly, through special reports that could be purchased from the league, and through the lecture circuit. Each issue of *News and Views* covered one subject, with issue titles such as "Socialism in the Churches," "The National Council's Program for Revolution," and "High Tide of Black Resistance, 1967." The Church League claimed that *News and Views* had a paid subscription of six thousand clergyman and fifty thousand laymen; unlike McIntire, Bundy's impact on the public at large was indirect. But what made the organization effective was that the information it collected and distributed was difficult to dispute—which mimicked McCarthy's methods. Moreover, its massive files made it and Bundy an important bridge between the secular right wing and militant fundamentalists.[71]

A close relationship between Bundy and McIntire developed in 1949. Bundy became a popular speaker to Christian and secular groups after he testified before the Senate Appropriations Committee on the Far East in 1949. He predicted the Communist attack on South Korea, and after the Korean War began, he became an "expert" on Communist aggression in Asia. He also preached to revival meetings, including an eight-week campaign in spring 1949 that ended with a speech to the ICCC meeting in Harrisburg, Pennsylvania. The twelve hundred attendees heard Bundy relate stories such as his confrontation with Dr. John Stamm, the bishop of the United Brethren Church and the FCC president. Because Bundy's maternal grandfather had been an Evangelical United Brethren Church minister, the seeming apostasy within that denomination greatly concerned him. Bundy joined the ACCC in the late 1940s, became a part-time public-relations officer and intelligence officer on McIntire's personal staff, and wrote articles for the *Christian Beacon*. In part because of his relationship with McIntire, the Church League's revenues expanded 600 percent over the next four years, becoming a major source of information for militant fundamentalists.[72]

In the mid-1950s, Bundy furthered his fame when he wrote *Collectivism in the Churches,* in which he argued that the ecumenical movement aimed to standardize Christian doctrine—creating a Christian collective—and that the Social Gospel of the FCC, NCC, and WCC was a front for a Communist attack on American freedom. For example, Bundy charged that the FCC's Commission on the Church and Social Service consistently made pronouncements sympathetic to socialism and communism, as in February 1951 when the Executive Committee issued a resolution arguing that communism traced a direct lineage to the Gospel of Jesus Christ.[73]

The third conservative who linked McCarthy and militant fundamentalism was John T. Flynn. Flynn began as a liberal newspaperman who exposed the corrupt practices of big business and who advocated isolationism. He opposed America's entry into the Second World War as an attempt by Roosevelt liberals to defend European imperialism and to spread secular liberalism. After the United States and Great Britain formed the alliance with the Soviet Union, he also turned anti-Communist and became a member of the Republican Party. In 1945, he joined the HUAC to expose communism within the Truman administration and six years later enlisted in McCarthy's anti-Communist crusade. Flynn wrote two books,

The Road Ahead: America's Creeping Revolution and *The Roosevelt Myth;* both became best-sellers and asserted the militant mantra that socialists were influential within the American government, unions, and churches.[74]

Published in 1949, *The Road Ahead* alleged that the FCC was a Communist-front organization, that a number of American church leaders were active Communists, and that Fabian Socialists, supported by liberal Protestant ministers, were pushing national planning as a precursor to fascism. The most important of these liberal Protestants were two Methodists: Dr. E. Stanley Jones, a missionary to India, and Garfield Bromley Oxnam, the bishop of the Washington, DC, area.[75] Flynn despised Jones for advocating a federal union of all Christian churches, for calling Gandhi and his pacifism "Christian," and for condemning capitalism as decadent and selfish. Flynn claimed that Jones referred to the Kingdom of God as a social order, not a theological system, and that Bishop Oxnam allowed the writings of pro-Communist Christians, such as Dr. Jerome Davis, to be sold in Methodist churches. In several pamphlets, Davis argued that Stalinist economic and social policies reflected the ideals of the Russian masses.[76]

In 1950, Verne F. Kaub from Madison, Wisconsin, formed the American Council of Christian Laymen to distribute copies of *The Road Ahead.* Kaub, a conservative writer similar to Matthews, Bundy, and Flynn, drew together the secular and religious strands of anticommunism. He wrote his own pamphlet, *How Red Is the Federal Council of Churches?* which charged not only that Oxnam and Jones were Communists, but that they followed in the tradition of important liberal Christians such as Harry Emerson Fosdick.[77]

McIntire and the ACCC led the militant fundamentalist attack on Jones and Oxnam, employing the press, the pulpit, and public protests. For example, members of the southern California branch of the ACCC picketed Dr. Jones's appearance at the Pasadena Council of Churches in 1950. The leader of the demonstration, Marion H. Reynolds of the Militant Fundamental Bible Churches and founder of the Fundamental Bible Institute of Los Angeles in 1936, approached Pasadena's two daily newspapers with information outlining the militant position. Although the *Star-News* refused to use the information, the *Independent* printed most of Reynolds's charges verbatim.[78]

The ACCC organized special meetings across the United States to publicize their charges against Bishop Oxnam. McIntire's tactics were effective: in early March 1953, the HUAC chairman, Representative Harold H. Velde of Illinois, went on the television show *Reporters' Roundup* and announced that an investigation into liberal and modernist churchmen, such as Oxnam, would shortly begin. Despite a public outcry that forced Velde to back down quickly, another HUAC committee member, Representative Donald Jackson of California, proposed the same idea on the House floor. Jackson charged that Oxnam "served God on Sunday and the communist front for the balance of the week." The following May, two hundred ACCC members traveled to Washington, DC, to hand Jackson a twenty-five-thousand-signature petition that demanded Oxnam be brought before the HUAC.[79]

The militant fundamentalists' tactics worked, and Bishop Oxnam insisted on a hearing. On 21 July 1953, the cleric voluntarily testified for ten hours. Major Bundy and several members of the ACCC attended the spectacle and were given front-row seats. Although the committee agreed that there was no concrete evidence against Oxnam—he only admitted that in the 1920s he was a member of groups that later developed ties with the Communist Party and that he supported the aims of the MFSA, but not its Communist leadership—the charges against the churchman gained credence within the world of militant fundamentalism. But because of the HUAC's inability to indict Oxnam as a Communist or to prove the same charge against Jack R. McMichael, the MFSA director, no other Protestant clergyman was brought before Congress.[80]

During the early 1950s, the American fear of communism and the Korean War enhanced the McIntire crusade and strengthened his relationship with Senator McCarthy and the HUAC. But after the Matthews fiasco in 1953 and McCarthy's Senate censure in 1954, McIntire's influence in national politics seemed to wane, and criticism of his tactics increased.[81] This reversal, however, was temporary, and new campaigns quickly revitalized McIntire and the ACCC: the fast rebound illustrated his vitality.

One important battle fought against the visit to the United States of Protestant and Orthodox clergymen from eastern Europe. Militant fundamentalists argued that the Communist-bloc clerics were not Christians, that their national governments controlled their theology and their churches' activities, and that these clerics were nothing but spokesmen for communism. The first attacks on the "Red" clergymen began in early 1954 when the WCC applied for visas to allow Professor Joseph L. Hromadka of Czechoslovakia and Bishop Albert Bereczky of the Reformed Church in Hungary to attend its Second Plenary session in Evanston, Illinois. After the US State Department granted the visas, McIntire petitioned Secretary of State Dulles and Attorney General Herbert Brownell to reverse the decision, citing the McCarran–Walter Immigration Act. The legislation barred entrance into the United States to citizens of Communist countries who did not openly disapprove of their totalitarian governments. McIntire further argued that the two clerics and their sponsor, the WCC, expressed sympathy toward socialism and communism.[82]

Although McIntire and twelve clerical supporters personally delivered a petition to Washington, the Hungarian and Czech Christians received their visas and appeared twice in Evanston, once at the plenary session and again at the WCC meeting the following August. But the militant fundamentalist opposition was loud, beginning with a Faith and Freedom Rally at the Collingswood Bible Presbyterian Church. McIntire and the ICCC imported their own foreign voices for the event: Norman Porter of Northern Ireland called communism and modernism the two biggest threats facing the Christian and secular worlds, and the Reverend Roman K. Mazierski, superintendent of the Polish Reformed Church in Great Britain, alleged that church leaders in Communist countries "proved to be perfect mouthpiece[s]" for Communist governments, which had "removed church officials and had them replaced by active Communists." The Reverend Samuel A. Jeanes of Merchantville, New Jersey, honored the numerous Baptist leaders imprisoned in Czechoslovakia for their faith, and McIntire charged that "Communist Governments in Iron Curtain countries have placed their own Communist agents in high ecclesiastical positions and are now using these agents in the church to deceive and mislead Christian people both behind the Iron Curtain and in the western world." Further protest in Evanston proved difficult when the ICCC failed to find a location to hold its own meeting and was forced to call its countercouncil at the Faith Theological Seminary in Elkins Park, Pennsylvania.[83]

The ACCC joined in the attacks against the visiting clerics after nine American clergymen associated with the NCC toured the Soviet Union. Although the NCC delegation reported that the Christian churches inside the Iron Curtain could not operate as freely as Western churches and that religious toleration was traded for political suppression, McIntire nevertheless ridiculed the visit as "beneficial to communism and in keeping with the Communists' new line to deceive the West."[84] When the National Council of Churches arranged for eight Soviet Orthodox, Baptist, and Lutheran clerics to come to the United States in an exchange visit two years later, they met public demonstrations. Supported by militant fundamentalists and Soviet émigré groups, protests were held on the arrival of the Soviets at New York International Airport, outside St. Nicholas Orthodox Cathedral in Manhattan, and at Wooster College in Ohio. Protestors appeared everywhere Metropolitan Nikolai of the Russian Orthodox Church preached. Militant fundamentalists charged that Nikolai was a Soviet secret agent who controlled the Soviet Union's Orthodox churches for the nation's Communist leadership, an accusation that the US Senate's Internal Security Committee took seriously. The largest group of protesters assembled as the visiting clerics visited Independence Hall in Philadelphia, less than ten miles from McIntire's church in Collingswood.[85]

Further ICCC activities included sponsoring a "truth squad" to protest Professor Hromadka's appearance at the Eighteenth General Assembly of the World Presbyterian Alliance in São Paulo in 1959 and a protest by ten ICCC leaders, including McIntire, at the WCC's Third Assembly in New Delhi in November 1961. In Brazil, McIntire held a Reformation Rally, and in India the International Council protested the presence of five official Roman Catholic observers and the admittance of two Pentecostal churches and the Russian Orthodox Church of Moscow as full WCC members. When McIntire and his group traveled to Brazil, it was not the first time the ICCC had ventured to South America to contest international gatherings of evangelical apostates. In July 1949, McIntire, Margaret Harden of the IBPFM, and Carl Matthews of the General Association of Regular Baptist Churches had protested the Inter-American Evangelical Conference in Buenos Aires, where the militant fundamentalists were refused entrance but held a protest meeting in a nearby church. And in

August 1958, the ICCC had held its Fourth Plenary Congress in Petropolis, near Rio de Janiero.[86]

Although McIntire placed increasing importance on his international crusade, the ACCC was still a vital part of his efforts. For example, when the WCC Central Committee met at Yale Divinity School in 1955 to discuss the role of religion in the nuclear age, a meeting that included two Hungarians and an East German church leader, the ACCC had protested outside the conference. Four years later McIntire organized ACCC rallies to denounce the visit to the United States by Soviet premier Nikita Khrushchev; the first rally, held at Connie Mack Stadium in Philadelphia, drew a sparse crowd and included many Soviet bloc immigrants. Other demonstrations included large protests at the Washington Monument in Washington, DC, and the Rose Bowl in Pasadena, California, as well as smaller ones in places such as Des Moines, Iowa, and Evansville, Indiana. Another rally was held in New York to oppose the United Nations' recognition of the People's Republic of China. The ACCC imported five clerics from Taiwan and South Korea to protest at the United Nations and to testify before the HUAC.[87]

Although McIntire was arguably the most famous and most vocal leader of American militant fundamentalism, the men he associated with in the 1950s widened the outreach and support that his crusade commanded; together they created the religious core of America's radical Right. Despite the numerous friends and allies that McIntire made through his ministry and through the ACCC and ICCC, three of his most important associates came from outside the two councils: Billy James Hargis, Fred Schwarz, and Harvey Springer.

Although all three men made a unique and substantial contribution to the radical Right, Hargis became McIntire's most important ally during the 1950s. The Oklahoma-based preacher boasted the largest and most widespread following because of his radio ministry and because of his willingness to work with the secular Right. Born in Texarkana, Texas, on 3 August 1925, as a teenager Hargis became an ordained minister of the Disciples of Christ and began a preaching career at churches throughout Oklahoma and Missouri. His ministry was unremarkable until 1948, when he resigned his pulpit at the First Christian Church in Sallisaw, Oklahoma, and relocated to Tulsa to found the Christian Echoes Ministry, Inc., better known as the Christian Crusade Against Communism. Hargis used the organization to attack modernism, communism, and racial integration.[88] He published a small eight-page monthly and began to make radio broadcasts but remained only a regional success. His rise to international fame began in the early 1950s when he managed to attract the attention of Senator McCarthy and the HUAC. In his autobiography, Hargis argues that McCarthy used Christian Crusade materials to prepare for the Oxnam hearings, and he claims to have written a Senate speech McCarthy gave against Bishop Oxnam.[89] Although the assertion seems plausible, there is no record of the speech in the *Congressional Record*. What is important, however, is that the militant fundamentalist community accepted the assertion, thus raising Hargis's stature.

Hargis's international status continued its dramatic rise when he, McIntire, and the ICCC hired Hargis to be chairman of the Bible Balloon Project. Begun in 1953, the project sought to evangelize the militant fundamentalist message in eastern Europe. Mimicking the use of helium balloons that the newspaper columnist Drew Pearson pioneered during his Crusade for Freedom scheme, Hargis and the ICCC proposed to airlift into the Soviet bloc Bibles printed in German, Russian, and various eastern European languages. To publicize the project, Hargis undertook a tour of Europe, preaching in Scotland, London, Amsterdam, Paris, and Geneva. The US State Department and the WCC initially opposed the Balloon Project as provocative, but after an appeal to President Dwight David Eisenhower the first 3,300 Bible tracts and 53,000 religious pamphlets left Nuremberg. The project continued for four years despite opposition from the West German government.[90]

During the six years that Hargis directed the Balloon Project, he used his new international notoriety, his connection with McCarthy, and the shrewd hiring of a local promoter to expand his radio revenues by more than 300 percent.[91] Correspondence between Hargis and Carl McIntire as well as extensive newspapers reports of the Bible Balloon Project show how important the project was to Hargis's new popularity. In 1960, air force education specialist Homer H. Hyde cited Hargis as an important source when Hyde authored a US Air Force training manual to instruct noncommissioned reserve officers on civil defense and security. The manual contained accusations of Communist infiltration into American churches and schools and the NCC's support for Red China.[92] Quoting Hargis, the ACCC, and the HUAC, Hyde blamed the infiltration on numerous organizations and modernist theological innovations, including the NCC and the new Revised Standard Version of the Bible.[93] By the early 1960s, Hargis's radio revenue surpassed McIntire's and other militant fundamentalists', and the Christian Crusade was broadcasting nine times per week, attacking targets such as the United Nations, the NCC, and the US Supreme Court.

Although Hargis cultivated friendships among the elite of the Christian Right—for instance, Bob Jones Sr. spoke at Christian Crusade meetings[94]—he differed from McIntire in his willingness to work with secular groups and right-wing politicians, many of whom McIntire refused to cooperate with.[95] The most notable of Hargis's allies was the John Birch Society, an organization founded in 1957. Robert H. Welch, the founder of the society, described democracy as "mob rule." To Welch, America was a republic; democratic rule was a prelude to a Communist dictatorship. A strong relationship developed between Hargis and the John Birchers; Robert Welch regularly spoke to the Christian Crusade, and Hargis publicly supported the work of Welch's organization. Welch and the John Birch Society echoed militant fundamentalism and charged that Communists held high positions in the US government and had dictated American foreign policy since 1941 and that many "Reds" were among the clergy of America's mainstream denominations. The society, many of whose members were fundamentalists, used militant tactics; it organized protests to heckle disliked speakers and formed public-pressure groups to harass stores that carried merchandise made in Communist countries. It also opposed the civil rights movement and racial integration and believed that American foreign aid not only hurt Christian missionary work but aided the crusade of atheist communism.[96]

There was a limit to Hargis's cooperation with other militant fundamentalists, however. Although he still collaborated with ACCC and ICCC activities, he resigned from the Bible Balloon Project, and by the late 1950s the Christian Crusade leader had little personal contact with

Carl McIntire. Hargis and McIntire's relationship became distant owing to both intense rivalry over the project and theological differences. McIntire was upset that most press releases from the project focused on Hargis's role and did not mention McIntire or the ICCC. Both militants, however, maintained the appearance of being close associates. This perception led the public at large and the two ministers' clerical adversaries to regard them as the leaders of a united militant fundamentalist movement.[97]

In 1948, McIntire began a relationship with Harvey Springer, an anti-Catholic and anti-Semite who pastored the First Baptist Church and Tabernacle in Englewood, Colorado, and ran the Independent Bible Baptist Missions to support separatist missionaries. Springer published a widely read separatist publication, the *Western Voice,* which he started in opposition to what he considered to be Jewish-inspired modernism. In the early 1950s, Springer and the newspaper turned to anti-Catholicism. In spite of the rise of Senator Joseph McCarthy and his alliance with militant fundamentalism, Springer viewed the Roman Catholic Church as a stronger threat to America's Protestant constitution than Jewish-led communism. To him, Catholics far outnumbered Communists in the United States, and, in addition, Catholics were loyal to the Vatican, a dictatorial foreign government. Catholics represented a fifth column, a threat of which many Americans were ignorant. The fellowship between Springer and McIntire was based on a shared separatist theology, and both frequently spoke at each other's meetings and churches. Beginning in 1948, the Coloradan held a popular annual revival that the Collingswood Bible Presbyterian Church sponsored. For example, in February 1949 Springer spoke to three thousand at the nearby Camden, New Jersey, armory. The close relationship became apparent to the militant community when the ICCC appointed Springer to head its Commission on Information and Publicity during the 1948 conference in Amsterdam.[98]

The relationship between militant fundamentalism and Dr. Frederick C. Schwarz, an Australian, began in 1950 when in the midst of a two-month tour of Asia McIntire and T. T. Shields of Canada heard the doctor speak. Son of an immigrant Viennese Jew, Schwarz had converted to Christianity and become a Baptist lay preacher. In the 1940s, he had begun a crusade in Australia against communism. McIntire and Shields were impressed enough to sponsor a speaking tour in the United States, during which the doctor was well received. Within two years, Schwarz returned to America, gained residency status, and began a radio program out of Waterloo, Iowa. He started the Christian Anti-Communist Crusade, which he moved to southern California, a hotbed for McCarthyism. After an extensive but short speaking career in local churches, he gained sufficient publicity to testify before the HUAC. Schwarz was considered an expert on communism, and the US Information Agency chose to distribute his book *You Can Trust the Communists (to Do Exactly as They Say).* Schwarz initially aligned himself with McIntire, the ACCC, and separatism. He appeared on McIntire's radio show and lectured in churches belonging to the organization. But Schwarz was not a fundamentalist, separatist, or premillennialist—only conservative and anti-Communist. As his popularity grew, he began to distance himself from militant fundamentalism, and his religious rhetoric became decidedly moderate. McIntire's initial link to Schwarz, however, demonstrates the internationalism of the Bible Presbyterian ministry and McIntire's willingness to work with nonmilitants if it suited his agenda.[99]

These relationships set the stage for McIntire's international crusade, which after the formation of the ICCC in 1948 increasingly took more of his attention. Although McIntire and the Bible Presbyterian Church already maintained an international fellowship through their support missionaries and through the foreign students studying at the Westminster and Faith seminaries, the ICCC's activities and agenda increased the scope of such activism. The International Council elevated McIntire's stature within militant fundamentalism, transforming him from an important American figure into an international crusader. It also enabled him to travel to Northern Ireland to meet the young Ian Paisley and thus to influence the development of Paisleyism. The international fellowship gave many of McIntire's militant allies—including Hargis and Springer—the opportunity to develop relationships with Paisley and other fundamentalists in Northern Ireland.

3

The Theological and Political Background to Ulster Protestantism

The factors that led to Paisleyism were not limited to American militant fundamentalism or to Irish revivalism and theological issues. The political, cultural, and economic history of the British Isles—from the Reformation through the mid-1950s—augmented the effects that fundamentalism, revivalism, and the transatlantic schisms within Presbyterianism contributed to Irish militant fundamentalism. This is clear from the historical references Paisley made throughout his ministry and the images he consistently used to connect his militant religiosity with Protestant martyrdom and traditional Calvinism. The political, cultural, and economic development of Ireland and Great Britain—a process that began with the English Reformation and continued through the spread of Protestantism into Scotland and Ireland and into modern Irish history—coalesced with American fundamentalism to set the stage for the career of the Reverend Ian Paisley.

The Plantation of Scottish Presbyterianism in Ulster

The Scottish Reformation was inextricably linked to the ministry of John Knox. A self-proclaimed prophet, Knox was the principal theologian of the Scottish Reformation. He helped to establish the Church of Scotland and was largely responsible for the success of Calvinism in Scotland. Knox argued that kings were subservient to the Bible and recognized the authority of civil government only if such authority did not contradict scripture. To Knox, the church and state must work together, although Scottish Calvinists could rebel against an ungodly ruler. Militant fundamentalists, including McIntire and Paisley, supported Knoxian principles; Knox's theology is evident in the American and Irish militant fundamentalist demand that government act in accord with the Bible. The *Protestant Telegraph,* a Free Presbyterian periodical, noted on several occasions the importance of Knox's theological and political stances to the Protestant cause in Scotland: "Such a man as Knox was used of God to further the Reformation in Scotland. . . . Knox believed that if civil rulers became tyrannical they could be deposed by their subjects."[1] Knox also taught that scripture was the inerrant Word of God, that proper church discipline required a trained and structured ministry, that the church had the duty to punish immorality and uphold the Sabbath, and that the Roman Catholic Church was the Whore of Babylon described in the biblical Book of Revelation. Ministers accordingly must proclaim the gospel while exposing apostasy and denouncing rulers who contradicted scripture.[2] In a sermon in 1963, Paisley argued that John Knox was as important to the Reformed faith in Ireland as were Martin Luther, Ulrich Zwingli, and John Calvin: "No Knox, No Kirk of Scotland, No Protestant Ulster."[3]

In spite of (and to a degree because of) the success of Calvinism in Scotland, the Scottish Kirk was afflicted with theological and political problems after the English, Irish, and Scottish crowns were united in 1603. Following his ascension to the throne, James I inserted bishops into the Presbyterian structure and imposed the Articles of Perth on the Scottish Church, which included Anglican sacraments such as private baptism and the celebration of festivals. James, an aspiring absolutist, forced these changes onto the Church of Scotland and an unwilling Scottish population—in part because he understood that Scottish bishops would strongly support the English monarchy. The religious situation within Scotland became more complex when Charles I pursued the Arminian theology of William Laud, the archbishop of Canterbury. Laudism denied predestination and revered the Eucharist and sacraments as the main channel to salvation, two tenets that were considered pro-Catholic and in diametrical opposition to Calvinism. Scottish Presbyterians detested Laudian theology. Charles supported Laud because the king wanted to make religious devotion uniform throughout his three kingdoms, so

Laud sought to elevate Charles's authority over the churches of England, Ireland, and Scotland.[4]

Both Charles and Laud believed that Calvinists were disloyal to the Crown and they sought to eradicate Reformed theology. When the king and his archbishop tried to impose the new Anglican Book of Common Prayer on Scotland and began to repossess the church property previously sold to Scottish nobles, Scottish Presbyterians were driven to rebel. Meeting in Glasgow, the rebels made an alliance with sympathetic nobles and swore an oath to the National Covenant of 1638. Although the covenant conditionally supported the king as the head of state, it did not accept James as the leader of the Scottish Church. It was a virulently anti-Catholic statement that condemned both the Laudian Book of Canons and the Articles of Perth and reconfirmed the Calvinist principles of John Knox. Laud's religious policies in Scotland not only drove the Scottish Covenanters into open rebellion but weakened the king's position with the English Parliament. In August 1643, in exchange for their military aid, the Scots forced the English Parliament to sign the Solemn League and Covenant. The document called for the Church of England to abandon its episcopal structure and to adhere to Calvinist doctrine. The Covenanters swore to defend Presbyterianism to the death and saw their fight against the Stuarts as a struggle for religious liberty and against despotism. Three years later Parliament and the Covenanters agreed to the Westminster Confession of Faith, which became a defining tenet of the Scottish Church, but which the Church of England repudiated after the Restoration.[5]

The success of Protestantism in England enabled a Calvinist Anglican Church to be established in Ireland. A majority of the Irish population stuck adamantly to the Catholic faith, however. Only a minority of the Anglo-Irish nobles and gentry and a small colony of Englishmen centered in Ireland's major towns accepted the new Church of Ireland. Because Irish Catholics were considered disloyal to the English Crown, the subjugation of Irish Catholicism and the augmentation of the Irish Protestant population became important aspects of English security. To accomplish this goal, English, Welsh, and Scottish Protestants were transplanted into the four provinces of Ireland through a program that began during the reign of Elizabeth I and continued throughout the seventeenth century. Although the plantation was only partially successful on most parts of the island, the arrival of thousands of lowland Scots—who brought their Presbyterian heritage and Reformed religion—in Ulster ensured that the population was largely Protestant and nonconformist.[6]

The Plantation of Ulster had a special significance; prior to the Scottish immigration, England's jurisdiction in Ulster was weak and the Protestant Reformation less successful than elsewhere in Ireland. In 1595, Hugh O'Neill, the Catholic earl of Tyrone and the strongest power in Ulster, rose in revolt to thwart further English encroachment. With support from chieftains throughout Ireland and with Spanish help, the earl initially appeared victorious. But when a Spanish expedition could not hold the southern port of Kinsale, O'Neill's army became overextended and was defeated attempting to relieve their Spanish allies. However, realizing that England's position in Ireland remained insecure, Elizabeth ordered her representatives to sign a peace treaty, which allowed a weakened O'Neill to retain his lordship and most of his traditional lands. When Elizabeth died, the treaty had yet to be finalized, and the new king, James I, ordered the administration in Dublin to change policy. The English Crown again moved against Ulster, and, understanding that his power had declined, O'Neill and several allies fled to the continent.[7]

The so-called "Flight of the Earls" left a vacuum in the North, enabling James I to confiscate O'Neill's and his allies' lands. As the king of the Scots and the English, James awarded the new property to new planters from both realms; undertakers from England and Scotland cleared the estates of the native Irish and recruited suitable settlers. The plan aimed to neutralize Ulster, to lessen the threat of foreign invasion, and to strengthen the Protestant position in Ireland. But an uneven balance developed: Scotland sent a larger number of poorer emigrants, but the smaller number of English brought more capital. Moreover, the undertakers did not always follow the orders of the English Crown and hired a substantial number of Gaelic Irish as tenants and laborers.[8]

Although O'Neill's defeat strengthened the Crown's control over Ulster, the strong presence of Scottish Presbyterians created a theological division within the Protestant population. In response, the Stuarts followed a religious policy in Ireland that established an Episcopal hierarchy and liturgy for the Church of Ireland but also accepted Presbyterian ministers. The Irish Church combined Anglicanism with Reformed theology: the Irish Articles of 1615, which established the tenets of the Irish Church, installed the five basic points of Calvinism, an episcopal structure, and the Book of Canons. The system temporarily allowed for a harmonious theological relationship between Anglicans and Presbyterians in Ireland; Irish Presbyterians felt that the state church considered their theological views.[9]

In Ulster, however, Scottish Presbyterians clung to the Covenanting tradition that gave a conditional support to the English Crown. After a majority of Scots Presbyterians swore allegiance to the National Covenant, Thomas Wentworth, the first earl of Strafford and the new lord deputy, required all Ulster Scots to repudiate the covenant. The Ulster Presbyterian ministers working within the Church of Ireland had to attest that the English king was the head of the church, a requirement that Calvinists could not accept. Wentworth's policy drove a majority of the Ulster Scots clergy out of the province; some of these ministers returned to Scotland, but others immigrated to the American colonies.[10]

Religious disaffection fused with political discontent. Needing new additional fiscal resources, the king ordered Wentworth to impose arbitrary fines on Presbyterian and Anglican planters and on the Irish Church. The fines alienated the entire spectrum of Irish Protestantism. Sensing that the weakness of the English Crown offered them an ideal opportunity to retake their lands and to strengthen Catholicism in Ireland, in 1641, Ulster's Gaelic and Catholic lords arose in rebellion. The rebels took their anger out on the entire Protestant community, massacring the English as well as Ulster Presbyterians. The 1641 massacres left a crucial legacy among Ulster Presbyterians, as one description testifies:

> Infant children were murdered before their mother's eyes. . . . Protestant parents had their eyes gouged out. Women were ravaged. . . . The priests and the bishops of Rome incited their parishioners to commit devilish acts. . . . It has been calculated that in Ulster alone 154,000 Protestants were massacred or expelled . . . where retaliation was possible the

> Protestants stood their ground. . . . [T]he foundations of the militant Protestant faith in Ulster were cemented with the blood of our forefathers. . . . They paid the price so that we could enjoy Protestant liberty.[11]

The massacres added fear to Ulster Scot anti-Catholicism; the Roman Catholics' treachery, perceived as a struggle between good (Protestantism) and evil (Catholicism), became a vital part of the Ulster Scots' cultural identity. To subdue the Catholic rebels, Charles raised an army in Scotland. This army also enabled Ulster Presbyterians to form the nucleus of an Irish church: the army brought along five Presbyterian chaplains and their congregations, who at Carrickfergus organized themselves into an Irish presbytery, the first official Presbyterian structure on the island.[12]

The situation in Ireland became increasingly complicated after the English Parliament formed an army and entered into civil war with Charles. The "Long" Parliament despised the king's autocratic rule and felt threatened by Charles's control over the Scottish army in Ireland. Ulster Scots, however, were uncomfortable in resisting the Stuart monarchy—a majority of Ulster Presbyterians opposed Oliver Cromwell and the parliamentary army during the following eight years—arguing that the execution of Charles I in 1649 was illegal. But the formation of the Confederate Catholics of Ireland (the Confederacy) in Kilkenny in October 1642 placed Ulster Presbyterians in a precarious position, and Irish Presbyterians were also forced to fight against Catholic military power. Order in Ireland was restored after Cromwell's New Model Army defeated both the royal army and the Confederacy and implemented a harsh system of land confiscations, transportations, and religious repression. Catholic priests were imprisoned, and Catholic worship outlawed; Presbyterian ministers were expelled to Scotland, and Presbyterian practices restricted. To strengthen English control over Ireland, Cromwell granted new lands in Ulster to English adventurers, most of whom were English Baptists and Independents and who had fought for or financially supported the Parliament.[13]

But Paisley, in his defense of Ulster's Protestant legacy, rehabilitated Oliver Cromwell into a man of God and a "Christian warrior who defended all Irish Protestants." Paisley's use of historical imagery could be revisionist in order to reinforce militant Protestantism in Ireland: "Oliver Cromwell's mission to Ireland has never been completed. He hoped and prayed for the conversion of the Irish, and he preached Protestantism wherever he went. Catholicism, as in Cromwell's day, has no right to exist in Ireland at all, the priests are intruders who have instigated numerous rebellions. They are poisoning their flocks with false, abominable anti-Christian doctrine and practices. Today we should complete the task, and strive for the conversion of the Irish."[14]

After the Restoration in 1660, however, Charles II imposed new legal restrictions on Presbyterians. The Act of Uniformity of 1662 required all Presbyterian ministers to use the Book of Common Prayer and to be ordained in the Episcopal manner, and the Test Act of 1672 required all officeholders to take the Oath of Supremacy and Allegiance to the King and to the Church of Ireland. The political and theological events of the early to mid-1600s, however, gave the Ulster Presbyterian Church enough confidence to withstand repression and to assure its existence. Cromwell instituted a policy of toleration for Ulster Presbyterians. Many of the Presbyterian ministers who had fled to Scotland a few years earlier were allowed to return and work as itinerant militant missionaries. Ulster Presbyterian ministers were granted *regium donum,* a royal stipend paid to Presbyterian clergymen. Tying the political developments with an entrenched Ulster Presbyterian Church was the revivalism that many Ulster Presbyterians favored. The Ulster Scots steadfastly adhered to the Covenanting tradition, the Westminster Confession of Faith, and revivalism.[15]

In spite of the new Ulster Presbyterian self-assurance, events in England and Scotland continued to influence the course of Ulster Presbyterianism. Charles II repudiated the Westminster Confession and the Solemn League and Covenant and reintroduced bishops into the Scottish General Assembly, causing many ministers to object and once again dividing the Scottish Church. Some Presbyterian ministers would not submit to Episcopal reordination or Episcopal authority, whereas others acquiesced. Although the objecting ministers were deposed for nonconformity, the existence of a semiorganized church enabled the Presbyterian ministers remaining in Ulster to retain their positions. The Carrickfergus Presbytery became the nucleus of an expanded Irish Presbyterian Church.[16]

When James II ascended to the British throne in 1685, the question of religion and parliamentary rights once again rose to the forefront of English and Irish politics. James's preference for Catholicism alarmed Protestants throughout the British Isles, but his new Irish policies gave dispossessed Irish Catholics the hope that they could regain both their property and their political power. In England, an alliance of seven powerful parliamentarians and nobles chose to thwart James and invite Prince William of Orange, the Dutch Stadtholder, to seize the English Crown. William's wife, Mary of Modena, had been first in line to the English throne until the birth of James Francis Edward Stuart in June 1688. On 6 November, William landed his Dutch army at Torbay on the southwest coast of England, and after James took flight to France, the Dutchman took control of England. But James had supporters in Ireland: in the southern provinces, Catholics seized control of the towns and garrisons. After solidifying his base, the deposed king swept into Ulster. Protestants in the North, however, rallied long enough to give William of Orange the opportunity to land his army at Carrickfergus. While Ulster Protestants held two vital towns—Londonderry (under siege for 105 days) and Eniskillen—William deployed his entire army against James. William's victories at the Battles of the Boyne and Aughrim impelled James II's second flight to France, secured the English Crown for William, and ensured that the monarchy of the British Isles would forever be Protestant.[17] The events of 1689, in particular the Siege of Derry and the Battle of the Boyne, took on mythical significance for militant Protestants, as Paisley's newspaper columns made clear: "There has always been conflict between Children of God and the forces of evil. In Ireland, the conflict has been particularly prevalent, and the Protestant faith, since the days of St. Patrick, has fought with popery for its very existence. Ulster is now the last bastion of Protestantism in Europe, and perhaps the world. The battles of faith were mostly fought in Ulster, and one in particular is in our minds at the moment. That is the siege of Derry in 1689."[18]

To solidify support throughout the British Isles, William III agreed to the Revolutionary Settlement and granted a bill of rights to his Protestant subjects, widened religious toleration to include all subjects but Catholics and Unitarians, and conceded triennial meetings to Parliament. At the same time, the conclusion of the Williamite War and a severe famine in Scotland drove new emigration from western Scotland into Ulster, greatly increasing the number of Presbyterians in the North. William's victory and the tolerance that his reign professed—although limited to Irish Presbyterians—and the new influx from Scotland created an environment that allowed Ulster Presbyterianism to form into the Synod of Ulster.[19] But unlike Presbyterians in England and Scotland, Irish Presbyterians did not gain complete toleration after the Revolutionary Settlement. The Church of Ireland saw Ulster Presbyterians as a threat—there were more reformed ministers per capita than Anglicans could produce, and so the *regium donum* was increased. Dissenting ministers could not legally perform marriages or baptisms, making it difficult for the children of Presbyterians to inherit family property. The Sacramental Test denied offices to dissenters who refused Anglican Communion.[20]

William allowed his Dublin administration to enact stronger penal laws to thwart a future Catholic rebellion. Additional land owned by Catholics was confiscated, and by 1700 Catholic ownership of Irish land fell to 14 percent of the total acreage. Enforcement of the penal laws began slowly, but after William's death in 1702 a new vindictiveness appeared. Catholics could not own guns or a horse worth five pounds, buy land, or enter into leases longer than thirty-one years. Catholics were barred from education and employment as lawyers, army officers, or public officials, and priests and bishops were persecuted. The enforcement of the penal laws was not as strong because Irish Anglicans lacked the resources and will to impose Protestantism throughout Ireland, and a fear of Presbyterian numbers existed. Frozen out of land ownership, Catholics joined the merchant class and were tenant farmers, and the Catholic Church survived. As the number of priests, Mass houses, and Catholic schools steadily grew during the eighteenth century, the Catholic gentry and urban middle class swore allegiance to the British Crown.[21]

As Catholics gained economically and politically during the eighteenth century, Ulster Presbyterianism began a political and cultural alignment with the English Crown despite the Anglican ascendancy's intolerant attitude. Presbyterians asserted Calvinism, their notion as God's chosen people and Catholics as God's damned, and a heritage of revivalism to assert a culture and religiosity different from Irish Catholicism. As Marilyn Westerkamp argues, the Ulster Scots' religious identity coalesced during the seventeenth century—a character built around revivalism and proto-evangelicalism. This religiosity played an important role in dividing Irish Presbyterians from their Catholic neighbors.[22] Revivalism accentuated communal divisions in Ulster. John Brewer and Gareth Higgins assert that Ulster anti-Catholicism was unique and differed from the anti-Catholicism in England and Scotland. In Ireland, anti-Catholicism was based on theological differences and on economic and cultural relationships, whereas in Great Britain it was based on politics. An overriding expression of Irish anti-Catholicism was manifest during revivals.[23]

Political Protestantism

After immigration to America abated in the 1720s, Ulster entered a period of prosperity. Over the subsequent eighty years, the combined impact of the British Industrial Revolution, the political revolutions in America and France, and Catholic emancipation upset both the economic and the political relationships within Ulster society. As a consequence, economic competition between Catholic and Protestant workers as well as between the merchants and industrialists of both traditions created new sectarian strife as Ireland industrialized. During the first four decades of the eighteenth century, Ulster was transformed from Ireland's poorest province into its wealthiest. The cultivation of potatoes and other foodstuffs was profitable, and the ready supply of food aided Ulster's industrialization. Access to water and the construction of new roads and canals stimulated the growing of flax, which enabled the establishment of a local linen industry. Protestants, however, were concerned that Catholics were gaining from their new role in the linen trade. Most linen manufacturing took place east of the Bann River, within the triangular geographic area bounded by Belfast, Lisburn, and Newry, which led to sectarian violence in areas containing a large mixed population.[24]

The impression of local labor and the imposition of new taxes for infrastructure improvements incited agrarian outrages, such as the houghing of cattle, while increased competition for rural tenancies and the proximity of linen manufacturers increased rents. The growing strife led to the formation of rural defense organizations, most notoriously the Catholic Defenders and the Protestant Peep O'Day Boys. The violence was random but consistent, taking place as nighttime hit-and-run attacks in which lightly armed Catholics were effective and as occasional set battles that Protestants always won. The sectarian strife led to the Battle of the Diamond on 21 September 1795. The battle, fought outside the town of Loughall in County Armagh, illustrated the nature of the conflict: although Catholics had the superior numbers, Protestants held most of the armaments and easily routed their neighbors. The Protestant victors celebrated their victory by forming the Loyal Orange Institution. Originally an organization of Anglican weavers and farmers expressing allegiance to the Crown and a militant evangelicalism, the order slowly expanded to include all sections and classes of the Protestant community.[25]

The republican and democratic philosophy imported from America and France encouraged some Presbyterians to reconcile their differences with their Catholic neighbors. Many Presbyterian radicals adopted the ideals of Thomas Paine and Jean-Jacques Rousseau, although support declined when France allied with the American revolutionaries. And when the threat of a French invasion spurred the English government to arm the Protestant Irish militia gentry, many Presbyterians rallied to the defense of Ireland. But the new militia, the Volunteers, was a mixed blessing for the English government: many Volunteers supported republicanism and used the threat of insurrection to demand legislative independence in Ireland and the easing of the discriminatory laws against Catholics. In 1782, Ireland gained parliamentary independence and the majority of the remaining penal laws were repealed. Moreover, two further laws increased religious tolerance in Ireland: the Sacramental Test was revoked in 1780, and the Relief Act of 1793 gave Catholics the right to an education at Trinity College, Dublin, and the ability to purchase land. Catholic property owners obtained the franchise; the right to bear arms; the ability to join the civil service, to serve as officers in the military, and to sit on grand juries. However, the act did not placate all Catholics and was too liberal for most Protestants, with the exception of extreme, political New Lights.[26]

Although these actions appeased many Presbyterian radicals, those who wanted a republic took action to achieve their aims. In October

1791, dissidents formed the Society of United Irishmen to eliminate English influences from the Irish government and to lessen the power of the established Anglican Church. Ian McBride argues that Irish republicanism originated with Presbyterians centered on the towns of Belfast and Newry and within the counties of Antrim and Down. The United Irishmen accordingly were most numerous in northeastern Ulster, an area where the sizable Protestant population minimized the fear of Catholic political and economic gains. Guided by New Light ministers and ideals, the United Irishmen were a religious as well as political movement and believed that an Irish republic equaled God's Kingdom on Earth; a Republican triumph could bring revival and hasten the End Times. Popular among Presbyterian artisans, farmers, and radical ministers, the United Irishmen combined political with religious ideas and sought to eliminate the power of the Anglican ascendancy and to form an alliance with moderate Catholics. Therefore, the Dungannon Manifesto, proclaimed 15 February 1782, supported Catholic emancipation and political rights. The United Irishmen hoped to strengthen Irish Protestantism, however, and argued that combining Enlightenment rationalism and reform would encourage "emancipated" Catholics to embrace reformed Christianity. As Irish Catholics freed themselves from Rome, the Irish Catholic Church would accordingly become superfluous.[27]

When Britain joined the crusade against republican France in 1793, Presbyterian radicalism alarmed British prime minister William Pitt. The Dublin administration moved both to disarm the United Irishmen and to suppress their political aspirations. Expecting help from a French expeditionary force and seeking to impose a republican parliamentary government, the United Irishmen and Catholic republicans joined in revolt. But reports of Catholic atrocities in Wexford alarmed many Presbyterians, who thus abandoned the United Irishmen and joined with Dublin. Despite French assistance, the Rebellion of 1798 was defeated, and Presbyterian radicalism diminished.[28]

Presbyterian radicals still hoped to free Irish Catholics from popery and discriminatory legal restrictions, but Catholic "liberty" had to take place in a political union with Great Britain. Presbyterians who favored Arianism argued vehemently for a more comprehensive Catholic emancipation, whereas Presbyterian evangelicals sought a more restrictive franchise. After the rebellion, the "Irish Question" became one of Britain's most pressing political issues. British policy aimed to eliminate political and economic disadvantages for both Catholics and dissenters and at the same time to restrict Irish parliamentary independence. The Act of Union of 1801 abolished the Irish Parliament and made Ireland an integral part of the United Kingdom. Irish Protestants united to secure the union, and Protestant support for a separate Irish Parliament disappeared. A political coalition of Presbyterians, Anglicans, and nonconformists coalesced as Catholic political ambitions progressed. But Catholic emancipation and the Act of Union did not resolve the Irish Question. The nineteenth century saw the rise of Protestant unionism and Catholic nationalism as well as a widening political impasse. As Irish Catholics argued for emancipation, the Irish Education Act, and Home Rule, Irish Presbyterians and Irish Anglicans formed an alliance to resist British gestures toward their Catholic neighbors.[29]

Economic and political destabilization coalesced with the revivalism and anti-Catholicism of Ulster Protestantism to strengthen the division between the Protestant and Catholic communities. A public expression of the new Protestant solidarity began as early as the late eighteenth century. Protestant organizations began annual parades to celebrate important anniversaries and to mark territory; such demonstrations were intended to intimidate Catholic neighbors and to press a political agenda. The propensity for publicly demonstrating Protestant prowess established a tradition of religious-based political marching in Ireland. Moreover, parading played an important role within the Orange Order, enhancing members' identification with the organization, inspiring loyalty, and legitimizing Orange violence. At times, marches were designed to defy authority. For example, the prospect of Catholic emancipation inspired large Orange Order parades in July 1829, although the Orange Institution had only been reconstituted that year. Marching helped to unite the Presbyterian and Anglican traditions in Ulster and provided an important link between Anglican and Presbyterian radicalism in the 1790s, Unionist defiance to Home Rule in the 1880s, and Protestant political power between 1921 and 1972. The Reverend Paisley would employ similar marches in the

1960s to protest "apostasy" and Catholic civil rights; Paisley's marches continued the same spirit of Protestant defiance to enforce ethnic territorial boundaries and to assert political points.[30]

The alliance of Ulster Protestantism required that the Church of Ireland develop a tolerance to the Presbyterian and nonconformist minorities. Only then could a common front against Catholic political gains in Ireland be formed. The acceptance of evangelicalism throughout Ulster Protestantism, acquiescence to British democratic ideals and the union, and demands for social reform helped to make the new attitude possible. Bible reading, revivalism, new political organizations (such as Brunswick Clubs), and moral reform helped stimulate a movement to convert Catholics to Protestantism and to bring on God's Kingdom on Earth and the End Times. Anglican and Presbyterian clerics confidently proclaimed a "Second Reformation" but spurred the Bible War in 1824. Catholic and Protestant clergy and laity fought for control of educational facilities and to prevent the other from proselytizing. Moreover, the Catholic clergy intensely opposed the attempt to assimilate Catholics into the Protestant community. The new reform movement, however, helped to secure the coalition between Irish Presbyterian, dissenter, and Anglican that coalesced during the Home Rule crisis and the partition of Ireland.[31]

The evangelical movement in Ireland created new doctrinal conflicts within Irish Presbyterianism as a theological split developed between the hierarchy and the laity. As a general rule, the church-going laity supported conservative evangelical theology, the evangelistic efforts, and itinerant preaching, whereas clergymen tended to support theological liberalism and Unitarianism.[32] For instance, a controversy developed after Unitarians opened the Belfast Academical Institute in 1814 as a Presbyterian institution. In 1821, the Reverend W. D. H. McEwen, a teacher of elocution at the new school, brought the English Socinian John Smethurst to Ulster on a preaching tour, which upset denominational conservatives.[33] Henry Cooke, who succeeded McEwen as the minister of Killyleagh Presbyterian Church, objected to Smethurst's visit and began a campaign to eradicate Unitarians from the Synod of Ulster. Although Cooke was not universally supported within Irish Presbyterianism—many ministers were sympathetic to Smethurst—Cooke held enough stature to be elected moderator in 1825. Asserting his position and exploiting fears over Christian liberalism, Cooke ensured that for the next century all future Presbyterian ministers would publicly support the Trinitarianism of the Westminster Confession.[34]

Cooke and Ulster's evangelical Presbyterians wanted to maintain Protestant political unity against the threat of Catholic civil rights. Cooke made the argument that only a political pact between Irish Presbyterianism and the Church of Ireland would maintain the hegemony of Ulster Protestantism and assure the political union with Britain. Cooke campaigned to defeat the nonsectarian National Education System, which would have provided for uniform Bible teaching (with no Protestant bias); attacked Catholic emancipation and repeal; and crusaded against both the disestablishment of the Church of Ireland and the Party Processions Act. He instituted a new forceful style of preaching and organized confrontations that often incited sectarian violence. Moreover, in 1828, when Catholic emancipation became law, Cooke's sermons helped to incite numerous riots in Belfast and surrounding cities. His campaign had its apogee in 1832 when he was the featured speaker at a mass demonstration in Hillsborough organized by Anglican landowners. Although at least sixty thousand Protestants heard the minister plead for Anglican–Presbyterian unity, his friendship with the Anglican ascendancy alienated many Presbyterians who maintained an affection for republican radicalism.[35]

Cooke's greatest legacy was his ability to mix evangelicalism, political activism, and confrontation into the new method of militant preaching. A succession of Presbyterian and Anglican preachers who employed the same aggressive style followed in his footsteps. One such cleric, the Reverend Tresham Gregg, a Dublin-based evangelical preacher, formed the Belfast Protestant Operatives' Society in 1843 as a Protestant defense force to replace the temporarily banned Orange Order. Gregg's rhetoric during the Belfast Riots of 1843 incited sectarian violence within the Pound and Sandy Row communities. Rural Protestants and Catholics immigrated to Belfast with an entrenched ethnic bigotry, and Protestant ministers' evangelical campaigns and political agendas added to the city's sectarian troubles. Militant preaching increased during the 1840s and 1850s; at the same time, open-air preaching, which aimed to reclaim back-sliding

Presbyterians and convert Catholics, became a common form of evangelization throughout the Ulster countryside. The militant style appeared in Belfast, and public witness became an increasingly common sight within the city. Although only eight such preachers existed in 1851, four years later Belfast had approximately sixty of them. The rise can be attributed to new support from the Presbyterian General Assembly and from the Church of Ireland, which set up the Belfast Parochial Mission to witness to the city's poor and working class. Until the summer of 1857, open-air preaching was not considered political or provocative and only on rare occasions invoked Catholic violence.[36]

An anti-Catholic sermon by the Reverend Thomas Drew, the vicar of Christ Church in Belfast, preceded the 12 July Orange parades and increased tensions during the marching season in 1857. Drew organized the Christ Church Protestant Association to mobilize Protestant political action and created a stand-off between Protestants and Catholics outside Christ Church, where he joined with two Anglican ministers, the Reverends William McIlwaine and Thomas Wellesley Roe, in organizing a series of public sermons. Although street preaching by Anglican ministers was a relatively new evangelizing phenomenon, it was also an alternative to Protestant marching because Orange parades were banned. Their rhetoric helped to incite six days of intense rioting. Any open-air preaching insulted Catholic sensibilities. Outdoor sermons were cancelled by city magistrates in a move supported by the Anglican and Presbyterian hierarchies. The Reverend Hugh Hanna, an anti-Catholic zealot and disciple of the Reverend Henry Cooke, felt that Catholic mobs had forced the ban and vowed to uphold Protestant liberty. Any opposition to open-air preaching was seen as an attack on Protestant civil and religious liberties. In August and September, Hanna began a new open-air campaign that drew large, angry Catholic mobs in response. As a result, new rioting took place, the most violent in Belfast up to that date. Hanna, who was not supported by his Presbyterian or Anglican colleagues, asserted Protestants' right to evangelize publicly, regardless of the consequences—a tactic that the Reverend Ian Paisley would copy one century later. Mark Doyle has shown that Drew and Hanna's ministry represented Ulster evangelicals who wanted to take the battle to the Roman Church and to Catholic Ulstermen.[37]

The 1857 riots took place in the decade that witnessed a new outbreak of revivalism. Several years earlier, as a response to declining church attendance and urbanization, young Presbyterian ministers had advocated a return to revival and a more emotional style of preaching. Religious enthusiasm broke out in Antrim in March 1859 after two ministers sent by the General Assembly to investigate the American Awakening of 1857 returned to Ireland. Building on the open-air preaching campaigns, the Revival had both long- and short-term impacts on Ulster Presbyterianism. Liquor consumption dropped, and church attendance increased, inspiring a new piety in the Ulster Scot community and a demand for the independent gospel halls that would later help the young Ian Paisley's early career. Moreover, as Andrew Holmes argues, the 1859 Revival built on trends that had been developing within Irish Presbyterianism over the previous century but also changed how Irish Presbyterians understood revival. Instead of spontaneous events and a regeneration of the church body, revivals became more "planned" or man made, where an individual and instantaneous conversion was possible through the work of the Holy Ghost.[38]

During the second half of the nineteenth century, however, popular evangelicalism in Ulster became more pietistic in practice and premillennial in eschatology—two characteristics that influenced the Paisley family and fellow Irish fundamentalists. The alteration of Irish Protestant religiosity was owing to the reemergence of mass revivalism and to the introduction of Home Rule for Ireland by the Liberal Party at Westminster. The 1859 Revival also introduced a new invectiveness toward Irish Catholics. The secular and religious leadership of Protestant Ulster increasingly employed religious imagery in speeches and sermons. Evangelicalism and its anti-Catholic expressions were associated with radical street preaching and Unionist politics throughout the rest of the nineteenth century. The Revival accordingly further embedded evangelism within the Irish Presbyterian tradition and the Ulster Protestant identity and widened the religious and cultural differences between Belfast's Protestant and Catholic communities.[39]

Less than three decades later, as the Land War and Home Rule galvanized anti-Catholicism, Hugh Hanna denounced the first Home Rule Bill, encouraged rioting against the legislation and charged that police efforts to contain Protestant violence were risking civil war and bolstering Catholic political power: "Ireland at this moment is within arm's length of civil war. The possibility of an appeal to arms as the inevitable settlement of the Irish question is discussed in calm and heroic resolution at ten thousand homes in Ulster. Every capable Loyalist should be enrolled in a logical defensive union to meet any emergency that may arise."[40]

Paisley was well aware that his campaigns followed in this tradition of forceful preaching and confrontation and of pursuing evangelicalism, revivalism, antiliberalism, and anti-Catholicism: "Dr. Henry Cooke was an Evangelical Protestant; he announced Biblical Truth and denounced Popish errors. It is written of him that he preached with a Bible in one hand and a gun in the other. He knew that the cause of Christ was the only cause and it must be defended no matter what the consequences."[41] Through Paisley's tactics, the militant street preaching and politics of Henry Cooke and Hugh Hanna reemerged. There are two vital differences, however, between Paisley and his two historical mentors: the theology behind each preacher's politics and the style of street activism each pursued. First, Cooke's traditional Irish Presbyterian evangelism and Hanna's Anglican rhetoric reached out to all Ulster Protestants, whereas Paisley intended his militant fundamentalism strictly for a separatist minority. Second, Cooke, Hanna, and their associates incited Protestants, but they did not lead mobs themselves, whereas Paisley was willing to confront Catholic marchers personally. But there is a similarity between Hanna and Paisley's methods: whereas Henry Cooke never advocated a violent confrontation with the British government, Hugh Hanna certainly did. In the summer of 1886, Hanna incited riots against Gladstone's first Home Rule bill, and Lord Randolph Churchill spoke to an Ulster Hall audience urging violent resistance to the Liberal plan for Ireland: "Ulster will fight and Ulster will be right"; Home Rule equaled Rome rule. Nearly one century later Paisley would organize quasi-paramilitary movements to oppose British government policy in Northern Ireland.[42]

Another Protestant militant who helped build the bridge between Paisley, Henry Cooke, and Ulster revivalism was Arthur Trew, a fundamentalist lay preacher and labor activist. During the early years of the twentieth century, Trew attacked the Catholic Church and the Unionist ascendancy. Speaking from Belfast's Custom House steps, he led counter-demonstrations against Catholic marchers, which created sectarian violence—the largest example being a Corpus Christi procession that 4,500 Protestants harassed. For his efforts, Trew received a twelve-month jail sentence. Although Cooke and Hanna advocated Protestant solidarity and espoused anti-Catholicism, it was through preachers such as Trew that these tenets were fused with the working-class populism of tenants' and workers' rights and were centered on Belfast. Ulster's largest city accordingly continued in the radical tradition of the United Irishmen, although with a populist antagonism toward the Unionist ascendancy and with a philosophy that did not include a rapprochement with the Catholic community. The combination of Presbyterian radicalism and the promotion of evangelical Christianity became important factors during the 1920s, when an extensive evangelical crusade coincided with the partition of Ireland and the founding of the Northern Ireland statelet.[43]

Although the political and economic developments of the nineteenth century were essential to the formation of a modern Ulster Protestant identity, the evangelical tradition of Northern Ireland Protestantism was equally important. In Northern Ireland, evangelicalism served not only as an attempt to win converts, but also as a means to defend Ulster Protestantism. This was true across the entire spectrum of Northern Irish Protestantism, from the large majority of Anglicans and Presbyterians through the sizeable numbers of Methodists, Baptists, Brethren, and other nonconformist evangelicals. Within each church was a large group of evangelicals who contrasted their version of Christianity and their sense of British nationality with Roman Catholicism and Irish Catholic nationalism.[44]

The evangelical identity of Ulster Protestantism would become more radical in the twentieth century as evangelicalism in Ulster fractured. Critical of fundamentalism and separatism, some evangelicals remained in mainstream denominations, such as the Presbyterian Church in Ireland and the Church of Ireland.[45] Within the diverse family of Ulster evangelicals developed several small fundamentalist churches that shared the same desire to defend Ulster Protestantism, but that were more militant and separatist about the Protestant dimension to the Ulster identity. These Protestants saw their role as defending both the true Protestant faith and

Northern Ireland's political status. Ulster's equivalent of American fundamentalist militants, they included independent Baptists such as Kyle Paisley, evangelical Methodists, and, most important, the Reverend Ian Paisley's Free Presbyterians. Of all the Protestant denominations and religious leaders in Northern Ireland, no church or cleric professed a stronger desire to combine evangelical religiosity with political activism than the Free Presbyterians and Paisley. In the 1960s, this political evangelicalism became known as "Paisleyism."[46]

Paisleyism was the end product of the religious and political history of Ulster outlined to this point. Its religious dimension derived from three centuries of Irish Presbyterian evangelism and revivalism, its export to the American colonies and development into fundamentalism, and the repatriation of militant fundamentalism back to Northern Ireland. Paisleyism politically connected the English and Scottish Reformations and the relationship that developed between Westminster and Ireland through colonization, plantation, and imperialism with the Act of Union and the establishment of the Northern Ireland statelet. It theologically linked revivalism, the theological controversies within Irish Presbyterianism, and fundamentalism. Paisleyism would never have developed, however, without the uniquely Irish battle pitting Protestant Unionism and evangelical identity against Irish Catholic nationalism—Paisley's career exemplified this confluence of religiosity and political activity.

PART TWO

The New Testament

Premillennial Paisleyism

4

A Fundamental Defense of Ulster Protestantism

The first three chapters outlined the influences that were vital to the formation of Paisleyism: the emergence of American fundamentalism, the political and economic maturation of the Northern Ireland statelet, and the coalescence of evangelism and revivalism into the Protestant identity of Ulster. This chapter explores the intersection of these three developments. In history, timing and the sequence of events are important. The Reverend Ian Paisley's Christian and political viewpoints would have evolved in a different manner if American Protestant fundamentalism had not been introduced into Ireland and if it had not come during the 1920s, the contentious decade that gave birth to Northern Ireland as a political entity. Although the Irish clergy maintained a steady discourse with American counterparts and were well aware of the growing modernist–fundamentalist controversy of the early twentieth century, the Irish Protestant laity came into direct contact with the theological concept through the evangelist crusade of William Patterson Nicholson.[1]

Born in April 1876 in Cottown, Northern Ireland, Nicholson grew up in a devout Presbyterian family. Educated at the Bible Training Institute in Glasgow—an institution that D. L. Moody strongly influenced—Nicholson worked as an evangelist in Scotland and Australia before ending up in the United States on the eve of the First World War. Although the Presbyterian Church in the U.S.A. ordained Nicholson as a minister, he associated with fundamentalists of all denominations and adopted a militant theology. Most of his exposure to fundamentalism and separatism occurred during his stays at the Moody Memorial Church in Chicago and at the Los Angeles Bible Institute. In 1920, an illness forced him to return to Ulster, and after addressing a meeting of workers, he began the first of two interdenominational revival and tent campaigns. These efforts were aimed primarily at the Protestant working class; for instance, during his second campaign, which began in 1924, the evangelist helped to found the Irish Alliance of Christian Workers (an organization that has continued to exist and still sporadically conducts revivals) to spread the gospel among the Protestant working class. Many of the workers Nicholson attracted were not churchgoers.[2]

During his meetings, Nicholson espoused a theology that resonated with the Ulster Protestant community. Many Protestants were wary of the unstable political situation that partition created and were susceptible to the deliverance and millennialism that a revival promised. Working in areas such as the Shankill Road in West Belfast and employing unorthodox methods, such as rough, colorful, and "un-Christian" language, Nicholson made an immediate impact. Many Ulstermen amazingly—Ulster Protestants are historically Calvinist—accepted the message of universal atonement, the promise of being "born again," and premillennialism. In addition, extensive newspaper coverage ensured the campaign's popularity and Nicholson's notoriety. His revivalism employed populist anti-Catholicism; for instance, he preached that the Free State and the Catholic Church were conspiring to destroy Protestant Ulster—closely associating his message with the local political situation. During his initial campaign, his meetings were held amid a continual cycle of sectarian street fighting, and IRA violence ensured support from the Unionist leadership. In 1921 and 1922, Belfast experienced extensive sniping and street violence, and Northern Ireland endured Irish Republican attacks and an economic boycott in the South. Mark Sidwell argues that because Nicholson's preaching diverted attention from economic problems and encouraged Protestant workers to remain loyal to the UUP, the Protestant ascendancy tacitly supported Nicholson. Sidwell contends that the evangelist's second campaign received less evident support from the Protestant political and economic leadership because it came at a less contentious time.[3]

Nicholson's legacy and his near-prophetic status inspired a devotional renewal among a wide spectrum of Ulster evangelicals—including the

Reverend James Hunter, minister of the Knock Presbyterian Church in Belfast; James Kyle Paisley; and William James (W. J.) Grier, a young doctoral student at the Presbyterian College, Belfast. Grier had been "saved" during the Nicholson campaign. All three were conservative Calvinists, but because of Nicholson's strong attacks on liberalism and modernism, they overlooked his Arminian ideal of unlimited atonement. Like many Irish Presbyterians, Hunter, Paisley, and Grier were concerned with modernism in the Irish and Scottish churches. Until the early twentieth century, Irish Protestant theologians were overall conservative, and liberals did not publicly endorse higher criticism or Darwinism. Andrew Holmes attributes this stance to several considerations: the legacy of revivalism and the 1859 Revival, conservative leadership, and a general belief that defense of biblical authority equated with defense of the Protestant ascendancy in Ireland. An undercurrent of liberal and modernist ideas had developed in Irish Presbyterianism since the 1830s, but although many Irish ministers accepted the ideas, they did not include higher criticism into their preaching.[4]

Although the Presbyterian Church in Ireland officially condemned Unitarianism and liberal theology during the 1829 schism, support for modernism began to reappear in the late nineteenth century. For example, in 1888 Thomas Walker, a professor of Hebrew in Belfast, was found to support German higher criticism, and Magee College in Londonderry dropped its religious test for the academics of its Arts Department. During the first two decades of the twentieth century, the theological beliefs of many Irish Presbyterian clergymen and missionaries created friction. Modernist ideas—such as denying any limits on God's mercy,[5] insisting that the Bible was not infallible, and believing that miracles, the Virgin Birth, and the Resurrection were mythic truths rather than scientific facts—appeared in a number of Irish Presbyterian publications.[6]

In June 1905, Hunter and the Belfast Presbytery protested the Irish Presbyterian Church's decision to support the United Free Church of Scotland, a new denomination formed out of the United Presbyterian Church of Scotland and the Free Church of Scotland. The new Scottish church did not require its adherents to subscribe to the Westminster Confession.[7] Hunter took his concerns about the modernist ideas espoused by Presbyterian missionaries to the Presbyterian General Assembly and charged the Reverend F. W. S. O'Neill, a missionary to China, with heresy. O'Neill, who professed Arianism and rewrote biblical tracts in a simpler manner that the Chinese could more easily understand, successfully defended himself.[8]

Nicholson's campaign incited Hunter to further action. The "heretical" writings that irked Hunter the most were J. Ernest Davey's *The Changing Vesture of the Faith* (1921) and *Our Faith in God Through Jesus* (1922). Davey, who held the Chair of Biblical Criticism at the Irish Presbyterian College (later renamed the Chair of Old Testament Language, Literature, and Theology), argued that God's grace was available to all; that Christ was not sinless and while on the cross felt he had "let God down"; that the Bible was neither infallible nor the sole Word of God; that there is no original sin; and that Christians should not be required to accept the Trinity as a basis of faith. To Davey, the New Testament did not teach the doctrine of the Trinity. Moreover, Davey and Irish Presbyterian liberals supported the ideal of the freedom of the individual conscience, even for ordained clergymen. In *The Changing Vesture of the Faith*, Davey asserted: "Salvation is usually connected with the historic fact of Christ's death rather than the divine character which it reveals."[9]

Hunter took it upon himself to attack what he saw as apostasy and arrogance. In 1926, he began to speak out, drawing large crowds and receiving backing from diverse groups such as the newly formed (Presbyterian) Bible Standards League. Hunter and his followers initially opposed only the proposed changes to the ordination process in which new ministers would no longer be asked if they believed in the traditional interpretation of the Westminster Confession or if the confession faithfully reflected the Word of God. Nevertheless, support from the league did not prevent a motion of censure against Hunter from the Belfast Presbytery for his public statements, which the presbytery argued broke church protocol, or prevent the defeat of Hunter's appeal to the General Assembly. It was when Hunter charged Davey with heresy, however, that Hunter's relationship with the Irish Presbyterian Church took a fatal course. W. J. Grier, a student of Davey's, approached Hunter in April 1926 to complain about the liberal lectures given by both Davey and the Reverend James Haire, a professor of systematic theology. Using the information Grier supplied, Hunter and the Bible Standards League openly called for Davey's dismissal. Hunter was once again censured for his public charges and for abjuring the church's judicial procedures.[10]

In December 1926, Hunter sought his revenge and formally charged Davey with heresy for teaching theology contrary to the Westminster Confession and for questioning the infallibility of the Bible. Five charges were brought against the theologian, included in three lengthy indictments that Grier witnessed,[11] and under Presbyterian procedure the church was required to hold a trial at the next General Assembly. The following June Davey made his defense and asserted that Jesus was divine but that his humanity was consubstantial, that he accepted the Trinity but in a historical sense and not in the strict traditional and fundamentalist context, and that scripture and the Westminster Confession of Faith did not preclude scientific or historical criticism. Wanting to maintain denominational unity over theological purity, the assembly voted sixty-five to eleven for exoneration.[12]

Public interest in the Bible Standards League had been minimal until Hunter began his proceedings against Davey. Some Irish Presbyterians left their churches because their ministers voted for Davey. The league published a series of pamphlets outlining its heresy charges against him, and Scottish and English ministers spoke at meetings in Londonderry, Coleraine, and smaller towns.[13] Hunter and his fundamentalist allies were appalled at Professor Davey's victory and appealed the verdict, but the trial and Davey's victory convinced Hunter, Grier, and their supporters to withdraw their memberships in the General Assembly. In October 1927, they formed a new denomination, the Irish Evangelical Church, a move that preceded Machen and McIntire's denominational schism by a decade. But many fundamentalists within the Bible Standards League and the Irish Presbyterian Church were reluctant to follow Hunter into the new denomination.[14] Like some conservative American Presbyterians, these clerics chose to confront liberalism and modernism from within the mainstream Presbyterian Church. But Hunter and Grier represented other Presbyterian fundamentalists who perceived that communion with the church was no longer feasible. These separatists argued that it would be easier to continue to expose and confront Presbyterian liberal and modernist apostasy from outside the Presbyterian Assembly.[15]

The Davey trial also took on transatlantic implications and established another link, although indirect, between North American militant fundamentalism and the future career of the Reverend Ian Paisley. W. J. Grier had attended Princeton Theological Seminary, where he earned a master's of divinity, and had been a student of J. Gresham Machen.[16] Owing to this relationship and because Princeton and the General Assembly in America were experiencing their own theological rifts, Machen took an interest in the Davey trial. Grier wrote to Machen, in one letter asking the American to propose questions to ask Davey at his trial and in another for advice on the appeal after Davey's acquittal.[17] Machen's stature was high enough with British fundamentalists that he made a two-week tour of the British Isles, which included speaking engagements in Londonderry's Guildhall and at the Ulster Hall in Belfast on June 5, 1927. Machen's efforts also interested Davey and Irish Presbyterian liberals; several weeks after Machen's visit to Ulster, his tour was noted by Davey, who disliked the "American" theology (i.e., conservative Calvinism) taught at Princeton and who urged the Irish General Assembly to "say what we think . . . in spite of Dr. Machen."[18]

James Kyle Paisley and American Fundamentalism

The Paisley family was introduced to the international network of separatist fundamentalism through William Patterson Nicholson's revivals in Northern Ireland and through a personal relationship with T. T. Shields of Canada. Kyle Paisley's involvement with militancy grew after he became a regular reader of *The Gospel Witness,* the weekly newspaper that Shields published in Toronto. Shields, born in England, became a Baptist minister in 1894 and the pastor of the Jarvis Street Baptist Church sixteen years later. Within ten years, his Jarvis Street church had become the largest Baptist congregation in Canada. Shields turned his church into a bastion for militant fundamentalism, inviting such notables as the antiliberal and antisocialist J. Frank Norris of Texas to preach. Shields opposed modernism and the ecumenical movement and opened the Toronto Baptist Seminary for fundamentalist Baptists. His notoriety made him a popular speaker in North America, the British Isles, and Australia. For example, in 1915 he traveled to England to preach in Spurgeon's Tabernacle in London. During this visit, he established his militant credentials when he charged that Roman Catholics in Quebec were hindering Canada's efforts during war. It is through this fame and through *The Gospel Witness* that Irishmen such as Kyle Paisley came in contact with Canadian militant fundamentalism.[19]

T. T. Shields was a strict moralist and an aggressive evangelical. He preached a separatism that argued against modernism and the Roman Catholic Church. He demanded frequent Bible studies and revival campaigns and was initially well respected within the American and Canadian evangelical communities. Shields became the president of the Baptist Bible Union of North America, which he organized with two fundamentalist leaders in the United States, the antievolutionist William Bell Riley of Minneapolis and J. Frank Norris. The Bible Union's First General Conference met in Kansas City in May 1925 and included both Canadian Baptists and allies from the Northern and Southern Baptist Conventions. But Shields's theology and moral stance created conflict with North American liberals and fundamentalists alike: ten years after his election, the abrasive preacher created a split within his own congregation even as he fought the Baptist Convention of Ontario and Quebec over modernism. His denunciation of sinful living, such as drinking, gambling, and dancing, and his dictatorial style upset the more moderate (and wealthy) members of his flock. Moreover, in the 1920s Shields attacked McMaster University professors I. G. Matthews and L. H. Marshall for teaching modernist theology as well as the *Canadian Baptist* for printing liberal editorials. When the Baptist Bible Union purchased Des Moines University in Iowa in 1927, Shield's dictatorial management and insistence on militant fundamentalism impelled so many students to leave the university that the union had to sell it. Shields also lost support owing to his eschatological and amillennial stances. He was not a dispensationalist and espoused a Calvinist form of fundamentalism that leaned toward amillennialism. He saw an apostate and immoral world that needed the redemption of the Second Coming, but in the Calvinist sense that it would come only through God's grace. The Canadian did not believe that Christ would establish his Kingdom on Earth, but rather that after his return Jesus would combine heaven and Earth into Paradise. In 1931, Shields orchestrated the expulsion of strict premillennialists from the Baptist Bible Union.[20]

In 1933, Kyle Paisley welcomed Shields to Northern Ireland; Shields had crossed the Atlantic to take part in a preaching tour to commemorate the Charles Haddon Spurgeon centenary.[21] Shields took much of his preaching style and some of his separatism from Spurgeon, the famous nineteenth-century English preacher whom Kyle Paisley also emulated. A close friendship developed between Kyle Paisley and Shields, as was evident when Shields laid the foundation stone for the Waveney Road church in Ballymena despite Paisley's adherence to strict premillennial eschatology.[22] Like Shields, Kyle Paisley was a moralist and separatist evangelical. Paisley took part in similar struggles against the Baptist Union of Britain and Ireland and used the same aggressive style; the elder Paisley's message attacking apostasy resonated with his son. Three decades later the Reverend Ian Paisley would utilize this style of confrontation against theological foes and one-time allies alike. But the manner that Kyle and Ian Paisley deployed differed from Shields's approach: the Paisleys were willing to work with Calvinist separatists of diverse denominational and eschatological backgrounds. As a consequence, throughout the last two decades of Kyle Paisley's ministry, both father and son would support each other's careers despite the son's adoption of Presbyterianism. The elder Paisley was invited on numerous occasions to preach to Free Presbyterian congregations, and in 1966 the Waveney Road church joined Ulster's Free Presbyterian Church.[23]

Free Presbyterianism in Ulster

The Reverend Ian Paisley's religiosity, his crusade as a militant fundamentalist, and his career as a politician are rooted in his childhood and teenage years. Ian Richard Kyle Paisley was born on 6 April 1926 in the city of Armagh. Within the Northern Irish context, there was nothing unusual in the young Paisley's childhood. The Paisley family was not well off; the elder Paisley practiced old-fashioned stern discipline; and the family was pious. Most of young Ian's relationships were either with family or members of his father's church. It was not exceptional that the younger Paisley came to Christ—or became "saved"—as a young man, but it is unusual that he did so at age six and after hearing his mother preach. The event gave an early indication of the direction his life would take, and from a young age Ian seemed destined for the ministry. Schooling was unexceptional for Ian, although he did well enough to prepare himself for the nondenominational Barry School of Evangelism near Cardiff in Wales, a school run by a fundamentalist Baptist who was a friend of his father. Beginning his religious training at the age of sixteen and in the midst of the Second World War, the young Paisley stayed in Wales for a year before returning to Northern Ireland to attend the Theological Hall of the Reformed Presbyterian Church in Ireland as a guest student.[24] At both schools, he developed a good reputation for public speaking and preaching, skills he promptly made use of at the end of the war. Moreover, the Reformed Theological Hall taught premillennialism, which reinforced the eschatology that his father professed.[25]

In the aftermath of the Second World War, Britain saw a revival of church attendance, and in Northern Ireland the interest in Christianity was intense. In the most religious province of Great Britain, northern Irish newspapers routinely carried advertisements announcing church services, and local clergymen were active in social and religious campaigns. Paisley made important friends around Belfast, such as W. J. Grier, now a young minister of the Irish Evangelical Church. Paisley began his ministry as an itinerant, preaching to Irish evangelical and fundamentalist Baptist churches as well as to Christian Worker's Union meetings. He also knocked on doors, spoke to Orange lodges, and appeared at gospel halls and tent missions in Belfast, Lisburn, and the Ballymena area. He presented a simple, fundamentalist message based on old-fashioned revivalism.[26] During his early period of street preaching, he formalized his preaching and evangelizing technique, utilizing skills learned at school, from his father, and through practice. He combined the American-style emotionalism and "altar calls" used by D. L. Moody and W. P. Nicholson as well as the confrontational tactics of Henry Cooke, Thomas Drew, and Hugh Hanna with a strong Calvinist message against immorality, ecumenism, and modernism.[27]

In December 1945, the young evangelist's career took a fortunate turn when he received an offer to preach to the Ravenhill Evangelical Mission

Church. The membership of the independent evangelical Ravenhill congregation in East Belfast included fundamentalists who had left the Methodist, Baptist, and Brethren churches. The Mission Church had grown out of a split that took place within the Ravenhill Presbyterian Church ten years earlier. During this schism, conservative members withdrew, objecting that some of the girls in the church choir, including the daughter of the church's minister, were allowed to cut their hair short. Paisley quickly became popular with Ravenhill's congregants because of his strong evangelical and fundamentalist message, his Friday night meetings, and his canvassing of local households and pubs. He also became known for his virulent attacks on the Roman Catholic Church and his rants against the Irish Presbyterian Church's support for ecumenism. During the summer of 1946, Ian Paisley was invited, in spite of his youth, to become the pastor of the sixty-member Ravenhill Mission.[28]

Paisley's ordination had important connotations both for his own self-image and for how his future opponents viewed his qualifications as a Presbyterian minister. The installation service, which took place in an Irish Evangelical church in North Belfast on 1 August, was not unique, but the gathering included a wide range of participants, including his father, Kyle Paisley; W. J. Grier, representing the Irish Evangelical Church; the Reverend Thomas Rowan, a one-time associate of D. L. Moody and a conservative Presbyterian; and T. B. McFarlane, a professor of the Reformed Presbyterian Theological Hall. To Paisley and his supporters, his appointment fit into the Baptist and Brethren tradition. His detractors, however, asserted that his ordination did not follow proper Presbyterian procedure; in the future they would argue that Paisley's irregular appointment invalidated his Free Presbyterian ministry. Reformed churches demand a ceremony where the new minister's qualifications are tested under presbytery guidance, whereas Baptists leave selection to individual churches. As Steve Bruce points out in *God Save Ulster! The Religion and Politics of Paisleyism,* Paisley was trying to appeal to both the Baptists and the fundamentalist Presbyterians present. The question of the validity of his ordination was not important during his early career, but as his notoriety grew, his opponents increasingly pointed to his lack of proper credentials to discredit his theology and militancy.[29]

An even more important demonstration of Paisley's growing connection with militant fundamentalism and revivalism took place the following week when Paisley conducted his first service as an ordained minister. During this service, W. P. Nicholson offered a public prayer: "I have one prayer to offer this young man. I will pray that God will give him a tongue like an old cow. Go in young man, to a butcher's shop and ask to see a cow's tongue. You will find it sharper than any file. God give you such a tongue. Make this church a converting shop and make this preacher a disturber of Hell and the Devil."[30]

Early supporters of the Reverend Paisley portrayed him as the "new W. P. Nicholson"—a powerful orator proclaiming renewal and professing antimodernism—and claimed that the "cow tongue" prayer was a prophecy of Paisley's future career.[31] Nicholson's occasional attendance at Ravenhill in the 1950s bore witness to his belief in Paisley's potential. Nicholson had retired to Ulster, and Paisley had heard him preach in the Hamilton Road Presbyterian Church and during the evangelist's revivalist tours of 1946 and 1947. It is most likely that Nicholson's abrupt style inspired the young Paisley and that it was this style that attracted people to the young preacher's meetings. Clifford Smyth, a Paisleyite during the 1960s and early 1970s, argues that Paisley's prophetic oratory mimicked Nicholson's. The fundamentalism that was espoused in Northern Ireland in the 1920s and that had influenced Kyle Paisley was undoubtedly passed on to the maturing Ian Paisley.[32]

During the next five years, Paisley's ministry intensified with frequent prayer meetings, street evangelism around Belfast and an "Old Time Gospel Campaign," and the formation of the Free Presbyterian denomination in 1951. In May 1948, Paisley spoke to the Lissara Presbyterian Church in the small village of Crossgar under the auspices of the National Union of Protestants (NUP), a British political–evangelical organization. His sermon impressed the assembled laity enough that one member, George Gibson, asked him to preach a gospel campaign starting on Saturday, 4 February 1951. The congregation was in the process of appointing a new minister, however, a procedure that divided the conservative and more liberal members. Because the Reverend Geoffrey Chart, a conservative ally of Paisley and a speaker for the NUP, had been denied the ministerial post,

Gibson and other conservative members believed that they were being run out of the church.[33]

The invitation to Paisley widened the conflict. Expecting a large attendance for Paisley's gospel campaign, Gibson petitioned the Down Presbytery for use of the church hall. The presbytery initially agreed but reversed its decision several hours before Paisley was to begin the meeting, claiming that Paisley's appearance violated assembly protocol. (Assembly Rule 254 required prior approval from the presbytery for visiting clerics who were not members of the Irish Presbyterian Church.)[34] Although the rule was intended to prevent division when one part of a congregation objected to a visiting minister, it was not always invoked. Gibson and a fellow elder tried to countermand the Down Presbytery's order, and both were immediately suspended. The day after Paisley had been advertised to preach, he, the two suspended elders, and approximately thirty supporters picketed the Lissara church. They entered the Sunday service while the suspension order was being read and in a grandiose style compared it to the papal bull of 1523 that demanded Luther repent. Moreover, they denounced the timidity of the Irish Presbyterian leadership and invoked the memory of Samuel Rutherford,[35] who personified the traditional Presbyterian Church government: "You say it is the Church of our fathers. It is NOT the Church of our fathers. THEY were made of sterner stuff than to tolerate men who betray their trust, and violate their solemn ordination vows. Let us listen to one of these men, the sturdy Presbyterian and saintly Rutherford, who said: 'Give not a hair's breadth of truth away, for it is not yours but God's.'"[36]

Although Paisley did hold a gospel campaign in the Crossgar Mission Hall that evening, Gibson and three elders withdrew from the Lissara Presbyterian Church. At a meeting in the mission hall on Killyleagh Street, the four dissidents formed a new congregation. Five weeks later, on 11 March 1951, Paisley helped this small group to form the first congregation of the Free Presbyterian Church of Ulster after a series of exploratory conferences.[37] The articles of the new denomination proclaimed it to be fundamentalist and Reformed, and the accompanying manifesto blamed the schism on the liberalism spread by church leaders, most notably J. Ernest Davey. The document identified the professor's trial and the membership of the Irish Presbyterian Church in the WCC as the key moments in the transformation of Irish Presbyterianism from orthodoxy to liberalism. The new Free Presbyterian Church, however, allowed for a flexible interpretation of the End Times, a tenet that was designed to attract a wider spectrum of Ulster fundamentalists and that in the future would be useful to Paisley politically.[38]

On 22 April, the Ravenhill Mission became the second congregation of the new denomination, now constituted as the Ravenhill Free Presbyterian Church. Although not all members of Paisley's church were interested in becoming Free Presbyterians, most were swayed by the arguments made by Paisley and younger fundamentalists such as John Douglas, a future Free Presbyterian minister. When Paisley did maneuver Ravenhill into joining the Free Presbyterian Church, the more independent-minded members withdrew. Within eight months, two other Presbyterian churches suffered schisms, and in both instances a minority group seceded to join the Free Presbyterians. The Drumreagh Presbyterian Church in Ballymoney suffered an internal feud between its liberal minister, John Barkley, and evangelicals led by Sandy McAuley. When Barkley left to become the principal of the Assembly's Theological College in Belfast, McAuley accused William Hyndman, the new minister, of sexual immorality, drunkenness, and physical violence. As a consequence, McAuley held meetings outside the church with the help of John Wylie, a member of Ravenhill Free Presbyterian.[39]

This split was also preceded by a call for Paisley to preach at the Drumreagh church after McAuley and associated evangelicals heard the young evangelist during a gospel campaign in Crossgar. When McAuley and Wylie brought Paisley to the nearby Cabra Schoolhouse in April 1951, the evangelist spoke against Presbyterian modernism and the immorality within the Drumreagh church. His words inspired McAuley and a small group to form the Cabra Free Presbyterian Church, meeting at first in a large tent next to the schoolhouse. During the inaugural service for the new congregation, four hundred Presbyterians heard Paisley preach against Professor Davey, apostasy, and the WCC.[40]

Shortly thereafter, another congregation formed in Rasharkin when that church split over the minister's ill treatment of his wife. As at Drumreagh, Wylie and a few dissidents held meetings denouncing the minister, the Reverend Ernest Stronge. Wylie came from a militant fundamentalist background—his theology and willingness to confront apostates influenced by the Reverend James Hunter and the fundamentalist and revivalism that had spread during the 1930s. Wylie's militancy speaks for itself: he was asked to leave Dundonald Presbyterian Church for questioning the minister's modernism; he became an early member of the NUP, where he met Paisley, and he supported gospel tent campaigns and open-air preaching. After listening to Paisley, Wylie convinced a group of evangelicals to form another Free Presbyterian church.[41]

Some of Paisley's detractors have argued that the young preacher took advantage of nontheological disputes to build his new denomination.[42] This argument does not explain, however, why so many dissidents left the Irish Presbyterian Church. What can be determined is that Paisley's message resonated with those Presbyterians frightened by modernism, ecumenism, and the changing social mores of the postwar period. Steve Bruce correctly notes that fundamentalist Presbyterians respected the young Paisley, liked his preaching style, and were concerned about the apostasy in the Irish church.[43] From the start of his ministry, Paisley was interested not only in spreading the gospel, but also in preaching the proper gospel to those he considered to be God's Elect. Under Calvinist theology, doing so required a public stand against apostasy.

During 1951, the first five Free Presbyterian congregations were founded, but after Paisley was jailed for the first time, nine more Free Presbyterian churches were formed. When the Free Presbyterian Church did expand, it did so in a limited manner and in a restricted geographical area. The first Free Presbyterian churches were, with several exceptions, east of the Bann River and in areas with a substantial Presbyterian population. Bruce notes that Free Presbyterian growth took place in either Ulster's conservative and rural Bible belt—counties Antrim and Down—or in areas surrounding Belfast, Ireland's center of liberal Presbyterianism. The proximity to Belfast is important: fundamentalist and conservative Presbyterians in eastern Ulster were more exposed to the liberal Presbyterianism of the church's leadership—its ministers and professors—and were more willing to act against them than were their fellow Presbyterians in western Ulster.[44]

Although there is no overt proof that Paisley had a long-term strategy to expand his denomination, in May 1951 Crossgar Free Presbyterian Church began advertising alongside Ravenhill Free Presbyterian in the *Belfast Telegraph*—the only church outside the Belfast metropolitan area to do so. Crossgar is fifteen miles from Belfast and did not draw its congregation from the city, so the coordinated advertising was an omen of Paisley's future plan for his new church.[45] But once Paisley's new denomination began to expand, he was no longer an independent Baptist with Reformed Presbyterian training; he was in open competition with both the Irish Presbyterian Church and the Irish Evangelical Church. The one factor that inhibited the growth of the new church was a shortage of ministers. The exclusiveness of Free Presbyterian theology and its militant fundamentalism made it difficult to find competent ministers who strictly adhered to Paisley's convictions. As the Free Presbyterian Church and Paisleyism grew, Paisley needed ministers loyal to his message and crusade, followers who would propagate his interpretation of the gospel. An attempt to send candidates to the Free Church of Scotland theological college in Edinburgh, which the Irish Evangelical Church also used, did not produce the desired results. Within two months after the founding of the Free Presbyterian Church, the Edinburgh college agreed to take five Free Presbyterian students, but few were accepted afterward. This early shortage was solved in part in October 1952 after the new denomination opened its own Bible college, which became an important factor in church growth.[46]

During the first decade of the Free Presbyterian Church, Paisley's stature and notoriety in Northern Ireland grew at a slow but steady pace. Paisley was making a name for himself through his evangelizing efforts and his work with the NUP. But he was known primarily within the Protestant church and political community around Belfast and counties Antrim and Down and to a small but widening segment of the secular working-class community.

Militant Fundamentalism in Ulster

Paisley's rise within the Northern Irish fundamentalist community came during the same five-year period that the Reverend Carl McIntire expanded his international fellowship. Although McIntire's militant activism in Asia and Latin America proved important, he became interested in the religious and political situation in Northern Ireland and the British Isles. His attacks on modernist and liberal Protestant clerics and the Catholic Church—and to a lesser extent his assault on communism—resonated with Irish Protestantism and Northern Irish politics. Owing to these mutual interests, McIntire developed contacts with many fundamentalists in Northern Ireland—his early relationships with W. J. Grier and Norman Porter being the most notable. Porter, an unemployed engineer and a Baptist lay preacher, maintained substantial connections within American militant fundamentalism. When McIntire met Porter, the Irishman was the secretary and treasurer of the Orangefield Baptist Church in East Belfast and active in Northern Irish politics. In August 1950, Grier and Porter attended the ICCC Second Plenary Congress in Geneva.[47] The relationship between McIntire, Grier, and Porter continued in the 1950s as Porter helped to form the NUP, Ulster Protestant Action (UPA), and the Evangelical Protestant Society (EPS)—organizations that worked in conjunction with the ICCC. The NUP, founded in 1942 in England, attacked High Church practices within the Church of England and tried to thwart the perceived Anglican move toward Rome. The EPS affiliated with the British Evangelical Council and worked to propagate the Calvinist and fundamentalist Protestant faith, to combat the ecumenical movement, and to protect Ulster Protestant heritage. Porter's activism bore political fruit. In 1953, he was elected to the Northern Ireland Parliament as an Independent Unionist for the Clifton Ward, North Belfast, although he lost the seat five years later in the 1958 general election. Because both Porter and the Orangefield Baptist Church professed a strict conservative Calvinism and amillennial eschatology, these theological stances helped him during his political career. His being amillennial (and not premillennial) enabled evangelicals to support him more easily: if Porter had been a premillennial, his political activism would have made him vulnerable to charges of hypocrisy. Moreover, McIntire, a premillennial who shunned direct political involvement, could, when necessary to his crusade, endorse political preachers if they professed Calvinist, militant fundamentalism.[48]

McIntire visited Belfast in 1950 after the Geneva congress and a year later, in 1951, to preach to the Botanic Avenue Irish Evangelical Church. During this stop in Northern Ireland, the American crusader stayed with the Grier family, W. J. being the minister of the Botanic Avenue Church; he most likely stayed there again in 1952 on his way to the ICCC British Isles Regional Conference.[49] The conference, held in Edinburgh, was an important bridge between the militant fundamentalists of North America and the British Isles; not only did Grier, Porter (as an NUP representative), and the spectrum of British and continental militants attend, but so did McIntire, T. T. Shields, and the Australian-turned-American Fred Schwarz. The conference asked Grier, the Irish Evangelical Church, and the Free Church of Scotland to form the British Committee for Common Evangelical Action. Communist encroachments in the Far East and modernism throughout the Christian world were the major topics; ecumenism, Communist influence in Japan, the New Revised Standard Bible, and Billy James Hargis's Bible Balloon Project were also discussed. For reasons that will become apparent, neither Kyle nor Ian Paisley chose to attend the conference.[50] McIntire returned to Belfast again in 1955 for a two-day visit, where he spoke on the "W.C.C. attitudes to Romanism and communism" at an EPS-sponsored rally held at the Mountpottinger YMCA. At this meeting, billed as "A Special Protestant Rally," McIntire talked about the WCC's liberal attitude toward ecumenism and the Roman Catholic Church as well as the council's leanings toward communism. McIntire answered the Irish hospitality, and under his auspices Porter and W. J. Grier attended ICCC meetings in the United States. For example, in August 1954 Porter spoke to the ICCC meeting in Philadelphia; Grier presented a report, "The Situation in Great Britain Today," to the council; and Porter spoke to McIntire's Collingswood, New Jersey, church.[51] Invitations to visit and preach in another church, especially in an international setting, lent credence to the stature of any minister, lay or ordained.

It is not clear exactly when Paisley first met McIntire, but their earliest known correspondence started immediately after the Free Presbyterian Church was established and after McIntire had been in Belfast to preach to Greer's Botanic Avenue Church.[52] During this visit, the American militant met Paisley and several members of the Ravenhill church. By late 1951, Carl McIntire considered the young preacher a "personal friend" and in their correspondence expressed interest in developments within the Northern Ireland fundamentalist community.[53]

In the early 1950s, Paisley spent most of his efforts tending to the affairs of the Free Presbyterian Church and to evangelical crusades. He involved himself in the Belfast-based Spanish Christian Mission; both he and the Reverend B. S. Fidler of the Barry School of Evangelism were referees ("advisers") to the mission. Although Paisley channeled much of his energy into gospel missions or into trips to NUP meetings in England, some of his focus was directed toward the print media. In April 1955, the Free Presbyterian Church published the first issue of *The Revivalist,* a monthly periodical that gave Paisley and his church a new outlet to espouse Free Presbyterian theology and to attack immorality, Protestant apostasy, and the Catholic Church.[54]

The Reverend Ian Paisley was little known outside the fundamentalist and Presbyterian communities in Ulster until local newspapers noticed his activism in the mid-1950s. The most significant episode was the Maura Lyons controversy in 1957, which made headlines and increased Paisley's notoriety. In autumn 1956, evangelists from the Elim Pentecostal Church were active in the Star Clothing Company in Belfast, a company that employed both Catholic and Protestant women. They were able to convert Lyons, a fifteen-year-old Catholic clothing worker, whom they introduced to the Reverend David Leatham, the minister of Dunmurry Free Presbyterian Church. Leatham immediately turned the teenager over to Paisley and Norman Porter. The young girl was afraid to confront her family, and so several Free Presbyterians—including John Wylie—helped her flee to England and eventually to Scotland.[55]

When the press discovered the story, it not only became sensational news but attracted the attention of the police. Abetting Maura's flight to Great Britain was a criminal offense, but because Paisley was not personally involved in that aspect of the affair, he chose to publicize the controversy with little fear of prosecution. He held a large meeting at the Ulster Hall (a municipal auditorium in Belfast city center), where he played a tape recording of Lyons recollecting her conversion. Paisley received substantial publicity, and the press coverage continued as the girl remained in hiding. Despite an initial reluctance on the girl's part and possibly because of Paisley's continued attempts to publicize the affair, Maura Lyons returned to her family the following May. It is clear that Paisley knew more about Maura Lyons's whereabouts than he was willing to tell the police, but he refused to confirm this fact during her stay in Great Britain or to Belfast High Court during her custody hearing after she returned home. Paisley told the Ulster Hall crowd, however, that in order to support Lyons's conversion he would "do time for Protestant liberty."[56]

The Lyons affair not only began a string of confrontations between Paisley and the civil authority over the next fourteen years but also increased his notoriety among the local population, elevated his stature within the local and international communities of militant fundamentalists, and exposed his confrontational style. Ed Moloney points out that when a Catholic converted to Protestantism in Ulster, it was done quietly. But the publicity surrounding Maura Lyons embarrassed many evangelicals and helped to incite instances of anti-Protestantism in the Republic of Ireland. The most notable of these instances was the Fethard-on-Sea boycott. The Fethard-on-Sea controversy developed when a Protestant woman, Sheila Cloney, separated from her Catholic husband and took their two daughters to Belfast; Mrs. Cloney had objected when the local Fethard-on-Sea priest ordered her to raise the eldest as a Catholic. In retaliation to Cloney's action, Catholics boycotted the Protestant-owned shops in the town and the local music teacher for four months as a means to pressure Cloney into taking her children back to Fethard-on-Sea.[57]

The Maura Lyons case and the Fethard-on-Sea boycott took place in the midst of an evangelizing battle between Protestants and Catholics in Northern Ireland that intensified during the 1950s. Paisley and the Free Presbyterian Church, however, were not as active in the efforts directed toward Catholics as were other fundamentalists and evangelists in Ulster. Although Paisley was not afraid to confront the Catholic Church, as the Lyons case illustrates, Free Presbyterians did little to convert Catholics. Norman Porter, the NUP, and Catholic Evangelical Fellowship were much more involved in the battle to "save" Catholic souls and to confront Catholic missionary efforts. For instance, Norman Porter worked with the Catholic Evangelical Fellowship to convert Catholics to evangelical Christianity. It appears that Paisley and the Free Presbyterians were more interested in expanding their church and battling what they perceived to be Protestant apostasy.[58]

In addition to their religious angst, Paisley and the Free Presbyterian Church organized to deter a dual political and military threat from the Catholic Church and the Republican Movement. To militants (and to many in the Protestant community), the IRA's attacks on border outposts and Nationalist initiatives on partition and education threatened the constitutional status of Northern Ireland. Paisley and the Free Presbyterian Church tacitly helped organizations such as the NUP and UPA to confront political initiatives orchestrated by the Catholic Church, the Nationalist Party, and liberal Unionists. During the 1950s and early into the following decade, such issues included public expenditures on Catholic schools and public gestures to the Catholic community from moderate Unionist politicians. Liberal Unionists suggested that Catholics could join the UUP and agreed to talks between the Orange Order and the Catholic Nationalist Party.[59]

Paisley, Porter, and other evangelicals used Catholic attacks on Protestant evangelicals in Ireland as well as instances of political and religious persecution of Protestants in Catholic countries as evangelizing tools within the Protestant community and as political weapons against ecumenism. *The Revivalist, The Irish Evangelical* (the organ of the Irish Evangelical Church), and the *Ulster Protestant* (a periodical Norman Porter helped to found with Willie Wilton, a Unionist senator and a frequent speaker at NUP meetings) routinely carried stories about persecution of Protestants in Catholic countries—with particular interest on Colombia, Spain, and the Republic of Ireland.[60]

During the 1950s, however, Paisley's confrontation with what he perceived as apostasy in the Irish Presbyterian Church and with the ecumenical movement brought him the most public attention and elevated his stature among militant fundamentalists throughout the British Isles and with Carl McIntire. Paisley consistently attacked Irish Protestant denominations belonging to the WCC, most vociferously targeting the Presbyterian Church in Ireland.[61] He sincerely despised the WCC's goals. The

Presbyterian Church's membership in the WCC created a convenient rallying cry to attract the militant evangelicals of Northern Ireland. Paisley's public targets also included the British Council of Churches (the British branch of the WCC); J. Ernest Davey, who was made moderator of the Presbyterian General Assembly in 1952; and Donald Soper, president of the Methodist Church in England. These attacks were at first confined to Paisley's pulpit, but in early 1952—a year after he first met the Reverend Carl McIntire—he began orchestrating public protests.[62]

Paisley's first public demonstrations took place outside a British Council of Churches meeting at Grosvenor Hall in Belfast in April 1952 and in June 1953 in front of the General Assembly as Irish Presbyterians elected Ernest Davey moderator—protests not reported in the Northern Irish secular press. Paisley used Davey's installation to begin annual protests outside the General Assembly in Belfast. In front of the assembly, he burned copies of Davey's books and articles, a tactic mimicking those McIntire employed in demonstrations against the WCC. By 1953, Paisley had become a friend of the American militant fundamentalist. In a sermon delivered three years later, while the June 1955 General Assembly was in session, he appealed to Presbyterians to leave both their church and the Student Christian Movement. His message resonated with some students; those belonging to the Evangelical Union—a union of Presbyterian seminary students—denounced Davey and refused to pray with other members of the Student Movement. The attack drew the assembly's attention for its schismatic nature: in a speech to the assembly, the Right Reverend John Knowles, the outgoing moderator, blamed the students' actions on unnamed outside influences, an obvious reference to Paisley and the Free Presbyterian Church. It is interesting to note, however, that not all Free Presbyterians approved of Paisley's tactics, which shows that the he, like McIntire, was willing to confront dissidents and alienate members of his own church.[63]

Paisley's protests and demonstrations brought him the legal trouble he seemed to desire. His first arrest took place in 1957 in Donaghadee. When Paisley and John Wylie used loudspeakers to evangelize along the town's beaches, they were cited for making a public disturbance and summoned to court. Two days later both ministers were again cited in Donaghadee while speaking to three hundred people—Paisley's tactics were drawing more support. Their court appearance and the dismissal of the charges made the Northern Irish press, which increased Paisley's prestige amongst his militant followers.[64]

Because Irish Protestantism traditionally maintained theological and political links with Protestant churches throughout the British Isles, Paisley and his allies were also concerned with the modernism and social activism on the British mainland. At first, they confined their protests to Ulster. A major target was Dr. Donald Soper, who dabbled in politics, espoused socialism and a radical social gospel, and talked fondly of Russian premier Nikita Khrushchev. Soper had been an outspoken pacifist during the Second World War, was a member of the Labour Party, sat on the London City Council, and was active in left-wing social campaigns such as the Peace Pledge Union and the Campaign for Nuclear Disarmament. The Methodist liberal and future lord preached a modernist theology, including denying the divinity of Christ and the Virgin Birth. He was also a strong supporter of ecumenism. In August 1959, Soper came to Ulster and spoke at an open-air meeting in Ballymena. Paisley, Wylie, and Harold Magowan, the minister of the Antrim Free Presbyterian Church, arrived with banners attacking Soper. The protestors heckled and argued with the Methodist cleric for an hour, invoking a spirited response. Soper taunted the Free Presbyterians by calling them "intellectual rabbits" and praised Soviet Communists for being more Christian than Ulster's militant fundamentalists. During the confrontation, Soper was prevented from speaking to the audience, and one layman, Joseph Kyle of Ballymena, threw a Bible at the English Methodist. Paisley's notoriety was such that he was the one accused of throwing the Bible (a charge that Soper later repeated in the House of Lords). The following day Wylie and members of UPA again pestered Soper as he tried to speak at Carlisle Memorial Methodist Church in Belfast.[65]

Three weeks later Paisley, his Free Presbyterian accomplices, and the two laymen were summoned to court under the Public Order Act for interrupting a public meeting. Two hundred spectators watched Desmond Boal, a Loyalist barrister from the Shankill Road, Belfast, and future political ally of Paisley, defend the preacher while two hundred more would-be spectators waited outside.[66] Each defendant was fined five pounds, but the following Sunday Paisley told a packed Ravenhill church that he would refuse to pay. The size of the congregation and the three hundred who could not enter the church that morning indicated Paisley's growing support among militant fundamentalists in Northern Ireland. The next day George Allport, the owner of *The Unionist,* a small Belfast magazine, paid the fine for the three clerics, arguing that a prison sentence for either Paisley or the two ministers would upset Unionist solidarity during the upcoming British general election. Allport stated that he disagreed with Paisley's tactics but had some sympathy with his message.[67] Paisley was disappointed in his inability to become a Protestant martyr: "This is a complete surprise to me. Our prophecy that the people behind the persecution would pay the fine, has come true. My attitude is still the same. We wish to go to jail. I was not consulted about the payment, otherwise I would have opposed it stoutly."[68] The court case and Allport's payment made the front pages. The news reports were the biggest media coverage Paisley had enjoyed in his early career and was an ominous indication of the growing notoriety he had gained outside of Free Presbyterian churches.

Two months later the *Belfast Telegraph* reported a smaller incident in Coleraine that involved Free Presbyterians, but not Paisley. During a council meeting, the mayor of Coleraine charged that the Free Presbyterian Church allowed its ministers to attack other Protestant churches during public meetings and to use loudspeakers on top of moving cars.[69] The incident showed how easy it had now become for the new church to receive press. Such actions were previously seldom reported in Northern Irish newspapers. Such publicity could be a double-edged sword, however, and at times Paisley received a hostile response. In March 1960, he was jeered at Queen's University during a meeting sponsored by the University Labour Group where the Free Presbyterian discussed the aims of UPA. The Labour Group usually attracted 30 people, but because of Paisley the meeting drew a group of 350 students and visitors. Some shouted Republican slogans or asked questions such as "What about Maura Lyons?"[70]

In late October 1960, Paisley and John Wylie held a protest against Dr. George MacLeod, the moderator of the General Assembly of the Church of Scotland and another future British lord, during the Scotsman's short speaking tour of Ulster. MacLeod led an experimental ecumenical community on the island of Iona, where participants lived communally and traded ideas on how the church should deal with the modern, industrialized world. The Iona community also allowed visiting clerics to hold church services using their own rituals. Paisley and Wylie were particularly incensed that a Greek cleric had celebrated an Orthodox Mass there. The Free Presbyterians charged that MacLeod and Iona were promoting a return to Catholicism, and they organized a protest when MacLeod spoke at the Delrada Grammar School in Ballymoney. After he had finished his talk on the Iona community, they peppered him with questions. MacLeod was also prevented from speaking in Coleraine when the Elders' Fellowship of the Coleraine Presbytery, influenced by the Free Presbyterian protests, withdrew its invitation to him.[71]

In March 1961, twelve Free Presbyterians picketed the Donegall Square Methodist Church when Bishop Sante Uberto Barbieri, the Methodist bishop of Argentina and the WCC president, spoke. The following month they did the same to E. Stanley Jones, the American missionary attacked by McIntire and the HUAC, when Jones spoke to the Carlisle Memorial Methodist and McCracken Memorial Presbyterian churches in Belfast. Dr. Jones, who had sympathized with communism in the 1930s and denounced the bombing of Germany in the Second World War, also compared Free Presbyterian tactics to those of the Soviet Union.[72]

In May 1962, Paisley led a demonstration outside the General Assembly in Belfast to criticize the Irish Presbyterian Church's membership in the WCC. In October, he protested a talk in Coleraine by the Reverend Austin Fulton, in which the former Irish Presbyterian Assembly moderator discussed his trip to India to attend a WCC conference. Although many clergymen condemned Paisley as a religious bigot, he did find support from more traditional Presbyterians, who asserted that defending the Reformation was not intolerant. Most notable were the Reverend Donald Gillies of the Agnes Street Presbyterian Church in Belfast and Presbyterian members of the Evangelical Protestant Society. The church leadership's ecumenical efforts and overtures to the Catholic Church were inciting a more vocal opposition. By mid-1962, the efforts by the Free Presbyterians and their militant fundamentalist allies were creating serious divisions within the Presbyterian Church in Ireland.[73]

In March 1962, Paisley expanded his crusade to include the ecumenical activities of the Protestant churches on the British mainland. That month the new moderator of the General Assembly of the Church of Scotland, Dr. Archibald Craig, made a visit to Rome to attend the centenary celebrations at St. Andrew's Kirk, but he also held talks with the pope. It was the first of many pilgrimages that British clerics would make. To Paisley, Craig's trip was part of a larger conspiracy to sell out Protestantism to Rome. Paisley held such strong convictions that two years later he and Jack Glass of Glasgow joined with Scottish militant allies to protest outside the Scottish General Assembly.[74]

Political and ecumenical developments within the British Anglican community induced a closer relationship between Paisley and British militant fundamentalists. A movement of High Church Anglo-Catholics within the Church of England—which had been active since the 1920s—wanted to reinstall more Catholicism into Anglican practice and theology. Their support for sacraments, vestments, and a more Catholic prayer book worried Irish Anglicans, who were generally more evangelical and "Low Church." Irish fundamentalists were generally unconcerned with the new Anglo-Catholic friendship until the Church of England decided to send observers to the Second Vatican Council. The Church of Ireland initially planned to send observers but under pressure from Irish Anglicans decided against the move.[75] However, the English Anglicans' decision to attend the council upset Protestants in Northern Ireland, none more so than Paisley. Anglican theology was not the primary issue to the fundamentalist, dissenting Paisley; that an Anglican-Catholic rapprochement threatened the constitutional link between Northern Ireland and Great Britain was. To militants, a "Low" Church of England and the Protestant nature of the British monarchy were essential elements within the British Constitution and the British Empire as well as a historical connection to the English Reformation. Political overtures to Rome—such as the meeting in Rome in March 1959 between Princess Margaret, the queen mother, and the pope—threatened the status quo. (Queen Elizabeth also met privately with Pope John XXIII in Rome in May 1960.) To Low Church Anglicans and Paisley, the prospects of an Anglican–Catholic union could influence British politics, allowing for more Catholic presence in Parliament and the prospect of a Catholic prime minister.[76]

Militant alarm at the "Romeward" trend within the Church of England grew when Geoffrey Fisher, the archbishop of Canterbury, made his own trek to Rome. Although Fisher's talk with the pope in December 1960 lasted less than an hour, it was the first time that an Anglican leader had visited Rome. Moreover, Fisher's trip came only twenty months after that of the queen mother and Princess Margaret. When the one hundredth archbishop of Canterbury, Michael Ramsey, proposed to modernize the Book of Common Prayer, to use new experimental forms of worship for a period of seven years, and to decide these matters without the consent of Parliament, the concerns of Low Church Anglicans and North Irish Protestants seemed prophetic. Many Protestants viewed these steps as the opening shot of an Anglican-Catholic reunion. Paisley's opposition to the ecumenism between the Church of England and the Roman Catholic Church was a landmark in his transformation from a premillennial preacher who crusaded against modernism and Protestant apostasy into an amillennial politician concerned about Irish and British politics.[77]

In August 1962, Paisley announced he would counterattack and visit Rome during the Vatican conference, during which he would distribute fifteen thousand copies of the Gospel According to John written in Italian. His mission was clearly political as well as theological. He was accompanied by two Free Presbyterian ministers, John Wylie and John Douglas, and the British, Northern Irish, and Italian press extensively covered his trip to Rome in October. Most notably, the BBC interviewed Paisley in London while he was in transit to Rome, despite the preacher's protest on 7 October outside Broadcasting House in Belfast, the BBC's headquarters in Northern Ireland. Approximately one hundred supporters had watched as Paisley nailed two posters to the building, one proclaiming "The BBC, the Voice of Popery" and another denouncing the BBC's refusal to air his denunciations of the Vatican Council and the pope. The Italian and Vatican authorities were thus warned of Paisley's intentions, and they detained the three clerics for questioning.[78]

On return to Belfast, a welcome home rally held in the Ulster Hall and similar meetings across the province were well attended. The response was such that the Presbyterian Church in Ireland felt compelled to issue a statement to the *Belfast Telegraph* that Paisley was not and had never been a Presbyterian Church in Ireland minister. Such concerns have been historically vindicated because the militant fundamentalist crusade received substantial impetus and support. In retrospect, John Douglas argues that the trip to Rome "laid the foundation for the revival rallies of 1966 and after," and Paisley's Vatican trek impressed his American allies. As a consequence, Paisley and the Free Presbyterian Church were invited to the annual convention of the McIntire-led ICCC in Amsterdam. The focus of the militant fundamentalist meeting was to protest the WCC's Third Assembly, held in New Delhi the previous year. By attending the International Council meeting in Amsterdam, Paisley and the Free Presbyterian Church expanded their fellowship with American militant fundamentalists.[79]

Although the new friendship would add another dimension to the contentious triangular relationship between Paisley, northern Irish fundamentalists, and the clerics of the mainstream Irish Protestant denominations, it is interesting to note that during the 1950s there was one point on which Irish and British modernists, on the one hand, and militant fundamentalists, on the other, agreed: their opposition to American "New Evangelicals" (neofundamentalist revivalists and evangelists) who came to the British Isles, most notably the Reverend Billy Graham. At first, Paisley, Norman Porter, and McIntire cautiously supported Billy Graham, and the Free Presbyterians criticized J. Ernest Davey for denouncing Graham's gospel as "a rather old-fashioned form of the Protestant faith." Paisley, McIntire, and other militant fundamentalists (including the Bob Jones family) grew to dislike Graham, however, because of his willingness to cooperate with clerics and churches considered in apostasy and because of his opposition to predestination and segregation. Graham stood on the Arminian side of the orthodox theological spectrum and spoke to integrated audiences, even in the American South. His ministry became associated with the New Evangelism of the Fuller Theological Seminary in California, which pushed a theology of traditional evangelism and social action and utilized worship services that mixed a fundamentalist message with sentimental music and altar calls. It was because of their mutual opposition to Billy Graham and New Evangelicals that Carl McIntire and the Bob Jones family became allies. It was also during this period that a column on theology written by Bob Jones Sr. first appeared in the Free Presbyterian journal *The Revivalist.*[80]

The Billy Graham Crusade drew millions throughout the British Isles. Although Protestant churchmen across the theological spectrum supported Graham for the interest in Christianity that his revivals garnered, both militant fundamentalists and modernists were hostile to him. They disliked Graham for his revival techniques and considered his emotional conversion calls shallow and temporary. Paisley and militant fundamentalists particularly despised the advice Graham gave to converts. Crusade prayer leaders told new Christians that it was acceptable to remain within their home denominations, including the Roman Catholic Church. But jealousy might have been another motive for Paisley's dislike of Graham: during the 1950s, the press that the Free Presbyterians received was not as substantial or positive as the news reports on Graham's crusades.[81]

Billy Graham's popularity and the success of his crusades contrasted with the limited acceptance of the revivalist and militant fundamentalist message of the Reverend Ian Paisley and the Free Presbyterian Church. The latter made news only when they caused a disturbance, whereas Graham's Christian message drew millions and inspired a new born-again experience for thousands of attendees. The militant fundamentalist opposition to Graham's tactics and theology illustrates the parameters of what Paisley and like-minded fundamentalists considered true revivalism. Paisley and the Free Presbyterian Church would restrain emotionalism within church services and during public meetings. Moreover, a proper revival had to be based on a Calvinist message, which was designed to attract the Elect and to support Ulster Protestantism's position as a family within God's chosen people.[82]

A Fundamental Polemic within Militant Ulster

As the Reverend Ian Paisley's ministry grew and his fellowship with American militant fundamentalism became increasingly important, his relationships with Irish fundamentalists began to deteriorate. The most substantial friction was with the Irish Evangelical Church and Norman Porter, both members of the ICCC. During the early 1950s, animosity between Paisley and other Irish fundamentalists developed as he established his ministry and started to build the Free Presbyterian Church. Much of the conflict came down to a contrast in style. Whereas Paisley was willing to attack fellow fundamentalists he believed to be apostate, both in speech and in print, other Northern Irish fundamentalists thought such assaults should be limited to liberal and modernist Protestant clerics. Paisley was upset because the Irish Evangelical Church would not support his new church and would not let him preach to their congregations. He was also concerned over the Evangelical Church's contact with nonseparatist fundamentalists. For its part, the Irish Evangelical Church believed Paisley was divisive to the fundamentalist community, and despite previous support it would not let him preach in its churches. Moreover, the church argued that Paisley should have joined its small denomination and went so far as to denounce the founding of the first Free Presbyterian Church at Crossgar. Paisley in his turn accused the Irish Evangelical Church and Norman Porter of conspiring to force his resignation from the NUP. The Irish Evangelical Church had backed the NUP's new treasurer, Reverend Eric Borland of the Irish Presbyterian Church, despite the fact that the Irish Presbyterians belonged to the WCC, and had banned Paisley from speaking at its annual convention.[83]

The trouble with Porter and the Irish Evangelical Church had transatlantic implications. Carl McIntire tried to balance his interest in the new Free Presbyterian Church of Ulster with the ICCC's demands and took on the role of mediator. Although Paisley warned McIntire that not all members of the NUP supported the International Council's work, McIntire wanted the relationships between the Free Presbyterian Church, Norman Porter, and the Irish Evangelical Church to be harmonious; peace in Northern Ireland would benefit the ICCC. Shortly after meeting Paisley in 1951, McIntire wrote to the young clergyman inquiring why his new church had not joined the Irish Evangelical denomination. Paisley replied that the Irish Evangelical Church was not vibrant, that it despised his fervent style of ministry—for instance, his all-night prayer meetings—and that the *Irish Evangelical* refused to report on his ministry. Paisley also complained about the Irish Evangelical's semi-apostasy: "our greatest danger in Ulster is not the modernists, but professed evangelicals who try to malign our work, either because they are actuated by jealousy, or want to walk the middle road of compromise."[84] McIntire wrote later that he was concerned over Paisley's criticism of Porter and W. J. Grier and argued that all true evangelicals must work together: "We are brethren and by the grace of God we must and should get along together. I do not want to become involved in the differences and difficulties which you are having locally."[85]

When Grier chaired the ICCC conference in Edinburgh in 1952 and was reluctant to allow Paisley to attend, McIntire gave Paisley further conciliatory advice: "I do hope that you will go to him as a real brother. You are going to have to learn to work together with other brethren who differ with you in various matters but are agreed concerning the great doctrines of the faith. You can build your work without tearing down the Irish Evangelical work or their church. Ireland is big enough. We are Protestants."[86] This was curious advice from a cleric as divisive as McIntire. Although the American militant fundamentalist was willing to confront members of the ACCC that he found in apostasy, he appeared overly concerned with local infighting when it might harm the ICCC.

However, the dispute in Northern Ireland was of limited importance to McIntire until the Free Presbyterian Church began inquiring about membership in the International Council. The Irish Evangelical Church informed the ICCC that it would resign from the council if the Free Presbyterians were admitted. In a letter to Abraham Warnaar Jr., the ICCC director in 1953, W. J. Grier warned that that his church had lost respect for Paisley: "Ian Paisley is an ecclesiastical adventurer and changes his viewpoints when necessary, specifically his position on baptism. . . . First Paisley is a Baptist, then a pedobaptist, now Free Presbyterian . . . [which] leaves it an open question how he is a Presbyterian."[87]

Paisley had his own concerns about the company that the International Council was keeping in the British Isles. He wrote to the organization's headquarters in Amsterdam and questioned the theological orthodoxy of some ICCC members, complained that others were in the

World Presbyterian Alliance—to Paisley, an apostate organization—and asked why an ICCC vice president had preached in a Belfast church affiliated with the WCC. Kyle Paisley also wrote to McIntire and questioned why Norman Porter and the Irish members of the ICCC were trying to recruit the Baptist Union of Ireland into the council, a group from which Kyle had split in the 1920s. The elder Paisley further inquired why Grier, Porter, and the Irish Evangelical Church were working to stop attendees to the ICCC conference in Edinburgh from speaking at his and the Free Presbyterians' churches.[88]

In May 1956, Warnaar notified the Free Presbyterian Church of Ulster that its application to the ICCC would be denied as long as the Free Presbyterians feuded with both the Irish Evangelical Church and the EPS. Warnaar noted that the Free Presbyterian Church was doctrinally correct, but that it must cooperate with the other fundamentalists in fellowship with the ICCC. In Warnaar's words, Paisley could not "fight friends as well as enemies."[89] Although McIntire was on the ICCC's credentials committee, the board also included Grier and Porter, and the American militant had to acquiesce to the collective decision. McIntire was no stranger to controversy, and under different circumstances he might have taken Paisley's side. In the mid-1950s, however, the Irish Evangelical Church and the EPS were more important to his international crusade against apostasy and communism than were Paisley and the young Free Presbyterians.

The friendship between McIntire and Ian Paisley developed cautiously and grew out of a shared theology—a mutual dislike of Catholicism, modernism, and communism—which allowed for an interest in each other's theological and political activity. For example, in March 1952 McIntire inquired why the Free Presbyterian Church would no longer send students to study under the Free Church of Scotland. Paisley wrote back to complain that the Free Church had reneged on the promise of help it had made immediately after the Crossgar schism in 1951 and that the Scots were spreading false testimony about the incident.[90] Because they shared more devotional and political similarities than differences, Paisley kept McIntire informed of his demonstrations and activities against the Irish Presbyterian Church and the WCC, and he was invited to the ICCC's Third Plenary Congress in Philadelphia in 1954; however, there is no evidence that he attended. By the late 1950s, McIntire became increasingly interested in Paisley's campaign against modernism and ecumenism in Ireland. In 1957, the *Christian Beacon* reprinted articles taken from *The Revivalist* that denounced Billy Graham. But it was the Free Presbyterian attack on Donald Soper in Ballymena and Belfast that particularly sparked McIntire's interest. The affair drove McIntire to ask why "this valiant for the truth [Paisley]," who "courageously exposes the W.C.C.," was not in the ICCC.[91]

McIntire's enthusiasm for Paisley took another positive step in 1961 when the British Isles suffered its own controversy over new Bible translations. During that year, the work of four committees representing translators and literary advisers from all of Britain's major Protestant denominations was published. The New English Bible, which replaced the English Revised Version, went beyond a simple revision and retranslated the New Testament into modern colloquial English. Paisley promptly attacked the new translation, objecting to numerous items concerning the new translation. Most important, he despised the fact that Professor C. H. Dodd, a Welsh New Testament scholar whose views on eschatology militant fundamentalists considered heretical, was in charge of the project. Numerous colloquial retranslations caught Paisley ire; for example, in Genesis 1:1–2 "a mighty wind" replaces "the Spirit of God" and in Acts 20:7 "Saturday night" replaces "first day of the week." In April 1961, McIntire purchased seven thousand copies of Paisley's pamphlet, *The New English Bible: Version or Perversion?* to distribute to his followers and covered the event in the *Christian Beacon,* the earliest mention of the Reverend Ian Paisley in McIntire's periodical.[92] In a letter to Norman Porter, McIntire expressed his pleasure with Paisley's pamphlet, which must have pressed home to Porter Paisley's rising stature with the militant fundamentalist leader.[93] Christian clergymen honor each other in several significant ways: one is to invite a respected cleric to preach to their congregations; a second is to purchase another's writings. When a prolific writer and speaker such as McIntire do either, the symbolism is profound.

Although McIntire's interest in Paisley grew, he still had to consider the ICCC as a whole and take into consideration the different relationships the council created. McIntire wanted to retain a strong relationship with

Porter and the Irish Evangelical Church; in correspondence with Porter, he praised Grier: "we truly love that brother."[94] It appears in early 1961 that Paisley asked McIntire to come to Northern Ireland and take part in a joint evangelistic crusade, but McIntire declined the request because the ICCC would not back an effort to which Porter, the EPS, or the Irish Evangelical Church would object. In this manner, McIntire made an effort to retain the bond between Porter, Grier, and the ICCC. He reiterated to his northern Irish allies the ICCC's position that the Free Presbyterian Church could not join the international organization until Paisley reconciled with both men.

As early as 1957, the Irish Evangelical Church began to reappraise its commitment to the ICCC. In late February of that year, the Irish Evangelicals passed a resolution questioning the divisive developments within the ICCC.[95] By the spring of 1962, the Irish Evangelical Church had resigned from the council. Grier and his church had come to dislike the organization's strict exclusionist policy, McIntire's autocratic style, and Paisley's rising stature with the American militant. A frustrated Porter remained on the ICCC's executive committee but complained to McIntire that Paisley's public hostility was hurting his own (Porter's) attempts to convince the Baptist Union of Ireland to join the international organization. For his part, Paisley did not understand why Porter, the president of the Baptist Union of Ireland in 1962, would keep his denomination within the apostate Baptist World Alliance. He also inquired why Porter continued fellowship with subsequent Baptist Union presidents, especially Dr. Howard Williams, who espoused modernist tenets. He criticized the Baptist Union of Ireland for selling a booklet written by Reverend J. B. Middlebrook (also the British Missionary Society secretary) that denied that salvation came through Christ's crucifixion. Paisley claimed that Porter had begun a new behind-the-scenes campaign to discredit him. In 1951, Porter had sent a confidential letter to the NUP membership challenging Paisley's attacks on the Reverend E. M. Borland, an evangelical minister of the Irish Presbyterian Church and an NUP member. Porter did not feel that the theological integrity of any Presbyterian fundamentalist should be challenged, and so he wrote to Pastor William Mullan of Lurgan Baptist Church denouncing the Free Presbyterian. A closer look at the correspondence gives credence to Paisley's argument: in the letter dated April 1961, Porter argued condescendingly that the Free Presbyterians were acting as if they were ICCC members. To illustrate his point, he charged that Paisley's denomination regularly distributed ICCC literature even though it was not a member of the organization.[96] Such actions were common within the militant fundamentalist community, however, and rarely drew negative comment.

In the early 1960s, the Free Presbyterians were gaining more notoriety than Norman Porter or the EPS. At the same time, important events were happening within ecumenical discourse, and McIntire saw the need for the strongest allies, such as Paisley and the Free Presbyterians. The WCC held a third congress in New Delhi in late 1961, even as the Roman Catholic Church prepared for the Second Vatican Council. The aspects of the New Delhi assembly that upset militant fundamentalists the most were the WCC's proposal to merge with the International Missionary Council, the admittance of the Russian Orthodox Church as a member, and the renewed call for church unity.[97] To counter these threats, the ICCC organized its Fifth Plenary Congress in Amsterdam and geared up for a series of counterdemonstrations.[98] It was under these circumstances that McIntire invited the Reverend Ian Paisley and the Free Presbyterian Church of Ulster as well as Kyle Paisley and the Gospel Tabernacle to Amsterdam as observers. The elder Paisley was happy to accept the overture and planned to be present at the congress. Speaking for the Paisley family and their Ulster followers, he stated that they were "Bible Believers" who held the traditional Reformed faith. Noting the apostasy in Northern Ireland, Kyle stated that nothing short of aligning with McIntire and the Twentieth Century Reformation Movement would defend Bible Protestantism in Ireland.[99]

The invitation to the Free Presbyterian Church and J. Kyle Paisley to attend the ICCC's Fifth Plenary Congress in Amsterdam as observers was an important event in Ian Paisley's international ascent. During this conference, the Paisleys and the Free Presbyterians were formally asked to join the ICCC. It was also in Amsterdam that the Reverend Ian Paisley met Bob Jones Jr., most likely for the first time, a relationship that within six years would transcend the Paisley–McIntire friendship. As noted previously, Paisley was well acquainted with the ministry of Bob Jones

University; the Free Presbyterian organ *The Revivalist* had printed articles by Bob Jones Sr. as early as 1958.

Several months after visiting Amsterdam, Paisley traveled to Rome to protest the opening of the Second Vatican Council. The trek, which took place in October 1962, added to the exposure that Paisley and the Free Presbyterian Church received throughout the British Isles and within the international militant fundamentalist community. In a letter to McIntire written a month before the trip, Paisley inquired whether the American militant would be in Rome and invited McIntire to Northern Ireland for a gospel campaign.[100] McIntire and the ICCC replied and heartily supported the trip to Rome, believing that the trip would gain more international publicity than the Free Presbyterians' movement had earned from any single protest. McIntire lamented that he did not have the money to send one hundred men from Ireland to augment Paisley and his entourage.[101] He also wrote to Norman Porter about the crusade to the Vatican, arguing that, of all the places in the world, Ireland was where the crusade should come from. He believed that the growing Paisleyite crusade in Northern Ireland created an outstanding opportunity to confront the perceived tyranny of Rome and the WCC's apostasy.[102] Porter backed Paisley's effort with considerable caution, stating that his group would not accompany the Free Presbyterians to Rome—Paisley's planned demonstrations adequately represented Northern Ireland—and warned McIntire that overzealous support for the protest might hurt the ICCC's reputation among British Christians.[103]

After the Free Presbyterian Church was given a conditional ICCC membership in February 1963, the feud between Paisley, on the one side, and Norman Porter and the Irish Evangelical Church, on the other, intensified. Many militant fundamentalists in North America still supported Porter, and he continued to be a frequent speaker in the United States and Canada as well as a contributor to the militant press.[104] Moreover, Paisley's growing fame did not stop Harvey Springer, an ICCC member who was aware of the Paisley–Porter feud, from appearing with Porter. As an independent and fundamentalist Baptist, Springer still found common ground with his Irish counterpart. In August and September 1965, Springer preached to three churches and six venues—mission, town, and

Orange halls—in a crusade that traversed Ulster. In an interesting assertion of Northern Ireland's fundamentalist and revivalist history, Springer's newspaper, *Western Voice*, claimed that the Coloradan had drawn the largest crowds since Nicholson in 1923. The publication also ran an article on the Ulster revival of 1859.[105] American militants clearly viewed Northern Ireland as an important battleground.

In addition to the incessant cross-Atlantic fellowship between North American and Irish militants, Paisley was gaining increased support from militant fundamentalists within both the British Isles and the international community. Paisley's emerging power was such that leaders such as McIntire did not want to alienate the Free Presbyterians. The *Christian Beacon* began a more extensive coverage of the Free Presbyterian Church.[106] But Paisley showed little interest in finding common ground with Porter and the Irish Evangelical Church. Instead, in letters written to McIntire between November 1963 and February 1964, Paisley outlined his new complaints: Grier allowed ministers of the Irish Presbyterian Church to preach from his pulpit, most notably Donald Gillies, a fundamentalist who would not leave his denomination. Moreover, Porter and Grier had attended dinners at which Catholics and ecumenical professors from the Irish Presbyterian College were present, placing both Ulstermen in communion with apostates, and the Irish Evangelical Church had hired Robert Cleland, a former Free Presbyterian officer excommunicated for sexual immorality.[107] In these letters, Paisley attacked Porter and the EPS for their membership in the National Association of Evangelicals. Furthermore, Paisley did not like the fact that Porter was an officer in the British Missionary Society and was the chairman of the British Evangelical Council—two apostate organizations—and that Porter criticized the Strict Baptist Group of Churches, a group consisting of twenty-six congregations from throughout the British Isles.[108]

Paisley became irate after Porter failed to protest J. B. Middlebrook's talk to Belfast's Antrim Road Baptist Church. He claimed that Porter had once again been "smearing" his name among Irish Baptists, and he sent McIntire a copy of a secret letter Porter had mailed to various Baptist pastors and church secretaries. Porter's signature is typed, and it is difficult to determine its authenticity; however, Paisley was most likely libeled.

Paisley believed that these controversies were drawing sarcastic comments in Northern Ireland from clergymen associated with the WCC; he argued that the snide insinuations were embarrassing the Twentieth Century Reformation in Ulster. Another issue dividing Paisley from Grier and Porter was Paisley's premillennialist and separatist views versus the amillennialism that Grier and Porter professed, which allowed for some semblance of moderation.[109] The contention is ironic now, though, considering Paisley's move to amillennialism as his political career developed.

Formal ICCC memberships are voted on at plenary congresses. Paisley and the Free Presbyterian Church of Ulster became constituent members of the ICCC in July 1965 at the Sixth Plenary Congress in Geneva. The decision to admit Paisley elicited considerable objection from British and Irish members. As a result, the feud between Paisley and Porter finally culminated in May 1967 when the EPS officially withdrew from the ICCC.[110] However, McIntire needed to retain allies in the British Isles as well as for the Twentieth Century Reformation and the International Council of Christian Churches. His relationships with many militants—in America and elsewhere—had soured, so he was reluctant to break all fellowship with Norman Porter. He asked Porter to reconsider the EPS's withdrawal: "Please don't go away this way. You and Paisley are brothers in Christ, washed in His blood and with Paisley being used by God as he is today, there is a way of understanding on your local level. I am sure the Babylon Church is upon us and the current that is taking all back to Rome is broadening."[111] According to McIntire, the Catholic Church had orchestrated the feud between Paisley and Porter.

By the mid-1960s, Paisley's growing importance effectively sidelined Porter. By the spring of 1968, when Paisley attended his fourth Bible Conference at Bob Jones University, Norman Porter had ended his fellowship with the North American militant fundamentalist community and had restricted his religious and political affairs to the British Isles. During the summer of 1970, Porter immigrated to Australia.[112] To the international community of militant fundamentalists, the Reverend Ian Paisley had become the primary proponent of Bible Protestantism in Ireland.

5

The Crusade Against O'Neill and Ecumenism

Until the early 1960s, Paisley's notoriety was confined to the Northern Irish religious community and to a small group of militant fundamentalists in North America and Great Britain. But during the five-year period between 1963, when Terence O'Neill was elected the leader of the UUP and appointed the prime minister of Northern Ireland, and August 1968 when Northern Ireland civil rights activists took their message to the streets of Ulster, Paisley became well known throughout Canada, the United States, and the British Isles. Paisley's confrontation with O'Neill and the civil rights movements propelled him from a little-known but vocal proponent of militant fundamentalism in Northern Ireland to a respected figure among the international community of militant fundamentalists. Worldwide militant support helped to bolster his belief that O'Neill's overtures to the Catholic community constituted "political ecumenicalism." To Paisley, such a policy was tantamount to inviting the Roman Catholic Church into Northern Ireland's political, cultural, and economic relationships. He believed that coming on the heels of the Anglo-Catholic rapprochement and the Second Vatican Council, O'Neill's policies added a new and serious threat to the political union between Great Britain and Northern Ireland. He also believed that the Roman Catholic Church tacitly supported the IRA and together with Irish Republicans organized the Ulster civil rights movement. The combination of these beliefs transformed his religious crusade against Irish Protestant ecumenism and liberalism into a political campaign against the O'Neill administration and Catholic civil rights.

Before March 1963, Paisley's activism was concerned primarily with spreading the militant fundamentalist gospel and confronting apostasy in the Anglican, Methodist, and Presbyterian churches of the British Isles.[1] Although he took part in some political activities (the NPU and the UPA), during the 1950s the Free Presbyterian Church espoused a nonpolitical Calvinism and was interested in preaching the gospel, not in confronting political issues. At this stage, Paisley did not yet understand the political connections to his protests against the Church of England and the British royalty's flirtations with Rome. The Free Presbyterian Church addressed social issues only when they threatened Calvinist mores. Yet events were under way that galvanized Northern Irish fundamentalists and set the stage for Paisley's move into politics in the 1960s. The acceptance of the British welfare state in Northern Ireland, the reappearance of Irish Republican terrorist activity in 1956, and the revitalization of the ecumenical movement seemed part of a four-way political conspiracy organized by the Roman Catholic Church, Republicans, Communists, and ecumenical Protestants to destroy Irish Protestantism.[2]

Although Northern Irish militant fundamentalists did not see an urgency to political action in the 1950s, their viewpoint changed after 1963 when Terence O'Neill, the prime minister of Northern Ireland, began a campaign to modernize the Ulster economy and to find a rapprochement with Catholics throughout the island. The Protestant opposition to O'Neill and the "Catholic conspiracy" was diverse, but a small vocal group dominated the discourse: the "Paisleyites" led by the Reverend Ian Paisley. Paisleyites objected to "O'Neillism," a program intended to eliminate the economic and political divisions that beset Northern Ireland. O'Neill attempted to reconcile the policies of the Protestant-run Northern Ireland government—designed to maintain Protestant economic and political control—with the aspirations of the province's Catholic minority.[3]

The Northern Ireland Statelet, 1922–1963

To comprehend the onset of both O'Neillism and Paisleyism, it is necessary to understand the political and economic history of the Northern Ireland statelet. Created in December 1922 from six of Ulster's nine counties, the Northern Ireland statelet was a political arrangement designed to prevent a Catholic–Protestant civil war in Ireland. The agreement did not settle Ireland's sectarian problem, however, or create a harmonious relationship between the British Empire and the new Irish Free State. The partitioning of Ireland and the establishment of the Irish Free State were intended only as short-term solutions; both the British government and the Irish government reasoned that economic necessity and political reality would drive northern Irish Protestants to unify with the South. However, the creation of two parliaments, one in Belfast controlled by Protestants (Stormont) and the other in Dublin dominated by Catholics (the Dail), made reunification unlikely. Both parliaments were given the power to veto unification, and in order to retain the union with Great Britain the Protestants in the North needed to control a majority of the seats in the Stormont assembly. As a consequence, the British government could not force Stormont to unite with the Irish Free State against its will.[4]

Political developments over the following three decades did not help the impasse. In 1937, Articles 2 and 3 of the Irish Free State's new constitution asserted its jurisdiction over Northern Ireland. The withdrawal of the Free State from the British Commonwealth and the creation of the Republic of Ireland in 1949 reinforced Protestant defiance in Ulster and forced the British Parliament to pass the Ireland Act (1949), which reiterated Northern Ireland's political position within the United Kingdom. The British government felt the need to reassure Irish Protestants that Northern Ireland would not be forced out of the union.[5]

The Catholic identity of Irish nationalism grew more pronounced after partition as the Protestant element within Irish nationalism dissipated. The Irish Constitution of 1937 granted the Roman Catholic Church a special position in the nation's culture and politics. Although the Catholic Church in Ireland was denied a state endowment, Catholic social policy quickly interposed itself into government policy. The Censorship of Films Act (1929); the Criminal Law Amendment Act (1935), which prohibited the sales or importation of contraceptives; and the constitutional ban on divorce (1937) reflected Catholic morality. The Catholic Church oversaw the education of a vast majority of Catholic children, and the Catholic hierarchy objected to Catholics attending Anglican Trinity College (1927). The hierarchy's defeat of the Mother and Child Scheme in 1950 revealed its political power. The proposed legislation required free compulsory health testing for children and a choice of doctor, but the hierarchy attacked the scheme as contrary to Catholic social teaching and asserted that it would lead to abortion and birth control.[6]

Deeply threatened by the "Catholicization" of the Free State, Protestants in Ulster based their cultural identity on an affinity with British and imperial culture. The UUP and the Protestant ascendancy wasted little time in creating in Northern Ireland a Protestant state for a Protestant people. Protestants solidly voted for the UUP. The party, which retained power from 1921 until Stormont was suspended in 1972, imposed economic and political restrictions on the Catholic minority to impel Catholics to emigrate in order to seek employment. A vital part of the Protestant plan involved local government councils, which were reconstructed and their boundaries redrawn to ensure that Protestants maintained control over urban and rural councils with both substantial Protestant and large Catholic populations. To retain segregated working-class neighborhoods, public-housing allotments were doled out at the discretion of local councilors. Protestant and Catholic councilors gave preference to Protestant and Catholic constituents, respectively.[7]

The constant threat of IRA violence—despite a lull in the 1930s and 1940s—and the existence of a minority population disloyal to the new statelet created a sense of embattlement among Ulster Protestants. The murder of southern Protestants during the Anglo-Irish and Irish Civil Wars (1919–22) intensified these fears. To help combat the IRA, the armed Ulster Special Constabulary was established in September 1920 to supplement the unarmed local police forces. In April 1922, the Civil Authorities (Special Powers) Act (Northern Ireland) gave the government of Northern Ireland the authority to take any step necessary to preserve law and order, including the suspension of habeas corpus and the internment of suspected terrorists.[8]

Catholics in the North unwittingly helped the Stormont government; they insisted on a separate educational system for their children and accepted both the benefits of the public dole and ineffective political leadership. Catholic politicians acquiesced to the corrupt public-housing system and concentrated their political efforts on eliminating partition instead of fighting for Catholic political rights within Northern Ireland and improving Catholic living conditions. As the British welfare system implemented a standard of living better than in the Republic of Ireland, Catholics in Northern Ireland were generally complacent. Most rejected the IRA's border campaign (1956–62), and some quietly supported the union between Northern Ireland and Great Britain.[9]

However, the UUP's dominance did not go unchallenged. Economic problems weakened Protestant working-class support for the Northern Ireland government. During the 1930s, unemployment rose as high as 27 percent, inciting sectarian riots but also cooperation between Catholic and Protestant workers. Stormont's refusal to integrate Ulster's industrial base into Britain's government-controlled war production during the Second World War helped create a surge of Protestant electoral support for independent Unionist populists and the Northern Ireland Labour Party (NILP). The NILP won two seats in Belfast and forced the UUP to implement most British social welfare policies, although the British Treasury paid a majority of the expense. By the end of the 1950s, Northern Ireland's economy was in recession, and the NILP made significant inroads into the Protestant vote. In 1962, the vote for the NILP peaked, with the party receiving 28 percent of the votes cast in Belfast and capturing four Stormont seats.[10]

O'Neillism

When Terence O'Neill took office on 24 March 1963, he inherited the governance of a province that was at an economic, political, and cultural crossroad. On the one hand, the UUP's hold on power and the union with Great Britain seemed secure, and community relations had improved. Tension between the Protestant and Catholic communities had relaxed as sectarian violence declined. Most Catholics did not support the IRA campaign in the late 1950s; the Nationalist minority was increasingly complacent toward unification; and Catholics were more willing to accept the British welfare state. In the early 1960s, some moderate Unionists proposed that their party allow Catholic membership, and the Orange Order and the Nationalist Party—the constitutional Catholic party—were engaged in conversations over community relations.[11]

But the local economy faced difficulties. Employment opportunities within Northern Ireland's three main industries—shipbuilding, linen, and agriculture—were in sharp decline, which created a political-economic dilemma for the UUP. As the local economy stagnated, Northern Ireland's government strained to finance welfare benefits during a time of declining tax revenues. Northern Ireland increasingly relied on the British government to finance its budget. These economic difficulties translated into increased political competition in Belfast between the UUP and the NILP for Protestant working-class votes.[12]

To remedy the economic situation and to keep his party in power, O'Neill looked to foreign investment, which required both the support of the Catholic minority and improved relations with the Republic of Ireland. In order to achieve this goal, O'Neill proposed limited political, economic, and cultural gestures toward the Catholic community, such as visiting Catholic hospitals and schools and inviting the Catholic bishop of Down and Connor to the Belfast City Hall for a reception. Although these efforts might seem trivial, in the Northern Irish context they were significant indeed. O'Neill was the first Northern Ireland prime minister to reach out to the Catholic community, and many Catholics responded positively. In February 1965, the Nationalist Party decided to participate fully in Northern Irish politics and agreed to become the official opposition at Stormont.[13]

The O'Neill administration devised several economic plans to improve the province's infrastructure and developed programs for limited urban renewal and designs for a new university. Although many Catholics and moderate Protestants showed appreciation for O'Neillism, the far-reaching reform program created political and economic expectations within the Catholic community that Northern Ireland's government could not meet. What civil rights leaders and social activists demanded from O'Neill threatened to alienate a substantial segment within the Protestant community. Most important, O'Neillism did not address the minority community's core demands for more public housing, voting rights in local council elections for all citizens, the elimination of gerrymandering in Londonderry and other cities with a large Catholic population, and reform of the Royal Ulster Constabulary (RUC).[14]

To make matters worse, the Unionist leader could not restrain radicals within his party and the Protestant community. O'Neill was met with political opposition from the UUP right wing and from working-class Loyalists, but, more important, he inspired an outcry from Paisley. Of all the opponents to O'Neill's policies, Paisley made the loudest and most active response; he opposed virtually every liberal and conciliatory move made by the O'Neill government with denunciatory sermons, public speeches, and public demonstrations. The combination of O'Neill's inability to thwart Paisley's crusade against political liberalism and demonstrations against the civil rights movement, on the one hand, and the slow implementation of social and economic reforms, on the other, provoked a violent reaction from the Catholic community.[15]

The Paisleyite and militant fundamentalist assault on O'Neill began three months into the new prime minister's administration. On 3 June 1963, William Jenkins, the lord mayor of Belfast, flew the flags at city hall at half-mast to honor the death of Pope John XXIII, and O'Neill sent an official condolence to Cardinal William Conway, the Catholic archbishop of Armagh. The following day an outraged Paisley preached to four hundred supporters gathered at the Ulster Hall, after which he led an illegal march to city hall to protest what he described as the defilement of the building. Because the marchers had failed to get a police permit for traditional marches, Paisley and six supporters were summoned to court. Seven weeks later Paisley held another meeting at the Ulster Hall, where he threatened, "There is going to be trouble in this city before this whole matter is over."[16] The next day he led a procession of Free Presbyterians to the Belfast Petty Session Court, where he pleaded not guilty and made a spirited defense. The preacher cross-examined an RUC district inspector and demanded the appearance of the lord mayor to answer several countercharges. The whole event made good press, but Paisley was found guilty and given the choice of a ten-pound fine or two months in jail. Once again Paisley promised to accept the jail time, but an English businessman, Peter Courtney, anonymously paid his fine and those of his four colleagues.[17] Although skeptics in Ulster believed that Paisley knew who had satisfied the fines, he protested in a telegram to O'Neill that the Unionist administration had paid them to sabotage his attempted "martyrdom" and to minimize the impact his imprisonment would create: "Congratulations to you [O'Neill], the Minister of Home Affairs, the Crown Solicitor, the police and the Unionist Lord Mayor, on not permitting your own law to take its course, and on arranging for my fine to be paid. No Surrender!"[18]

Paisley's brush with authority inspired contentious acts from supporters and enemies alike. John Wylie and two evangelists from the Christian Workers' Union conducted a religious service near a Gaelic football pitch in predominately Nationalist Dunloy and were assaulted by Catholic residents. Because Gaelic football is associated with Irish nationalism (the sport is almost exclusively played by Catholics), and owing to the town's demographics, the service was seen as provocative. Despite the violence, Wylie held further meetings in the town. But Paisley's rising notoriety led to death threats, and the church on Ravenhill Road was vandalized—both of which acts the Free Presbyterians blamed on Catholic activists. In September 1963, windows at the church were damaged despite a police guard, and Paisley claimed to have received death threats through the mail.[19] The following April an edition of the *Belfast Telegraph* publicized Paisley's claims, which he reiterated to a crowd of two thousand supporters in the Ulster Hall who were commemorating the Larne gun-running incident of April 1914.[20] Paisley used the Larne commemoration to declare a "No Surrender" crusade against O'Neillism and to profess premillennial eschatology. Basing his assertion on the apocalyptic message in Daniel 3:18,[21] he interpreted the words "we will not serve thy gods" to mean "no surrender for Ulstermen"; O'Neillism equaled idolatry, and such irreverence would induce the destruction of Protestant Ulster.[22]

Paisleyites fought O'Neill and apostasy at every opportunity. When the Fisherwick Presbyterian and University Road Methodist churches in Belfast invited two Catholic priests to speak to the youth clubs of their respective congregations in the spring of 1964, Paisley threatened "monster" demonstrations. Thus, despite support from their church bodies, both churches felt it best to abort their plans. Reverend John Withers of Fisherwick explained his reasons:

> Fortunately it was not possible to record the strident, hysterical, even filthy abuse which has been hurled at me through the telephone, for such a

> record would be a grim embarrassment to my friends in the Presbyterian Church who differ from me in love and understanding. They would be ashamed of the company they are forced to keep. All persecution, apartheid, and discrimination are born of fear or insecurity, and my love of Christ, while not perfect, is strong enough to cast out all fear of the Pope of Rome or any other self-appointed Pope. I am so glad that the "monster demonstration" has been called off, for we already know the "Monster."[23]

Paisley found defenders within the Evangelical Presbyterian Church (formerly the Irish Evangelical Church—the denomination had changed its name in March 1964), in spite their past differences, but these Presbyterian fundamentalists argued that Paisley was not the only Protestant who objected to the presence of the Catholic priests.[24] Probably because of the notoriety he received and in part owing to the vindication he must have felt, Paisley wrote to Carl McIntire and boasted of his victory over Presbyterian apostasy and Roman Catholicism.[25]

Paisley's crusade against O'Neillism slowly became a political as well as a religious movement. In October 1964, Northern Ireland's political parties participated in a British general election that many expected Labour to win. Conservatives have historically been more attached than Labour to the British union with Northern Ireland, and during the run-up to the election campaign British Labour Party leader Harold Wilson made public comments promising to extend social justice to Catholics in Northern Ireland. Because of the economic difficulties, the UUP expected a strong challenge from the Northern Ireland Labour Party. Moreover, the mixed constituencies of Belfast expected unusually tense electoral battles. Owing to the British system of "winner takes all" for national elections, and because a majority of Protestants voted for the UUP and a majority of Catholics voted Nationalist, only the seats in constituencies with a mixed Catholic–Protestant population were strongly contested between the Unionists and the Nationalists. During the election, the UUP faced NILP opposition in Belfast for seats in areas with a Protestant majority.[26]

One of the bigger fights loomed in West Belfast, an area that included both Catholic and Protestant voters. The election put the Republican Billy McMillen, an NILP candidate, and Jim Kilfedder of the UUP, up against

Harry Diamond, a founder of the Republican Labour Party. Because of Protestant unemployment at the Belfast shipyards—which were located in the electoral district—the UUP was concerned over losing Protestant votes to the NILP. During the short election, the UUP looked for any situation that would help the Unionist vote. They found one when McMillen displayed an Irish tricolor in the front window of his campaign office, located on Divis Street, a small street close to city center. Although flying the Irish flag was not illegal, the RUC could cite the Flags and Emblems (Display) Bill (Northern Ireland) of 1954 and demand the removal of any flag or symbol that was deemed a threat to public order.[27] A *Belfast Telegraph* article publicized the appearance of the flag, and Paisley decided to take up the defense of Protestant honor. Holding a rally in front of city hall on 27 September, Paisley threatened to lead a march to seize the Irish tricolor, a move that would have undoubtedly created sectarian violence. Paisley backed down, however, when Minister of Home Affairs Brian McConnell banned the march. Although at this time Paisley was willing to confront what he considered apostate Protestant churches, he seemed unwilling to orchestrate public violence.[28]

Hoping to thwart the street fighting that would result and at the same time appease Paisley, the RUC removed the flag the following morning. A small group of Catholic teenagers who had been expecting the Paisley march were unfortunately waiting there, and a series of battles broke out. During the day, the number of Catholic rioters expanded to an estimated two thousand. Three days later serious trouble erupted again, when McMillen once again displayed the tricolor, and the RUC once again removed it. The fighting involved water cannons, petrol bombs, and reportedly a few members of the IRA. The trouble spread to other cities, including Enniskillen, Dungannon, and Coleraine; the violence on Divis Street was the worst that Northern Ireland had seen since the early 1930s. In retrospect, it has been shown that sectarian feeling became more intense: the Divis Street riots convinced some younger Catholics, such as Gerry Adams, the future IRA and Sinn Fein leader, to become interested in political and Republican activism.[29]

Paisley denied he had colluded with the Unionist government, but some Catholics believed that such an arrangement had been made. Gerry

Fitt, the Republican Labour member of Parliament (MP) for the Belfast Docks constituency, charged in a Stormont speech that Paisley and Minister of Home Affairs Brian McConnell had discussed Paisley's proposed march before the events took place and that the whole event was a conspiracy to attract votes for Kilfedder: "I say in this case and I suggested it when it happened that the Government, in collusion with Mr. Paisley, agreed to give him the credit for taking down the tricolor in Divis Street. They agreed to give him the credit and the Unionist Party in this country will someday live to regret that agreement which was reached between the parties."[30] Cahir Healy, the Nationalist Party MP for South Fermanagh, argued that Paisley was disrupting the democratic process: "Where is the freedom that people are supposed to enjoy at Imperial elections if Paisley is going to determine what flag can be used and what speeches are going to be made? I suppose that Paisley had some form of public opinion behind him but I would suggest that it is the least informed and indeed the most ignorant and provocative in the whole community."[31] Such assertions improved Paisley's stature within both the militant fundamentalist and the secular Protestant working-class communities—attacks on him were making headlines for both the militant and Loyalist causes. There were even hints that Paisley's tactics were similar to those of the American militant right wing. The August 1965 issue of *Focus* magazine referred to his growing power within the Unionist, Loyalist, and evangelical communities as well as to his McCarthyite tactics.[32]

However, not all Ulster Protestants were willing to elevate Paisley to the role of messiah. The bulk of the Protestant community and the government were supportive of the police; Edward Gibson, chairman of the Ulster Young Unionist Council, asked leaders of the UUP to disassociate the party from Paisley's activities and to back the RUC. He asserted to the Stranmillis Debating Society that a minority within the UUP was developing Paisleyite tendencies and that the trend must stop. Many Protestant leaders were far more forthright in their condemnation. Some clergymen, such as John Withers of Fisherwick Presbyterian Church, had been issuing warnings about Paisley for several years: "Some offer tolerance to Dr. Ian Paisley in Ulster to-day simply because they do not take him seriously. At worst, this is a form of personal contempt, and many who shrug their shoulders murmuring, 'Let him alone,' are guilty of just that—personal contempt."[33] Others seemed to awaken to the threat of Paisleyism for the first time. Professor Robert Corkey, the former moderator of the Presbyterian Church in Ireland, told the Northern Irish Senate that Paisley had won a following of "thoughtless people, who are as apparently as brainless as himself."[34] During a service in Belfast in early 1965, Eric Gallagher—who ran the East Belfast Mission and was a future president of the Irish Methodist Conference—warned Ulster Protestants of the road that lay ahead:

> 1965 will demand of the churches in Northern Ireland a clear and uncompromising stand. The threat of religious freedom and liberty is as great from Protestant fascism as from any form of Roman totalitarianism. . . . [T]he churches, by their silence, have unwittingly conspired to allow these self-appointed defenders of the faith to be regarded as the representatives of the authentic teaching of Christ. The good and decent folk in Germany—and there were far more of them than the other kind—woke up too late to what the Nazis were doing. Ulster Christianity could all too easily sell the past to the religious fascists.[35]

The Divis Street riots brought an unusual display of Christian unity when the Churches Industrial Council—an organization consisting of Catholic, Methodist, Presbyterian, and Anglican clergymen—publicly appealed for peace. According to Eric Gallagher, this plea was the first public initiative in Northern Irish history that included both Catholic and Protestant clerics. Paisley's response was in sharp contrast, when on 4 October he told a Sunday night service in the Ulster Hall: "Make no mistake we are in the battle and this is an evil day." He asserted that Protestant churches were appeasing Catholics and took the opportunity to attack the WCC, claiming that this international organization abetted the conspiracy.[36]

The press in the Irish Republic and throughout the British Isles noticed Paisley's growing popularity and Unionists' reluctance to denounce him. After Terence O'Neill gave a speech to the Royal Commonwealth Society in London, a reporter for the *Times* asked him about the riots. O'Neill would not disassociate himself from Paisley, however, and only asserted that the reverend's actions were "not commended." The reserved response is indicative of the respect that the UUP showed for Paisley's growing popularity; the Ulster Unionists did not want to alienate Paisley's followers. Whatever O'Neill thought of Paisley's crusade at this time, however, his insistence on a muted response would change in early 1965.[37]

At the same time, Paisley's opinion of the new policies of the O'Neill administration drastically altered when in mid-January 1965 O'Neill made what is arguably the biggest decision of his administration. Consulting only senior civil servants but not members of his own cabinet, the prime minister invited the Republic of Ireland Taoiseach (head of government), Sean Lemass, to Stormont for friendly consultations. Northern Protestants vilified Lemass for his role in the 1916 Easter Rising, for his past membership in the IRA, and for his previous militancy toward the Irish Free State. (The Free State had interned Lemass during the Irish Civil War in the 1920s.) As Taoiseach, however, Lemass had instituted a new economic program to increase industrial output, exports, and jobs and had lessened the political rhetoric aimed at Northern Ireland and partition. Just as O'Neill sought rapprochement with the Republic of Ireland, Lemass advocated similar approaches to the Unionist government even though the previous prime minister of Northern Ireland, Sir Basil Brooke, had ignored the overtures Lemass made to the Belfast government in the early 1960s. Brooke had followed the unwritten policy of the Stormont government that no official political or economic contacts would be made with the republic until the Dublin government recognized Northern Ireland's constitutional position. O'Neill, however, broke with this policy.[38]

In the late evening of 13 January 1965, Lemass appeared at Stormont for several hours of informal talks. Meeting with the press the following morning, O'Neill's cabinet publicly supported the talks, as did a majority within the Protestant and Catholic communities. Speaking to the Stormont assembly, Gerry Fitt noted that, besides Paisley, only two people in the North objected to the overtures: Desmond Boal and Edmond Warnock, both MPs and allies of the militant preacher. After a lengthy debate, the Northern Ireland House overwhelmingly passed a motion in support of the O'Neill–Lemass talks.[39]

During the following year, discontent over the talks developed within the UUP, and in April 1965 a dozen rebel MPs held a closed meeting to find a way to force O'Neill's resignation. O'Neill's autocratic style and refusal to appease the Unionist right wing constricted his power base. His preference for working with civil servants instead of with government ministers increased disaffection with his agenda. Although the opposition to O'Neill from within the UUP was not a serious threat at this time, it increased during the several months following the Lemass talks. For example, the decision to locate a new public university in Protestant Coleraine instead of in Catholic-majority Londonderry upset many Protestants and Catholics in western Ulster.[40] Nevertheless, the majority of Northern Ireland's public and the UUP, including Brooke and the Protestant ascendancy, continued to stand behind the prime minister. A special two-hour meeting of the UUP voted to back O'Neill, and in the provincial election the following November the number of votes cast for O'Neill and the UUP increased at the expense of the NILP.[41]

In contrast, Paisley and his supporters consistently and unanimously opposed the Lemass meeting. The afternoon following the talks, Paisley and two Protestant Unionist politicians, Belfast Alderman Albert Duff and Councilor James McCarroll, delivered a protest letter to the prime minister's private secretary. The letter charged O'Neill with dictatorial policies, appeasement toward the Irish Republic and the Republican movement, and the outright betrayal of Protestant heritage. Traveling the several miles to the Parliament building in a car covered with a large Union Jack and holding placards reading "No mass, no Lemass" and "I.R.A. murderer welcomed at Stormont," Paisley and his supporters were met by the press and television cameras on their arrival. The following week at a meeting in the Ulster Hall, Paisley referred to O'Neill as a "Lundy" (Ulster Protestant slang for a traitor), organized a sizeable protest march through the city center to the Belfast Telegraph building, and called for a general election to oust the prime minister. The O'Neill–Lemass talks were also denounced in *The Revivalist,* which commended Boal and Warnock for being the only two MPs to address the issue within the Northern Ireland Parliament. The magazine continued the old argument that the talks were part of a larger ecumenical conspiracy that aimed to reunite Protestant churches under Rome's authority.[42]

Paisley and his supporters were further incensed when on 9 February 1965, O'Neill made a reciprocal visit to Dublin. Preceded by a visit from Brian Faulkner, the Northern Irish minister of commerce, to discuss economic cooperation, this second round of talks was again exploratory and informal. O'Neill found it necessary to alleviate militant and Loyalist fears, however, and to assert publicly that no formal agreements were made. He called a meeting of the Ulster Unionist Council in Wellington Hall, Belfast, in order to have his new policies officially approved. In response, Paisley and his Free Presbyterian supporters once again hit the streets of Belfast and protested wherever O'Neill spoke publicly. They began a campaign to protest wherever the prime minister spoke. For example, John Wylie and a small group picketed O'Neill's talk at the Castlerock Orange Hall in West Belfast on 19 February, while hundreds of supporters protested the Lemass meetings in a march to the UUP's headquarters in Glengall Street. Because of the O'Neill–Lemass talks, and despite a lull in larger protests throughout the rest of 1965, the Reverend Ian Paisley and his followers—whom the *Belfast Telegraph* had now dubbed "Paisleyites"—began a concerted crusade against O'Neillism.[43]

The growing opposition to O'Neill and the Easter Rising commemorations planned for April caused sectarian and political tensions to rise in Northern Ireland in early 1966. Paisley's crusade exploited the situation. *The Revivalist* proclaimed "The Challenge of 1966," a militant fundamentalist program to thwart the perceived resurgence of Romanism and the expansion of ecumenicalism,[44] and Paisley wrote a pamphlet that urged Protestants to remember past Protestant sacrifices:

> Now there are voices raised in our Province today which advocate a course of forgetfulness. They tell us that the sooner we forget the great epochs of history, the sooner we forget about "Derry, Aughrim, Enniskillen and the Boyne" the better for us as a people. . . . Let it be said, and let me say it without fear of contradiction, that there are even leaders in Church and State who are apostles of this doctrine of forgetfulness. . . . This text says, "Remember, thou was a bondsman in the land of Egypt."

> . . . [I]f there's one thing Ulster needs to remember it is this, that four hundred years ago they were bondsmen and under the Egyptian slavery of pagan popery. Let me say this: wherever there is bondage, wherever there is tyranny, wherever there is superstition, wherever the people are subjugated, there you will find the iron heel of the Roman Catholic Church, the jack-boot of the Vatican.[45]

In spite of their new inclination toward political activities, Paisley and the Free Presbyterian Church of Ulster reasserted a revivalist message: "The Free Presbyterian Church is an evangelistic gospel preaching church. It believes in Revival and in the power of believing prayer. It has no desire to build on any other man's foundation. It seeks to win souls to Christ rather than members to a denomination."[46]

To Paisley, the answer to ecumenism and Catholic tyranny transcended the defeat of O'Neill's policies and the thwarting of a Republican resurgence; the response required a fundamentalist devotion to scripture and the practice of traditional, reformed Christianity. Paisleyites reacted strongly against the Catholic community's plans to celebrate the fiftieth anniversary of the 1916 Easter Rising in Dublin. Both moderate Nationalists and radical Republicans expected to hold marches to honor the anniversary, which Paisley and many in the Protestant community viewed as a challenge to Protestant ascendancy. Paisleyites were outraged when O'Neill commemorated the Rising in Ballycastle by delivering the opening address to a Protestant–Catholic conference at the Corrymeela Centre on Easter weekend. Billed as "Community 1966," the cross-community effort aimed to bridge sectarian differences over the upcoming celebrations. But there were also warnings that O'Neillism was losing moderate Protestant support: the select vestry of the Church of Ireland in Londonderry opposed the Anglican churches within the republic that planned to hold commemorative services, and the Evangelical Fellowship of Ireland formed to confront Irish Protestantism's "Romeward movement."[47] Nate Minford, the Unionist MP for Antrim, addressed Stormont on the possibility of a Paisleyite–Catholic confrontation: "We are approaching a period when in fact, unless the Government keeps very rigid control of our affairs, [Paisley] could inflame hatred in his own particular and peculiar way."[48] Minford expressed the angst of those moderate Protestants who did not want the commemorations to take place but also did not condone Paisleyite activities: "We want to be perfectly certain that those Protestant people, or seemingly Protestant people, who can inflame passions will also, if need be, be taken into account when we are trying to maintain peace at this time. There is a great fear in this country and in this House for anybody to mention the name of Ian Paisley, but he can do damage in this country. I am not doubting his loyalty, but we have got to understand that we are not going to have another Divis Street simply because Ian Paisley says such and such a thing is wrong."[49]

Many Ulster Protestants, however, believed that the Catholic community was making political advances at Protestants' expense; as a result, the Paisleyite crusade won growing Protestant support. To take advantage of the new support, Paisley created the Ulster Constitution Defence Committee (UCDC) and an auxiliary group, the Ulster Protestant Volunteers (UPV), to coordinate political and religious activities and to create an organization a secular Loyalist could join. The UCDC was the idea of Free Presbyterian printer Noel Doherty and was intended to be a political action group and to control Paisleyite marches and rallies. Paisley headed the organization and had ultimate authority over press releases, political candidates, and discipline. The group also contained a twelve-man committee, or the "twelve apostles" of militant fundamentalist political action. The UCDC set up the UPV as a subgroup constituted into divisions designed to correlate with Stormont's parliamentary constituencies. The UPV provided Paisley with secular working-class street activists willing to attack the O'Neill administration and the Northern Ireland civil rights movement. Both groups had strict membership requirements and bylaws: no Catholic or convert to Protestantism could join the UCDC, nor could any member of the RUC, except for "B" Specials, who were the police reserve. Those who joined the Volunteers were to be street soldiers for public demonstrations and a militia to confront the expected IRA resurgence during the 1916 Rising commemorations.[50]

With the formation of the UCDC and with steady recruitment into the UPV, Paisley was ready to confront the commemoration parades and planned a series of counterdemonstrations. Concerns over Paisley's marches and over IRA activity forced the Northern Irish government to limit the scope of the Easter Rising parades. The government mobilized ten thousand "B" Specials, canceled trains from Dublin, and set up numerous border checkpoints. Several Paisleyite marches were canceled in Armagh and Newry—two towns with sizable Catholic populations—but the demonstration Paisley led in Belfast curbed the corresponding Catholic parade that was to march from the city center to Anderstown in West Belfast. Paisley purposely chose a route that would pass the assembly point for the Catholic parade, forcing the Unionist government to restrict the route for the Catholic march. Although both the Easter Rising and the Paisleyite demonstrations were unauthorized and thus illegal, the government did not prevent Paisley's countermarch. The size of Paisley's parade, which the *Protestant Telegraph* estimated at ten thousand marchers and thirty thousand supporters, and the appearance of several Ulster politicians made the demonstration too large to stop. During the parade, several important comments were made: one symbolic, when a five-minute wreath-laying ceremony was held to commemorate the Ulster Volunteer Force of the 1910s, and the other verbal when Paisley declared war on O'Neillism. The bias the government had shown by limiting the Catholic march and the security measures installed during the week made some Catholics reevaluate their commitment to supporting O'Neill. In addition, Catholic activists became determined to thwart future Paisley marches and demonstrations.[51]

Another consequence of O'Neill's policies was the reformation of the Ulster Volunteer Force (UVF). Named after the Protestant militia that formed in 1912 to defend Ireland against Home Rule, the new paramilitary organization was founded in late 1965 by two opposing factions: small rural groups and Loyalists in urban Belfast who met in the Standard Bar on the Shankill Road. Because the UVF is a secret organization, it is impossible to determine the extent of its initial membership and to determine the powers behind its formation. One founding member, Augustus "Gusty" Spence, however, claimed that UUP members had recruited him. There is no evidence to prove Spence's assertion, and Steve Bruce points out that the UVF had a motive for claiming official support that did not exist.[52]

The UVF planned a two-pronged campaign: on the one hand, to murder known members of the IRA and to instill fear within the Catholic community and, on the other, to create the impression that O'Neill's policies were encouraging a resurgence of the IRA. After announcing the start of its campaign in a press release, the UVF went on a short-lived spree of shootings and petrol bombings. Two shots were fired into the house of John McQuade, the Stormont MP for the Shankill area, and the UUP headquarters were hit by an ineffective bomb, both attacks designed to be blamed on Republicans. On 7 May, a petrol bomb was thrown at a Catholic-owned pub on the Shankill Road, but the missile unfortunately killed an elderly Protestant woman who lived next door. Three weeks later a young and drunk Catholic laborer was shot after Spence and his UVF team failed to find their intended target, Leo Martin, a well-known Republican. And on 26 June, the UVF made an important mistake: three Catholic barmen were shot while drinking in the Malvern Arms, another pub near the Shankill Road, and one of the targets died from his wounds. Unfortunately for the Ulster Volunteers, several off-duty policemen were in the pub, and the UVF assailants were quickly arrested, tried, and sentenced to prison. As a consequence, the government proscribed the Ulster Volunteer Force, the first Protestant group to suffer this fate in Northern Ireland. The Stormont government believed the proscription had ended the problem, but it appears that the UVF continued as a small clandestine organization, training and recruiting members until it reemerged after the "Troubles" began.[53]

During the interrogation and trial of the Malvern Street assailants, direct links between the UVF, the UCDC, the UPV, and Paisley were insinuated. The RUC pointed out that UVF members were also active in the UPV, the UCDC, and the Free Presbyterian Church. Noel Doherty, for example, who helped to found the UCDC, had ties to the UPV and the UVF. In the summer of 1966, Doherty was charged with and convicted for plotting to steal gelignite in Loughall and expelled from the UCDC upon his arrest. O'Neill himself claimed during a speech to Stormont on 29 June that a leading member of the UVF was also a UCDC . In his speech, O'Neill cited police reports that Paisley had on at least two occasions welcomed UVF members to a meeting. Although Paisley did not deny making the statement supporting the UVF, he stridently claimed it was taken out of context—he welcomed all Protestants to his meetings, including members of the police forces. Moreover, he charged that the RUC secretly tape-recorded his public speeches, an accusation O'Neill publicly affirmed.[54]

Paisley's support for violence and his connection to the UVF remain a matter for debate. The UCDC and the UPV officially banned violence, and there is no proof that Paisley had a role in illegal activities. In addition, Paisley consistently and promptly denounced any person, such as Doherty, when they were arrested. Yet he offered tacit moral support and inspiration for the UVF through his rhetoric, speeches, and sermons. In an off-repeated statement that was used later to discredit Paisley, one of the Malvern Arms assailants, Hugh McClean, reputedly told the police interrogators: "I am terribly sorry I ever heard of that man Paisley or decided to follow him." But it was a policeman who placed the statement in the police report, and McClean's attorney asserted to the court that his client never made it. Moreover, Gusty Spence and the Ulster Volunteer Force have denied a direct link between Paisley and their group and have offered an alternate argument: Paisley only partially inspired members with his political-religious rhetoric, and the motivation for violent action came largely from secular sources within the Loyalist community.[55]

The General Assembly Creates a "Martyr"

By the mid-1960s, the Paisleyite community's political angst transcended O'Neillism. Protestant ecumenism, especially within the Church of England, was a growing concern. Paisley and militant fundamentalists in Northern Ireland viewed the developing relationships between the government of Great Britain and the Vatican as well as between the High Church Anglicans in England and the Catholic Church as threats to Irish Protestantism and the British Constitution. When Prime Minister Harold MacMillan arranged for an audience with the pope, and when Queen Elizabeth II sent a Catholic peer to represent the Crown at the funeral of the archbishop of Westminster, Cardinal William Godfrey, in January 1963, the Free Presbyterian Church sent a telegram to 10 Downing Street protesting the government's betrayal of the Act of Settlement and of Britain's Protestant heritage. Carl McIntire published the Free Presbyterian protest in his American media outlets, which were now giving substantial publicity to the new ICCC member.[56]

Alongside his attacks on the O'Neill administration, Paisley took every opportunity to protest or to lead marches against ecumenicalism and Protestant apostasy. In October 1964, he and the Return to the Reformed Faith Council of Great Britain and Ireland, which included Jack Glass and Brian Green, sent a cable to the United Nations secretary-general, U Thant, complaining that the pope had flown over Northern Ireland; because of bad weather, Pope Paul VI's flight to New York had been diverted across Ulster. The cable charged: "Adherents of the reformed faith refuse to recognize the validity of the Pope's right to be an advocate of peace. The past alliance of the Vatican with the Fascist dictators, Hitler and Mussolini, and its present alliance with Franco indicate the true nature of the Papacy."[57] In mid-October, Paisley protested the invitation to a Catholic chaplain to attend the dedication of the new wing of the Royal Maternity Hospital in Belfast. In January 1966, he wired Queen Elizabeth II attacking the decision to allow Father Thomas Corbishley, a Catholic priest, to say the closing prayers at Westminster Abbey. Then he led a protest outside the abbey that included twenty-three ICCC members and directed a march that passed Whitehall and Trafalgar Square. On his return home, Paisley stated to the press that the protest was "worthwhile. It has made this matter known to English people, who know nothing about Protestantism and will help to rouse them to their Protestant heritage."[58]

Despite the extensive coverage he and his actions were receiving, Paisley complained that the Northern Irish press was not fair to fundamentalist Protestants and that Protestant-owned newspapers were under the control of ecumenical laymen. Printed media was important to Paisley because he could not express his views on the radio. In Northern Ireland, use of the airwaves was not available to smaller sects or clergymen deemed controversial by the BBC's Central Advisory Body in London. Spurred in part by the refusal of the Ulster press—most important, the *Belfast Telegraph*—to place ads for Paisleyite rallies, a plan was laid in early 1966 for publication of the *Protestant Telegraph* and the establishment of a Free Presbyterian printing company (Puritan Printing, run by Noel Doherty). Paisley adopted a tactic that American militants and UPA employed: he wanted a printed outlet that solely expressed militant fundamentalist positions, however, and so his publication emulated the *Christian Beacon.* The first issue of the militant *Telegraph* was published that April.[59]

One month before the launch of his new print media, Paisley went to London on the first leg of a trip to Rome. He intended to protest the decision by Michael Ramsey, the archbishop of Canterbury, to visit the Vatican and meet with the pope—the first meeting between the heads of the Anglican and Catholic churches since the 1500s.[60] At the time, Ramsey was publicly promoting the idea of reuniting the English and Roman churches. The ICCC picketed Lambeth Palace and marched through London, and the ICCC delegation heckled Ramsey and Bishop John Moorman at Heathrow Airport as they boarded their plane for Rome. Paisley, John Wylie, and Belfast councilor James McCarroll flew on the same flight with Ramsey, and after landing in Italy met Jack Glass from Glasgow and two Londoners, Brian Green and Robert Hood (an Anglican vicar). Paisley and Wylie were denied entrance into Italy, although their four companions were granted visas. Glass, Green, and McCarroll heckled Ramsey while he celebrated communion in All Souls Anglican Church in Rome. The protests generated substantial publicity but did not prevent the Anglican–Catholic talks from taking place.[61]

At the end of the three-day meeting, the pope and the archbishop issued a statement promising that serious dialogue over theological issues would begin between their two churches. Carl McIntire and the ICCC took great interest in Ramsey's activities and the protest; for instance, in September 1962 the ICCC staged a protest against Ramsey during his visit to the United States. Not only did the *Christian Beacon* run several articles about the visit to Rome—reprints of information that British militant fundamentalists provided—but McIntire also took the opportunity to publicize and condemn the ecumenism within the worldwide Anglican community. He wrote a letter to Ramsey deploring the Church of South India's expulsion of fundamentalist Anglicans who belonged to the ICCC.[62]

Paisley returned home to a mixed reception, getting ridicule and condemnation in the secular press and a lukewarm response from Irish fundamentalists, but a hero's welcome at the Ulster Hall. Some evangelicals thought Paisley had gone too far, however, and were reluctant to give the militant additional publicity. For example, one man attending the talk in Belfast had the courage to question Paisley's protest against Ramsey, as did Dr. T. A. B. Smyth, a former Irish Presbyterian Church moderator. Although the *Evangelical Presbyterian* (the new name of the *Irish Evangelical*) covered the archbishop's visit to Rome and condemned the road to reunion, it did not mention Paisley, his companions, or their protests.[63]

Paisley's continuing protests were affecting his opponents: prior to the Divis Street riots, most Protestant clerics chose to ignore Paisley. But as Paisley's crusade became more visible and political, more Protestant clergymen spoke out. While Paisley was on his way to Rome, the Reverend A. H. McElroy, the president of the Liberal Association of Northern Ireland, denounced Paisleyism as an old and intolerant idea that was part of the Irish Protestant heritage traceable to the 1700s. McElroy charged that Ulster Protestants did not have a Protestant religiosity but were secular Britons who espoused a cultural anti-Catholicism. Moreover, he asserted that Paisleyism was based on a secular neofundamentalism acceptable to 80 percent of Ulster Protestants, many of whom never attended church services.[64]

The rapprochement between the Church of England and the Roman Catholic Church was not the only political and ecumenical apostasy upsetting Paisleyites. Paisley and militant fundamentalists were also concerned with developments in Irish Presbyterianism. For example, the leadership of the General Assembly and of the Presbyterian education system supported the ecumenical movement and refused to denounce liberal and modernist ideas. The Irish Presbyterian Church was a member of the WCC and had not officially condemned Ramsey's trip to Rome, and so Irish Presbyterians were an object of Paisley's scorn.[65]

Every June the Presbyterian Church in Ireland holds its annual assembly in Belfast, and in 1966 Paisley was determined to make his opinions known to that church body. Although he and his Free Presbyterian supporters had held annual protests outside the assembly since 1953, the protest in 1966 and his subsequent arrest and imprisonment elevated his stature within the international fellowship of militant fundamentalism. He became the foremost defender of Bible Protestantism in the British

Isles. After the General Assembly began its annual convention in Belfast city center in June 1966, Paisley organized an intensive campaign of denunciation and harassment. On 6 June, he announced that he would lead a protest march from the Ravenhill Free Presbyterian Church in East Belfast to the General Assembly. The march was provocative to the Catholic community because it passed through the Catholic Markets neighborhood, an area situated between Ravenhill and the city center where no Protestant march had been allowed to pass since the 1930s. Although the Ministry of Home Affairs reluctantly approved the route—arguing that the government did not see the potential for violence—the Free Presbyterian marchers aggravated the situation by carrying anti-Catholic placards. When Paisley and his supporters passed through the Markets, approximately two hundred Catholics formed a human wall in front of the Albert Bridge and refused to let the Paisleyites into Cromac Square.[66]

The march proceeded after the RUC dispersed the Catholic crowd, but this police action provoked a lengthy battle with the local Catholic community. Catholic politicians, such as Eddie McAteer, the leader of the Nationalist Party, and moderate Protestant supporters of the O'Neill administration questioned the home affairs minister's judgment. The Presbyterian General Assembly also attacked the government and passed a resolution denouncing Paisley's extremism. Anti-O'Neill Unionists and Paisleyites were nevertheless jubilant. They blamed Catholics for the violence, asserting that the Paisleyites had been barraged with bricks, glass, and other missiles. Paisley boasted his accomplishment: "This is the first Protestant parade through the market area for 30 years. It is quite a victory."[67] Paisleyite demonstrators approached their original target that evening when the preacher and a large group of followers picketed the General Assembly. Attendees to the assembly, including the Northern Ireland governor Lord Erskine and his wife, were verbally abused as they entered the assembly building. The protest alienated moderate Presbyterians, who were shocked at the treatment of their church leaders and the harassment of the Erskines, but gained Paisley new supporters from anti-ecumenical Protestants and from within the Orange Order.[68]

The Paisleyite march and demonstration as well as the reactions from the Presbyterian Church in Ireland and the Catholics of the Markets neighborhood set Northern Ireland firmly on a course toward communal, sectarian violence. From June 1966 forward, there was little the O'Neill administration could do to thwart the rise of Paisleyism, the onset of a Catholic civil rights movement, and the collision between both movements. Therefore, it can be argued that the Northern Ireland Troubles began that month.

On 6 June 1966, Stormont began a week-long debate on the Markets and assembly disturbances. The *Belfast Telegraph* published an editorial that called the debate a crucial test for Stormont and O'Neillism and asked whether the institution would stand for law and order or for civil disobedience. Most of the comments made within the Northern Ireland Parliament were against Paisley. Pro-O'Neill MPs, such as Nate Minford, questioned why the minister of home affairs had allowed the march to proceed, and Nationalists and Republicans, such as Gerry Fitt, asserted that Paisley's antics were harming community relations. Minford called for a public inquiry and personally attacked Paisley for a statement that the UCDC telegrammed to McConnell denouncing the police for their actions against the protestors outside the Assembly Hall.[69]

The strongest condemnation of Paisley came from O'Neill, whose lengthy comments not only questioned the preacher's patriotism but argued that continued British support for the status quo in Northern Ireland required responsible government in Ulster. A substantial portion of O'Neill's speech is included here because it gives an accurate description of why moderate Unionists disliked and feared Paisleyism:

> I am not prepared to accept lectures on loyalty from such a source [Paisley]. . . . I have been accused of "selling our Constitution down the river bit by bit and inch by inch." But respect for the Ulster Constitution can only be founded on respect for Ulster. If a Fascist movement were to be allowed to rule the roost in Ulster then our Constitution might indeed be in danger. Of course there are a few misguided people who believe in the infallibility of Mr. Paisley. Let us, then, recall a couple of his former threats. A year ago, when Mr. Lemass came to Stormont, this man threatened that any Unionist candidate who spoke in favour of that visit would be opposed at the next election. . . . Another threat

> was to the effect that if I visited Dublin I would never be permitted to return. Well, here I stand, Mr. Speaker. . . . Now, I understand members of this House are being threatened with personal violence if they dare to raise their voices. Respectable citizens lift their telephone receivers and are forced to listen to a torrent of disgusting language followed by threats of violence, or their telephones ring all night so that they cannot sleep. These are not the activities of a political party seeking the support of the electorate but the sordid techniques of gangsterism. To those of us who remember the thirties the pattern is horribly familiar. The contempt for established authority; the crude and unthinking intolerance; the emphasis upon monster precessions and rallies; the appeal to a perverted form of patriotism; each and every one of these things has its parallel in the rise of the Nazis to power.[70]

O'Neill's eloquent and—to his supporters—well-argued speech, which detailed the Paisleyite tactics and accused Paisley of intolerance and fascism, was received well in the Catholic and moderate Protestant communities. But many anti-O'Neill Unionists and Loyalists felt that the prime minister's portrayal of Paisley amounted to appeasement. Although few MPs dared defend violence, they did accuse the Catholics of the Markets community of provoking it and wondered why they had been ready for Paisley and his marchers with a large stockpile of missiles. Edmond Warnock of St. Anne's, Belfast, went so far as to blame O'Neill's policies for the rise in sympathy toward Paisley.[71]

Some Unionists called on the government to prevent further outrages, and Minister of Home Affairs Brian McConnell asserted that the government would not allow such disturbances and marches to happen again. Paisley would not back down, though, and in the week leading up to the Stormont debate over the Cromac Square and assembly disturbances he held meetings at the Ulster Hall to assert his defiance. He also announced a 16 June parade of UPV divisions to take place in Belfast. McConnell rejected the call from a Nationalist MP to ban Paisley's public appearances. The Belfast City Council overturned a Nationalist proposal to bar Paisley use of the city-owned Ulster Hall by a vote of thirty-three to eleven. Despite the ban on parades and public meetings, Paisley held a rally at the

Ulster Hall to denounce O'Neill and the Unionist government and led a march on 16 June that went from the Shankill Road to the City Center.[72]

The protest at the General Assembly led to summonses against Paisley, the Free Presbyterian reverends John Wylie and Ivan Foster, Belfast city councilor James McCarroll (who had accompanied Paisley to Rome), and three lay supporters. On 6 July, the Belfast Magistrates Court issued a charge of unlawful assembly, yet the new legal trouble dramatically increased Paisley's popularity among Northern Irish Protestants disenchanted with O'Neillism and the ecumenical discussions of Protestant churches. Due to appear in court on 18 July, Paisley planned a pretrial march through the city center. The government initially threatened to outlaw the march but allowed it with a ban on offensive placards. Preparing for his case, Paisley's legal advisers managed to get magistrate Albert Duff, a Belfast City alderman and Protestant Unionist, to issue summonses to Lord and Lady Erskine, Prime Minister O'Neill, Home Affairs Minister McConnell, and assorted other luminaries, including the lord chief justice. Moreover, Dr. Alfred Martin, the Presbyterian General Assembly moderator and several Presbyterian clergymen were called to court.[73]

On 18 June, Paisley held a short service at the Ravenhill Road Free Presbyterian Church and then proceeded solemnly to the Magistrates Court with hundreds of supporters and spectators following behind. By the time the court case began, spectators occupied every seat in the court, and more than one thousand Paisleyites were locked outside the court singing hymns. Paisley and his codefendants called no witnesses for their defense, and neither O'Neill nor McConnell nor the Erskines appeared, nor did any of the summoned Presbyterian clergymen show up. Paisley made a statement to the court that he and his codefendants had been unfairly maligned in the press and in the Stormont debates and that it was unjust that Lord and Lady Erskine were not compelled to appear, considering that many of the charges thrown at him and his fellow defendants concerned their alleged abuse of Lady Erskine.[74]

The court held for the police and argued that although the protest had not begun as an unlawful assembly, the defendants' actions had deteriorated into a criminal offense. Paisley, Wylie, Foster, McConnell, and two supporters were fined thirty pounds each and required to post a bond binding them to keep the peace for two years. Only the defendants could sign the bond, and if they failed to comply, they were to be imprisoned for three months.[75] The next morning Paisley, Wylie, and Foster took the stage in the Ulster Hall and declared that they would not pay the fines or sign the peace bond. Paisley stated that he "chose to go to prison and make a martyr of himself."[76] The Free Presbyterian Church published an article in the *Protestant Telegraph* several weeks later to explain its moderator's defiance: his imprisonment would publicize the bias that Northern Ireland's legal system showed toward Loyalists, would bring further pressure against the policies of the O'Neill government, and would show that the case against him had no merit. Paisley further charged that he was given the option of a peace bond so the O'Neill government would not have to imprison him, leaving only a small fine to pay that the Unionist administration would once again take care of.[77]

On 20 July 1966, Paisley, Wylie, and Foster were remanded to Crumlin Road Jail. For the first two nights of Paisley's sentence, several thousand Paisleyites assembled outside the jail, holding a vigil. On the third night, rioting broke out, which the police ended with a water cannon. On 23 July, approximately two thousand Paisleyites assembled at the West Belfast Orange Hall to begin a march to the city center, but because of the trouble at Crumlin Road Jail the previous night the police restricted the march to the Shankill area. In spite of the efforts made by Dr. Stanley Cooke, the acting moderator of the Free Presbyterian Church, to prevent trouble, the marchers proceeded to the city center. They were stopped at Peter's Hill at the end of the Shankill Road, and again the RUC used a water cannon to disburse the crowd. According to police reports, most of the hooligans arrested during the Shankill riots were teenagers and not members of the Free Presbyterian Church.[78]

To prevent further trouble, O'Neill and his cabinet invoked the Special Powers Act and imposed a three-month ban on all marches and parades within fifteen miles of Belfast City Hall and on any public meeting consisting of four or more persons. Only traditional parades by organizations such as the Orange Order, the Ancient Order of Hibernians, and the Salvation Army received an exemption. Moreover, all marches outside the excluded area would be closely scrutinized, and three parades in Glengormley,

Lisburn, and Hillsborough, called by the UCDC to protest Paisley's imprisonment planned, were banned. But Home Affairs Minister McConnell agreed to meet with a twenty-man Paisleyite deputation at his home in Lisburn on 28 July, and O'Neill met a contingent of Free Presbyterian ministers and the Reverend Brain Green on 10 August. Although the meetings with the home affairs minister and prime minister did not secure Paisley's release or alter the special order, it is indicative of Paisley's growing stature that McConnell and O'Neill felt the need to talk to both groups.[79]

Paisley, Wylie, and Foster's fines were once again anonymously paid, but because all three clergymen would not sign the peace bond, they remained in jail. This time they were civil, not criminal, prisoners, and this status gave them better rights. One important concession was the ability to write a weekly letter, which Paisley used to address his church and to explain his plight to friends in the United States. These letters were read to capacity audiences at weekly services held at the Ulster Hall. In addition to the letter to his church, Paisley wrote a commentary on the New Testament book of Romans as a theological statement of his fight against Terence O'Neill. In *An Exposition of the Epistle to the Romans: Prepared in the Jail Cell,* a lengthy treatise on God's sovereign grace, Paisley argued that his imprisonment was God's will and preordained as part of God's plan for Free Presbyterians, an important family within God's Elect. According to Paisley, throughout history God has blessed "special" men with imprisonment, during which they wrote about the love and spirit of God. As had the Apostle Paul, Paisley suffered jailing as a way of evangelizing for his church and for the benefit of militant fundamentalism.[80]

Paisley turned what was a minor criminal act into a case of martyrdom for the defense of Bible Protestantism. Within a year, seven new Free Presbyterian congregations were founded, and Paisley proclaimed that God had brought revival to Ulster. Free Presbyterian ministers were invited into churches across Ulster to explain Paisley's martyrdom; between June 1966 and New Year's Day 1968, the number of Free Presbyterian congregations virtually doubled. In addition, more of the secular Protestant working class began to look to Paisley as a Protestant savior.[81]

On 19 October, Paisley became the first Free Presbyterian prisoner released from Crumlin Road Jail. Although only a small crowd was on hand at the prison, he received a hero's welcome from the Ulster Loyalist community and from the international militant fundamentalist fellowship. The new minister of home affairs, William Craig, banned a larger celebration planned by the Free Presbyterian Church, but the following Sunday, 23 October, the Free Presbyterians were allowed to hold a "welcome back" rally in the Belfast suburb of Dundonald. This meeting included the Reverends Wylie and Foster, who had also been released.[82]

Northern American militant fundamentalism rejoiced in Paisley's release. Not only did they publicize the event within their newspapers, but a number of Americans came to Northern Ireland to take part in the celebrations. Bob Jones Jr. and six ACCC ministers attended a Reformation Rally at the Coleraine Free Presbyterian Church on 5 November and along with two thousand supporters took part in a Sunday night service at the Ulster Hall two days later. Jones participated in daily prayer meetings at the Ravenhill Road Free Presbyterian Church and spoke at the city hall in Armagh. Paisley and Bob Jones Jr. claimed that the Catholics protesting the meeting hurled insults and stones at them as they left the church service. On Jones's return to the United States, Bob Jones University began planning a major speaking tour for Paisley, including a stop in Tulsa, Oklahoma, to address the Christian Crusade. The Joneses believed that the amount of press coverage given to the Irishman's imprisonment would draw extensive interest.[83]

The expanded curiosity Americans showed to British speakers had become apparent earlier during a rally organized by the American Council of Christian Churches for Harrisburg, Pennsylvania. On 24 September 1966, the Second Convocation on Religious Freedom highlighted the trouble that McIntire, the ACCC, and Paisley were having with government authority. The Reverends Brian Green from London and William Beattie from Northern Ireland gave their testimonies about the protest at the Presbyterian General Assembly in Belfast. Green argued that true Bible Christians in both the British Isles and North America faced religious persecution from the government, the mainstream secular media, and a resurgent Roman Catholic Church.[84]

The concurrent meetings in Northern Ireland and North America and the juxtaposition of American militants in Ulster and of British militants in the United States were a turning point. The fellowship between militant American fundamentalism and the Reverend Ian Paisley had come full circle. Moreover, the transatlantic solidarity showed Paisley that his jailing was a landmark in his career.[85] The strength of the international bond became apparent when Paisley wrote to both Bob Jones Jr. and Carl McIntire from prison; he gleefully praised his imprisonment as God's will and as a new martyrdom for Protestantism:

> How real is the Lord's presence! How sweet is communion with him! How blessed is the Book! How wonderful are the doctrines of gospel grace! We sang for we cannot be silent, His love is the theme of our song, with the prisoner Samuel Rutherford we can say now with deeper meaning: "with mercy and judgment; my web of time we wove; and aye the dews of sorrow; were listed by his love; I'll bless the hand that you did, I'll bless the heart that planned; when throwed [*sic*] where glory dwelled, in Immanuel's land."[86]

Paisley had grown from a leading figure within Ulster fundamentalism and the religious life of Northern Ireland into an important member of the international militant fundamentalist movement. His legal trouble also sparked a sudden increase in the membership of Free Presbyterian churches. Between July 1966 and the end of 1969, twelve new Free Presbyterian congregations were formed in Londonderry, Lisburn, Dungannon, and nine smaller towns. Paisley's popularity grew among secular and Loyalist working-class Protestants, augmenting Paisleyism as an alliance between rural evangelicals and urban secular Protestants. This partnership would be of immense importance as Paisleyites took to the streets of Ulster to confront Northern Ireland's civil rights movement.[87]

6

Civil Rights for the Green, the Black, and the Orange

As Paisley and O'Neill awoke to New Year's Day in 1967, it likely seemed to both that they had strengthened their stature among their respective supporters. Paisley had become an important martyr within the international fellowship of militant Protestantism, and the Free Presbyterian Church was beginning to expand its membership and plan new congregations after a decade of limited growth. O'Neill, meanwhile, retained UUP support as well as the moderate leadership of the Protestant and Catholic communities. Most local Unionist associations upheld O'Neill when the party took a special vote on 24 September 1966, and Unionist MPs unanimously backed him three days later.

However, O'Neill would soon see his career shortened. Dissidents within the UUP and the Grand Orange Lodge of Ireland (Orange Order)—whose members solidly supported the UUP—and Catholic activists within the newly formed Northern Ireland Civil Rights Association (NICRA) in January 1967 began a series of events that put intense pressure on the O'Neill administration that weakened its ability to introduce reforms or to alleviate Protestant concerns. Although the erosion of support for O'Neill within the UUP and the Protestant community as well as from his moderate Catholic supporters was not yet outwardly evident, from the day Paisley walked into the Crumlin Road Jail, the Northern Ireland prime minister could never simultaneously satisfy Paisleyites and the Catholic community. New factors now entered the arena.[1]

The Green and the Black

During the closing years of the 1960s, the focus of Paisley's crusade shifted from opposing Christian apostasy and the policies of the O'Neill administration to battling the emerging civil rights movement in Northern Ireland. To Paisley and militant fundamentalists, the movement was nothing more than a thinly disguised coalition of Irish Republicans, Communists, and the Roman Catholic Church. They were convinced that the movement threatened the constitutional status of Northern Ireland and the existence of Bible Protestantism in Ulster. Between August 1968 and the outbreak of sectarian violence one year later, Paisley turned the efforts of his crusade against civil rights activism.[2]

In January 1967, both the United States and Northern Ireland were contending with indigenous civil rights movements, which were moving in different directions. In America, the movement for racial equality ebbed as African Americans gained voting rights and access to integrated schooling and as civil rights activists radicalized. The civil rights movement of large street marches and local activism had largely run its course, and Americans were beginning to accept the reality of integrated schools and public facilities. Proponents of social change now focused on implementing the Great Society and confronting Black Power and the Vietnam War. Across the United States, civil rights activists were turning from direct-action protests to antiwar and antiestablishment activities.[3]

In Northern Ireland at the same time, Catholic activists were beginning to escalate their demands for political and economic equality. Civil rights activism had been the vocation of a small group of middle-class Catholics and a coalition of Labour and Liberal MPs in Westminster who had been willing to give Terence O'Neill time to affect meaningful reforms. In January 1967, however, the Northern Ireland civil rights movement gave notice that its patience had run out. Over the next thirty months, the events that transpired in Northern Ireland and the United States transformed the careers of both the Reverend Ian Paisley and Prime Minister Terence O'Neill.[4]

The civil rights campaign within Northern Ireland began in 1963 and in a manner much quieter than its American counterpart. The pressure for reform came from two organizations that were founded to publicize Catholic discrimination complaints and to lobby the British government to take a more active role in Northern Ireland's internal affairs: a private group, the Campaign for Social Justice in Northern Ireland (CSJ) formed in Dungannon in 1963, and the Campaign for Democracy in Ulster (CDU), a group of Labour and Liberal MPs, was established at Westminster two years later. The CSJ consisted of middle-class professionals who disseminated discrimination statistics to the British and Irish press as well as the British government. It avoided a violent or religious theme within its pamphlets and press releases. It had grown out of housing protests that a group of Catholic housewives undertook in front of the Dungannon Urban Council. Although Catholic and Protestant councilors awarded houses within their respective districts, no new homes had been built in Catholic neighborhoods since 1945, and the appearance of 140 new dwellings in Dungannon's Protestant wards aroused indignation. An ad hoc organization to lead the protests, the Homeless Citizens' League, developed under the leadership of Patricia McCluskey, the wife of a prominent local doctor and a cofounder of the Social Justice campaign. As a forerunner to the CSJ—but with more limited goals—the Citizens' League enjoyed only a short-term existence.[5]

Although the CSJ and the CDU sustained long lifetimes, both organizations faced obstacles they could not overcome. An early court action against the Dungannon Council was abandoned because of a lack of funds, and Westminster rules prevented the CDU from raising issues about Northern Ireland on the floor of the House of Commons. Most important, Harold Wilson's Labour government carried on the British political tradition that had existed since 1921: it largely ignored the situation in Ulster. Hence, CSJ's nonviolent and secular strategy and the CDU's democratic approach drew little notice from the British government or the British public. The CSJ had a more direct effect on Catholic nationalism because its quiet strategy did not satisfy a group of left-wing housing and community workers and student leaders, who demanded a more radical approach, including confrontational direct-action protests. These activists noticed the effectiveness of the Selma-to-Montgomery march and other major American civil rights protests—broadcast on British television and reported in the Northern Irish and British press—and demanded a stronger civil rights movement.[6]

Moreover, the CSJ's early work did not satisfy the political aspirations of the Republican movement, and the political-military coalition of Sinn Fein and the IRA pushed a more radical agenda. Because of the failure of the IRA's border campaign, in the early 1960s Republicans transformed their basic strategy. Communist political activity replaced a political agenda based on partition. The Republican movement also made overtures to the Protestant working class, hoping to win Orange converts to a united Irish workers' republic. Republican activists formed the Wolfe Tone Society in October 1964 as discussion groups to promote republicanism and civil rights, and in Ulster the group became active in cities such as Belfast and Londonderry. Desmond Greaves of the Connolly Association in London—a British-based group of Irish workers linked to the British Communist Party—along with two members of the Wolfe Tone Society, Roy Johnston and Anthony Coughlan, formulated the new Republican strategy; they argued for a left-wing agenda to implement a worker's republic in Ireland and to eliminate sectarianism in Ulster. Johnston, the education officer of the Republican Army Council, and Coughlan, a lecturer in social administration at Trinity College, Dublin, asserted that the focus of Republican political efforts should turn to social activism and support for civil rights activities. In 1967, Cathal Goulding, the chief of staff of the IRA's Army Council made the policy official when at the annual Republican meeting in Bodenstown he attacked the tradition of physical-force violence. The threat of violence was not entirely eliminated from the Republican agenda, but it was in those years relegated to a secondary role. Goulding argued for a campaign of socialist-based social action groups. His attempt to transform the IRA accentuated militant fundamentalist fears of a resurgent Roman Catholicism in Northern Ireland. Militants wanted the Irish Left to push civil rights as a precursor to a Communist revolution and an Irish socialist state and the Roman Catholic Church to acquiesce to the plan in an attempt to become the state church.[7]

Despite some small successes in Londonderry and Belfast, through the mid-1960s Catholic civil rights activism in Northern Ireland was a disjointed effort between Republicans, radical leftists, and moderate Catholics who employed legal methods. By late 1966, however, the mood began to change. A civil rights meeting in Belfast in November heard Ciaran Mac an Aili, president of the Irish Pacifist Association, argue for a civil disobedience campaign. On 29 January 1967, the CSJ helped to form the NICRA as a partnership between Republicans (which included the IRA, the Wolfe Tone Society, and the Republican Clubs that had been formed to circumvent the proscription of Sinn Fein), left-wing housing activists and Communists, and a spectrum of nonviolent Catholic and labor organizations. NICRA sought to coordinate Northern Ireland's rapidly diversifying civil rights efforts and accepted known members of the IRA and nonaligned Republicans who sympathized with the violent assertion of Catholic political ambitions. The civil rights group met monthly and opened branches throughout Northern Ireland; any person or group who accepted the new organization's constitution could join. It even included three Protestant participants: Unionist Stormont senator Nelson Elder, Robin Cole of Queen's University Young Unionists (and chairman of the university's Conservative and Unionist Association), and the Ulster Liberal Party. NICRA agreed to a policy that supported the O'Neill administration and, along the lines of the CSJ, did not advocate public protests.[8]

However, the loose nature of its structure mandated that NICRA would never have a strong and domineering leadership and allowed its membership the freedom to promote competing agendas. This concept proved to be important when some members argued that support for O'Neill should not to be open-ended and gave the prime minister one more year to implement effective reforms. The social demographics of civil rights activists also weakened NICRA's effectiveness: the movement divided along class lines, with Catholic middle-class members such as the McCluskeys advocating a moderate movement, but Catholic workers advocating a more militant approach. The majority of Republicans and leftists within NICRA were from the Catholic working class, and between January 1967 and August 1968—when the first civil rights march took place—they pushed for radical protests in support of housing reform. The civil rights movement altered its nonconfrontational style in June 1968 when Austin Currie, the Nationalist Party MP for East Tyrone, at his party's annual conference not only argued for direct-action protests but followed through on his demands.[9]

Because NICRA did not initially advocate street protests, Paisley and his militant fundamentalist supporters paid little attention to the organization. This did not mean they totally ignored the issue of Catholic civil rights. Paisley and organizations such as the EPS kept a vigilant eye on the emerging civil rights movement as well as on Republican activity in Northern Ireland and the Republic of Ireland—arguing that both movements worked in collusion. In March 1967, the *Protestant Telegraph* and the *Ulster Protestant* denounced as treasonous proposed marches that planned to commemorate the 1867 Fenian Rising despite a temporary ban on parades by Home Affairs Minister William Craig. Implementing the Special Powers Act, Craig placed a month-long proscription on all public processions and meetings unless authorized by the RUC—permission difficult for Nationalists and Republicans to obtain. Because the temporary law did not prevent Junior Orangeman bands from marching during the same period, Catholic MPs charged that the government was appeasing Protestant extremists. Craig also outlawed the new Republican Clubs set up to circumvent a similar ban on Sinn Fein and the IRA.[10]

The same feeling of outrage over discrimination that Northern Ireland's Catholic politicians expressed also germinated within three important groups: politically minded students attending Queen's University, the NILP, and moderate Protestants who supported Catholic civil rights demands. During the 1967—68 academic year, civil rights in Northern Ireland and the United States, the war in Vietnam, the student riots in France, and the Soviet invasion of Czechoslovakia awoke some Ulster students to the need for political activism. Simon Prince argues that civil rights for Catholics were a minor battle in a larger global revolt against imperialism, capitalism, and the establishment. On 8 March 1967, Queen's students formed a Republican Club in defiance of the government ban, and two days later eighty students staged an illegal march through Belfast's city center. Paisleyites and the police ignored these two efforts, but in mid-November a Paisley-led counterdemonstration blocked a smaller march to the UUP headquarters. In response, several thousand students protested in front of Craig's house.[11]

Both the O'Neill administration's policies and the militant fundamentalist effort to thwart these policies inspired calls for reform from diverse elements within the Unionist community. During its 1967 General Assembly, the Presbyterian Church in Ireland issued a statement against religious discrimination that showed an increasing willingness to address the problem,[12] and the NILP passed a resolution at its annual conference in Newtownards calling on the British government to investigate discrimination in Northern Ireland. Paisley denounced both initiatives. The NILP strongly supported the CDU and the two-day visit to Ulster by Paul Rose and Stan Orme, two important figures within the CDU. In September 1966, the NILP and the Irish Congress of Trade Unions submitted a report to the Northern Ireland government calling for business votes in provincial elections and Queen's University seats to be eliminated and for Stormont constituencies to be redrawn. The receipt of the report marked the first time that a Unionist administration had agreed to consider civil rights grievances.[13]

Westminster ignored the call for reform despite demands from the CDU to discuss discrimination in Northern Ireland within the British House of Commons—such debate would break parliamentary convention. The push increased in strength when Gerald Fitt of the Republican Labour Party and a Stormont MP won the Westminster seat for West Belfast in the March 1966 British general election. The British government's apathy and inaction proved to be a major mistake. As Vincent Feeney argues, the lack of interest in Ulster's affairs prior to the summer of 1968 forced NICRA to adopt direct-action protests. Ulster politicians, however, did not ignore the new civil rights activism or Paisley's counterefforts. During Stormont debates, Austin Currie, Harry Diamond (the MP from Falls Road, Belfast), Gerry Fitt, and James O'Reilly (the MP for Mourne) denounced previous Paisleyite actions, such as the proposed march to Divis Street in 1964 and the protest outside the Presbyterian General Assembly two years later, as intimidating to the government and condemned both Paisley and the *Protestant Telegraph*. The Paisleyite newspaper had called for Fitt's arrest and supported the ban on the Republican Clubs.[14] O'Reilly contrasted Irish Presbyterians who advocated liberty in 1798 to those who pandered to extremist Protestants 170 years later: "Now in 1967 we have so-called Free

Presbyterians. In my view their attitude to freedom is repugnant to the principles for which those earlier Presbyterians fought and died. We have people whose creed is a creed of hatred and whose actions are a mockery of Christianity and whose aim is the setting up of a ruthless direction of State policy and control over the forces of Government."[15]

In North America, militant fundamentalists took a strong stance against the American civil rights movement, which they attacked as Communist inspired and backed by liberal, apostate Protestant clergymen. Militants viewed both racial integration and theological liberalism as Communist-inspired efforts to eradicate "true" biblical Protestantism. For three decades, from the Second World War through the Vietnam conflict, McIntire, Hargis, and the American militant fundamentalist community focused much of their efforts on the perceived threat that theological modernism and atheistic communism posed to Bible Protestantism and American democracy. They believed that God had ordained the United States, as a Protestant nation, to defend the Bible, capitalism, and private property. The Supreme Court's landmark *Brown v. Board of Education* decision in 1954, which outlawed segregated school systems, alarmed segregationists and militant fundamentalists, and set in motion massive resistance from the American South. Although militants as a group condemned civil rights efforts, Billy James Hargis and Carl McIntire led the militant fundamentalist attack on the civil rights movement. This opposition increased their notoriety among the American public, who responded with either increased financial support or an outcry.[16]

Hargis and McIntire initially confined their opposition to meetings, sermons, and editorials; the federal courts' inability to implement the *Brown* decision made a stronger reaction unnecessary at this point. The situation changed dramatically on 1 February 1960, however, when four African American college students sat down at the Woolworth's whites-only lunch counter in Greensboro, North Carolina. Their courageous action inspired a wave of civil disobedience across the southern United States, provoked a violent response from southern whites, and forced the Kennedy and Johnson administrations to implement civil and voting rights legislation. As liberal Christians supported both federal policy and civil rights activism, McIntire, Hargis, and their fundamentalist associates intensified their campaign against liberal Christian and civil rights organizations. The most notable targets were the NCC and the National Association for the Advancement of Colored People.

Militant fundamentalists argued that a plot existed to use integration, civil rights agitation, and black street violence to destroy America's Protestant churches and establish a godless America. Logical incoherence was a hallmark of the militant argument. For example, militants asserted that civil disobedience violated God's command to "be subject unto higher powers" (Romans 13:1),[17] yet McIntire and Paisley were willing to undertake public protests against both the American and Northern Irish governments. Militants insisted that scripture allowed Elected Christians to attack the civil authority of apostate governments. In other words, any action was divinely ordained if it supported the militant fundamentalist position.[18] In the 1960s, McIntire used the *Christian Beacon* and his *Twentieth Century Reformation Hour* radio broadcasts to highlight the connection between civil rights actions and clerics in the NCC. Billy James Hargis employed the traveling Anti-Communist Leadership Schools run by his Christian Crusade for the same goal. Hargis and McIntire attacked the Supreme Court decision in 1963 to outlaw prayer and Bible reading in America's public schools and the Civil and Voting Rights acts the following two years, thus gaining new financial and moral support from Americans who were not militants but were concerned over school integration, black voting power, and the perceived promotion of atheism in the school system.[19]

Although the American and Northern Ireland civil rights movements developed independently, there was a transatlantic correspondence. Historians, participants, and observers of the Northern Ireland civil rights movement acknowledge the influence of its American counterpart. The Homeless Citizens' League in Dungannon in 1963 was one of many organizations to notice, admire, and imitate publicly the tactics of groups such as the Student Non-Violent Coordinating Committee and Martin Luther King Jr.'s Southern Christian Leadership Conference. The forty women who picketed the Dungannon Urban District Council held placards with slogans such as "They talk about Alabama, why don't they talk about Dungannon?" and "If our religion is against us, ship us to Little

Rock."[20] When NICRA began its marches, participants routinely sang "We Shall Overcome," the anthem of the American movement. NICRA leaders admit that they copied American tactics. For instance, Michael Farrell, the leader of the People's Democracy who helped organize the Long March from Belfast to Londonderry in early January 1969, acknowledged that the three-day protest was modeled after the 1965 Selma-to-Montgomery March in Alabama.[21]

In his comparative study of the American and Northern Irish civil rights movements, Brian Dooley chronicles several examples of direct transatlantic contacts. In a November 1966 speech, Ciaran Mac an Aili, the Irish pacifist leader, urged Republicans to emulate Martin Luther King Jr., and in the same year Eamonn McCann—a leading Catholic activist in Londonderry—met Stokely Carmichael in London at the Dialectics of Liberation Conference. Fionnbarra O'Dochartaigh, another Catholic activist from Londonderry, subscribed to magazines that black American civil rights activists produced and rearticulated their arguments in the *Irish Democrat,* the Connolly Association's paper. Although such direct exchanges were uncommon, Gerry Adams, the Sinn Fein leader, argues that many Irish Republicans identified with American blacks.[22]

The international news media had the biggest impact on Ulster militant fundamentalists, moderates, and radicals alike. Ulstermen kept abreast of the news from America; the British and Northern Irish press consistently covered the important events of the American civil rights movement. The publications of Northern Ireland's major Protestant denominations frequently carried articles on the American civil rights movement and were generally sympathetic to the demands of the black minority. For example, the *Irish Christian Advocate,* the organ of the Methodist Church in Ireland, included stories about the Freedom Riders in 1961 and the integration of the Universities of Alabama, Georgia, and Mississippi and noted the violence segregationists employed and the federal reaction. These secular and religious reports taught activists in Northern Ireland that direct-action protests not only made the news but brought government intervention.[23]

Coverage of the American civil rights movement in the Northern Irish militant fundamentalist press, in contrast, was negative. These periodicals emulated America's militant fundamentalist segregationists who denounced the civil rights movement and black preachers, arguing that both dispensed political propaganda, not Christian tenets. A good example is the reports on Martin Luther King Jr.'s civil rights crusade. Militant fundamentalists despised King not only for his popularity and effectiveness, but for his connections with left-wing activist groups, his social theology and alleged communism, and his attacks on Christian fundamentalism. They charged that King's ministry did not "save" souls but promised a postmillennial, man-made kingdom of heaven on earth. Moreover, they attacked civil rights leaders such as King and the Reverend Ralph Abernathy for their (lack of) personal morality. Stories on the assassination of Martin Luther King Jr. exemplify the depth of militant disgust. Even after King's assassination, militants assailed him as the purveyor of lawlessness, not the proponent of racial justice.[24] The *Protestant Telegraph* described King's ministry:

> He laid great emphasis upon the brotherhood of man rather than the Kingship of Christ. He chose liberal theology rather than fundamentalism. He chose ecumenism rather than separation, he chose pacifism, looking to Ghandi [*sic*] as his guru, and to the Pope as his friend, but his pacifism could not adequately be transmitted to his followers. The people that he led have now taken to riot, looting and murder. The smoldering racial tensions have once again been rekindled. The communist agitators have whipped up grief and emotion into xenophobia and uncontrollable rioting; and America is on the brink of civil war. There can be no integration or equality of the races, no peaceful coexistence, no international harmony, until and when nations and men submit to Christ—the Prince of Peace.[25]

Militants insisted that King's legacy was not the elimination of racial barriers, but rather the violence that followed his death. The *Protestant Telegraph* featured articles with headlines such as "Violence the Fruit of King's 'Non-violence' Campaign."[26] To militants, King's advocacy of civil disobedience was not only un-Christian, but directly responsible for racial riots and communal violence—a self-serving argument considering Paisley's willingness to defy Northern Ireland's civil authority and the sectarian strife he helped to create. In contrast, the secular press and liberal

Christian press in Northern Ireland and much of North America backed King and the goals of the civil rights movement. After his death, Ulster's secular and moderate religious press eulogized him and welcomed his legacy. Both the *Church of Ireland Gazette* and the *Presbyterian Herald* supported the Martin Luther King Memorial Fund that the WCC set up for the benefit of the Delta Ministry in Mississippi and for Freedom City, a housing estate for unemployed cotton plantation workers.[27]

The Orange

The spread of Paisleyism within the Orange Order played an important role in how the opposition to O'Neillism and Catholic civil rights developed throughout the Protestant community. The extent of Paisley's rising influence and O'Neill's decline can be illustrated by looking at the new support Paisley received from members of the Orange Order and increasing attacks by Orangemen on O'Neillism. The Orange Order included members from all segments of the Protestant community, including important businessmen and clergymen, and many Unionist politicians belonged to the fraternal organization. Moreover, annual processions of Orange Lodges were community events, and the Orange marches on 12 and 13 July each year, which celebrated the Battle of the Boyne, were public holidays in Northern Ireland. Thus, the Orange Order had an important influence on the political, cultural, and economic life of Ulster.[28]

It is prudent to point out that although there are important similarities between Paisleyite and Orange practices—for example, both Paisleyite meetings and Grand Orange Lodge of Ireland gatherings began with a prayer; both Paisleyite and Orange Order marches included Bible readings; and the Orange Order required its members to uphold the Protestant religion—the relationship between Paisley and the Orange Order was complicated and often hostile. Paisley's ecumenical efforts and his vocal position on temperance created dissension within the Orange Order. Many Orangemen agreed with Paisley's populist argument that working–class Protestants were also entitled to civil rights and that the Protestant working class also suffered high unemployment and their housing conditions were substandard,[29] but Paisley's attacks on Protestant apostasy and immorality divided the Orange Order. Paisley was the chaplain of the Apprentice Boys' Belfast and District Amalgamated Committee (No. 6 District) until replaced after the Crossgar schism. Many Orangemen were Presbyterians who did not appreciate noncommunicants attacking their church, and in December 1951 the Orange Order and the Apprentice Boys of Derry Association excluded Free Presbyterian chaplains from most lodges. These Orangemen did not support militant fundamentalism. Moreover, there is good evidence that the Orange leadership wanted to thwart Paisley's popularity and his religious and political aspirations. But Paisley remained a member for another decade and continued to denounce individual members of the Orange Order as ecumenists, WCC supporters, and drunkards. For example, in 1958 the Orange Order censored Paisley for accusing the Reverend Warren Potter, chaplain of the Mountpottinger Orange Lodge, of apostasy. Paisley was upset that Potter had resigned as a member of the Irish Evangelical Church and the NUP to return to Irish Presbyterianism. Furthermore, in 1962 when the Orange Order refused to expel the lord mayor of Belfast, Robin Kinahan, after Kinahan attended a Catholic funeral mass, Paisley quit the fraternal organization in protest but continued to address the North Antrim Lodge of the Independent Loyal Orange Institution during 12 July celebrations. Although these events were little noticed by the public, they were important in widening the gap between Paisley and Protestant authority.[30]

During the mid-1960s, the relationship between the Reverend Ian Paisley and the Grand Orange Lodge of Ireland took on a new dimension. Although the Orange leadership and moderate Orangemen disliked Paisley, many of the rank and file became Paisleyites; a large section of Orangemen supported Paisley's attacks on the ecumenical movement and on O'Neill. In the contentious atmosphere of Ramsey–Rome talks and the assembly protest, Paisley, his fame rising, became a favored speaker during the 12 July celebrations. His influence could be seen throughout the Orange Order: the Grand Lodge of Ireland issued a statement denouncing the attendance of Protestant clergymen at Catholic dedication services, declared that ecumenical Protestant clergymen were not welcome at the upcoming 12 July parades, and attacked the WCC.[31]

During July 1966, twenty-eight resolutions targeted Stormont policy toward Easter Rising celebrations, and ten specifically denounced

Archbishop of Canterbury Michael Ramsey's trip to Rome. Throughout the summer of 1966, Paisley was invited to speak to the Orange service at Knockadona on 12 June, to the Apprentice Boys in Dromara the next day, and to a large crowd at Castlewellan on 1 July, which included eight Orange bands. Moreover, anti-O'Neill heckling was heard at six Orange demonstrations during the 12 July gatherings. As a result, the tensions within the Orange Order exploded in violence during the 12 July celebrations of 1967. Orangemen attacked George Forrest, the Ulster Unionist Westminster MP for mid-Ulster, when he proposed a resolution in support of the prime minister. The level of animosity was unprecedented: Forrest was physically assaulted while speaking from the platform at Coagh. Similar pro-O'Neill declarations at Belfast Fontana, Lisburn, and Tandragee were also denounced. In addition, traditional Orange resolutions supporting the prime minister were omitted during numerous celebrations, including the one at Enniskillen that Lord Brookeborough (Basil Brooke), the former prime minister, presided over. Brookeborough expressed the concerns of many Unionists who were upset over O'Neill's firing of Harry West, the minister of agriculture from County Fermanagh, for corruption and over the consistent banning of Protestant parades over the previous year. West, a right-wing hard-liner and opponent of O'Neill, had used privileged governmental information to purchase land in County Fermanagh. Although Paisley and the Orange Order had their differences in the past, from the mid-1960s on the two worked in a loose alliance to defend Irish Protestantism.[32]

But there was a limit to Orange Paisleyism: the Orange Order's leadership remained resistant to Paisley's crusade, and tensions within the order grew during the mid-1960s. In 1965, Sir George Clark, the grand master of the Grand Orange Lodge of Ireland, broke with Orange tradition and made conciliatory comments toward the Catholic community during his 12 July speech at Finaghy. All Orangemen did not accept Clark's viewpoint, and the following year Northern Irish dissidents and a large number of Scottish bands made a loud pro-Paisley showing at Finaghy.[33] In the summer of 1966, internal dissension forced the Orange Order to reconfirm its commitment to the Anglican Thirty-Nine Articles of Faith and the Westminster Confession, while simultaneously denouncing the violence that the Paisley protest provoked. Led by Clark, the Orange leadership wanted to show support for O'Neill by allowing a limited outreach to the Catholic community. Two leading Orangemen, Ulster Unionist MP Phelim O'Neill (the prime minister's cousin) and Colonel Henry Cramsie, attended a Catholic mass in Ballymoney, and Nat Minford, a vocal opponent of Paisley and a prominent Unionist politician, appeared at the opening of a Catholic school in Anderstown. These gestures to the Catholic community violated the Orange Order's rules, so many rank-and-file Orangemen sought to discipline the violators. In the past, the order had rarely upheld such sanctions, but in June 1967 Phelim O'Neill and Minford were summoned before their lodge to answer the charges, an action both men considered insulting. Neither MP was immediately forced to leave the Orange Order, but the incident showed that the influence of moderates within the order had waned. As a result of the controversy, the Grand Orange Lodge of Ireland amended its by-laws and ordinances, enabling the order in the future to expel any member who attended a Catholic service or ceremony.[34]

Paisley received a larger degree of support from the smaller Independent Loyal Orange Institution of Ireland (also called the Independent Orange Order). Trade unionists who felt that the Orange Order leadership did not look out for working-class interests established the new organization on 11 July 1903, in East Belfast. The dissidents institutionalized a movement that opposed Unionist leadership and that Paisley copied. In one example of Paisleyite posturing, the Independent Orange Order approved of Paisley's attack on Fisherwick Presbyterian Church in 1964 and that same year made the first open attacks on ecumenism during its 12 July celebrations.[35]

The Moorman controversy provides another example of Paisley's growing influence within both the Orange Order and the Independent Orange Order. The dispute also illustrated Paisley's move toward politics and how the Orange–Paisley relationship helped to determine the growth of Paisleyism. In August 1966, the Church of Ireland announced that the Irish Church Association had invited John Moorman, the Anglican bishop of Ripon, to speak at St. Anne's Cathedral on the dialogue between the Church of England and the Roman Catholic Church. Moorman had attended Vatican II as an observer and in 1966 accompanied Archbishop Ramsey to Rome to talk with Pope Paul VI. As a counterprotest, a coalition of Protestant groups, including Paisley's Free Presbyterians and the Orange Order, held Reformation Services across Ulster to reaffirm the Protestant faith and to defend the Protestant political identity of Northern Ireland and Great Britain. Dr. F. J. Mitchell, the Anglican bishop of Down and Dromore, asked Anglican churches to refuse permission for these services. The evangelical element within the Grand Orange Lodge and the Independent Orange Order supported Paisley's antiecumenical and anti-O'Neill stances and Paisley's defense of Ulster's political status quo. The Independent Orange Order replied to Mitchell that no evangelical Protestant should be denied use of a Protestant church and charged that his stance against the Reformation Services was a part of the Anglican move toward unity with Rome.[36]

The controversy over Moorman's visit aroused intense interest outside the ranks of the Orange orders and further strengthened Paisley's growing influence among Ulster Protestants. In October 1963, Moorman told interviewers from the Roman Catholic Church that he supported a reunion of Christian churches and that "there will have to be a central head of the Church, and that head will clearly have to be the Bishop of Rome."[37] Such a statement added fuel to the Paisleyite fire. Moorman's apparent support for the Anglo-Catholic goal of one united Christian Church under the head of the Roman pope provided further evidence of growing Roman Catholic influence in Britain.[38]

Paisley did not initially react to Moorman's planned visit—he was in jail at the time—but as the visit approached, militant condemnation erupted. The *Protestant Telegraph* denounced the visit as an attack on the Reformation and the Revolution Settlement of 1689 and dismissed Moorman as a traitorous quisling. Paisley promised to stage a protest outside St. Anne's during Moorman's talk. The threat worked: under additional pressure from the Orange Order and after a personal request from Terence O'Neill, the Very Reverend Cuthbert I. Peacocke, the dean of Belfast, withdrew permission for the Irish Church Association, an ecumenical organization, to use the cathedral. Moorman canceled his visit.[39]

To Paisley and his supporters, Moorman's visit provided a rich opportunity for public protest against the ecumenical movement in Northern Ireland. Paisley appeared on Ulster TV, stating: "All who saw the Bishop of Ripon could not fail to see the satanic composure of that face."[40] The leaders of the Church of Ireland and the Irish Presbyterian Church in their turn attacked the opponents of the Moorman visit and of ecumenism. The *Church of Ireland Gazette* denounced "forces that would deny freedom of speech in Northern Ireland";[41] the House of Bishops issued a statement denouncing Paisley's planned protests; and in a sermon to St. Anne's, Reverend Brian Harvey argued that militants had no right to determine whom the cathedral invited.[42]

Paisleyism was once again a topic of discussion in the Northern Ireland Parliament and a cause of dissension between Irish Protestant churches and the Free Presbyterian Church. O'Neill was forced to deny the charge when Nationalist MP Patrick Gormley claimed that the government had pressured Peacocke to cancel Moorman's visit. Moreover, Paisley's threat to protest increased tensions between fundamentalists and evangelicals, on one side, and ecumenists and liberal Christians, on the other. The *Protestant Telegraph* proclaimed the cancellation of Moorman's visit as a "great victory for Ulster Protestants."[43] The Church of Ireland, to distance itself from its more ecumenically minded English cousins, issued a statement entitled "The Church of Ireland and Other Churches" that reconfirmed its commitment to the British Constitution, the Thirty-Nine Articles of Faith, and the Book of Common Prayer and expressed its support for the traditional Apostolic and Reformed Protestantism of Irish Anglican theology. Nevertheless, the Irish Anglican bishops supported the talks between Anglicans and Rome, including the first meeting that was held in early January 1967 at Gazzoda, Italy, to discuss scripture, tradition, and liturgy. They also expressed support for an ecumenical meeting held in the National Stadium in Dublin, attended by Eamonn De Valera and the Apostolic Nuncio, and for the Greenhills Conference on Christian marriage, which met in the Presentation Convent in Drogheda and was attended by 150 Anglican, Methodist, Non-Subscribing Presbyterian, and Catholic clergymen as well as by the Salvation Army.[44]

The fight against liberalism and modernism within the Irish Presbyterian Church continued to concern Paisley as much as the Church of England's rapprochement with Rome. The invitation to Moorman, then, appeared as yet another step toward a return to Roman rule over the Anglican churches. In spite of his arrest in 1966, Paisley led protests outside the Presbyterian General Assembly the following two years. Home Minister William Craig banned a threatened march to the General Assembly in 1967, but Paisley, several Free Presbyterian ministers, and a small crowd of hymn singers and placard holders picketed outside the assembly building, jeered dignitaries as the latter left the assembly, and skirmished with the police. Paisley charged that O'Neill had made a deal with the Catholic community to prevent another Paisleyite march through Cromac Square.[45]

The protest outside the 1968 assembly was a repeat of that of the previous year with the exception that Paisley kept his plans a secret until the day before the assembly was scheduled to begin. He canceled his proposed march because he did not like the route the RUC had allowed, but he was able to publicize his concerns about the assembly's agenda: *The Revivalist* and the *Protestant Telegraph* denounced the plan for the Judicial Committee to review the Westminster Confession of Faith and condemned the introduction of a report on interchurch relations that acknowledged the Catholic Church as Christian.[46] The Paisleyite press also attacked the election of John Withers of Fisherwick Presbyterian Church as assembly moderator. Paisley despised Withers for his outreach to the Catholic community, for his friendly communion with Catholic priests, and for his support for modernist professors, such as J. L. Haire of the Presbyterian college. As discussed in chapter 5, in 1964 Paisley had forced Withers to cancel the visit of a Catholic priest who was to speak to a youth group at Fisherwick Presbyterian Church. Four years later Wither's election as moderator confirmed for Paisley the apostate intentions of Irish Presbyterianism.[47]

In conjunction with their attacks on Protestant apostasy, militant fundamentalists kept constant pressure on the O'Neill administration; Paisley and his allies took the lead with a combination of street protests, articles in the militant media, and attacks from the pulpit. Paisleyites denounced O'Neill at virtually every public appearance the prime minister made. A thousand-man Paisleyite parade in Portadown to protest O'Neill's speech at the local Orange Hall opened 1967; although the march was not banned, it was stopped by the RUC. The year ended with a protest against O'Neill's December meeting with the new Irish Taoiseach, Jack Lynch.[48] Paisley and supporters met Lynch outside Stormont with a barrage of snowballs and placards accusing O'Neill of selling out Irish Protestantism to the Catholic Church. In a *Protestant Telegraph* editorial entitled "O'Neill the Dictator," Paisley laid out his current charges against the prime minister: he was arrogant and a liar, ignored the wishes of Stormont, placed himself above the law, and used the police to further his political aims.[49]

Paisley condemned the RUC as an agent of O'Neillist repression when it worked against his interests or those of the Free Presbyterian Church. In one notable case, the Reverend John Douglas, the Free Presbyterian minister of Portavogie, was arrested under the Public Order Act for an open-air speech made on 8 September 1966. Paisley charged that the police lied in presenting their evidence. In September 1967, a small crowd of Catholics attacked Paisley's wife, Eileen, a Belfast City councilor. Paisley accused the RUC of failing to protect her. Although it is speculative and difficult to prove whether the O'Neill administration and the RUC conspired to thwart Paisleyism, they were definitely very concerned over the militant movement. The home secretary kept a secret file on the "Paisley Faction," which included a fairly accurate list of "incidents and demonstrations" involving Paisley, a list of suspected UPV and UVF members, and information on the official contacts between the Unionist government and Paisleyites. The file does contain important errors, however—most notably an assertion that the UVF was the military wing of organized Paisleyism—which illustrates the Unionist administration's fears that Paisleyites were a potential physical threat.[50]

Paisley and British Militants

As the O'Neill administration continued to advance its political ecumenism, Paisley increasingly perceived himself as the primary defender of British Protestantism. He decided to strengthen his fellowship with British militants as an alternative means to thwart the perceived constitutional threat to Northern Ireland. In 1964, Paisley and Reverend Jack Glass, a militant Baptist fundamentalist from Glasgow, began annual protests outside the Church of Scotland Assembly in Edinburgh. In large part owing to Paisley's influence, Glass had begun a long career of public demonstrations in Scotland. In 1966, he protested against diverse unity services in Glasgow and traveled to Rome, where he interrupted the service Ramsey was taking part in at St. Peter's Cathedral. Glass was good at inciting reprisals; he was detained for three hours in Rome and on several occasions beaten up in Glasgow. He led protests against Princess Margaret's visit to the new Catholic cathedral in Liverpool in November 1967 and against the Church of Scotland moderator for supporting unity talks with the Roman Church. Furthermore, Paisley and Glass coordinated their campaigns and attacked the conversations between the Church of England and the Roman Catholic Church. When an Anglican–Roman Catholic joint commission proposed talks with the specific intention of church reunification in August 1967, Paisley, Glass, and militant fundamentalist allies in England organized a united response. For Glass's efforts, in May 1968 Paisley ordained Glass as pastor of the Zion Sovereign Grace Baptist Church in Polmadie, a suburb of Glasgow.[51]

The Free Presbyterian Church of Ulster and the Sovereign Grace Baptists joined the British Council of Protestant Christian Churches (BCPCC), a small organization that Paisley and the Reverend Brian Green of London set up to counter the British Council of Churches and that the ICCC funded. The BCPCC included the Strict Baptist Group of Churches (Green's denomination), the Latvian Lutheran Churches in Britain, and the small Polish Reformed Church in Exile. Membership gave Paisley both new militant allies and a new avenue in the British Isles for high-profile protests. Paisley's first interest in Green arose after reading a pamphlet the English militant had coauthored in 1962, advising British Baptists not to join or have fellowship with the WCC. Paisley invited Green to preach at the Free Presbyterian Church's 1963 Easter Convention.[52] In September 1967, Paisley, Green, and Councilor Ronald Henderson of the Liverpool Protestant Party protested Anglo-Catholic unity talks with a demonstration in Trafalgar Square and a deputation to 10 Downing Street. The same month Paisley and Green protested outside Huntercombe Manor in Maidenhead, where the Anglican-Catholic talks were taking place. The following January the BCPCC heckled Archbishop Michael Ramsey as he arrived at the Catholic Westminster Cathedral in London to preach within the cathedral, the first Anglican bishop to do so.[53]

On the eve of Northern Ireland's first civil rights marches, Paisley emerged as the most prominent proponent of militant fundamentalism in the British Isles. His notoriety was such that in November 1967 he was invited to the Oxford Union to debate the proposition "that the Roman Catholic Church has no place in the twentieth century" with Norman St. John-Stevas, a British Tory MP and prominent Catholic layman. Brian Green also spoke at the debate, supporting the militant position.[54] Although most of the students attending the debate voted for the Catholic viewpoint, Paisley and Green were given a prestigious forum to denounce Catholic tenets. At the same time, the *Belfast Telegraph* took a poll on Paisleyism, an unusual step with respect to a nongovernmental public figure. Although the paper happily announced that there was overwhelming opposition to Paisleyism throughout Northern Irish society, 30 percent of the Ulstermen surveyed stated that they agreed with the Free Presbyterian moderator. The poll included the Catholic community, so it can be argued that more than 50 percent of Protestants backed Paisley. No militant fundamentalist in the United States or elsewhere in Great Britain could claim the same level of public support.[55]

7

Paisley, the Elijah of Ulster

In August 1966, the Reverend Carl McIntire sent a telegram to Queen Elizabeth II, protesting the jailing of Paisley and his associates that followed the Paisleyite demonstration in front of the Presbyterian General Assembly. McIntire argued that the convictions of Paisley, John Wylie, and Ivan Foster constituted religious persecution and that their arrests had been carried out at the request of the WCC and the Presbyterian Church in Ireland. McIntire based his claims on the fact that it took the authorities in Northern Ireland almost a month after the General Assembly to bring charges. We can assume that McIntire's wire had little effect on the royal family (or on the British government), but the action was meant as publicity—and it succeeded. The mainstream and militant American press reported the story, and Paisley's star rose higher. On his way to Beirut for a conference of the Middle East Bible Council, McIntire stopped in Belfast and was permitted to see Paisley, Wylie, and Foster in Crumlin Road Jail. McIntire, the most avid promoter of Paisley's "martyrdom," pushed Paisley's cause to militant fundamentalist allies and within the ACCC and ICCC.[1] The result was that Paisley's time in jail—or, more specifically, his selfless willingness to suffer for the cause—raised his stature among not only militant fundamentalists and secular Loyalists within Northern Ireland, but also among the wider community of militant fundamentalists within the British Isles and the United States.

The previous August, the bond between Paisley and McIntire drew closer after Paisley attended the Sixth Plenary Conference of the ICCC in Geneva and made a short trip to the United States. McIntire wrote to Norman Porter shortly after Paisley's American trip concluded, boasting that the Ulsterman had been received at Bob Jones University and at the

Collingswood Bible Presbyterian Church. He noted that Paisley made a strong impression in churches affiliated with the Independent Fundamental Churches of America that he spoke to. According to McIntire, Paisley spoke emotionally with the "big lungs of Elijah and the sound of the rushing of wind."[2]

During the Thirtieth General Synod of the Bible Presbyterian Church in October 1966, held at Cape May, New Jersey, the perceived persecution of the Free Presbyterians and their moderator was made a prominent subject of discussion. The synod passed two resolutions: one to support Paisley's martyrdom and the other to protest the United Press International's (UPI) reports on his imprisonment. The Bible Presbyterians were upset that the UPI portrayed Free Presbyterians as extremists, not evangelists of the correct gospel, and that it depicted Paisley's imprisonment not as a protest, but as a staged charade to seek publicity.[3]

The *Christian Beacon* printed the letter Paisley wrote to McIntire from his jail cell (also intended for the Bible Presbyterian Church and the ACCC) that explained the Cromac Square and General Assembly disturbances as the result of government persecution, not a criminal act, and thanked McIntire for his support. The *Christian Beacon* expanded its coverage of the fundamentalist–ecumenical battle within the British Isles. McIntire's paper reported on the International Christian Youth's picketing of the British embassy in Washington, DC; Donald Soper's attacks against Paisley during a Methodist conference in Wolverhampton, England; and the Orange Order's 12 July resolution against British Anglicans.[4] To the militant fundamentalist press, Paisley had become a modern-day prophet.[5] The Irish crusader became a constant and featured subject in the *Christian Beacon*. Beginning with an article that covered Paisley's protest trip to Rome in March 1966, McIntire's paper chronicled the Ulsterman's arrest, trial, and imprisonment and complained about the biased press coverage of the events. McIntire wrote a long article on the persecution that Paisley and Bible Protestants suffered in Northern Ireland.[6]

The *Christian Beacon* reprinted a copy of McIntire's letter to *Life* protesting the magazine's August 1966 article "The Unholy War of Preacher Paisley." McIntire charged that the *Life* story attempted to discredit opponents of the ecumenical movement. He did have a point: the article employed innuendo to compare Paisleyism to McCarthyism and Chicago-style gangsterism and to link Paisley's rhetoric directly with Protestant paramilitary and communal violence. *Life* blamed Paisley for inciting two Catholics to toss projectiles at the British monarch when she appeared in Belfast to open the Queen Elizabeth II Bridge. According to Hugh Moffett, the article's writer, Northern Ireland had been on the brink of a Catholic–Protestant reconciliation until Paisley intensified his crusade in early 1966. The article restated the unproven charges of Paisley's complicity in the 1966 UVF murders and included a picture showing the front of the Malvern Arms pub juxtaposed with a picture of Paisley and the archbishop of Canterbury. The overt image connected Paisley to the murders and hinted at his politicalization.[7]

Reports of Paisley's "persecution" spread throughout the media of militant fundamentalism in North America. For example, *The Gospel Witness* printed an article in its 18 August 1966 edition that charged that the widespread criticism of Paisley was intended to discredit the entire international militant fundamentalist fellowship. In "An Innocent Preacher in Prison," *The Gospel Witness* asserted that it was the Catholics and Protestants who were opposed to Paisley's crusade who had incited violence. Furthermore, Paisley's only crimes were to be an energetic evangelist and crusader in the mold of D. L. Moody and Martin Luther, to expose apostasy, and to bring Ulstermen to Jesus Christ. The periodical *The Sword of the Lord,* published by John R. Rice in Murfreesboro Tennessee, included a letter from Bob Jones Jr. defending Paisley.[8]

Although Paisley's relationship with Carl McIntire was still his most important friendship in the United States, the building relationship with Bob Jones University became increasingly valuable as the 1960s progressed. The imprisonment improved the growing friendship between the Free Presbyterian Church and the Bob Jones family of Greenville, South Carolina. In a second trip to the United States in April 1966, Paisley traveled to South Carolina to attend the annual Bible Conference at Bob Jones University, speaking on the direct link between the Reformation, Scottish Calvinism, and Free Presbyterian theology. He had spoken at the same conference in April 1965, preaching on the ministries of John Calvin and John Knox.[9] At the 1966 conference, Paisley was a featured but not prominent guest, but because of his imprisonment he was granted an honorary doctorate of theology from Bob Jones University that September and received new support for evangelizing engagements in the United States.[10] It is noteworthy that Paisley used one of his weekly prison letters to correspond with Bob Jones Jr. In this letter—which Paisley knew would be disseminated throughout the university and featured during the Joneses' radio broadcasts—he thanked the South Carolinian for the gifts and letters that were sent to his wife and mentioned that three students from Bob Jones University had visited him in jail. He reiterated the persecution directed at him and his supporters but was jubilant that the Northern Irish press had published a report asserting that two hundred thousand Ulstermen supported his crusade. He also noted that his imprisonment was bringing him closer to God.[11]

The Twentieth Century Reformation and Bob Jones University worked energetically to bring Paisley to the United States for new and larger speaking tours.[12] Paisley's talks and sermons impressed McIntire, who argued that the Ulsterman was God's primary voice in Ireland. Immediately following Paisley's imprisonment in June 1966, McIntire and Bob Jones Jr. began to organize a series of engagements for him the following spring. Plans were laid for Paisley to visit churches that had fellowship with Bob Jones University, Baptist and Methodist churches that professed militant fundamentalism, as well as small denominations that were ACCC members. Within most of these churches, Paisley's anti-Catholicism was not a concern, although when it did arise—as with Billy James Hargis's Christian Crusade in Tulsa, Oklahoma—Paisley was reconstructed as a separatist anti-Communist crusader. Hargis was enthusiastic at the prospect of Paisley's visit and did not see a problem arising from it among his own Catholic supporters. According to Hargis, "Most of the conservative Catholics in the United States are fully aware that the Catholic hierarchy, worldwide, is growing more and more pro-Communist. Everywhere I travel I find more and more out-spoken anti-Communist Catholics that are concerned about their own hierarchy. There is an interesting development taking place in the Roman Catholic Church itself [against its hierarchy]."[13]

Paisley's third speaking tour in the United States began 28 March 1967 at the Collingswood Bible Presbyterian Church before moving to the annual week-long Bible Conference held at Bob Jones University. Paisley was one of the seven featured speakers, a privilege also given to Bob Jones Jr. and four nationally known militant fundamentalists. Paisley's talk, "Lessons on Revival Gleaned from the Life of Elijah," was mostly theological and antiecumenical; he correlated the apostasy of Israel to that of Irish Protestantism in the twentieth century. He compared the Israelites' introduction of Egyptian idolatry with the interaction between evangelicals and the Roman Catholic Church. His extensive itinerary included engagements throughout the country.[14] Paisley also made a number of stops in Canada, including three in the Maritime Provinces, one in Vancouver, and another as the featured speaker in Toronto at the Annual Convention of the Canadian Council of Evangelical Christian Churches. The convention was held in the Jarvis Street Baptist Church—the church that T. T. Shields pastored for most of his ministry—and included both McIntire and Bob Jones Jr. as eminent speakers.[15]

Paisley appeared as the featured speaker at the national ACCC convention in Harrisburg, Pennsylvania, where the Irish militant fundamentalist argued that the current problems facing humanity resulted from the failure to respect scripture. Publicity for his tour followed a pattern—each engagement was promoted to the church's membership or convention attendees and advertised in the local press.[16] Although not an unusual practice, such ads were reserved for prominent visitors. There unfortunately is no record of what Paisley preached to each separate church. Unlike today, when most churches record their services, in the 1960s such recordings were unusual, and congregants recorded sermons by hand or made notations in their Bibles. But what can be determined is that Paisley denounced the ecumenical movement in Northern Ireland and the threat the Roman Catholic Church posed to Protestantism, intermixing both topics in a premillennial message based on the Old Testament Book of Daniel. According to him, ecumenism and the Roman Antichrist were hastening the End Times. Citing chapter 11, verse 32, he preached that apostate Irish Protestants were working against the Covenant. For this indiscretion, God would inflict retribution and captivity on His people—a premillennial reading of the Second Coming. To Paisley, Catholic civil rights and the resurgence of Irish Republican violence had not yet emerged as significant factors.[17]

Paisley's tour of the United States aroused both protest demonstrations and shows of support, thus illustrating his rising international stature. At Philadelphia International Airport, several hundred hymn-singing supporters met the Irishman, but on the same night hecklers positioned themselves inside the Collingswood church. The coverage of his antiecumenical crusade in Ireland in publications such as *Life* and the *New York Times* had incited interest in Paisley in American cities with large Irish American populations. McIntire charged that the protesters appeared because Philadelphia television misrepresented Paisley as the leader of a "lunatic fringe" in Ireland and that America's press had distorted his protest at the Presbyterian Church General Assembly in the summer of 1966 as anti-Catholic. Paisley caused a controversy in Fort Worth, Texas, when the 9 April edition of the St. Anne's Episcopal Church weekly bulletin contained Reverend Norman V. Hollen's lengthy attack on Paisley's career. Hollen did not like the joint appearance at Castleberry Baptist Church of Paisley and Major Edgar C. Bundy of the Church League of America, fearing that any attack on the papacy or liberal Christian doctrine would provoke a backlash from local Catholics and Protestant clerics.[18] Although the episode in Texas passed quickly, the incident illustrated Paisley's growing international stature and his prominent position within the American militant fundamentalist community.

In a departure from previous tours, Paisley made several radio appearances. An important interview took place on the *Heart-to-Heart Hour* broadcast from Phoenix. He not only explained his view of the situation in Northern Ireland but prophesized that modernism, the ecumenical movement, the Irish Council of Churches, and the WCC would hasten the Second Coming of Christ. Paisley returned to the American airwaves in the summer of 1968 with Pastor Brian Green to begin a two-week evangelistic campaign at the Christian Admiral Conference Hall in Cape May, New Jersey. The crusade was broadcast back to Northern Ireland through McIntire's short-wave radio station WINB in Red Lion, Pennsylvania.[19]

Until the Reverend Ian Paisley began making annual trips to the United States, he had showed little interest in America's political and civil rights issues. Likewise, the Reverend Carl McIntire had not been overly concerned with Northern Ireland's constitutional issues until Paisley was jailed for the first time. Although Paisley sympathized with American fundamentalists and saw communism, black rights, and integration as mutual threats to the United States, and although McIntire and Bob Jones Jr. empathized with the danger that the IRA's Marxist and Catholic rights agenda posed to Ulster, the transatlantic relationship centered on religious issues. These attitudes reflected the worldview of North American and British militant fundamentalists who after the Second World War saw the ecumenical movement and Protestant apostasy as co-conspirators in a worldwide Roman Catholic–Communist coalition. In the late 1960s, however, the mutual fear of civil rights added a new element to the "Red"–Roman conspiracy and transformed the relationship between Paisley and American militants from a theological union into a broader Christian–political crusade.[20]

The fear of a Roman Catholic and Communist union was not new and had existed since the fundamentalist–modernist battles of the 1910s and 1920s. According to militants in North America and the British Isles, both the Roman Catholic Church and Communist regimes such as the Soviet Union were repressive dictatorships, working in unison to implement a totalitarian one-world government. Communism and Catholicism aimed to divide the world, but in order to do so they had to eradicate Protestantism—the voice of Christian liberty. To achieve this goal, the Catholic–Communist–ecumenical axis backed Communist insurgencies and civil rights movements. In Ireland, IRA terrorism bolstered the Catholic Church's anti-Protestant agenda, while in the United States social changes and an attack on segregation threatened America's white, Protestant hegemony. In the 1960s, the international fellowship of militant fundamentalists accordingly believed that civil rights activism had entered the Roman–Communist coalition in a concerted effort to wipe out international Protestantism.[21]

To militants, the threat to Protestantism heightened in 1968 and was apparent in many of the important battlegrounds of the Cold War, including the wars in Vietnam and Biafra, as well as Rhodesia's declaration of independence. Behind these conflicts, militant fundamentalists saw a partnership between the Catholic Church and Communist forces to expand communism and Catholic totalitarianism: "Romanism and communism on the surface appear to oppose each other; in reality they are both working towards the same end, which is the totalitarian control of the people."[22]

To expand the Vatican's power, the Catholic Church had to suppress local Protestant communities and fundamentalist Protestant churches. Militants believed that, just as US foreign policy used local "brush wars" to fight the Cold War, the Catholic Church employed indigenous Communist revolutions to suppress Protestant liberty. For instance, Paisley and his American allies argued that Ian Smith's regime in Rhodesia was a Christian and Protestant government threatened by both Communist-inspired African revolutionaries and Rome-directed British imperialists. Billy James Hargis helped to promote the All-Africa Christian Crusade Congress in Salisbury, Rhodesia, in January 1969, where the Rhodesian prime minister—the featured speaker—asserted that his country's racial policies were enacted to thwart atheistic communism. In another example, militants insisted that Rome pushed Biafran independence because the rebel leader, Lieutenant Colonel Oduniegwu Ojukwu, was Catholic and thus the Catholic Church's dupe. Militant fundamentalist theories could be complex and flexible, however—in Southeast Asia, the Roman Church and the Moscow–Beijing axis were on opposite sides: the American involvement in Vietnam was a Catholic crusade to back the Kennedy administration's appointee, Prime Minister Ngo Dinh Diem.[23]

Militant fundamentalists perceived all these conflicts as part of a loose conspiracy between the Soviet Union, the Catholic Church, and the WCC to divide the world between Moscow and Rome. The Roman Catholic Church used Communist movements to eliminate the major threat to their ambitions, usually Bible Protestantism. Militants believed that the totalitarian nature of Roman Catholicism and Eastern Orthodoxy allowed communism to breed; only Protestant countries, such as the United States, the United Kingdom, and the nations of the British Commonwealth, could thwart international communism. American militant fundamentalists articulated this viewpoint at numerous Bible conferences, including those that Paisley attended in New Jersey, South Carolina, and Canada.[24]

As his international contacts grew, Paisley tacitly supported the segregationist and anti-Communist positions of American politicians and anti-Communist laymen who were important to the militant fundamentalist crusade. The most significant were Senator Strom Thurmond of South Carolina, Governor Lester Maddox of Georgia, John Stormer, and General Edwin Walker; all except Maddox spoke alongside Paisley at Bible conferences. John Stormer, who made his name as the author of *None Dare Call It Treason* (1964), a chronicle of the Communist conspiracy to destroy American democracy and Protestantism, was a frequent speaker at militant churches and Bible conferences. According to Stormer, America was losing the Cold War because of the internal Communist threat. Described by Erling Jorstad as the "far-right bible," Stormer's book sold seven million copies, with Free Presbyterians in Ulster, Bible Presbyterians in New Jersey, and numerous other militant fundamentalist churches worldwide serving as retail outlets. McIntire and his organizations bought twenty thousand copies. Because of his notoriety, Stormer became a sought-after speaker and was active within the ACCC and ICCC. On several occasions, he accompanied Hargis overseas. He spoke at the ACCC conference in 1967 and at the Bob Jones Bible Conference in 1968, both places where Paisley also preached. Most of Stormer's writings addressed right-wing political issues, but he also pastored several Baptist churches and was awarded honorary degrees from the Manahath School of Theology in western Pennsylvania and from Shelton College, a New Jersey–based school affiliated with the Reverend Carl McIntire.[25]

Paisley shared platforms with General Edwin A. Walker, a veteran of both the Second World War and the Korean War and the commander of the airborne troops that forced Little Rock's Central High School to integrate in 1957. A valued speaker at Bible conferences and at militant fundamentalist churches, Walker became radicalized after witnessing the brainwashing of American prisoners of war in Korea and the use of federal power in Little Rock. Because of his activism, he had found trouble while serving with the Twenty-fourth Infantry Division in Augsburg, Germany.[26] In October 1960, he had initiated the Pro-Blue Program, which he wrote to educate soldiers about Communist infiltration into American institutions. Inspired by the National Security Council's Cold War Directive of 1958 that allowed officers to issue anti-Communist literature to their commands, the Pro-Blue Program utilized conservative publications (including John Birch Society material), employed speakers such as

Edgar C. Bundy, and advised soldiers how to vote in American elections. Starting with its 16 April 1961 issue, the *Overseas Weekly,* a liberal tabloid aimed at American soldiers, began a relentless attack on Walker's program. Liberal clergymen in America and the NCC quickly joined the assault. Worried over parallels to France's Secret Armed Organization—a group of militant European colonists supported by elements within the French military, which used terrorist tactics to fight against Algerian independence—and the joint appearance of American fundamentalists and military officers at right-wing seminars, the Kennedy administration retracted the Cold War Directive.[27]

The administration ordered Defense Secretary Robert A. McNamara and the acting judge advocate of the army, Major General Robert H. McCaw, to charge Walker with violation of the Hatch Act, which prohibited anyone in the military from influencing how American soldiers voted. Senators Strom Thurmond and Barry Goldwater denounced the reversal on the Senate floor, as did militant fundamentalists in their newspapers and radio shows and from their pulpits. Thurmond introduced Senate Resolution 191 calling for the Senate Armed Forces Committee to investigate the military's attack on Walker. Removed from his command, Walker resigned and became an active anti-Communist crusader as well as an instant celebrity on the militant fundamentalist circuit. McIntire, Hargis, and Bob Jones University strongly supported Walker during his military career and after his resignation.[28]

Walker played a prominent role in the controversy over the enrollment of James Meredith at the University of Mississippi (Ole Miss) in 1962. Meredith's action incited thousands of Mississippi segregationists to rush to Oxford to defend the racial integrity of the university and aroused a call to segregationists across the South. Walker was one of those who made haste to northern Mississippi. In Oxford, he not only urged rioters to attack the marshals but publicly called for a volunteer force to oppose the federal action. Arrested for inciting insurrection against the American government and assaulting federal marshals, the retired general was imprisoned and given psychiatric testing.[29]

These events elevated Walker from one of many speakers on the militant fundamentalist circuit into a celebrated "martyr" and a man of action.

In February 1963, Walker and Billy James Hargis jointly conducted a cross-country crusade called Operation Midnight Ride, which held meetings in twenty-nine cities, including Greenville, South Carolina, and at Bob Jones University and warned about the Communist encroachment in America and liberals' acquiescence to it. At each rally, Hargis made a short speech, followed by Walker, who talked on various subjects, most prominently the federal "invasion" of Mississippi and the Ole Miss riots.[30] Thurmond and other conservative politicians appeared with Walker at Bible conferences and meetings of the Christian Crusade's Anti-Communist Leadership Schools. For instance, on 4 July 1968 Bob Jones Jr. gave the invocation at a dinner at the Fifth Annual New England Rally for God, Family, and Country, a dinner in Boston honoring Walker. The earliest known meeting between Paisley and Walker occurred in May 1967 when both men spoke at the Jarvis Street Baptist Church to the Canadian Council of Evangelical Protestant Churches. Walker informed the Reverend McIntire that "he enjoyed his short visit with Dr. Paisley."[31]

Senator Thurmond and Governor Maddox were also activists on the militant fundamentalist Bible conference and church circuit that helped shape Paisley's anti–civil rights movement in Northern Ireland. For example, Thurmond addressed the Twentieth Century Reformation Hour Freedom Rally in Cape May, New Jersey, on 14 June 1968 on familiar themes: the US Senate promoted federal authority over the Constitution and God's divine will, and the American government was not effectively fighting communism. To Thurmond, America could solve all its problems by returning to a fundamentalist and "true" Christian faith in God. Thurmond maintained a close personal friendship with McIntire and spoke at the ACCC conference on several occasions. The senior senator from South Carolina appeared at the Christian Crusade's Anti-Communist Leadership Schools and publicly advised Christians to support Hargis and the ACC and to leave the apostate NCC. Support from a US senator, especially one with Thurmond's stature, is no small matter for any religious figure.[32]

Although it is certain that Paisley and Thurmond knew each other during the 1960s, the relationship between Paisley and Lester Maddox is more intriguing. Elected governor of Georgia in 1966, Maddox had made his fame two years earlier when he had prevented African Americans from eating at his Pickrick restaurant in Atlanta, chasing them into the street with hand guns and ax handles. The restaurateur was known for his outspokenness on civil rights agitation in Atlanta; he helped to found the People's Association for Selective Shopping to boycott and picket white businesses that served African Americans. After a court order closed his restaurant, Maddox insisted that a conspiracy of the federal government, Communists, and the NCC had targeted him. He adopted McIntire's tactics and picketed the White House, protesting President Lyndon Baines Johnson's refusal to meet with him.[33]

Maddox was another politician with strong militant fundamentalist beliefs. After receiving the Democratic gubernatorial nomination in 1966, he asserted that "God put me where I am today."[34] When he won the election, he held prayer sessions in the governor's office and argued that America's economic, social, and moral troubles could be solved with a fundamentalist Christian revival. To Maddox, America suffered from spiritual poverty: "Such a revival would restore states' rights, property rights, free enterprise and liberty—which were part of our spiritual heritage."[35] God and the Bible would win over Communists and atheism and defend private enterprise, capitalism, and private property. Maddox appeared at numerous churches throughout the country, where he supported Christian involvement in politics and compared the defense of capitalism with the will of God: "Nowhere in the Bible do I find the teaching that when a person is elected governor he is supposed to stop serving Christ. When the enemies of God, of America and of freedom fill the streets with their calls for the abolishment of private property, for government takeover of the private free enterprise system and for an end to constitutional government, then the hard-working, law-abiding Christian patriots of this country must take their stand for what they know is right."[36]

Maddox attended Bible conferences and militant fundamentalist events where, like Thurmond, he publicly opposed liberal church theology and clerics. Moreover, in April 1969 he issued a public statement opposing the Consultation on Church Unity meeting held in Atlanta. Six months later he took part in the McIntire and ACCC-led Bible-Believers

March in Trenton, New Jersey, organized to support the war in Vietnam.[37] He went on the *Twentieth Century Reformation Hour* broadcast to explain his decision:

> The goal of Dr. McIntire, the goal of Lester Maddox, and the goal of Christian patriots in this country is one and the same. We are publicly and unashamedly letting the nation and the world know that we do believe in the living God and that we are loyal to our country. There are those in our midst today who would seek the solution through asking us to place our faith in the Democratic Party, the Republican Party, the Governor, the President, or expanded social programs. We've tried all these but still have a nation grasping and seeking the answer. That answer is Christ and in the living God. . . . We seek victory, not surrender, over Communism.[38]

Paisley was clearly impressed with Maddox, a politician with militant fundamentalist beliefs. The *Protestant Telegraph* reprinted the full text of a speech the governor made to the Christian Crusade convention in Tulsa, Oklahoma, in August 1967. The Free Presbyterian paper proudly proclaimed it was the first in the British Isles to do so. In the speech, Maddox asserted that his administration was intimately Christian and that his election as governor of Georgia was part of a backlash from conservative Americans against atheistic government, the implementation of the Great Society, and integration. Maddox called the racial rioting across American cities a Communist conspiracy abetted by liberals within the US government. By devoting nearly half of his bimonthly eight-page paper to Maddox's speech, Paisley signaled his whole-hearted endorsement of Maddox's position and intimated that such a scenario could happen in Northern Ireland if the O'Neill administration did not stamp out the civil rights and Republican movements. It is conceivable that admiration for such Christian politicians strengthened Paisley's resolve to enter politics.[39]

In the spring of 1968, as the American South implemented integration, Paisley paid closer attention to the events in the United States. During March and April, he witnessed firsthand the traumatic transition in the South during a speaking tour of twenty-three cities that included Natchez, Mississippi; Decatur and Huntsville, Alabama; Augusta, Georgia;

and several cities in northern Florida. However, the most influential event of the trip took place on 4 April 1968 during the annual Bible Conference held at Bob Jones University. In the midst of the conference, James Earl Ray assassinated Martin Luther King Jr. in Memphis, Tennessee. Although the conference had begun on Sunday, 31 March, with a general call for a worldwide Christian revival to compel the eventual Second Coming of Jesus Christ, four days later the End Times appeared to be more imminent. That evening, news of Martin Luther King's death and reports that intense racial riots had broken out in forty-six American cities reached the university, as did the image of the machine guns placed on the steps of the US Capitol Building. Paisley spoke on the morning of 6 April, and although he avoided mentioning King's assassination and its violent aftermath, it is clear from his conference speech that he considered Irish and American Protestantism to be facing similar threats of apostasy and paganism, two important factors leading to the apocalypse: "The heart of both systems [referring to the NCC and the WCC as well as to Babylonian paganism] is idolatry; that is materialistic worship with the denial of the spirituality of God. Both are satanic attempts to build a way to God, and as such constitute anti-Christianity, the religion of anti-Christ. Both these systems have the seed of religious intolerance."[40]

Paisley argued that Christ was a separatist—"He separated us from darkness"—and quoted from Daniel and Revelation to connect the ecumenical movement with the End Times. Dr. Archer Weniger, a California preacher and ardent anti-Communist, followed Paisley to the platform and spoke on the earthly situation at hand. Weniger addressed the rioting. He blamed the turmoil in America on ecumenical apostasy, immorality, and the Communist-led radicalization of the American civil rights movement. To Weniger, all these elements were part of an interconnected conspiracy, a message that Paisley and other fundamentalists readily approved.[41] John Stormer, who also spoke at the conference, expanded on Weniger's message. He charged that King had promoted racial discord and racial rioting and had helped Communists take advantage of America's social problems. He contrasted the America of 1968 with the America of the 1930s, when a majority of Christian churches had practiced sound biblical theology and the government had taken action against social disorder. During his talk, Stormer quoted from Matthew 5:13[42] and argued: "The nation that forgets God shall be turned into Hell. . . . America is sick."[43] While Paisley patiently listened to his American militant fundamentalist allies' comments, he underwent what would be his second political (and eschatological) epiphany: any and all civil rights activism in Northern Ireland had to be squashed.[44]

A Footnote on Prejudice: Paisley and Segregation

Paisley's close relationship with Bob Jones University and Carl McIntire brought Ulster militant Protestantism into the American civil rights debate. In America, militant fundamentalists argued not only that segregation was the best social solution, but that scripture revealed it as the Will of God. Many militant fundamentalists opted for an anticlerical position, arguing that the leadership of mainstream denominations and seminaries—not the church body—were supporting civil rights as part of a liberal social gospel. Some public statements defending the militant position were made; for example, in 1958 the annual ACCC convention passed a resolution declaring that segregation and apartheid were Christian and that interracial marriages were unbiblical. In 1964, the ACCC urged black Christians to denounce the leaders of the civil rights movement, asserting that the NCC's support for the civil rights movement violated scripture. In these arguments, militants were careful not to advocate racial superiority, but to attack integration as a component of the Social Gospel and contrary to Old Testament teaching.[45]

The Anti-Communist Leadership Schools sponsored by Billy James Hargis and the Christian Crusade made the defense of segregation a major topic at its seminars. Speakers at the schools quite often did not hide their racism: R. Carter Pittman, a radical Georgia lawyer, consistently used the word *nigger* as well as imagery that would have been welcomed at Ku Klux Klan rallies. Although Hargis never openly expressed such views and did condemn Pittman, the Georgia racist was a frequent speaker at the Anti-Communist Leadership Schools. Such were the men that the Reverend Ian Paisley fraternized and prayed with during Bible Conferences in America.[46]

The Civil Rights Act of 1964 ordered the Department of Health, Education, and Welfare to withhold federally backed student loans from the students at segregated schools, such as Bob Jones University. The latter university also lost its tax-exempt status as a religious and educational institution granted under the Internal Revenue Code of 1954; donations to the university and the school's profits became taxable. Bob Jones University argued that the law was satanic and socialist and would lead to federal interference in their curriculum. The school's administration refused to comply with the act. Because one-third of its students used the federal loan program, the university organized its own Freedom Loan Fund to help with its student body's financial needs.[47]

During the 1960s and throughout the climax of the American civil rights movement the following decade, Bob Jones University denied admission to African American students. The university, even while claiming it had no prejudice against blacks as individuals, prescribed to the biblically inspired segregation of traditional southern society and the religiosity that God forbade the integration of races. On 17 April 1960, Bob Jones Sr. articulated this argument on his weekly radio show and in the pamphlet *Is Segregation Scriptural?* "If you are against segregation and racial separation, then you are against God Almighty. God is the author of segregation."[48] Five years later Bob Jones III was quoted in *The Nation:* "A negro is best when he serves at the table. When he does that, he's doing what he knows how to do best. The Negroes who have ascended to positions in government, in education . . . have a strong strain of white blood in them. Now I'm not a racist and this school is not a racist institution. I can't stress that enough. But what I say is purely what I have been taught, and what I have been able to study [in] the teaching of the Scripture."[49] It was illegal in South Carolina and Tennessee to operate an integrated school until the laws were revoked in 1964, but even when the Jim Crow laws of the American South were overturned, Bob Jones University did not change its racial policies.

As the civil rights movement abated, Bob Jones University attempted to thwart criticism and federal policy. The school admitted a few married African American students and employees of the university in 1971, although interracial dating was prohibited—a policy that lasted into the 1980s. Among a cross-section of American Christianity, Bob Jones University became a pariah, but militant fundamentalists supported its stance. As late as 1985, Bob Jones Jr. argued that he could support only "two or three" African American preachers because all other black ministers promoted political propaganda (i.e., the National Association for the Advancement of Colored People) and their theology was contrary to scripture.[50] Paisley was certainly aware of the university's racial policy, given his yearly trips to the Greenville, South Carolina, campus in the late 1960s, but he never denounced it in the *Protestant Telegraph.* Considering that Paisley had no reservation in indicting moderate fundamentalist Protestants for fellowship with liberals or Terence O'Neill's economic and social policy and overtures to the Irish Catholic community as appeasement, his silence in this case is incriminating.

8

Christian Disobedience in Ulster

When Paisley returned to Northern Ireland in May 1968, his rhetoric against NICRA dramatically increased: attacks on civil rights took prominence over those against O'Neillism. Moreover, his tactics changed in a very important way. Before the summer of 1968, Paisley had harassed numerous "apostate" opponents but had never physically prevented an opponent from protesting or attending any church service, meeting, or conference. Instead, his counterdemonstrations and marches were designed to have the RUC and the Stormont government accomplish this task. In August 1968, however, when Catholic protestors hit the streets of Ulster, Paisley decided to personally stop NICRA from marching. Aware of the reputation that American civil rights marches had won and with an understanding of the threat that a radicalized movement presented, he could not allow the Catholics in Northern Ireland to emulate the African Americans of the southern United States. He knew that federal legislation had effectively bolstered civil rights in the United States, and he accordingly hoped to prevent that success from being repeated in Ulster.

Paisley has never publicly stated that the events of the American civil rights movement overtly influenced his reaction to the Northern Ireland civil rights movement. There is little doubt, however, that after several years of fellowship with segregationists and anti–civil rights American militant fundamentalists, after being a witness to the changes that the American civil rights movement inflicted on American society, and after his relationship strengthened with Bob Jones University, the situation in America had a profound impact on him. Four months after the assassination of King and after witnessing the resulting violence, Paisley felt a sense of urgency in resisting NICRA when Catholic activists decided to hit the streets of Ulster. It is not a coincidence that the strongest and most vocal opponent of NICRA was the man who had seen firsthand what a strong civil rights movement supported by a sympathetic press could accomplish. Thus, in August 1968 the defense of Bible Protestantism in Ireland meant the defeat of the Catholic civil rights movement.

When the summer of 1968 began, Northern Ireland's political and communal relationships could have proceeded in either of two directions. The UUP's immediate implementation of reforms acceptable to the Catholic community or the setting of a realistic timetable for their future appearance might have eased minority activism. Such a move would have encouraged the civil rights movement to work through the parliamentary process and to shun street protests. The Stormont government unfortunately chose a second course: the O'Neill administration decided to maintain the status quo and only promised limited reforms. Because the second scenario prevailed, radical elements within the civil rights movement pressed for direct action, and moderates within the civil rights movement agreed to back a limited campaign of civil rights marches and local protests. Catholic politicians understood that the new direction of the civil rights movement would arouse a reaction from Protestant extremists, and the Nationalist Party leadership refused to endorse direct-action protests—except when they were unavoidable—which enabled radicals to influence the direction of the campaign. The emergence of Catholics marching on Northern Ireland's streets proved too much for Paisley and his followers, and so between June 1968 and August 1969 Northern Ireland witnessed an escalating battle between Paisleyites and the Catholic civil rights movement.[1]

The direct conflict between Paisley and the civil rights movement began in June 1968 when housing activists in Caledon made the fateful decision to begin direct-action protests. Over the previous year, the Republican Club in County Tyrone (an illegal organization) had encouraged Catholic families to squat in the new housing built in Caledon's Protestant ward. However, each time a house was occupied, the RUC evicted the trespassers. Austin Currie, the Nationalist MP for East Tyrone, brought up the matter during a Stormont debate, and after receiving little support from the government, he personally joined one of the squatting families. The house Currie chose to squat in was assigned to a single, nineteen-year-old Protestant secretary who had been selected over Catholic families that had been on the housing list for ten years.[2]

The overt act of discrimination and Currie's resulting arrest reminded Catholics how little the O'Neill administration had changed Northern Ireland. Many Catholics concluded that more drastic action would be required. After a small NICRA protest in Dungannon on 22 June, Currie asked both NICRA and the CSJ to support a larger protest to march to go from Coalisland to Dungannon. Both organizations reluctantly agreed to support Currie's plan, and on 24 August Currie and the NICRA assembled four thousand marchers in Coalisland to begin the five-mile walk to Dungannon. Despite the marchers' peaceful demeanor, the RUC redirected their route to avoid a counterdemonstration that the UPV had orchestrated.[3]

Paisley saw that the Coalisland campaign signaled a new radicalism within NICRA and argued that Irish republicanism and the Catholic Church were the true culprits. The *Protestant Telegraph* noted that the march took place on the 396th anniversary of the Saint Bartholomew's Day Massacre of Huguenots in France and asserted that it was not a protest for civil rights, but an assault on Irish Protestantism.[4] To many in Ulster, the claim was absurd, but not to Free Presbyterians and Paisley's militant fundamentalist supporters. To press his point, Paisley organized a march of two hundred members of the UPV in Maghera in early September. Maghera was chosen because Kevin Agnew, a local solicitor and member of NICRA's executive committee, had called for more civil disobedience in the area.[5]

After the Coalisland–Dungannon march, civil rights activism in Northern Ireland focused on Londonderry, a city important to the Protestant cultural identity in Northern Ireland. Londonderry is Protestant Ulster's Kosovo, the site of an important battle—the siege of Derry in 1689—but a city numerically dominated by a cultural and religious enemy.[6] Because of the city's Catholic majority, retaining Protestant control over it required blatant gerrymandering and extensive housing and employment discrimination. Catholics constituted 70 percent of the city's population but controlled only eight of twenty council seats and suffered two and a half times the rate of Protestant unemployment. Moreover, Londonderry's division of the RUC owned Northern Ireland's strongest reputation for hostility toward Catholics.[7]

The city also contained some of Northern Ireland's most radical civil rights activism. Eamonn McCann, who formed the Derry Housing Action Committee (DHAC) in partnership with local Republican Clubs, organized Northern Ireland's most dynamic housing unrest. The DHAC's primary tactics were conducting street protests and disrupting the proceedings of the Londonderry Corporation. At the end of August 1968, the DHAC asked NICRA to take part in a civil rights march in Londonderry set for 5 October. Because of the tension within the city, NICRA initially denied McCann's request, and only radical and Republican groups agreed to participate. NICRA wanted to retain a moderate influence in Londonderry, however, and after an internal debate reluctantly agreed to support the march. Moreover, when Protestant organizations in Londonderry also complained, Home Affairs Minister William Craig banned the demonstration. Because of the ban, the entire spectrum of civil rights groups in Northern Ireland agreed to participate, and what would have been a small protest turned into a march of four hundred, including three British Labour MPs and several Nationalist MPs from Stormont.[8]

The choice of Waterside Station as a staging point was made to reinforce the parade's nonsectarian appearance. However, the parade route added another challenge to the government. Because the station sits within a Protestant neighborhood, and because the march proceeded into the city center, the route seemingly was designed to make the RUC overreact. On cue, the RUC stopped the marchers with water cannon and a baton charge as they neared the city walls. Both the BBC and Ulster television broadcast the police violence; this publicity further increased support for civil rights within the Catholic community and demands from the British government for O'Neill to act. On the evening of the march, Catholic and Protestant gangs in Londonderry began several days of street fighting, which convinced Paisley that the marchers had intended to instigate violence.[9]

Many within Northern Ireland's Protestant community now concluded that the RUC needed help to maintain law and order on the streets of Ulster; more Protestant extremists joined Paisley's counterdemonstrations.

Encouraged by Paisley, Protestants demanded tougher action toward civil rights marches. The tactics used by Paisley and Protestant extremists made it impossible for O'Neill to implement meaningful reforms. To make matters worse, after 5 October an increasing percentage of the Catholic community accepted radical civil rights protests as a necessity, and the Nationalist Party withdrew as the official opposition at Stormont. To the Catholic community, O'Neill was using the dual threat of Catholic civil disorder and Paisleyite reactions as an excuse to block reforms.[10]

During the last two months of 1968, a series of civil rights protests in Londonderry, Belfast, and Armagh met a growing reaction from Paisleyites. A new ad hoc organization in Londonderry, the Derry Citizens' Action Committee (DCAC), organized the largest civil rights protests. John Hume, a leading moderate politician, and Ivan Cooper, a liberal Protestant, directed the DCAC in a moderate direction, widening the moderate–radical split within the civil rights movement and alienating radicals such as Eamonn McCann. When Hume and the DCAC organized a second march on 2 November, retracing the route used one month earlier, their protest incited the Loyal Citizens of Ulster to instigate a larger Paisleyite countermarch.[11] A third civil rights march planned for 16 November brought threats of a second Paisley counterdemonstration in Londonderry and forced William Craig to ban for one month any marches within the city. Catholics from across Northern Ireland responded with anger, and fifteen thousand took part in an illegal demonstration. However, Hume's moderate leadership and a cautious RUC attitude prevented violence.[12]

The success of these civil rights marches and the size of the turnout on 16 November inspired Catholic dock and factory workers to mount a series of small processions within Londonderry's walls. The sight of these marchers increased the Protestant desire to stop further civil rights protests. To Paisley and many Protestants, the O'Neill administration's apparent impotence against the civil rights movement and Stormont policies invited intervention from the British government. Paisley's counterdemonstrations took on the aspects of a revival and combined political speeches with his own and other fundamentalist preachers' religious sermons. The use of religious oratory was important because it inspired violent defiance both from Protestants who claimed to have a relationship with God and from secular working-class extremists. Secularized workers respected Paisley and believed that following a man of God vindicated their radicalism.[13]

On the night of 30 November 1968, two thousand Paisleyites assembled in Armagh, sang hymns, and waited for a planned civil rights march to proceed. Paisley's aggressive intentions were clearly announced in fliers posted by the UPV: "Ulster's Defenders. A friendly warning. Board up your windows. Remove all women and children from the city on Saturday, 30th November. O'Neill must go."[14] Despite the RUC's efforts to search Paisley supporters before they entered Armagh, many Paisleyites produced weapons. As a consequence, the civil rights march had to be diverted around the city center where Paisley had assembled his followers. Although Paisley and an aide, Ronald Bunting, were subsequently arrested for disturbing the peace, and many observers felt that the RUC had acted fairly toward the civil rights marchers, the diversion of the march appeared to Catholics as a concession to Paisleyism.[15]

The escalating tension in Northern Ireland alarmed both Irish church leaders and the British government. The Catholic and Anglican primates issued a joint appeal for peace, a rare display of Catholic–Anglican unity, although not surprising to militant fundamentalists who had long suspected both hierarchies of ecumenical aims. As the intensity of civil rights marches increased, the British government paid more attention to the affairs of Northern Ireland and took a new, aggressive stance in its intercourse with O'Neill. Over the previous four decades, the UUP had manipulated contact between Northern Irish and British officials, and Unionist–British discussions had focused on financial matters. Westminster now started to reevaluate its policy toward Northern Ireland and insisted that O'Neill begin to institute reforms. Prime Minister Harold Wilson threatened to reconsider Britain's financial and political relationship with Northern Ireland if Catholic demands were ignored or if the UUP right-wing replaced O'Neill. Wilson's response tightened the difficult position in which O'Neill was placed. Too much reform risked a backlash from Paisley and the UUP's right-wing, whereas limited reforms could not placate a majority of the Catholic community and would escalate civil rights activities.[16]

On 22 November 1968, the British government forced O'Neill to announce a series of reform measures: the reorganization of the Londonderry Corporation as a development commission that would include Catholic members; the establishment of a fair-housing program that would take control of the waiting list for new houses from the lord mayor; the appointment of an ombudsman to investigate complaints against the Northern Ireland government; and the elimination of the company vote in Stormont elections. Many Catholics thought that the reforms were inadequate and insincere and that the O'Neill government would avoid implementing them. The reforms did not satisfy the civil rights demand for "one man–one vote" in local council elections, nor did they eliminate the Special Powers Act or promise new housing. Nevertheless, the civil rights movement had gained in two months more rights for Catholics than the Nationalist Party and the IRA had achieved in forty-seven years. Radicals within the civil rights movement believed further pressure on the O'Neill government would bring additional concessions.[17]

The new initiatives enraged Paisley and his followers. Because Paisley considered all civil rights organizations to be fronts for Republican activities and the Catholic Church, he believed that placating these groups constituted treason against Irish Protestantism. He argued: "None of us need be a qualified psychiatrist to conclude that the present spate of unrest in Ulster, under its convenient label of Civil Rights . . . is in reality a united Roman Catholic protest—not against our Unionist Government—but rather and indisputably against centuries of oppression and repression by the Roman Catholic hierarchy and its Italian dictators in the Vatican. . . . [C]ivil rights marchers are . . . in actual fact screaming against the many centuries of injustice meted out to them by their Vatican dictators."[18]

The escalating confrontations between Paisley and Catholic radicals increased the pressure on O'Neill. After Paisleyites violently disrupted a civil rights meeting in Dungannon, O'Neill went on television to address the increasing violence. O'Neill's "Crossroads" speech on 5 December 1968 promised a new commitment to implementing reforms that were acceptable to the Catholic community. O'Neill asked the civil rights movement for a moratorium on marches and the Protestant community to support his government's policies. But NICRA, the DCAC, and a majority of civil rights activists announced only a temporary halt to all marches. The O'Neill government made two other important moves: the attorney general adjourned all summonses for all outstanding civil rights offenses until the following May—thus including those given to Paisley and Bunting—and O'Neill fired William Craig in an attempt to thwart right-wing dissension within the UUP. Craig now aligned himself with the Paisleyites, and Paisley temporarily confined his activities to church matters.[19]

O'Neill's efforts at reconciliation foundered as a new student-based group from Queen's University, People's Democracy, decided to wreck the truce. The confrontations between Paisley and civil rights marchers over the previous four months as well as the RUC's reactions in Dungannon and Londonderry aroused a coalition of radical, leftist, and moderate student groups into organizing their own movement. After ten students picketed Craig's house on 6 October 1968, and Craig publicly insulted the group, a meeting was called at the Students' Union to plan a protest march. Three thousand students marched from the university to Belfast City Hall three days later but were diverted around Shaftsbury Square to avoid a large gathering of Paisleyites. At an impromptu meeting that evening, Queen's University students formed the People's Democracy to press for the same civil rights demands as NICRA. What made the group different were its anarchic structure and its independence from the civil rights movement. People's Democracy was open to all students, faculty, and alumni of any British university, and each member had an equal say in the group's decisions and organization. A small group of radicals, however, manipulated the organization's decisions and made sure that the group was less spontaneous and democratic than it proclaimed. Several charismatic and well-known political activists directed the organization's course, the most important being Eamonn McCann of Londonderry; Michael Farrell, a lecturer with an extensive background in radical activities; and Bernadette Devlin, the future Westminster MP. Farrell was also a leader of the Young Socialist Alliance, a group that violently confronted the police during civil rights marches and along with McCann was a member of the Irish Workers' Group, which aimed to unite Ireland into a socialist worker's republic.[20]

Farrell, McCann, and Devlin wanted to implement a socialist revolution, and they believed that only a radical movement could change

Northern Irish society. All three viewed NICRA as a middle-class attempt to maintain the basic class structure. The best way to accomplish their goal was to provoke the O'Neill government into overreacting to civil rights protests, to incite Paisley into violent counterdemonstrations, and to provoke intervention from the British government. Farrell did not support the moratorium on civil rights marches and feared that the November reforms might actually satisfy the Catholic community. So on 1 January, he, along with two hundred radical supporters, began the Long March, a four-day protest march from Belfast to Londonderry. The route chosen passed through a mostly Protestant-dominated region and was designed to provoke a violent reaction from Paisley and his followers and to force the O'Neill government to protect Catholic civil rights marchers. From the moment the marchers set out from Belfast City Hall, they met a constant barrage of Protestant harassment. The RUC was forced to reroute the Long March several times to avoid hostile counterdemonstrators. Paisley did not join the protesters but assigned Ronald Bunting, Bunting's Loyal Citizens of Ulster, and the UPV to lead the Protestant extremists. On the evening of 3 January, Paisley and Bunting held a prayer meeting at the Guildhall in Londonderry, calling on their audience to defend Protestantism and to attack the marchers.[21]

When the marchers arrived the following morning at Burntollet Bridge a few miles outside Londonderry, three hundred Protestant extremists attacked them with clubs, sticks, and paving stones. The marchers' police escort refused to intervene. Later that afternoon the marchers were again attacked as they entered Londonderry, setting off several days of rioting within the city's Catholic neighborhoods. Catholics had expected the Long March to meet some resistance, but they did not anticipate the indifference the police exhibited that day. During previous civil rights marches, the RUC had rerouted marches to secure the marchers' safety, but this time the police appeared to direct marchers into a trap. Reports that the new minister of home affairs, Captain William Long, had met with Paisley and Bunting on 2 January led to accusations of government collusion in the incident. Although no direct complicity has ever been proven, it appeared to Catholics that the O'Neill government had become more interested in placating Paisley and Protestant extremists than in pushing reforms and seriously considering civil rights complaints. The *Protestant Telegraph* only exacerbated tensions when it triumphantly applauded the attack at Burntollet Bridge and predicted a new awakening in the Protestant community against the civil rights movement.[22]

On 5 January 1969, Terence O'Neill went on television again. This time, however, he accused the civil rights movement of promoting anarchy but only mildly criticized Paisley, Bunting, and the UPV: "I think we must also have an urgent look at the Public Order Act itself to see whether we ought to ask Parliament for further powers to control these elements which are seeking to hold the entire community to ransom. Enough is enough. We have heard sufficient for now about civil rights, let us hear a little about civic responsibility."[23] This speech lost O'Neill what moderate Catholic support he still retained and ended most dialogue between the government and the civil rights movement. The events of December and January convinced most Protestants that Catholics were overemphasizing civil rights demands and were actually interested in political power. Many Protestants who had supported O'Neill and flaunted "I Back O'Neill" buttons after the Crossroads speech now embraced Protestant radicals and Paisley. A majority of Protestants discounted O'Neill's assurances and the British government's promises that civil rights reforms would not come at the expense of the Protestant community.[24]

As a result of escalating violence, O'Neill proposed the Public Order (Amendment) Bill to supplement the Special Powers Act. The amendment banned all protests and counterprotests and made it harder to obtain police permission to hold marches. Although the bill met stiff resistance and did not become law until February 1970, it stifled Paisley, whose claim to support legal government authority meant he had to back down from new counterdemonstrations. O'Neill introduced the Public Order Bill to deter growing opposition to him within the UUP. Not only were Protestants from outside the UUP, such as Paisley, demanding that O'Neill resign, but a growing movement within the party publicly advocated his removal. Many Protestants believed that his government could not maintain law and order.[25]

In late January 1969, the right-wing Unionist attack on O'Neill intensified when twelve backbenchers met at a hotel in Portadown to formulate a strategy to oust the prime minister. In response, O'Neill decided to call a general election to demonstrate his popular support. Paisley decided to run as a candidate against O'Neill in the militant fundamentalist's first election campaign. He lost the election but drew enough votes to embarrass O'Neill, and the UUP split its vote, with twenty-nine pro-O'Neill Unionists winning seats and ten anti-O'Neill candidates victorious. It was the first electoral split in the party's history. Moreover, the Nationalist Party's loss of three seats to civil rights activists, including John Hume, illustrated the waning of its influence within the Catholic community. Radicalism was becoming increasingly popular among Ulster's Catholic and Protestant voters. O'Neill was reelected as leader of the UUP, but the erosion of support for his policies was obvious. He and the UUP suffered another significant election defeat in April when the death of George Forrest, the Unionist Westminster MP for mid-Ulster, prompted a by-election. To assure the defeat of a Protestant candidate, Republicans, the Nationalist Party, and the People's Democracy agreed to support Bernadette Devlin as the representative of all non-Unionist parties. Devlin won on a nonsectarian, radical socialist platform that attacked both the UUP's discriminatory policies and Paisley's religious viewpoints.[26]

The Stormont and mid-Ulster by-elections were not the only new troubles facing O'Neill. Between 30 March and 24 April 1969, the Ulster Volunteer Force orchestrated a series of bombings that damaged electrical and water facilities throughout Northern Ireland. Both the government and Paisley blamed the IRA, and the RUC initially could not provide evidence of UVF complicity. The *Protestant Telegraph* asserted that the civil rights campaign had begun its second phase: the bombings signaled the start of a new round of Republican violence that aimed to topple the Northern Ireland government.[27] Despite the RUC's claims to the contrary, Catholics suspected that Protestant extremists had committed the bombings. Later in the year the Northern Irish authorities arrested members of the UVF for the attacks, but by then it was too late to placate the Catholic community.

After determining that his policies had split the UUP, O'Neill resigned as prime minister on 28 April 1969. Unionist moderates retained enough power, however, to elect Major James Chichester-Clark as the new party leader over Brian Faulkner, the Unionist right wing's choice. Throughout the summer of 1969, Chichester-Clark continued the basic O'Neill policies and so did not win the confidence of either the Catholic community or Paisley and Protestant extremists. To all three, the new prime minister appeared indecisive, inarticulate, and awkward. Catholics did not believe that Chichester-Clark could deter Paisley or the Unionist right wing, and Paisley and Protestant extremists were dissatisfied when the prime minister continued O'Neill's policies.[28]

From the end of the Long March until the start of the marching season in the summer of 1969, both the Northern Ireland civil rights movement and Paisley continued their campaigns. Most of the civil rights actions were either small People's Democracy protests or larger protests led by radicals, not by NICRA members. These protests included the four-thousand-person demonstration in Londonderry on 28 March that again covered the ground between Waterside train station and the Diamond in the center of the city and the march in Omagh in mid-April that counter-demonstrators confronted. NICRA had earlier backed off from supporting demonstrations but, frustrated by the lack of reforms, announced on 2 June that it would start marching again in six weeks.

The tensions within the province were augmented by both the street violence and sectarian intimidation that was occurring on a regular basis in Belfast and Londonderry between Catholics and the RUC and by the appearance of neighborhood vigilante committees in Catholic and Protestant neighborhoods. The Shankill Defence Association that John McKeague founded was one notorious Protestant group that used intimidation and threats of fire-bombing to "convince" Catholics to leave predominately Protestant areas. McKeague was a former Free Presbyterian and member of Paisley's Ravenhill congregation.[29]

Protestant marching was the final straw that ushered in a new and deadly era in the history of Northern Ireland—and in Paisley's career. In 1969, the 12 July Orange Order parades proceeded with sporadic violence in Belfast, although the RUC established an uneasy truce. Serious sectarian fighting broke out near the Shankill Road after Catholics attacked a Junior Orangeman parade that passed in front of the Unity Flats housing estate. The Shankill Defence Association counterattacked, but a massive

RUC presence stopped the Protestant onslaught. Nevertheless, residents of Unity Flats accused the police of aiding the Protestant extremists.

Stormont expected trouble to be repeated during the annual 12 August Apprentice Boys parade in Londonderry. Robert Porter, the new minister of home affairs, began discussions with the British government for the use of the British army if serious violence did occur, and several British army units were dispatched to bases in Northern Ireland as a precaution. Porter refused to ban the Apprentice Boys march, and the parade proceeded without incident until fighting broke out between Catholic and Protestant youths that afternoon. The tensions created during the previous ten months of civil rights marches and protests proved too much, and the sporadic street fighting escalated into two nights of vicious rioting. On the third day of rioting, the Northern Ireland government conceded that it had lost control of law and order, and at 4:15 PM on 14 August 1969 troops of the Prince of Wales' Own Regiment were deployed onto the streets of Londonderry.[30]

The Second Jailing

Although Paisley's campaign against the Catholic civil rights movement in Northern Ireland became his primary concern, he continued to fight British ecumenism throughout the fall of 1968 and the spring of 1969. As a consequence, his crusade against the ecumenical movement, theological liberalism, and the Anglican Church's "Romeward trend" continued to elicit a negative reaction from moderate Irish and British clerics and increased admiration from American and European militant fundamentalists. The contrasting reactions were never more apparent than after the Northern Ireland authorities jailed Paisley for a second time in March 1969.

In early July 1968, Paisley and associates in the BCPCC—once again involving Brian Green and Jack Glass—picketed the WCC assembly in Uppsala, Sweden. Paisley and Free Presbyterian ministers, including the Reverend John Wylie and Ivan Foster, joined the BCPCC and John Walsh of America to protest the imprisonment of Protestant clerics in Cameroon and the presence in Uppsala of the archbishop of Canterbury, Billy Graham, and Catholic observers. Militant fundamentalists championed the case of the Presbyterians in Cameroon, claiming that the group had been imprisoned for their refusal to join the country's state-ordained ecumenical church. They also attacked the new WCC resolutions against the Vietnam and Biafran wars as well as "avant-garde" theological conceptions such as "touch-and-feel" prayer sessions where participants prayed as well as expressed physical affection. Militant fundamentalists equated these practices with recycled pagan orgies. Paisley, Wylie, and Foster held placards announcing their martyrdom two years earlier and confronted delegates from the Irish Presbyterian Church and the Irish Methodist Eric Gallagher at the entrance to the assembly.[31]

The following January Paisley led another BCPCC protest in London against Cardinal John Heenan, the Roman Catholic archbishop of Westminster, who spoke at St. Paul's Anglican Cathedral as part of a week of prayer for Christian unity. Heenan was the first Catholic archbishop to preach in a British Protestant church in four hundred years. Although Paisley, Green, and several associates were able to enter the churchyard, several hundred opponents trapped them and for two hours shouted abuse at them, such as "Paisley go home" and "Fascist." London police officers had to protect the militant fundamentalists.[32]

As the episode reveals, Paisley's public stature had incited a stronger response from his critics throughout the British Isles; Paisleyites had never before inspired preplanned counterprotests. In early December 1968, Lord Donald Soper attacked Paisley in the British House of Lords as a "man with a loud voice" and claimed that "his doctorate is self-inflicted. He is purely dogmatic and has no scholarship. He is a rabble-rouser, he has a raucous approach and a dogmatic gesture."[33] This is the second time that Soper had mentioned Paisley in the House of Lords. In December 1966, during debate over the racial and religious discrimination bill, Soper had stated that the situation in Northern Ireland was dangerous and called Paisley "evil and wicked." He had used Paisley as an example to argue that religion must be included in the bill. However, the new attack two years later had an elevated sense of urgency. Eric Gallagher, who publicly supported NICRA's aims and condemned extremist actions such as Burntollet Bridge, expressed the feelings of many moderate Protestants when he argued that Protestant churches in Ireland should have been denouncing Paisley in a stronger tone.[34] The General Assembly of the Presbyterian

Church in Ireland harshly criticized Paisleyism, although it would not mention Paisley by name:

> Those who provoke violence reactions have themselves a share in responsibility for the results and have also paved the way for the followers less disciplined than themselves. Whatever the faults of demonstrators, a far greater disservice has been done to Northern Ireland by those who have banded themselves together to prevent, by physical resistance, the peaceful expression of opinion, instead of answering it with a greater reason and self-discipline. By violence of speech and action, by person[al] vilification and harassment, they have dishonored the cause they professed to defend. . . . Such treatment of those who were protesting against what they believed to be wrong has been a grievous betrayal of the Protestant and Presbyterian principles of civil and religious liberty and respect for conscience.[35]

Other Irish Protestants were taking a neutral position, however, opposing both civil rights activism and Paisleyism. Although not supporting Paisley's methods, these moderates argued that Irish Protestants had legitimate grievances. The *Church of Ireland Gazette* urged Irish Protestants to support civil rights in the North but also printed an editorial proclaiming that Protestants in the Republic of Ireland also needed civil rights and attacking the anti-Protestant policies of Irish Catholicism. The *Gazette* pointed out that Protestants in southern Ireland could not get divorces or buy contraceptives and that the Ne Temere decree—requiring that the children born out of mixed Catholic–Protestant marriages be raised Catholic—was a major obstacle to ecumenism between Protestant and Catholic churches.[36]

Throughout the spring and summer of 1969, Paisley's voice was somewhat muted in Ulster because of the pending court case that resulted from his counterdemonstration in Armagh the previous November. Although Paisley and Bunting first appeared in court on 27 January 1969 and were convicted of unlawful assembly and sentenced to ninety-day imprisonment, both were released on appeal and not jailed until the end of March. At that time, the appeal was heard by a judge who happened to be Catholic: the original sentence doubled. But both Paisley and Bunting were released early after Chichester-Clark announced an amnesty for all civil rights offenses that had taken place after 5 October 1968.[37] Paisley's second jailing further elevated his status within the international community of militant fundamentalists, and his ordeal became standard reading in newspapers such as the *Christian Beacon* and *Western Voice*.[38]

Throughout the spring and summer of 1969, Paisley's fellowship with militant fundamentalists in the British Isles and North America strengthened, and Ulster witnessed a steady stream of militant visitors. In February 1969, Bob Jones Jr. appeared with Paisley in a series of meetings in Ulster to support Paisley's anti–civil rights and antiecumenical crusades but also tacitly to support his political campaign. Bob Jones III appeared at the Tandragee Free Presbyterian Church and the Ulster Hall.[39] After Paisley's jailing in March 1969, the ACCC passed a resolution commending him as a "great Protestant leader" and denouncing the Northern Irish civil rights movement for inciting violence. Because of his second imprisonment, Paisley could not attend the annual Bob Jones Bible Conference, although Brian Green, who spoke in his place, fully detailed his martyrdom and the "spiritual conditions in Great Britain today." Green argued that the civil rights movement in Northern Ireland and the Catholic Church were the culprits behind Paisley's legal trouble.[40] The Bob Jones conference organizers sent a telegram to President Richard M. Nixon condemning Paisley's second incarceration as an assault on Bible Protestantism. McIntire also added direct support, with guest editorials in the *Protestant Telegraph* and telegrams to the queen of England that denounced the treatment of Paisley.[41]

American support bolstered Paisley's campaign against apostasy and ecumenicalism within the Irish and British churches. In early June 1969, Paisley led six Free Presbyterian ministers in a protest against the appearance of Dr. John Carson, the new moderator of the Irish Presbyterian Church, at the Trinity Presbyterian Church in Bangor and planned a visit to Geneva with sixteen ministers to protest Pope Paul VI's visit to the WCC headquarters. Geneva was the home of John Calvin, so the choice of venue for the pope's visit galled militant fundamentalists. In spite of a ban by the Swiss authorities—who cited a supposed (but false) death threat against the pontiff from Jack Glass—Paisley and his entourage left for Geneva.

He and five others were detained at the airport, but the remainder of the group was able to stage a protest outside the WCC building.[42]

Following the protests, Paisley returned to Belfast to prepare for the upcoming 12 July celebrations and to prepare for the new wave of NICRA marches. Whether he was prepared for the outbreak of sectarian fighting is speculative, but he had spent two decades warning Ulster Protestants and militant fundamentalists throughout the world that apostasy and the Roman Catholic Church threatened Ulster Protestantism. To many Irish Protestants, his dire predictions appeared to be becoming true. As the marching season in Ulster in the summer of 1969 began, Paisley was the most revered defender of Bible Protestantism within the international militant fundamentalist fellowship.

PART THREE

The Second Coming

Paisley and Amillennial Politics

9

The Genesis of Ulster Amilitant Politics

This final section examines Paisley's career in politics and his transformation from a premillennialist fundamentalist crusader into an amillennial politician. During his early career as a campaigning antimodernist and antiecumenical militant fundamentalist, he showed a basic interest in politics, but more concern with the signs forecasting the Second Coming and revival. He focused his political activities on constitutional issues, such as defending the union between Northern Ireland and Great Britain, protecting the Protestant identity of the Church of England and the British Constitution, and on local controversies, including education grants to Catholic schools and state-mandated sabbatarianism. As a novice politician, he took a populist stance in opposition to the policies of the ruling UUP. Politics for Paisley in these early years was a means to an end: political action could be used to establish a godly, Calvinist state, to arouse a new religious revival within Ulster, and to thwart the aspirations of Irish Catholicism.[1]

Reflecting on his propensity for Unionist populism during an interview in 1996, Paisley reminisced over his disposition to independent Unionism and stated that he had developed an early dislike for the official Unionist Party. He asserted that the UUP did not act in the best interests of the Protestant working class and that it was unnecessarily antagonistic to the Nationalist Party and the Catholic community. During his career as a crusading militant fundamentalist, Paisley attacked the UUP as consistently as he did Catholic politicians and political demands. This animosity toward "Big House" Unionism continued through his service in the Northern Ireland, British, and European parliaments. As a Northern Irish and British MP, however, Paisley protected the social and economic needs of his entire constituency, both Catholic and Protestant. And as a European MP, he worked to protect the interests of the entire Northern Ireland community. It is conceivable that a fundamentalist Protestant who grew up in a social position outside the Protestant ascendancy would feel some compassion for the well being of the Catholic as well as Protestant community as long as Northern Ireland remained securely within the United Kingdom and as long as Protestant dominance within Northern Ireland remained unchallenged. Although this position might seem contradictory in light of Paisley's vehement opposition to Catholic civil rights actions, such as the Coalisland-to-Dungannon march in August 1968, he had no problem allowing Catholics to rent public homes or to receive any other government-provided privileges as long as Protestant power in Northern Ireland was not threatened. Civil rights marches had to be challenged, however, because they imperiled the Protestant control of the province and Northern Ireland's constitutional position as a province of the United Kingdom.[2]

The National Union of Protestant Action

Paisley came from a subsection of Ulster Unionism that supported independent political action against the Protestant ascendancy. These Unionists, primarily working class, followed a tradition that had begun in the late nineteenth century and continued through the Home Rule crisis and the establishment of the Northern Ireland statelet. The alternatives to the UUP became more numerous and aggressive in the period between the partition of Ireland and the 1940s. Populists supported movements independent of the UUP; for instance, the Protestant Action Society was formed to help Protestants buy property and to thwart Catholics from doing the same. Moreover, the Ulster Protestant Defence and Propaganda Society fought to ensure that the Protestant religion would be taught within the new Northern Ireland public-school systems, and the Ulster Protestant League was set up to defend Protestant jobs. Independent and populist Unionists won parliamentary seats in the late 1940s with the election of Tommy Henderson and J. W. Nixon in Belfast, candidacies that both the largely secular urban working class and pious Protestants supported. Working-class and evangelical Protestants were concerned over the UUP leadership; the working class accused Unionists of engaging in class politics, and evangelicals asserted that the party expressed little evangelical fervor. The UUP employed anti-Catholic rhetoric and economic discrimination against the Catholic community to maintain the economic division between the Protestant and Catholic working classes but showed little interest in improving Ulster's economy or in revivalism and evangelical efforts.[3]

Paisley's first foray into Unionist politics came in January 1949 as the campaign agent for UUP candidate Tommy Cole during Cole's run for the Stormont Ward of Belfast, Dockside. By all accounts, Paisley argued a sectarian and antisocialist message. Not only was the area divided between working-class Protestants and Catholics, but it had also previously elected NILP candidates. This was part of a larger trend in Belfast politics, which saw five socialists, including two from the NILP, elected in Belfast after the Second World War. But during the 1949 election, the UUP made the border the primary political issue after the Irish Free State declared itself a republic. Paisley attacked the antipartition stance of the NILP candidate and orchestrated a campaign that promoted Protestantism, ensuring Cole's victory. Because the area experienced consistent sectarian trouble in the past and because of Paisley's campaign efforts, the campaign was the most violent in the constituency since 1921.[4]

In spite of Cole's victory, the process affected Paisley negatively; he concluded that he should concentrate on his ministry. In January 1949, an event that Paisley considered an epiphany diverted his attention from politics and back to religious matters. He claimed that during an extended prayer meeting with members of the Ravenhill Mission he encountered the Holy Ghost, who asked him to inspire a revival among Ulster's true Christians—those who professed Calvinism and took a fundamentalist view of the Bible—and to forego politics. The divine visit, however, did not prevent Paisley from working on the Westminster candidacy of the Reverend James MacManaway, a Church of Ireland minister who held a Stormont seat for Londonderry. MacManaway won the House of Commons seat for West Belfast in February 1950. But Paisley's spiritual revelation shaped his own career during the 1950s and early 1960s: he primarily evangelized, and when he did involve himself in political issues, he worked indirectly with organizations such as the National Union of Protestants and Ulster Protestant Action and in a manner that used political action to promote religious concerns.[5]

During the late 1940s, Paisley expanded his ministry into political and social issues but subordinated those issues to religious concerns. He helped to establish the Ulster branch of the NUP and became the organization's treasurer. It was in part through his uncle, the Reverend W. St. Clair Taylor, who was the general secretary of the organization in London, that Paisley involved himself with the NUP, but also through the relationships he developed in Ulster. The most important was Norman Porter, the Baptist lay preacher and associate of Dr. Carl McIntire, with whom Paisley attended evangelical meetings.[6]

Organizations such as the NUP widened the scope of both Paisley's religious activities and his political connections. As the NUP's Northern Ireland treasurer and secretary, respectively, Paisley and Porter used the group as a platform for political activism that benefitted evangelical Christians. The NUP sought to maintain Protestant unemployment and to thwart Catholic evangelizing and ecumenical efforts. It also worked to uphold the traditional Protestant character of public life in Northern Ireland. Alarmed by the growing secularization of British society and the loosening of public morals, Paisley and the NUP opposed the liberalization of laws governing alcohol consumption and sales on the Sabbath. Because the Northern Ireland Parliament and local councils held the right to legislate on local issues such as education, local voting rights, and alcohol sales, these institutions were subject to constant NUP pressure. For example, in May 1948 Paisley spoke at an NUP meeting denouncing the attempt to open the Belfast Museum and Art Gallery on Sundays. Two years later Paisley and the NUP petitioned the Belfast Corporation, the city's administrative body, to ban alcohol ads on city-owned buses, and in 1958 Paisley and Porter opposed the Intoxicating Liquor and Licencing Bill (Northern Ireland), which permitted new alcohol licenses and increased sales in hotels. During the confrontation with the Belfast Corporation, Paisley made a personal attack on Unionist senator Joseph Cunningham, who was also a county grand master of the Orange Order and chairman of the corporation's transport committee, at a protest meeting. In the style of former Ulster Protestant demagogues, Paisley exhibited a willingness to confront Unionist leadership. Although his propensity to attack apostate Unionists and Protestant leaders predates his introduction to Carl McIntire, it was not until he met the American that he began denouncing fellow fundamentalists.[7]

Following the Second World War, Northern Ireland maintained a semipuritanical society that limited the number of bars and the hours they could operate and kept sabbatarian "blue" laws. The opening of public buildings, conveniences, and parks were outlawed on Sundays. Although evangelical Protestants—essentially from rural and small town areas, but with a sizable urban base—supported the law, the system faced local pressure. The Catholic community did not share the Protestant concept of the Sabbath—Catholics routinely petitioned for permits to stage football matches and to open bars on Sundays—and the urban, Protestant working class was less inclined to attend church and more likely to visit pubs or public events on Sunday.[8]

To Paisley and the NUP, Catholic evangelization was as serious a threat as public morality. A protest was made to the ministers of health and local government claiming that Catholic employees of local hospitals were preventing Protestants from evangelizing within state-run hospitals. Paisley joined NUP street protests, such as demonstrations against the mission that Redemptorist priests held in Belfast to convert non-Catholics. In October 1950 and April 1951, Norman Porter and Paisley appeared at NUP rallies in Pomeroy, County Tyrone, a contentious and divided town with an active Republican sector. Six years later the town's Republican community would become an important force behind the IRA's border campaign. During these rallies, a converted Australian Catholic, Monica Farrell explained the evils of Catholicism to the local Protestant community. Whereas Paisley shunned elected office, Porter used his leadership in the NUP to propel him into a Stormont seat. In October 1953, Porter ran as the independent Unionist for the Clifton ward of North Belfast and won on a Loyalist, anti-Catholic, and anti–Big House platform.[9]

Paisley's adherence to militant fundamentalism and his divisive accusations against Protestant allies, however, upset his coalition with Porter and the NUP. As shown in chapter 4, during the early 1950s Paisley began attacking Porter and fellow Irish fundamentalists, such as the Irish Evangelical Church, for their relationships with Irish and British Protestants who were not militants as well for Porter's and the Irish Evangelical Church's amillennialism. Paisley's cooperation with the NUP thus lasted barely five years. In 1952, Paisley resigned from the NUP after a controversy involving the Reverend Eric Borland of Bangor, the organization's vice president and a Presbyterian minister. Borland argued that Paisley threatened to create trouble for any NUP minister whose theology differed from strict militant fundamentalism. Paisley's willingness to attack fellow evangelical clergymen led Borland, Porter, and the NUP to vote him off its Ulster executive. But because he retained support from the main office in England, he was able to regain the organizational name for use in Ulster. It is interesting to note, in light of his future political career, that Paisley attacked Norman Porter for his political activity after Porter was elected to Stormont. Paisley argued that no practicing Christian minister (including lay preachers) should be an elected and paid public official, a position that the Reverend Carl McIntire supported.[10]

Despite their theological differences, Porter and Paisley temporarily joined forces again in 1956 to form UPA. Purportedly founding UPA at a meeting inside the headquarters of the UUP, the group's original organizers included a wide range of militant Loyalists from Belfast, notably Desmond Boal, a secular barrister and member of the UUP, and Billy Spence, whose brother would help to resurrect the UVF ten years later. UPA was established to defend Belfast against the expected IRA attacks, but when the IRA threat was contained to the Northern Ireland border, UPA concentrated on social and economic issues. For example, one UPA branch worked to prevent Catholics from obtaining public housing in North Belfast. The organization supported Protestant employment and pressed for unrestricted marching by Protestants because many Orange parades in the 1950s were banned or rerouted to avoid Catholic neighborhoods, most notably the Bovevagh Flute Band's procession through Dungiven (a heavily Catholic town) and the march down the Longstone Road near Annalong. The Public Order Act (Northern Ireland), passed in 1951, required forty-eight hours' notice to the RUC in order to obtain a parade permit; the act allowed the police to suppress marches deemed a threat to public order. Paisley articulated the Free Presbyterian position in July 1959 when during an early "Twelfth" held at the Belfast shipyards, Paisley and Wylie spoke to more than one thousand workers. The two clerics denounced the bans as an attack on Bible Protestantism and assailed Northern Ireland's home affairs minister and the pope for their complicity.[11]

His relationships with UPA and the NUP as well as his willingness to confront Unionist authority earned Paisley a reputation as an independent, a populist, and a demagogue. In March 1958, UPA became involved in local political campaigns, in one instance helping Albert Duff—who ran a gospel mission on Aughrim Street in Loyalist Sandy Row—to run for Brian Maginess's Stormont seat. Maginess, the minister of education and the husband of a Catholic, was attacked for policies the UUP introduced at Stormont, including state financing for Catholic schools and the withdrawal of the Family Allowances Bill, a plan that would have penalized larger and mostly Catholic families. Paisley also supported Duff, Charlie McCullough, and Free Presbyterian minister John Wylie in city council elections the following May. Cautiously disregarding his encounter with the Holy Ghost almost two decades earlier, Paisley became Duff's election manager after declining an offer to run for the office himself.[12] Maginess won the Stormont election with the help of Prime Minister Brookeborough, and Duff and the two others were elected to the Belfast Corporation. All three ran as Protestant Unionists, a loose political organization that Paisley helped to establish. In 1960, UPA put its support behind Desmond Boal to win election to Stormont, representing the Loyalist Shankill Road ward in West Belfast. But the success of UPA political activities was inconsistent: in the March 1958 Stormont election, Norman Porter lost his seat.[13]

In the May 1961 Belfast Corporation elections, the UPA ran five candidates, two of whom won—Albert Duff and James McCarroll, a Free Presbyterian layman. But Paisley's tactics, including directing the UPA to accuse rivals of employing Catholics, once again caused dissension. Paisley quit UPA several years later, although he continued to work with the group. For example, during the 1964 British general election, he and UPA supported James Kilfedder and helped foment the Divis Street riots. The NUP controversy and his membership in UPA had an important early impact on his political and evangelical outlook. Paisley was convinced that attacking enemies could bring political advantages and help maintain militant fundamentalism.[14]

However, many Free Presbyterians did not approve of their moderator's political activism. This attitude was pervasive in spite of John Wylie's election to the Ballymoney Urban District Council in May 1958. Wylie had run for office after the council revoked use of the city hall for Wylie and a Spanish former priest, Juan Juarte Arrien, to hold a mock Mass.[15] Nevertheless, the NUP and UPA became useful fronts to distance Paisley the emerging politician from his dual roles as a pastor and Free Presbyterian Church of Ulster moderator.[16] Moreover, Ulster Protestant Action inspired Paisley to form new political organizations in early 1966 that eventually led to the formation of a formal political party. The UCDC and the UPV, two organizations that were vital to Paisley's campaign against O'Neill and the Northern Ireland civil rights movement, played important roles in his politicization. (Paisley dissolved UPA almost at the same time that he developed these two organizations.) Both groups expanded his support base beyond the boundaries of the militant fundamentalist community; but many of these street activists were interested in maintaining Protestant political power and economic rights for the working class, not in protesting against the ecumenical movement or Christian modernism.[17]

Paisley proclaimed his political ambitions when he formally organized the Protestant Unionist Party (PUP). In the March 1966 British general election, Paisleyites campaigned against O'Neill's supporters within the UUP, standing as "Protestant Unionists." *Protestant Unionist* was previously an informal moniker employed after the city council and Stormont elections in 1958. The PUP was in essence Paisleyism as a political action group and a coalition between the Reverend Ian Paisley and the solicitor Desmond Boal, Paisley's new political ally. The PUP platform combined economic populism, anti-O'Neillism, and evangelicalism: the party opposed the appeasement of the Catholic Church, the civil rights movement, and the IRA; called for the defense of the union; and demanded new housing, local voting reform, and a program to ease unemployment. During the first days of the PUP, Paisley hinted at higher political ambitions: in an Ulster Hall rally in July 1966, he announced, "With the help of God and the Protestants of Ulster . . . the day is coming when I will be in the House of Commons [Stormont]."[18]

Four Paisleyite candidates stood for election in Belfast in 1966 in opposition to the UUP. All four lost, but in West Belfast their candidacy ensured the defeat of the Unionist James Kilfedder, who came in second to Gerry Fitt of the small Republican Labour Party. This was the same Unionist candidate Paisley had supported two years earlier and over whom serious rioting had occurred on Divis Street. Despite their complicity in the election, Paisleyites denounced Fitt's success as another victory for O'Neillism.[19] The PUP experienced a few early successes, such as Eileen Paisley's election to the Belfast City Council in May 1967 and the election of two councilors in Lisburn. In the February 1969 Stormont elections, called by O'Neill as a mandate on his policies, the PUP fielded six candidates. Paisley himself ran against O'Neill. Although none of the PUP candidates was elected, Paisley's showing was strong enough to embarrass the prime minister.[20]

After the election, the UUP voted to back O'Neill, but the UVF's bombing campaign, the election of Bernadette Devlin as the Westminster MP for Mid-Ulster in a by-election, and continuing civil rights activism led to O'Neill's resignation as prime minister on 28 April 1969.[21] Paisley viewed O'Neill's departure as an act of God, yet he, his militant fundamentalist allies, and his PUP supporters initially backed the new administration of Major Chichester-Clark, who tried to continue O'Neill's policies. The outbreak of sectarian street fighting in August 1969 and the deployment of the British army to the streets of Northern Ireland caused Paisleyites to reverse course. Since November 1968, when the British government had forced O'Neill to implement a reform program, many within Northern Ireland's Protestant community viewed British policy as appeasement of the civil rights movement and the Republic of Ireland. It seemed to Loyalists and supporters of the union that the actions of the British government were facilitating the resurgence of the IRA and that the British were considering abandoning Northern Ireland to the southern republic. Paisley and the PUP articulated these concerns.[22]

In October 1969, the British government released the *Hunt Report*, which blamed Unionist policies for Northern Ireland's outbreak of sectarian violence.[23] The report called for the disbanding of the Ulster Special Constabulary; the disarming of the RUC; the appointment of Sir Arthur Young, the London police commissioner, as Northern Ireland's chief constable; and the formation of an Ulster Defence Regiment as a unit of the British army. After implementing these reforms, London still did not have adequate control of security. Ken Bloomfield argues that the British government, by not implementing direct rule in August 1969 and assuming complete control of security policy, put too much pressure on Unionist–Catholic relations and allowed political Paisleyism to mature. For instance, the RUC and the "B" Specials were placed under the general officer commanding when deployed in riot control. To Northern Irish Protestants, British security policies seemed ineffective and too conciliatory toward the Catholic community. They particularly abhorred the existence of "no-go" areas; the British army agreed that the army and the RUC would not enter Catholic working-class neighborhoods and left the local residents to police themselves (mainly through the IRA). These areas became safe havens from where the IRA could plan attacks on security forces and organize a bombing campaign.[24] Yet British security policy was strong enough that the British army's action (for example, arms searches and the Falls Road curfew in July 1970) alienated many within the Catholic community. The IRA bombing campaign slowly intensified, and when the internment of Republicans was badly implemented, the IRA resurrected itself as a potent terrorist organization. After the "Bloody Sunday" shootings in Londonderry, during which the Parachute Regiment killed thirteen unarmed marchers protesting internment, British government policy foundered. For the duration of the "Troubles," no policy could simultaneously satisfy both Catholic and Protestant interests.[25]

The Fourth Year of "Trouble," the First Year of Amilitant Politics

During the months following the British army deployment in August 1969, militant fundamentalists in the United States showed a renewed interest in Paisley's crusade. It was imperative to this Calvinist fellowship to defend law and order in Ulster and to protect Bible Protestantism. To militants, Northern Ireland had become an important battlefield in the struggle between the Roman Catholic Church and militant fundamentalism.

Moreover, the appearance of Westminster MP Bernadette Devlin in the United States in late August on an extensive speaking tour to press the case of the Catholic community and the Northern Ireland civil rights movement made support for Paisley a vital exercise. Devlin, a Trotskyite but also the darling of Irish Americans, was given a warm reception and the key to the city in major cities such as New York, Philadelphia, Los Angeles, and San Francisco. A "truth squad" consisting of a two UUP politicians followed Devlin to the United States, holding news conferences and television appearances to refute Devlin's assertions about the situation in Northern Ireland and to expose the Bolshevik basis to the Northern Ireland civil rights movement.[26] The messengers were moderate Unionists—William Stratton Mills, who sat in the British House of Commons, and Robin Baillie, a Stormont MP—but were supported vigorously by American militants and were reminiscent of the "truth squads" that McIntire and the ICCC had employed to protest "Red" clerics in 1959. Two weeks later Paisley himself came to North America and retraced Devlin's route. Standing alongside the Reverend Carl McIntire, he belied to the American press Devlin's claims of discrimination in Ulster. Both the Unionist and Paisleyite truth squads made a political defense of Ulster Protestantism, although Paisley and McIntire did articulate some theological rhetoric.[27]

McIntire and Paisley presented the militant fundamentalist position. Paisley received more secular copy than he had during his previous tours of the United States as well as extensive coverage in Northern Ireland. In New York, Paisley and McIntire were refused an audience by Mayor John Lindsay despite the mayor's previous meeting with Devlin. In Los Angeles, Paisley argued at the Los Angeles Press Club that the Catholic Church was essentially a Communist organization. In Philadelphia, McIntire made sure that hymn-singing supporters met Paisley at the Philadelphia International Airport and that he received a warm welcome at the Bible Presbyterian Church in Collingswood, New Jersey. But Paisley's most important stop was in Greenville, South Carolina, where on 12 September he made a speech to the student body of Bob Jones University, a largely political message that talked about the escalating trouble in Ulster. He denounced Catholic attacks on Protestants, but not Protestant violence toward the Catholic community.[28]

The deployment of the British army was an important development in Paisley's metamorphosis from a premillennial preacher into an amillennial politician. The army's presence on the streets of Ulster gave the British government the responsibility for security and law and order, but the continued existence of the Northern Ireland Parliament gave Unionists legislative power over civic affairs. This dual control proved unworkable and helped the IRA to expand its support within the Catholic community, which in turn increased the support for both Protestant paramilitaries and political Paisleyism in response. In many ways, it became inevitable that IRA violence would escalate, that the Northern Ireland Parliament would be suspended in 1972 and direct rule from London imposed, and that Paisley's political activity would increase. As Westminster sought a political solution involving Ulster Nationalists and Dublin, Paisley and a wider segment of Unionism moved into a position of opposition to the British government.[29]

With British troops on the streets of Ulster and the British government seeking to thwart the growing violence with a political solution, moderates within the UUP could not simultaneously satisfy the British and fulfill the demands of the Loyalist and fundamentalist communities. Its failure created a political opening for new leadership that could articulate the demands of the Protestant working class and evangelical communities. At the same time, Ulster's secular warfare elevated Paisley into an even higher position within militant fundamentalism. In Northern Ireland, militant fundamentalists had fought a long rhetorical battle against civil rights, communism, ecumenism, and the Catholic Church. Now Northern Ireland became a physical battleground.[30]

In a show of support for Paisley and Irish Protestantism, McIntire and Bob Jones Jr. returned to Belfast in early October 1969 to open the new Martyrs Memorial Free Presbyterian Church. After visiting Belfast and viewing the damage from the riots of the previous month, McIntire held a press conference in the United States to announce that Irish Christian Relief (ICR) would raise money for Northern Irish Protestants affected by the violence. McIntire used his *Twentieth Century Reformation* radio program to raise five thousand dollars for the ICR. The militant fundamentalist media in America made the situation in Northern Ireland a prime topic. John R. Rice, editor of *The Sword of the Lord,* documented McIntire's trip to Belfast, expressed amazement that a substantial revival was taking place despite the violence, and urged American Protestants to pray for Northern Ireland.[31] Such support from prominent American militants bolstered Paisley's international stature. No longer just a martyr, Paisley was hailed as a "prophet," a description he did not discourage. As the safety and economy of Ulster faltered, he asserted that he was a modern-day Amos and warned of increasing violence and financial hardship. In control of the largest congregation in the British Isles and the most important European spokesman for militant fundamentalism, he turned his attention to the security situation in Northern Ireland.

10

The Second Coming

Paisley and the "Civil" Religion of Democratic Unionism

Throughout the first six months of the British army's deployment in Northern Ireland beginning in August 1969, Paisleyites remained fairly complacent. During that fall and winter, however, a previously dormant foe reemerged that impelled Paisley into action: the IRA.[1] The ineffectiveness of British government policy and the escalation of Republican violence accelerated Paisley's move into politics. His second jailing, the opening of the Martyrs Memorial Free Presbyterian Church, and his increased stature within the international fellowship of militant fundamentalists furthered his prestige among both church-going and secular Ulster Protestants and eased his transition into politics. From the 1970s on, Paisley's crusade slowly but steadily transformed from one against ecumenicalism and the civil rights movement into a political campaign. In early February 1970, the Protestant Union Party (PUP) fought two by-elections for Belfast City Council seats, winning both against UUP candidates.[2] Paisley's personal foray into politics came during the Stormont by-election in April 1970, when he won the Bannside seat that Terence O'Neill had vacated; the former prime minister had become a British peer. Although Paisley won only 43 percent of the vote, he outpolled Dr. Bolton Minford, the UUP candidate, and Pat McHugh of the NILP.[3] The voters ignored Minford's plea: "A Protestant Unionist government has nothing to offer the people, but fist shaking and words of hate. By voting for that party a Unionist is abandoning reason for a future of fear and uncertainty, and is turning his or her back on fifty years of solid achievement by the Unionist

Party."[4] Instead, many Protestant voters accepted Paisley's plea that Ulster needed deliverance. The April 1970 Stormont election gave the PUP two victories (Reverend William Beattie also won in South Antrim) and confirmed Paisley's new vocation as a politician.[5]

Paisley's victory accelerated the process that turned him from a premillennial crusader against Irish Protestant apostasy and Catholic civil rights into an amillennial politician. Militant fundamentalists in the premillennial tradition regarded the conflict in Northern Ireland as quite possibly the skirmish that would lead to the upcoming Battle of Armageddon. But how and when Jesus would return to rule God's Kingdom on Earth became less important to Paisley than defending the union between Northern Ireland and Great Britain—and hence Ulster Protestantism—through the political process. Instead of campaigning against apostasy in expectation of the Second Coming—a premillennial proposition that demanded the salvation of souls rather than political action—Paisley began working for political solutions, a tactic more in line with the amillennialist emphasis on temporal reforms. He never publicly articulated this view, but his conversion was exposed by his actions. Moreover, the Articles of Faith of the Free Presbyterian Church of Ulster, published in *The Revivalist* in November 1969, took an ambiguous stance on the Second Coming, calling it "the visible and personal return of our Lord Jesus Christ," a position that both pre- and amillennialists could take.[6] The Free Presbyterian Church mimicked the eschatological policy that Bob Jones University had adopted in the 1960s: any view of the millennium was acceptable, although the church discouraged postmillennialism and its liberal-modernist connotations. Thus, the theological relationship between Paisley and the Joneses strengthened, and Bob Jones University could support Paisley's political activity.[7]

No longer did Paisleyism constitute a crusade against apostasy and ecumenicalism; it became a political movement working to prevent a British withdrawal from Northern Ireland, to thwart Catholic political gains and the unification of Ireland, and to defeat Republican violence. It is one thing to protest against government actions as a concerned citizen, but another to be an elected participant within the political process. Although Paisley the MP continued in opposition to the Ulster Unionist Party, as a sitting MP he was required to offer workable solutions. His election to the British House of Commons in June 1970 made him part of the national government, enhancing his political dilemma.[8]

Paisley's victory splintered the UUP into Paisleyites, official Unionists, and the Alliance Party, a new coalition of moderate Unionists and Catholics. This fragmentation became official in September 1971, when Paisley and Desmond Boal turned the PUP into the new Ulster Democratic Unionist Party—the DUP. The new party was set up to articulate the political demands of evangelicals and the secular working class; the party name was changed to differentiate it from Protestant Unionism and to widen its base beyond Free Presbyterianism. Paisley's religiosity continued to overshadow his politics. In September 1971, he and Boal began regular meetings with right-wing Unionists and Martyn Smyth of the Orange Order—the Unionist Alliance—as a means to coordinate militant Unionist action. However, Paisley's prospective allies were wary of his militant fundamentalism.[9]

Paisley promptly embarked on a religious-political crusade as the DUP followed two tracks—one political, the other populist and based on Christian ethics. A four-headed political policy was pursued: to maintain the union with Great Britain, to denounce Unionist rule in Ulster as treasonous and incompetent, to reject any consideration of unification of the North and the South as the Republic of Ireland, and to defeat the IRA. The DUP social and economic platform sought to improve the economic lives of the working and middle classes, to thwart the liberalization of Ulster society, and to defend Irish Protestantism. The DUP proved popular to Free Presbyterians as well as to secular Loyalists. There is evidence that many former supporters of the NILP joined with the Democratic Unionists.[10] As an alternative to Ulster Unionism, Paisley and the DUP showed a willingness to promote contentious and unpopular policies. For example, they came out against internment because the policy could be used against Protestants as well as Catholics. Paisleyite opposition to internment was politically shrewd because the policy was ineffective; it did not seriously harm the IRA but instead helped Republicans recruit new volunteers.[11]

The "Bloody Sunday" shootings in late January 1972, the pending entry of Great Britain and the Republic of Ireland into the European Economic

Community, and criticism of British policy by important American politicians, notably Senator Ted Kennedy, placed enormous pressure on the British government. The Irish question had to be solved; devolved Unionist rule in Northern Ireland was accordingly doomed.[12] In March 1972, Prime Minister Brian Faulkner and his Unionist government were given an ultimatum—either Stormont with no control over security or direct rule. After the suspension of the Northern Ireland Parliament, Paisley and the DUP began a strong political offensive against the UUP and the British government, and the IRA military campaign surged. When it became known that William Whitelaw, the first British secretary of state for Northern Ireland, had secretly negotiated with the IRA in early 1972, members of the DUP felt vindicated; it was conceivable that the British government would abandon them to the Republic of Ireland. There were also indications that Westminster was alarmed over political Paisleyism. It has been argued that one of the many reasons that the Heath administration dissolved Stormont was a fear that Paisley was gaining political support and could conceivably become the Northern Ireland prime minister.[13]

At first, the DUP backed direct rule and integration as the best way to maintain the union with Great Britain and argued that a weakened Stormont could not maintain the political alliance. Paisley and the DUP asserted that the union would best defend "Gospel liberty" and preserve the Christian witness of the Free Presbyterian Church in Ulster. When this stance proved unpopular, the DUP developed a platform calling for devolution, with the largest party to be the head of government. In contrast, the UUP wanted to restore the Stormont Parliament. But when this policy appeared unrealistic, the UUP reversed course and advocated integration with Great Britain as the best way to protect Ulster Unionist control of Northern Ireland.[14]

The rise of the DUP coincided with the formation of Loyalist paramilitary organizations. Protestant paramilitarism was a response to the increased IRA terrorist activity and to direct rule imposed from London; a Protestant terrorist campaign began because Loyalists did not think British policies could defeat Republican violence. The same month that the DUP was formed saw the founding of the Ulster Defence Association (UDA), an organization that Paisley occasionally but cautiously worked with, but whose violence he consistently denounced. The UDA asserted a mutual reluctance and would not allow clergymen to join its ranks.[15]

On 21 July 1972, the IRA exploded twenty bombs in Belfast within sixty-five minutes, forcing the British army to invade the Catholic no-go areas in order to restore police control. Although the army's Operation Motorman compelled the IRA to retreat into a cell system that could only terrorize Britain into a stalemate, British security measures appeared to be a failure. With the mounting violence and Northern Ireland under direct rule, it was vital for the British government to find a political solution in Ulster. Although Catholic civil rights demands were being satisfied—Westminster introduced legislation to alter electoral boundaries, to promote equal voting rights in local elections, and to address housing and Catholic employment concerns—finding a provincial settlement that both fulfilled Catholic political aspirations and minimized Protestant dissent proved impossible. Protestant and Catholic positions appeared irreconcilable. The Unionist parties wanted an internal solution with majority rule and without Dublin's participation, whereas Nationalists looked to a settlement that included the Republic of Ireland. At the first intraparty talks held in England at Darlington in September 1972, only the NILP, the UUP, and the Alliance Party took part. The DUP refused to attend unless the British government began an official inquiry into several incidents in which the British army had shot Protestant civilians on the Shankill Road. The newly formed Social Democratic and Labour Party (SDLP), a Catholic party that advocated unification through the political process and pushed socialist policies, would not participate while internment continued.[16]

From this point forward, British government policy focused on five objectives: to defeat the IRA; to form a Northern Ireland Assembly, giving Catholics a role in government; to involve all political parties that denounced violence; to assure Protestants that the union with Great Britain would continue as long as a majority in the province wanted it; and to involve the Republic of Ireland in the political and security processes. The first solution proposed was three-part devolution: Northern Ireland would have an assembly elected by proportional representation, an executive containing Protestants and Catholics, and a Council of Ireland representing the British, Northern Irish, and Republic of Ireland governments.

The council would involve itself in cross-border matters such as tourism.[17] Over the next three decades, the British government consistently pushed variations of this scheme, and the DUP constantly rejected all such proposals, especially involvement of the Republic of Ireland in all-party talks and a rapprochement with Sinn Fein.[18] The UUP took a pragmatic stance, however, and was more willing to negotiate. Brian Faulkner, the new leader of the UUP, accepted power sharing and argued that preserving the union required compromising with the SDLP. Faulkner claims that his coalition with the SDLP worked well, but that the disruptive tactics utilized by the Unionist and Catholic grass roots doomed their efforts. For example, many Social Democratic supporters sustained a rent-and-rates strike, which undermined the policies of the SDLP leadership.[19]

The British government passed the Northern Ireland Constitution Act (1973), transferring the veto over unification from the Northern Ireland Parliament to the province's electorate; voters were given the same veto over unification that Stormont had reserved since 1921.[20] In the first Assembly elections, held on 28 June 1973, a coalition of the DUP, dissident Unionists, William Craig's newly formed Vanguard Unionist Progressive Party, and Protestant paramilitaries won twenty-six of seventy-eight seats. The UUP won only twenty-four seats, and the SDLP nineteen. The DUP took part in the election, although it asserted that it would not join the assembly if it won. It further argued that the election was a concession to the IRA and should have taken place after the IRA was defeated. An executive was nevertheless formed without the DUP, Brian Faulkner serving as chief executive and SDLP's Gerry Fitt as his deputy.[21]

To implement British government proposals, a new conference was held in December 1973. Out of the discussions came the Sunningdale Agreement, an accord calling for a Council of Ireland and a new power-sharing executive under Faulkner. The executive sought to bring the UUP, SDLP, and Alliance Party into a coalition government. The British government demanded a power-sharing government be formed—one that included constitutional Catholics (the SDLP)—as a condition for restoring a devolved parliament in Northern Ireland.[22]

In response, Loyalist paramilitaries formed the United Ulster Army Council and joined with dissident Ulster Unionists and the DUP to reject the agreement. When the first Council of Ireland met at Stormont, Paisley and DUP deputies protested inside the building and chained themselves to several benches, only to be physically removed. Professor Kennedy Lindsay jumped on the Speakers' Table and shouted that Democratic Unionists "have driven the money-changers from the temple." The UUP officially also turned against Sunningdale. The agreement suffered a major blow when Taoiseach Liam Cosgrove, under local pressure, denied that Sunningdale required the republic to give up its claim to Northern Ireland. In the February 1974 British general election, the DUP, the UUP, and Vanguard united into the United Ulster Unionist Council to oppose Sunningdale, winning eleven of the twelve Westminster seats.[23]

Frozen out of the Sunningdale Agreement, Paisley and the Democratic Unionists united with conservative Ulster Unionists and the right-wing Vanguard movement to support the Ulster Workers' Council Strike, which had begun in mid-June 1974. The strike aimed to shut down all public services as well as private business and force the British government to abandon Sunningdale. Paisley and Vanguard initially opposed the action, and as the strike started, Paisley quickly departed for Canada to attend a funeral. When it became obvious that the strike would be successful, both the DUP and Vanguard reversed course and publicly backed the Loyalists. For fifteen days, Protestant paramilitaries manned roadblocks and intimidated workers and businessmen into participating in the strike, severely restricting the delivery of electricity, gasoline, fresh food, and piped water. Although the British army refused to intervene, Prime Minister Harold Wilson went on British television and called the strikers undemocratic rebels and "spongers" on the British Treasury. Wilson's comments infuriated a wide section of the Protestant community and ensured the strike's success.[24]

The Ulster Worker's Council Strike and the British government's weak response not only wrecked Sunningdale but also effectively ended Protestant paramilitary political power and helped to drive these groups into a stronger military campaign and criminal gangsterism: if the paramilitaries could not be politicians, they would rule their neighborhoods as gunmen. Although many working-class Protestants looked to the UDA and the UVF as a defense against IRA violence, they were wary of voting for and giving power to men of violence. In the long run, the political impotency of Loyalist paramilitaries helped the DUP. Loyalists who disagreed with Paisley's theological crusade nevertheless now saw the DUP as the only legitimate alternative to the UUP. After the Ulster Workers' Council Strike, the DUP began to receive more votes from the secular working and middle classes and from evangelicals outside the Free Presbyterian Church.[25]

The Vanguard Party began to fall apart in May 1975 when Craig proposed the idea of an emergency coalition with the SDLP. Vanguard argued that the British government planned to withdraw from Northern Ireland and that only a compromise with moderate nationalism would thwart the IRA. Vanguard's fall from grace left the DUP as the only radical Unionist party outside of the small paramilitary parties.[26] Vanguard's argument proved unpopular; moreover, many Unionists were wary of Vanguard owing to its pro-independence stance and its association with paramilitarism. The demise of the Vanguard coalition took place four years later when Peter Robinson, the DUP's deputy leader, won William Craig's East Belfast seat. Over the next decade, Unionist political support divided between the UUP, the DUP, the Alliance Party, and a small electorate who still voted for the parties aligned with Protestant paramilitary groups. However, the need for Unionist political solidarity and the DUP's position as the second-largest Protestant party restricted the DUP's political fortunes: it cooperated with the UUP and agreed not to contest elections where a split Protestant vote would ensure a Sinn Fein or SDLP victory.[27]

Support for the DUP rose and fell depending on the security situation and on Paisley's ability to offer viable alternatives to British policy and paramilitary violence. For example, when Paisley organized a second Loyalist strike in 1977 to demand more security measures, the action failed because paramilitaries would not support it and because the British government acted quickly to defeat the strike.[28] At least twelve hundred new British soldiers were deployed to Ulster. Although the strike failed, the DUP doubled its number of councilors and won control of Ballymena—its first council—during local elections one week later. During the short campaign, the DUP effectively attacked the UUP for not supporting the second worker strike. But in the 1979 British general election, the DUP won only 10 percent of the vote, although it is fair to note that the DUP did not contest every seat. Several months later, however, Paisley was elected to the European Parliament.[29]

Paisley launched the short-lived Third Force in 1981, a group of armed Paisleyites formed to aid the RUC, the British army, and paramilitary groups against the IRA.[30] For a short period, Third Force rallies drew substantial crowds, especially in November 1981 after the murder of Unionist MP Reverend Robert Bradford. In Ballymena, Paisley displayed five hundred armed men to journalists, but support dwindled in the following year. Third Force activities also had limited political value. Graham Walker argues that the Third Force and its paramilitary persona temporarily restricted the growth of the DUP at the provincial and national levels.[31]

During this period, Sinn Fein also enjoyed new electoral support, a result of the blanket protests that Republican prisoners began in 1976 and the series of hunger strikes begun in late October 1980 that brought Republicans substantial Catholic sympathy. The leader of the strike, Bobby Sands, died during the protest. The fortunate timing of a by-election enabled Sands to be elected to the British House of Commons. Because of this political success, the IRA and Sinn Fein reassessed their schema that pressed military force to the virtual exclusion of political initiative and began their "ballot box and Armalites" strategy: the Republican movement would participate in the political process while continuing with its terrorist campaign. When Gerry Adams took Gerry Fitt's West Belfast seat during the June 1983 British general election and Sinn Fein won 43 percent of the Catholic vote, the policy appeared successful. The increasing vote for Sinn Fein forced the SDLP to radicalize its platform. For instance, after the 1982 election for the Northern Ireland Assembly, the SDLP refused to take its seats.[32]

Sinn Fein's expanding electorate and the continuing concerns over IRA violence forced a closer relationship to be formed between the British government and Dublin. After a summit in Dublin on December 1980, British prime minister Margaret Thatcher began a new attempt to implement power sharing in Northern Ireland and to find a role for the Republic of Ireland. The British government had previously opposed involving the Dublin government in Northern Ireland's internal affairs, including the Sunningdale Conference. The DUP objected to the Prior Initiative in 1982 to establish the Northern Ireland Assembly, and, as a result, in the 1982 council and Assembly elections and the 1983 British general election the DUP vote once again increased.[33] The London–Dublin rapprochement culminated in the Anglo-Irish Agreement, signed 15 November 1985 in Hillsborough Castle. The new agreement did not differ from the Council of Ireland in structure, but the Republic of Ireland was given a consultative role in Northern Ireland affairs, although the republic would not acknowledge the constitutional position of Northern Ireland as a part of Great Britain.[34]

The secrecy behind the Anglo-Irish Agreement dialogue and Margaret Thatcher's sudden acknowledgment that the republic must be included in a Northern Irish settlement shocked all Unionist parties. The DUP and UUP once again united to denounce the Anglo-Irish Agreement. The DUP led protests outside Stormont and at Maryfield, the offices of the secretariat set up under the agreement. On 23 November 1985, Paisley and the UUP leader, James Molyneaux, appeared on the same platform in Belfast in front of one hundred thousand Protestants and together held a meeting with Thatcher at 10 Downing Street. All Unionists resigned their Westminster seats in protest, and both the DUP and the UUP supported a Protestant civil disobedience campaign that shunned contact with British government officials, withheld rates, and disrupted the business of Unionist-controlled councils.[35]

The refusal of the two main Unionist parties to take part in cross-community political agreements and the reluctance of the British government to call a referendum on the Anglo-Irish Agreement furthered the political impasse. Although electoral support for Sinn Fein declined, IRA activity continued and Loyalist violence rose after 1986. Many Protestants believed that the agreement was offered to the Catholic community only because of the IRA campaign and argued that Protestants must apply the same pressure on the British government. Paisley once again employed the specter of paramilitarism. In 1986, he and the DUP leadership supported Ulster Resistance, an organization with objectives similar to those of the Third Force. At the same time, members of both parties joined the Ulster

Clubs set up by the United Ulster Loyalist Front, a paramilitary front group that threatened to take up arms against the British government. On 10 November 1986, Paisley and two DUP leaders, Peter Robinson and Belfast mayor Sammy Wilson, appeared on the same platform with Alan Wright, the chairman of the Ulster Clubs, to attack the Anglo-Irish Agreement. Paisley reputedly made comments that suggested nonconstitutional action. But the increased paramilitary violence and Paisleyite political rhetoric did not help the DUP; between 1986 and the April 1992 Northern Ireland elections, the DUP vote fell.[36]

In February 1987, Paisley and Molyneaux established the Unionist Task Force to better coordinate Unionist policy. The group produced *An End to Drift,* a report cowritten by Peter Robinson. The task force argued that Unionists must continue to negotiate, but to maintain majority rule and to push for devolution. The report only resulted in further Unionist fissure, however, and gave credence to the new political initiatives from Protestant paramilitarism, most notably the UDA's *Common Sense* proposals. *Common Sense* called for an independent Ulster with a new constitution and a provision for minority (Catholic) rights. The new threat of Protestant paramilitary violence and the continued DUP and UUP resistance to power sharing with Nationalists created an atmosphere that made the British government abandon the Anglo-Irish Agreement.[37] But the Unionists were not running the show: British government policy became more flexible toward the SDLP, the Republican movement, and the Republic of Ireland. On 9 November 1990, Peter Brooke, the British secretary of state for Northern Ireland, made the first of two speeches that argued British interests in Northern Ireland were not selfish and tacitly giving Irish republicanism political legitimacy. The same month that a back-channel dialogue between the British government and the IRA began, public discussions with Unionists, Nationalists, and the Dublin government continued. On 26 March 1991, the Brooke Initiative argued for a multistrand approach to all-party discussions. In the first strand, Northern Ireland's Protestant and Catholic parties would conduct direct talks, which would be followed by talks between Stormont and Dublin and finally by talks between Great Britain and the Republic of Ireland. In the final strand, Unionists would be considered part of the British team. The

Brooke Initiative was important: it set a precedent for future talks, sparked the first direct discussions between Unionists and Nationalists since 1973, and marked the first time the British government made public overtures to the Republican movement.[38]

In the early 1990s, electoral support for the DUP stagnated, and frustration within the DUP toward the party's inflexible policies became more evident. Its opposition to the UUP and British policies appeared ineffective. The loss of votes in April 1992 and the ineffectiveness of the party's boycott of Westminster and the Northern Ireland Office created dissatisfaction with Paisley's leadership: because all party decisions had Paisley's backing, he was personally rewarded or blamed for the party's successes and failures. To regain lost electoral support, in April 1992 the DUP joined with the UUP in the talks Peter Mayhew, the new secretary of state for Northern Ireland, organized between the SDLP, the Unionists, the British government, and ministers from the Republic of Ireland. The Free Presbyterians within the DUP were opposed to participation in the Mayhew talks, whereas the secularists saw the pragmatism in negotiations. The discussions led to another proposed assembly, to be elected by proportional representation based on the number of seats each party won, and for an executive appointed by the Northern Ireland secretary of state. Unionist ranks split as the DUP once again took a harder stance toward Dublin. The DUP did not want any involvement by the Republic of Ireland, whereas the UUP was willing to accept Dublin's involvement in committees that the Assembly established. The DUP temporarily boycotted the talks set for Dublin Castle in September 1992 and then followed an obstructive policy when the party returned to the negotiating table.[39]

The Brooke and Mayhew talks led to the Downing Street Declaration. Announced on 15 December 1993, the declaration continued the basic policy that the British government had pursued since 1973. But for the first time the Republic of Ireland confirmed the right of the people of Northern Ireland alone to determine Northern Ireland's future, and Sinn Fein and Protestant paramilitaries were brought into the political process. Following the Downing Street Declaration, the IRA and most Protestant paramilitaries declared cease-fires; both Protestant and Catholic paramilitary groups decided to join the peace process.[40]

The DUP, however, continued its defiance toward the British government. Paisley protested against the declaration with a demonstration outside the prime minister's office. During a meeting at 10 Downing Street, Paisley upset British prime minister John Major to such a degree that Major had Paisley physically removed. The DUP leader refused to believe that the British government had not made a secret deal with the IRA. His ire grew stronger after the British and Irish governments produced the *Frameworks for the Future* document in February 1995, calling for an Irish dimension—stronger cross-border institutions—and a strong pro-Nationalist agenda. *Frameworks* also made decommissioning a precondition for Protestant and Catholic paramilitaries to enter talks while negotiations continued. An independent commission, the International Body on Arms Decommissioning, was formed to address disarmament. Unionist opposition to *Frameworks,* however, ended Molyneaux's tenure as UUP leader.[41]

The DUP displayed its open contempt of British authority in a more threatening manner. Both Paisley and Unionist MP David Trimble—soon to be the leader of the UUP and future Nobel Peace Prize winner—shared a platform at Drumcree in July 1995 to denounce the restrictions on the Orange march through the area. The Drumcree standoff began when Catholic residents on the Garvaghy Road near Portadown petitioned to have the local Orange parade banned, and the RUC prevented the march from taking place. At one point, Billy Wright, the leader of the Loyalist Volunteer Force (an offshoot of the UVF that did not participate in the cease-fire), threatened to destroy police barricades with construction equipment. Called to Drumcree to ease tensions, both Paisley and Trimble made speeches demanding that the Orange bands be allowed to march, and the two joined hands after the parade was allowed to proceed. Paisley called the march "a great victory for Northern Ireland Protestantism." The Drumcree standoff continued in 1996 and threatened to end the new all-party negotiations chaired by George Mitchell, the former governor and senator from Maine. During the next ten years, the parade became a major flashpoint between Loyalists and the British government.[42]

Out of the Downing Street Declaration came a new round of all-party talks, which began in June 1996. From these talks developed the Mitchell Principles, a template for future paramilitary participation in Northern

Irish political talks. The principles included total and verified disarmament, the ending of punishment killings and beatings, and the acceptance of a peaceful political process. Parties that had not accepted the Mitchell Principles—the PUP and the DUP (two Protestant parties associated with paramilitaries) as well as Sinn Fein—were not invited. In his book on the negotiations, *Making Peace,* George Mitchell argues that the DUP worked aggressively to disrupt the talks and even boycotted the discussions, during which Mitchell was appointed chairman. The absence of the DUP made the UUP the sole agent for Unionism. The Belfast Agreement, announced on Good Friday in 1998, restated the basic principles of the Downing Street Declaration. Moreover, the British government repealed the Government of Ireland Act (1920); the Act of Union once again became the constitutional basis for the political existence of the Northern Ireland state. Direct rule from Westminster was to end as soon as a Northern Ireland Assembly was elected; three consultative councils that included Dublin, Scotland, and Wales established; and a referendum scheduled for both Northern Ireland and the Republic of Ireland. The latter tacitly acknowledged Northern Ireland's constitutional position as part of the United Kingdom when its government agreed to put the question to its citizenry. For the Belfast Agreement to be implemented, more than one-half of Northern Irish voters had to vote for its implementation, and a majority in the Republic of Ireland had to agree to change the republic's Constitution. All parties in Northern Ireland except the DUP accepted the provisions of the agreement, although a substantial minority in the UUP also opposed them.[43]

A majority of Northern Ireland's Protestants detested the Belfast Agreement, and the UUP was penalized for its support of it with a declining vote. In the Assembly elections of May 1998, the party won just a little more than 21 percent of the vote, its worst showing in any election since the establishment of Northern Ireland, although it still managed to win twenty-eight seats to the DUP's twenty. However, when David Trimble—formerly the radical Unionist of Drumcree but now the more moderate head of the UUP—agreed to form a Northern Ireland Executive that included Sinn Fein before the IRA agreed to disarm, UUP domination of Protestant votes was doomed. Paisley and the DUP adamantly insisted that they would never act as Trimble and the UUP had. Over the following five years, DUP votes steadily increased, and during the November 2003 elections for the Northern Ireland Assembly the DUP became the largest Unionist party. It advanced with the electorate because its platform best articulated Protestant fears and because it successfully argued that they could renegotiate the Belfast Agreement with the British government. Protestants were worried that the agreement meant unification, and many believed that the IRA's refusal to destroy its weaponry made any talks with Sinn Fein treasonous.[44] Protestant angst increased as substantial changes to Northern Ireland's administration were implemented. Unionists and Loyalists alike viewed policing (the Police Act [Northern Ireland] of 1998), judicial reform (the early release of paramilitary prisoners), stronger government action on Orange parades (the Independent Parades Commission), the new police badge, and the elimination of the Union Jack from police stations as concessions to the Catholic community and Republican violence. But the Belfast Agreement created a turning point in Northern Irish politics: in order for Unionists to continue to participate in Northern Ireland's political talks, all parties—including the DUP—would have to negotiate with Dublin.[45]

The Second Coming: Paisley and Amilitant Fundamentalism

As Paisley's political involvement grew, it took a toll on his theological commitment. In a significant episode in February 1970, the Reverends Jack Glass and Brian Green as well as thirteen Free Presbyterian ministers were arrested in London during a BCPCC protest against Queen Elizabeth II's audience with a French cardinal. They handed out a petition on behalf of Paisley, but the Ulsterman himself did not attend because he was preoccupied with the election for two vacant city council seats in Belfast. Moreover, two months later a third coast-to-coast preaching tour of the United States—to visit nineteen states and Canada—was canceled owing to his electoral campaign. Paisley was clearly beginning to focus on political matters.[46]

However, Paisley maintained his strong relationship with American militant fundamentalists and continued to make trips to the United States. The militant press continued its coverage of his political-religious crusade.[47] But because of his political workload as well as the deteriorating relationships between Carl McIntire and Billy James Hargis and within the American militant fundamentalist community as a whole, Paisley limited his visits to the annual Bible Conference at Bob Jones University and the meetings of the World Congress of Fundamentalists after the organization was founded in 1976.[48] These visits were interrupted in 1971 and 1972, however, when the US State Department denied him a visa, citing his inflammatory speeches and sermons. The ban, which added to Paisley's reputation among supporters as a Christian martyr, forced him to confine his visits to Canada and to push his message through intermediaries such as his wife.[49] The US State Department revoked Paisley's visa for a second time on 21 December 1981, citing his role in the formation of the Third Force. In the mid-1980s, Paisley used the political connections he had established in the 1960s and traveled to Washington, DC, to meet with Senators Strom Thurmond and Jesse Helms. Accompanied by Dr. Rod Bell of Virginia Beach, Paisley met with both senators to discuss the political situation in Northern Ireland.[50] Much of Paisley's transatlantic ministry was taken over by other Free Presbyterians. For example, the Reverends Ivan Foster and William Beattie made trips to the United States, speaking at militant fundamentalist churches and at Bob Jones University, and the Reverend Alan Cairns immigrated to Greenville, South Carolina, and pastored the second Free Presbyterian church in North America in 1976.[51]

Following his elections to the Northern Ireland, European, and British parliaments, the Reverend Paisley continued to use Christian themes in his political speeches and to employ militant disruptive tactics in religious and political settings. For example, his public statements began to contain a political as well as a theological message. He asserted that Britain and Northern Ireland were in an economic slump and facing IRA violence because the British had turned from God—Britain was nearing judgment.[52] Such Christian rhetoric helped Free Presbyterians to support Paisley's political fundamentalism. Paisley was concerned that Great Britain's secularization and changing public morality had brought God's judgment in the form of the IRA campaign. He compared himself to Amos, the prophet who warned Israel: "Prepare to meet thy God."[53] In October, 1972, the Free Presbyterian Church denounced British prime minister Edward

Heath's talks with the pope as illegal. Paisley, along with Free Presbyterian ministers and laymen, protested the archbishop of Canterbury's visit to Northern Ireland in the spring of the following year; denounced the talks between Irish Republicans and Anglican, Presbyterian, and Methodist clergymen at Feakle in December 1974; and opposed Margaret Thatcher's audience with the pope two years later.[54]

Preoccupation with Rome and the Irish Catholic Church remained a priority. Paisley—as both MP and minister—disrupted the first Catholic Mass held in the British House of Commons celebrated by Cardinal George Hume, the archbishop of Canterbury, in July 1978. During the fall of 1979, the Free Presbyterians and the DUP opposed the proposed visit of Pope John Paul II to Northern Ireland and a decade later (September 1989) led a new protest in Rome, which included Bob Jones Jr. and Brian Green, against the meeting between the pope and the Anglican archbishop of Canterbury as well as their attendance at a Catholic Mass.[55] In 1985, DUP councilors refused to attend an official function in Belfast because Cardinal Tomas O'Fiaich was to attend—sitting with a Catholic cleric was equated with sitting at public galas with Sinn Fein. A decade earlier three DUP councilors in Ballymena boycotted a Remembrance Day service when a Catholic priest was scheduled to take part. In December 1986, Paisley interrupted Thatcher's speech in the European Parliament, objecting to her rapprochement with Ireland and Britain's new diplomatic relations with the Vatican. He was ejected. In October 1988, he protested the pope's visit to the Strasbourg assembly, so vehemently that his microphone was turned off. Paisley, his church, and his party also attacked purely religious matters.

As the Troubles dragged on, Paisley and the DUP consistently combined fundamentalist and political rhetoric. For example, in 1981 the Free Presbyterian Church and the Democratic Unionists led an attack on the European Court of Human Rights; the court had sanctioned Britain for not extending rights to homosexuals in Northern Ireland. The DUP published an advertisement in the 18 November 1985 issue of the *News Letter* attacking the Anglo-Irish Agreement: "For God and Ulster, Dr. Ian Paisley M.P. as an Elected Representative, Calls on all Bible Believing Protestants to set Aside Next Lord's Day 24th November, as a Special day of Prayer for our Beloved Province. Psalm 107:27-28; Hebrews 11:6."[56]

Free Presbyterians and the DUP campaigned together on sabbatarian and moral issues during the 1980s, contradicting the premillennial opposition to a social gospel: Paisley's party developed a Save Ulster from Sodomy Campaign when the British government drafted the Homosexual Offences (Northern Ireland) Order; DUP deputy leader Peter Robinson protested the opening of sex shops in Belfast; and the DUP opposed extending the British 1967 Abortion Act to Northern Ireland.[57] They also picketed a gay festival in Londonderry and the showing of *Jesus Christ Superstar* at the Belfast Grand Opera House in the 1990s and protested the Heineken Cup rugby match held in Belfast on a Sunday in January 2004.[58]

In contrast to Paisley's rise through his ability to mix politics and militant fundamentalism, the careers of Carl McIntire and Billy James Hargis declined after 1966 because of their political activity, internal dissension within their ministries, and conflict with fellow militant fundamentalists. Major difficulties were the US government's restrictions on their radio ministries and financial capabilities and the waning interest in the threat that communism and the civil rights movement posed to Christians in America. Fighting the American government did not provide the long-term political benefits for McIntire and Hargis that opposing the British government had earned for the Reverend Paisley.

After John F. Kennedy won the US presidency in November 1960, McIntire came out aggressively against the election of a Catholic president whose willingness to negotiate with the Soviet Union made his administration's anti-Communist credentials suspect. Militant fundamentalists opposed Kennedy's cautious support for civil rights and social welfare, disliked his appointment of moderate and liberal cabinet members, and despised his handling of the Bay of Pigs and the Cuban Missile crises. Militants were also incensed at federal efforts to enforce court rulings over civil rights: for example, the registration of James Meredith at the University of Mississippi in 1962, the stand-off with Governor George Wallace in Alabama in June 1963, and the protection of civil rights activists during the Selma-to-Montgomery march in 1965.

However, militants such as McIntire and Billy James Hargis expected to pay a price for their militant activities. Immediately after Kennedy's election, McIntire wrote to Norman Porter expressing a fear that the

Kennedy administration would start a campaign to shut down McIntire's radio programs, a position that proved correct.[59] The political activism of militant fundamentalism inspired a federal counterattack. The Internal Revenue Service (IRS) investigated the tax-exempt status of militant fundamentalist organizations, and the Federal Communications Commission placed restrictions on radio broadcasts, the militant fundamentalist's primary mouthpiece and source of revenue. In January 1962, the Bible Presbyterian Church lost its tax-exempt status for its political activities; donations, which were no longer tax deductible, began to decline.[60]

Billy James Hargis and his Christian Crusade went through their own battle with the IRS after Hargis's attacks on the American government intensified in the mid-1960s. On the air, Hargis charged that Communists had infiltrated American domestic and foreign policy and denounced liberal policies such as the progressive income tax and the Great Society. On 22 September 1966, the IRS revoked the tax-exempt status of Christian Echoes Ministry, Inc.[61]

In 1964, the Johnson administration began to enforce the Federal Communication Commission's Fairness Doctrine, the policy that required broadcasters to offer free rebuttal time to those they attacked on the air. Washington also instructed the IRS to monitor the religious groups that engaged in political rhetoric. If such a station continued to present a political agenda, it would lose its license. The commission and the IRS investigated both the Christian Crusade's and McIntire's radio ministries. After a two-year court battle ended in October 1966, the Christian Crusade lost its tax-exempt status. In 1967, the Federal Communications Commission held hearings on the renewal of the radio license of McIntire's Pennsylvania station WXUR after numerous groups—including the Anti-Defamation League, the American Baptist Convention, and the Pennsylvania Labor Federation—opposed the militant fundamentalist programming. When the US Supreme Court in 1973 finally heard both the WXUR and the Christian Crusade cases, it upheld both the commission and the IRS. WXUR was forced off the air. The loss of commission licenses and denial of tax-exempt status meant not only the loss of important outlets to espouse the militant fundamentalist viewpoints, but the loss of vital financial income.[62]

McIntire's political and financial problems were aggravated by problems with other militant fundamentalists. On 31 October 1969, the ACCC passed a resolution condemning McIntire's leadership and his attacks on several council leaders—McIntire had argued that they were "soft on liberalism." Dissidents in the ACCC assailed McIntire's political views as well as his racial and civil rights biases. His opponents also did not like his excessive administrative expenses and questioned the transfer of an ACCC relief fund to the ICCC. The ACCC ultimately dropped McIntire from the organization's executive committee, and in November 1970 the Bible Presbyterian Church and several allies were expelled from the ACCC.[63]

McIntire retreated into his role as the leader of the ICCC and for a while maintained a good relationship with both Bob Jones University and Paisley; during the 1970 Bible Conference in Greenville, South Carolina, the university awarded McIntire one of the first Bob Jones University Memorial Awards.[64] However, strains in the relationship between McIntire and Paisley began to appear. For instance, the *Christian Beacon* did not mention Paisley's electoral victory in April 1970. McIntire did not approve of clergymen's becoming politicians—that is, except when it served his purposes (e.g., Norman Porter's election to Stormont in 1953). The stance contrasted with Bob Jones University's support for Paisley's political activities. Another source of contention was McIntire's adherence to premillennialism and disdain for post- and amillennialism.[65]

The relationship became problematic by the mid-1970s when Bob Jones Jr. and Paisley resigned from the ICCC and in June 1976 founded the World Congress of Fundamentalists. Although McIntire was invited into the new council, he declined the offer because he knew that he would not have a leadership role. Instead, he and the rump ICCC began to attack the new congress and its "neofundamentalist" form of militancy, causing Bob Jones Jr. to denounce McIntire and his organization at the Edinburgh meeting. A seemingly broken man, McIntire in his turn criticized the new militant fundamentalist group and its founders, proclaiming: "You do not have any right to call yours a world congress—I am the man who has world congresses."[66] McIntire wrote to Paisley with an ultimatum: apologize or all fellowship would cease. Neither the McIntire Collection at the Princeton Theological Seminary Libraries nor the

Fundamentalism File at Bob Jones University contains any record of an apology from Paisley.[67]

Paisley and Bob Jones Jr. disassociated themselves from direct fellowship with Carl McIntire after the World Congress of Fundamentalists came into existence. The new World Congress carried on the militant fundamentalist campaign against modernism, ecumenism, new evangelicals, the Catholic Church, and communism. In Edinburgh, Paisley met little objection from the attendees when he called for fundamentalists to involve themselves in political matters. He argued that it was God who chose which men would lead the Lord's battle, implying that he was divinely selected.[68] In this manner, militants could thwart the secularization of society and the modernization of Christian theology. Paisley easily won approval from his North American and British associates for his new political and religious crusade. For example, the World Congress passed a resolution in 1999 denouncing the British government's negotiations with Sinn Fein.[69]

When useful, however, Paisley, the Joneses, and McIntire would cautiously work together. Bob Jones University still supported the ICCC's work and would speak at the organization's conferences. For example, in the early 1980s McIntire joined the militant fundamentalist condemnation of Paisley's visa revocation,[70] and both Paisley and McIntire spoke in Toronto in January 1982 at a meeting of the Evangelical Protestant Churches held to protest Paisley's exclusion. In the summer of 1983, Paisley and Bob Jones Jr. shared a platform with McIntire in Vancouver to protest the WCC meeting in that city, although refusing to make it an ICCC protest.[71]

As fundamentalist involvement in American politics escalated, Bob Jones University had no trouble supporting Paisley's increasing participation in Northern Irish politics and his moderating Calvinism. However, other allies in the British Isles did. Jack Glass, the Glaswegian whom Paisley had ordained in May 1968, began to turn on his mentor in the early 1970s. At first, Glass imitated Paisleyite theological politics by addressing political issues and publishing his own reformed newspaper. He also ran for the British Parliament seat for Glasgow Bridgeton in the 1970 British general election, winning nearly 7 percent of the vote as an Independent Protestant, and for Glasgow Hillhead in May 1982. However, Glass soon accused Paisley of abandoning true Calvinism and adopting the more moderate Calvinism taught at Bob Jones University. Protesting that Paisley and Bob Jones failed to preach the gospel of John Knox, Glass and several congregants picketed the World Congress in Edinburgh.[72] The charge illustrated the split between Glass and his former militant allies—at Glass's ordination in 1968, Bob Doom, an American and fundamentalist Baptist and Bob Jones University graduate, had given the opening prayer. Although the Glass-led protest signaled a break with Paisleyism, Paisley and Green were able to set aside their differences in June 1982 when they led a protest march that condemned the visit of Pope John Paul II to Edinburgh. With his political actions, though, Glass betrayed his own leaning toward amillennial politics.[73]

The Bob Joneses and Paisley remained allies owing to their flexible theology and their mutual ability to avoid scandal. Both approaches enabled Paisley to become a successful politician. In contrast, other militant fundamentalist leaders of the 1950s and 1960s lost their power. As shown, McIntire's ego and management style alienated former allies. Moreover, the relationship between Billy James Hargis and his militant fundamentalist allies soured. As early as 1964, militant fundamentalists felt uncomfortable with Hargis's new theological positions and associates. He approved of new Evangelicals, such as Pat Boone—who were suspect for their Arminianism and charismatic services—and hired the Jesuit, anti-Communist crusader Father Daniel Lyons as editor-in-chief of the *Christian Crusade Weekly*. A decade later Hargis faced charges of hetero- and homosexual improprieties with five students and was forced to resign as president of both the American Christian College and the Christian Crusade. His ministry effectively ended. He refused to accept his fall from militant fundamentalist grace, and in October 1975 he announced his intention to revive the Christian Crusade to its previous glory. Despite a vigorous effort that continued until his death in 1997, he could never restore his ministry to more than a fraction of what it had once been.[74]

The Second Coming: Paisley, the Amillennial Politician

So how did the DUP transform itself from a party that espoused predominantly Free Presbyterian and populist policies into a pragmatic party willing to sit with Sinn Fein in government? What propelled it from a position subordinate to the Ulster Unionists to a position as the leading political organization in Northern Ireland? And what role did amillennialist politics and religiosity play in both changes? In retrospect, in the early 1970s there were indications that Paisley was destined to transition from a premillennial crusader to an amillennial politician. Clifford Smyth argues that in 1971 Paisley and Boal intended to form a political machine more secular than Protestant Unionism so that they could promote "earthly" politics and receive fairer coverage from the mainstream media. But at first this platform proved difficult: many DUP activists were Free Presbyterians who wanted only "saved" Christians to be eligible for membership, and the Free Presbyterian Presbytery's decisions could impact party policy. In June 1973, a church resolution allowed the Reverends James McClelland, William McCrea, and Ivan Foster to run for the Northern Ireland Assembly, thus expanding denominational influence over the DUP. The presbytery had previously only officially endorsed the candidacies of Paisley and the Reverend William Beattie. Smyth further asserts that the Free Presbyterian activists' religious commitment made them zealous proponents of Democratic Unionism and encouraged strong financial contributions. Moreover, during the 1970s Paisley would not allow DUP policies to violate the doctrine of the Free Presbyterian Church, and his "political fundamentalism" took on the demeanor of a fundamentalist revival.[75]

Despite the Democratic Unionist political revivalism, a fundamentalist–secular split developed within the DUP during the 1980s over the direction of party policies. Militants generally dictated the party's course, which limited the DUP's political effectiveness. For instance, the party's political and moral agendas made taking advantage of the defeat of the Anglo-Irish Agreement difficult. In the mid-1980s, the DUP was not ready to compromise its Christian ethics to gain votes from secular Protestants. In another example, Deputy Party Leader Peter Robinson temporarily resigned in September 1987, upset over the party's refusal to accept the Unionist Task Force report he coauthored and frustrated over Paisley's insistence on combining religion and politics. The militant fundamentalist influence was temporary and illusionary.[76] Fergal Cochrane asserts that during the 1980s the DUP increasingly secularized as it attracted more urban and professional voters and as Robinson turned the party away from Free Presbyterian morality. For example, Robinson convinced Paisley to rename the *Protestant Telegraph* to make the newspaper appear more secular: *The Voice of Ulster* was markedly more political in its news coverage, and *The Revivalist* became the sole Free Presbyterian mouthpiece, although it continued to print articles of a political nature (e.g., one on the H-Block issue in November 1982).[77] Moreover, DUP-run councils accepted Sunday openings and pushed the local option on alcohol consumption and sales, and moderate Democratic Unionist activists would attend political functions where Catholics and apostate Protestants were present and alcohol was served. The DUP's secular wing had made these accommodations to political necessity, but Free Presbyterians within the organization did not like them. The party could previously raise revenues only at fund-raisers that did not have alcohol, use games of chance, or allow secular music or musicians from liberal and charismatic churches. Paisley, as party leader, balanced the aspirations of both DUP wings and sought to hold the party together.[78]

In spite of the DUP's secularization—or possibly because of it—votes for the party steadily grew after 1998. The new support came mostly at the expense of the UUP—from 2001 through 2007, the DUP vote increased at every election owing to the popularity of its platform, both its economic populism and a hard stance toward Republican involvement within the political process. The DUP continued to support the counterterrorist activities and the local police forces' Protestant identity (which working-class Loyalists liked)[79] and pursued a hard-line political policy that restricted the Republic of Ireland to a consultative position in Northern Ireland's affairs. It maintained that Sinn Fein would be allowed to enter political talks only after the IRA disarmed and denounced terrorism. The DUP also opposed the Mitchell Talks, arguing that George Mitchell, as a Bill Clinton appointee, was biased in favor of the Irish Catholic position.[80]

For a while, the DUP maintained its hard-line politics. It denounced the Belfast Agreement and declared that, if elected to power, it would renegotiate the agreement, a position that attracted new voters. During the November 2003 Northern Ireland Assembly elections, it argued that it was the only Unionist party capable of revising the Belfast Agreement to Protestant advantage and in a manner that would restrain Sinn Fein's ambition. Many members of the UUP and the Orange Order accepted the DUP's shift; three UUP politicians, including Jeffrey Donaldson, became Democratic Unionists. The Orange Order's leadership campaigned against the Belfast Agreement and was hostile to the Parade Commissions, set up to monitor and control Orange and Loyalist marching. The Orange Order and the UUP became political opponents. In March 2005, the Grand Orange Lodge of Ireland voted to sever its link with the Ulster Unionist Council, and a majority of Orangemen switched their votes to the DUP.[81]

As the Democratic Unionist vote grew, however, the party began a subtle but important shift in its position toward Sinn Fein. Although the party had insisted it would not talk with Sinn Fein, in February 2004 DUP members attended a meeting at Stormont to review the progress of the Belfast Agreement despite the presence of Sinn Fein. Furthermore, when the DUP attended the Leeds Conference in December 2004, it made a significant alteration to its platform. It understood that Britain's price to reestablish a Northern Ireland parliament was a power-sharing agreement that would include Republicans (if the IRA decommissioned its arms). The DUP subsequently notified the British government that it would consider entering a devolved government that included Sinn Fein. But Republican criminal activity delayed the decision: IRA volunteers robbed the Northern Bank five days before Christmas and murdered Robert McCartney, a Catholic, in a Belfast bar fight in early January 2005. This violence allowed the DUP to rescind its decision. During the 2005 British general election, the DUP again insisted that it would never share power with Sinn Fein.[82]

At the St. Andrews talks in October 2006, however, Paisley and the DUP indicated they were ready to work with Sinn Fein. After the conference, Paisley stated: "Today we stand at a crossroads. We stand at a place where there is a road to democracy and there is a road to anarchy. I trust that we will see in the coming days the vast majority of people taking the road to democracy."[83] This statement was reminiscent of Terence O'Neill's Crossroads speech, which Paisley had ridiculed nearly thirty-seven years earlier. It showed Paisley's new willingness to violate both the principles of his five-decade campaign against "Roman tyranny" and traditional DUP policy. On 9 October 2006, Paisley drank tea and ate scones at Stormont with Sean Brady, the Catholic archbishop of Armagh, without an opening prayer being said first (usually a DUP requirement for any meeting).[84] In May 2007, the DUP agreed to form a government with Sinn Fein. But opposition within the party was strong: during party meetings, DUP leadership was attacked, and Paisley was heckled, forcing the DUP to cancel its annual conference for the first time. Many DUP activists and supporters, however, did not believe that DUP policy would change no matter what sort of speeches Paisley made; in the 7 March 2007 Northern Ireland Assembly election, the DUP won thirty-six seats to the UUP's eighteen.[85]

Throughout the DUP's history, the party has had to strike a balance between its Free Presbyterian support—which made up the bulk of the party in 1971—and members who either attended other Protestant churches or who wanted a more secular party. The internal relationship between these two groups has defined not only the party's personality and politics, but its relationship to the Protestant electorate in Northern Ireland. The interconnection illustrates what the party's soul had been for three decades: a compromise between Paisley's Loyalist, amillennial politics and his premillennial Christianity. His pragmatism exposed a trend that had been redefining Ulster's evangelicalism since the revivalism of the nineteenth century: the abandonment of hyper-Calvinism and the acceptance of earthly solutions to man's depravity and the work of the Holy Ghost. What made the transformation possible within Democratic Unionism and for many Free Presbyterians were the personality and leadership of the Reverend Ian Paisley. In the beginning of its eschatological transition, the DUP platform and persona conformed to Free Presbyterianism.[86] But when the party grew in voting strength and Paisley's politics began to alienate Free Presbyterians, longtime supporters of his antiecumenical and antimodernist campaigns muted their opposition in reverence to their party leader and church moderator. But dissidents appeared. The most notable was the Reverend Ivan Foster—the loyal Paisleyite jailed along with Paisley after the General Assembly protest in 1966 and a longtime participant in Paisleyite demonstrations, the DUP, and the Free Presbyterian Church. In the late 1980s, Foster began to express concerns over DUP politics. His attacks, argued in *The Burning Bush*, intensified after the Leeds Conference in December 2004. After January 2005, the Free Presbyterian Church itself condemned the DUP reversal, saying it was contrary to scripture.[87]

Paisley's transformation to amillennial politics was complete when in May 2007 he became first minister of the Northern Ireland government. His appointment set up the final battle in his political-theological transition; four months later the Free Presbyterian synod gathered to discuss the "new Paisleyism." To the Free Presbyterian Church, there was a limit to the cooperation between premillennial Christianity and amillennial politics. Many Free Presbyterians believed that the moderator of a "true" Christian church could not simultaneously be first minister of Northern Ireland, and so Paisley was forced to step down as the Free Presbyterian moderator. That Paisley resigned as the Free Presbyterian moderator instead of stepping down as Northern Ireland's first minister reveals the nature of his amillennial politics. For Paisley and his wife, the action taken by the Free Presbyterian Church of Ulster appeared painful. In a May 2007 *Revivalist* editorial, he denounced his critics and called himself "God's Anointed." Eileen Paisley referred to her husband as a modern-day Moses and attacked Ivan Foster and other dissidents.[88]

The reasons for Ian Paisley's rise as a prominent politician in Northern Ireland and for McIntire and Hargis's fall were similar: all three were men of strong personalities who could attract both passionate supporters and rabid opponents. Moreover, all three maintained antagonistic relationships with their respective national governments and their fellow fundamentalists. But as a member of the Northern Irish and British governments, only Paisley had the political acumen and stature to influence national affairs and to withstand government pressure; as a prominent militant fundamentalist "prophet," only Paisley retained the support of his denomination until the twilight of his ministry. His political ascent ended, however, when in May 2008 he resigned as first minister, and Peter Robinson replaced him as leader of the DUP. In the new world of amillennial politics, Paisley had played the political game expertly and risen to the top. But his success was short-lived; he paid the ultimate sacrifice and descended Mount Stormont into political retirement.

A revealing statistic that illustrates how Paisley was willing to build up his political career at the expense of his ministry is the status of the

Free Presbyterian Church in the twenty-first century. While the Reverend Ian Paisley's political fortunes skyrocketed, Free Presbyterianism stagnated. From 1971 through 1991, Free Presbyterian Church membership grew from approximately 7,300 to a little more than 12,300; in 2001, membership dropped slightly to around 12,000. The decline came in spite of—or possibly because of—the improved relations between the Free Presbyterian Church in Ulster and other fundamentalist churches and organizations in Ireland, including the EPS and the Evangelical Presbyterian Church.[89]

That many Free Presbyterians were frustrated with Paisley's politics is illustrated in the decline in attendance at Martyrs Memorial Free Presbyterian Church. In October 1969, Paisley attracted 1,800 worshippers every week; only several hundred attended Sunday services in 2008. Moreover, dissident Free Presbyterians picketed the annual DUP conference two years earlier, upset at the party's reversal on fundamentalist politics. The premillennial crusader of the late 1960s would never have let politics interfere with his primary religious mission: the return of Jesus Christ was expected any day, and the pretribulation argued by premillennialists meant that saving souls preempted earthly politics. In contrast, the amillennial politician of the twenty-first century could not allow evangelical work to interfere with the political process; the Christian church needed revival, but all the Elect had to do was contain evil and maintain a moral society, not establish God's Kingdom on Earth. It is ironic that the militant fundamentalist and evangelical reverend of 1947, the antiapostasy and anti–civil rights crusader of 1967, and the populist Democratic Unionist politician of 1987 would have opposed First Minister Paisley of 2007.[90] Although Paisley's transformation has simultaneously fascinated and bewildered observers of Northern Ireland, it has dismayed his former supporters. Ivan Foster articulated the intense feelings of betrayal and disappointment that long-term supporters felt after the DUP announced its agreement with Sinn Fein in May 2007:

> None who loved Ian Paisley would have wished him to end his political life with the godfathers of IRA murder and terror firmly entrenched in the joint leadership of Northern Ireland. . . . That is not what Ian

> Paisley entered politics to achieve and it is not what his early supporters expected. He leaves in power the very forces he rallied the Protestant people of Ulster to oppose, even unto the death. The memories of the man that I would wish to retain and cherish are those of his days as a mighty preacher when it was my privilege to sit under his ministry in gospel missions in tents and halls from one end of Northern Ireland to the other. Those were the days of conversions, of God's people separating from the apostasy of the ecumenical churches and an exposing of the Romeward trend.[91]

There has been much speculation as to why the Reverend Ian Paisley, after years of political and theological opposition to power sharing with Republican and Nationalist parties, chose to make a political about-face and enter into government with Sinn Fein. It is possible that someday Paisley will explain his decision; historians can only speculate until then. Ed Moloney presents a wide range of possibilities: either a long-term plan (derived in the early 1950s) or egotism and power or a desire to join the Unionist and British establishment or the influence of Eileen Paisley, who was in favor of such a move.[92] These proposals make good copy but trivialize Paisley's long career as both a political and militant fundamentalist crusader. In contrast, Patrick Mitchel comes closer to the truth when he hints that Paisley's political shift has theological underpinnings. Mitchel contends that as Paisley became more political, he relinquished his separatist, pessimistic premillennialism; he changed his theology as he adapted his politics.[93] The rumor of a second epiphany during the September 2004 Leeds Castle negotiations—that the Holy Ghost wanted revival through politics—is intriguing but difficult to corroborate. Moreover, the argument that Paisley has moved toward the position advocated by the Evangelical Contribution on Northern Ireland (ECONI) is too recent to analyze properly. ECONI was formed after Protestant resistance thwarted the Anglo-Irish Agreement as a means for Anabaptist and Arminian evangelicals to advocate cross-community political and spiritual dialogue. ECONI argued that Northern Ireland's Protestants had turned their back on God through their paramilitary, political, and theological support for Ulster as an "Elect" Protestant nation. Whether Paisley meant to or not, his politics after the Belfast Agreement took the same course. Perhaps the key to the shift lies in Ian Paisley's personal sense of destiny: although his belief that he had been anointed as "God's man" for the salvation of Ulster stayed constant, his understanding of what salvation meant changed significantly.[94] Furthermore, Paisley's continued references to his militant fundamentalist roots make his amillennial political transformation difficult to ascertain. As late as October 2000, he denounced the meeting between Queen Elizabeth II and the pope in a sermon called "None Dare Call It Treason," borrowing the title of John Stormer's militant bible of the early 1960s.[95]

Although the reasons behind Paisley's decision to accommodate Irish republicanism remain opaque, the consequences are clearer. Paisley and Free Presbyterians gained socially from the move, and the Paisleys were accepted into the British establishment. Ian Paisley was invited into the British Privy Council, and his wife, Eileen, was nominated to the House of Lords. Moreover, many opponents applauded Paisley's willingness to compromise, and the relationship between the Free Presbyterian Church of Ulster and Irish evangelicals improved. But Paisley suffered theologically when he lost his standing in the Free Presbyterian Church of Ulster and alienated many long-term supporters in Northern Ireland, as Ivan Foster testifies. To many fundamentalist Protestants, the Reverend Ian Paisley was no longer a prophet and a martyr, but an apostate and a Lundy. In contrast, Free Presbyterians in North America, who are now a separate presbytery from their Ulster brethren, reacted more favorably to Paisley's decision. Although the Free Presbyterian Church of North America had no official position on the power-sharing agreement, those who understood its significance took a more practical stance and backed Paisley.[96] One such supporter argued:

> I support his action. I believe he (probably to his own surprise) accomplished what no other power-sharing politician had done: he was able to have the IRA repudiate its armed campaign, Sinn Fein declare its support for the Ulster police service and court system and commit itself to the democratic process. Since Sinn Fein had gained substantial electoral support and had met the apparently unfulfillable standards set by

> the DUP, and since what the British government was about to do would have been disastrous for Ulster (abandon power sharing), I believe that Dr. Paisley made a wise and right choice.[97]

This statement expresses a reasonable assessment of the Reverend Ian Paisley's political accomplishments.

Paisley's decision to share power culminates his dual career as earthly politician and godly theologian. Like numerous political dissidents in Irish history—including Irishmen such as Eamonn DeValera and Michael Collins—Paisley accepted power when offered it. And, like them, he accommodated past principles for pragmatic politics. As a militant and fundamentalist minister, Paisley had to compromise his militant beliefs. Although it is practical to be a premillennial preacher and an oppositional politician, the head of a government must focus on the fundamentally amillennial task of building a better society in the here and now. However, to accept the Reverend Ian Paisley as a Christian of militant fundamentalist but sincere religiosity—and there is no theological or historical reason not to—one must accept that he believed he was doing God's will. In spite of his legacy as an anti-Catholic bigot and crusading Loyalist, by entering into government with Sinn Fein, Paisley has offered Northern Ireland its best chance to date for lasting peace.

NOTES

WORKS CITED

INDEX

Notes

Introduction

1. "7,000 See Church Opened," *Protestant Telegraph,* 11 Oct. 1969; Bob Jones Jr. to John R. Rice, undated, Fundamentalism File, Bob Jones Univ., Greenville, SC. Within his letter, Jones reported not only on the opening of the new church, but also on the British army's threatening attitude; Jones accused the army of preventing many worshippers from attending. But Jones was upbeat: that day 150 men and women gave themselves to God and became "saved."

2. In Northern Ireland, Loyalists proclaim a conditional loyalty to the British Crown (as long as the royal family remains Protestant) but will oppose the British government if British policy contradicts the Loyalist political agenda; their British identity is essentially imperial. Unionists support the political union between Great Britain and Northern Ireland and are loyal to Westminster. There is also a class distinction: Loyalists tend to be working class, whereas Unionists are primarily from the upper and middle classes. Complicating these identities, a working-class Loyalist can also be a Unionist, but it is rare for upper- and middle-class Unionists to consider themselves Loyalists.

3. "New Evangelicals," who wanted a dialogue with liberal Christians and who were willing to compromise with ecumenists, appeared after the Second World War—Billy Graham being the most relevant to militant fundamentalists. The WCC was formed in August 1948 as an ecumenical forum to eliminate the theological differences between various Christian denominations.

4. Ian H. Murray, *Spurgeon v. Hyper-Calvinism: The Battle for Gospel Preaching* (Carlisle, PA: Banner of Truth Trust, 1951), 66–99.

5. Robert G. Clouse, "Introduction," in *The Meaning of the Millennium: Four Views,* edited by Robert G. Clouse, 7–13 (Downers Grove, IL: InterVarsity Press, 1977); George Marsden, *Fundamentalism and American Culture: The Shaping of Twentieth-Century Evangelicalism: 1870–1925* (Oxford: Oxford Univ. Press, 1980), 66–68.

6. Bob Jones Jr., *Fundamentals of Faith: A Series of Chapel Messages on the Bob Jones University Creed* (Greenville, SC: Bob Jones Univ. Press, 1964), 5–56; Carl McIntire, *The Testimony of Separation* (Collingswood, NJ: Christian Beacon Press, 1952); Ian R. K. Paisley, *Christian Foundations* (Greenville, SC: Bob Jones Univ. Press, 1971); Ian R. K. Paisley,

For Such a Time as This: Recollections, Reflections, Recognitions (Belfast: Ambassador, 1999), 12–49.

7. Marsden, *Fundamentalism and American Culture,* 4–6; Ernest Sandeen, *The Roots of Fundamentalism: British and American Millenarianism 1800–1930* (Chicago: Univ. of Chicago Press, 1970), ix–xix; David N. Livingstone and Ronald A. Wells, *Ulster-American Religion: Episodes in the History of a Cultural Connection* (Notre Dame, IN: Univ. of Notre Dame Press, 1999), 7–10.

8. "Ulster Needs Deliverance," *Protestant Telegraph,* 13 June 1970. To Paisley and like-minded militant fundamentalists, "Bible Protestants" are those Christians who base their faith and practice on a literal interpretation of scripture and are for the most part independent of mainstream denominations.

9. "Were the Reformers Right in Separating from the Church of Rome at Reformation? By Ian R. K. Paisley," "The Pope's Pedigree," and "John Knox," *Protestant Telegraph,* 22 Oct. 1966, 28 Oct. 1967, 12 Dec. 1970.

10. Because Catholics suffered discrimination in public-sector jobs and Protestant-controlled companies, O'Neill needed to create better employment opportunities (E. A. Aunger, "Religion and Occupational Class in Northern Ireland," *Economic and Social Review* 7 [1975], 16).

11. Steve Bruce, *God Save Ulster! The Religion and Politics of Paisleyism* (Oxford: Oxford Univ. Press, 1989); Ed Moloney, *Paisley: From Demagogue to Democrat?* (Dublin: Poolbeg, 2008). In the 1960s, Loyalists opposed both the liberalism of the O'Neill administration and Catholic civil rights, while supporting the political union between Northern Ireland and the United Kingdom. In the 1970s, Loyalist political activism expanded to include opposition to British government policy; Loyalists detested Westminster's efforts to bring Ulster's Catholic community and the Republic of Ireland into a political settlement in Northern Ireland and thought British security policy ineffective.

12. Marsden, *Fundamentalism and American Culture,* 1–61. Fundamentalists opposed the loosening of public morality, liberal intellectual ideas, and the cultural influences that arose out of Roman Catholic, Eastern Orthodox, and Jewish immigration.

13. Livingstone and Wells, 101–37.

14. Steve Bruce, *Paisley: Religion and Politics in Northern Ireland* (Oxford: Oxford Univ. Press, 2007), 20–21.

15. James Morris, *The Preachers* (New York: St. Martin's Press, 1973), 189–231.

16. "Bible Conference Notes," *Fellowship News,* 27 Apr. 1968.

17. Tim Pat Coogan, *The Troubles: Ireland's Ordeal, 1966–1995, and the Search for Peace* (London: Hutchinson, 1995), 60–82; Jonathan Bardon, *A History of Ulster* (Belfast: Blackstaff Press, 1992), 664–72.

18. "Dr Paisley Held in Custody for 3 Hours by British Army," *Protestant Telegraph,* 27 Sept. 1969.

19. "Ulster Needs Deliverance," *Protestant Telegraph,* 13 June 1970. Although no author is attributed to this article or to most other articles from the *Protestant Telegraph,* all opinions expressed in the paper follow those of the editor—Paisley—or were directly written by him.

20. W. J. Grier, *The Momentous Event: A Discussion of Scripture Teaching on the Second Advent* (Edinburgh: Banner of Truth Trust, 1976), 16–17.

21. "Exclusive Interview with the *Observer*" and "Dr. Paisley Acceptable as Prime Minister," *Protestant Telegraph,* 9 May 1970 and 16 Oct. 1971; Patrick Mitchel, *Evangelicalism and National Identity in Ulster 1921–1998* (Oxford: Oxford Univ. Press, 2003). In his interview with the *Ballymena Observer,* Paisley was asked how a Protestant clergyman could be involved in politics. He replied, "[A minister] should be a Christian in his home, in his business, in society and in politics. Politics is a very important part of society. In normal times I do not think that a Christian minister should stand as a Member of Parliament, but when the situation is such as it is in Ulster today, when the very heritage of our Protestantism is at stake, Protestant ministers, I feel, should be giving a lead to their people." The October 1971 article cites the *Spectator,* which argued that because Paisleyism was such a popular force, Ulster Protestants in the future would demand Paisley as their prime minister.

22. To Free Presbyterians, however, such a scenario would have been of immense historical and theological importance.

23. "U.D.U.P. Election Manifesto," "DUP Says No to Power-Sharing," and "A Short History of the D.U.P. by David Calvert," *Protestant Telegraph,* 23 June 1973; Apr. 1980; 20 June, 11 July, and 8 Aug. 1981.

24. "Sharing with Murderer—Right or Wrong?" "Press Statement from the Presbytery of Ulster," and "Presbytery Statement of Rededication Following the Election of a New Moderator," *The Burning Bush,* July 2007 and Sept. 2007. In 1951, the Free Presbyterian Church of Ulster did employ a temporary moderator until Paisley took over.

25. Email message to the author from the Reverend Ian Foster, 19 Mar. 2008.

26. Anders Boserup, "Contradictions and Struggles in Northern Ireland," *Socialist Register* (1972), 174; John Darby, *Conflict in Northern Ireland: The Development of a Polarised Community* (Dublin: Gill and MacMillan Books, 1976).

27. J. R. Archer, "The Unionist Tradition in Ireland," *Eire-Ireland* 15 (1980): 47–53; David Gordon, *The O'Neill Years: Unionist Politics, 1963–1969* (Cork, Ireland: Athol Books, 1969), 7–9; Arend Lijphart, "The Northern Ireland Problem: Cases, Theories, and Solutions," *British Journal of Political Science* 5 (1975): 92–94.

28. Aunger, 16; Derek Birrell, "Relative Depravation as a Factor in Conflict in Northern Ireland," *Sociological Review* 20 (1972): 321–25.

29. Paul Bew, Peter Gibbon, and Henry Patterson, *The State in Northern Ireland, 1921–72: Political Forces and Social Classes* (Manchester, UK: Manchester University

Press, 1979); Michael Farrell, *Northern Ireland: The Orange State* (London: Pluto Press, 1976); Liam Paor, *Divided Ulster* (Harmondsworth, UK: Penguin, 1970).

30. A. T. Q. Stewart, *The Narrow Ground: Aspects of Ulster, 1609–1969* (London: Faber and Faber, 1977).

31. Ed Moloney and Andy Pollak, *Paisley* (Dublin: Poolbeg Press, 1986); Patrick Marrinan, *Paisley: Man of Wrath* (Dublin: Anvil Books, 1973); Clifford Smyth, *Ian Paisley: Voice of Protestant Ulster* (Edinburgh: Scottish Academic Press, 1987); Steve Bruce, *No Pope of Rome! Anti-Catholicism in Modern Scotland* (Edinburgh: Mainstream, 1985); Bruce, *God Save Ulster!*

32. Bruce, *God Save Ulster!*

33. Owen Dudley Edwards, *The Sins of Our Fathers: The Roots of Conflict in Northern Ireland* (Dublin: Gill and MacMillan, 1970), 44–49; Martha Abele MacIver, "Militant Protestant Political Ideology: Ian Paisley and the Reformation Tradition," Ph.D. diss., Univ. of Michigan, 1984, 263; F. Eugene Scott, "The Political Preaching Tradition in Ulster: Prelude to Paisley," *Western Speech Communications* (Fall 1976): 249–59. See also Martha Abele MacIver, "Ian Paisley and the Reformed Tradition," *Political Studies* 35 (Sept. 1987): 359–79. Paisley's connection with McIntire and the Jones family is also briefly mentioned in Don Abbott, "Ian Paisley: Evangelism and Confrontation in Northern Ireland," *Today's Speech* (Fall 1973): 49–55.

34. A select historiography of the studies published after the Good Friday Agreement includes: Arthur Aughey, *The Politics of Northern Ireland: Beyond the Belfast Agreement* (New York: Routledge, 2005); Kenneth Bloomfield, *A Tragedy of Errors: The Government and Misgovernment of Northern Ireland* (Liverpool: Liverpool Univ. Press, 2007); Brian Barton and Patrick J. Roche, eds., *The Northern Ireland Question: The Peace Process and the Belfast Agreement* (Houndmills, UK: Palgrave MacMillan, 2009); Derek Birrell, *Direct Rule and the Government of Northern Ireland* (Manchester, UK: Manchester Univ. Press, 2009); Colin Coulter and Michael Murray, eds., *Northern Ireland after the Troubles: A Society in Transition* (Manchester, UK: Manchester Univ. Press, 2008); Paul Dixon, *Northern Ireland: The Politics of Peace and War* (Houndmills, UK: Palgrave, 2001); Christopher Farrington, *Ulster Unionism and the Peace Process in Northern Ireland* (Houndmills, UK: Palgrave MacMillan, 2006); Carolyn Gallaher, *After the Peace: Paramilitaries in Post-accord Northern Ireland* (Ithaca, NY: Cornell Univ. Press, 2007); Michael Kerr, *Transforming Unionism: David Trimble and the 2005 General Election* (Dublin: Irish Academic Press, 2006); Roger MacGinty and John Darby, *Guns and Government: The Management of the Northern Ireland Peace Process* (Houndmills, UK: Palgrave, 2002); Catherine O'Donnell, *Fianna Fail, Irish Republicanism, and the Northern Ireland Troubles, 1968–2005* (Dublin: Irish Academic Press, 2007); Brendan O'Duffy, *British–Irish Relations and Northern Ireland: From Violent Politics to Conflict Regulation* (Dublin: Irish Academic Press, 2007); Henry Patterson and Eric Kaufmann, *Unionism and Orangeism in Northern Ireland since 1945* (Manchester, UK: Manchester Univ. Press, 2007); Graham Spencer, *The*

State of Loyalism in Northern Ireland (Houndmills, UK: Palgrave, 2008); Graham Walker, *A History of the Ulster Unionist Party: Protest, Pragmatism, and Pessimism* (Manchester, UK: Manchester Univ. Press, 2004); and Ian S. Wood, *Crimes of Loyalty: A History of the UDA* (Edinburgh: Edinburgh Univ. Press, 2006).

35. Gladys Ganiel, *Evangelicalism and Conflict in Northern Ireland* (Houndmills, UK: Palgrave, 2008); Gladys Ganiel, "Ulster Says Maybe: The Restructuring of Evangelical Politics in Northern Ireland," *Irish Political Studies* 21 (June 2006): 137–55.

36. Moloney, *Paisley,* 499–516; Bruce, *Paisley,* 163–66; Patrick Mitchel, "Unionism and the Eschatological 'Fate' of Ulster," in *Protestant Millennialism, Evangelicalism, and Irish Society, 1790–2005,* edited by Crawford Gribben and Andrew R. Holmes (Houndmills, UK: Palgrave, 2006), 226.

37. Steve Bruce and Martha MacIver appear to be the only scholars of Paisleyism to have extensively researched the archives at Bob Jones University.

1. The Transatlantic Background to Fundamentalism

1. Bruce, *God Save Ulster!* 27–30; Ian R. K. Paisley, *My Father and Mother: A Loving Tribute by Their Younger Son* (Belfast: Martyrs Memorial, 1976), 4–5.

2. Bruce, *Paisley;* Moloney, *Paisley,* 3–6.

3. Bruce, *God Save Ulster!* 27–30; Moloney, *Paisley,* 7–8; Paisley, *My Father and Mother.* Ballymena maintains a temperate reputation owing to its numerous Presbyterian churches and its devout Puritan and evangelical morality. It is no coincidence that the 1859 Ulster Revival began near the town.

4. Ian R. K. Paisley, *Nicholson Centenary 1876–1976: From Civil War to Revival Victory* (Belfast: Martyr's Memorial, 1976). I discuss Nicholson's ministry in Northern Ireland in chapter 4.

5. Reverend R. J. Beggs, *Great Is Thy Faithfulness: An Account of the Ministry of Pastor James Kyle Paisley and a History of the Separatist Testimony in Ballymena* (Ballymena, Northern Ireland: Ballymena Free Presbyterian Church, n.d.), 5–15; Bruce, *God Save Ulster!* 28–30; Paisley, *My Father and Mother;* Joshua Thompson, *Century of Grace: The Baptist Union of Ireland, a Short History 1895–1995* (Belfast: Baptist Union of Ireland, 1995), 107–12. A Puritan influence can be attributed to Kyle Paisley's Scottish-born wife, Isabella Turnbull, who was conceived into a Covenanter background and who despised modern things such as cinemas and lipstick. Although raised in a Reformed Presbyterian household, Turnbull became a staunch Baptist while still a teenager. After immigrating to Northern Ireland, she occasionally preached to the Lurgan Baptist Church.

6. Quoted in Beggs, 18.

7. I. Murray, *Spurgeon v. Hyper-Calvinism,* 66–99; Craig Skinner, *Spurgeon and Son: The Forgotten Story of Thomas Spurgeon and His Famous Father, Charles Haddon Spurgeon* (Grand Rapids, MI: Kregel, 1999), 79–96.

8. Quoted in Beggs, 17. As a preacher, the Reverend Ian Paisley made numerous references to the Reformation: "The Reformers knew from personal experience that Rome turned the Pardon of God into a Profanity. . . . As Protestants, we must remember the past. What happened when Rome ruled supreme? . . . [H]istorians, both Roman and Reformed, call this period the 'Dark Ages'" ("Protestants Remember!" *Protestant Telegraph,* 16 July 1966). Also see Ian R. K. Paisley, *The Battle of the Reformation: Why It Must Be Fought Today* (Belfast: Puritan, 1967).

9. Paisley, *My Father and Mother,* 5–7.

10. Leigh Eric Schmidt, *Holy Fairs: Scotland and the Making of American Revivalism* (Grand Rapids, MI: Eerdmans, 2001), 11–21.

11. David W. Miller, "Religious Commotions in the Scottish Diaspora: A Transatlantic Perspective on 'Evangelicalism' in a Mainline Denomination," in *Ulster Presbyterians in the Atlantic World: Religion, Politics, and Identity,* edited by David A. Wilson and Mark G. Spencer, 22–38 (Dublin: Four Courts Press, 2006).

12. Marilyn J. Westerkamp, *The Triumph of the Laity: Scots-Irish Piety and the Great Awakening, 1625–1760* (Oxford: Oxford Univ. Press, 1988), 15–42.

13. Ibid., 43–73; Schmidt, 32–41.

14. R. F. G. Holmes, *Our Irish Presbyterian Heritage* (Belfast: Presbyterian Church in Ireland, 1985), 124–31.

15. The Westminster Confession of Faith professes belief in the Trinity; the Atonement and Resurrection of Jesus; double predestination (the idea that God predetermines not only who will be saved, but who will be damned); and the argument that the pope is the Antichrist foreseen in Revelation.

16. Peter Brooke, *Ulster Presbyterianism: The Historical Perspective 1619–1970* (New York: St. Martin's Press, 1987), 93–103; Ian McBride, *Ulster Presbyterianism and Irish Radicalism in the Late Eighteenth Century* (Oxford: Clarendon Press, 1998), 72–83; David W. Miller, "Did Ulster Presbyterians Have a Devotional Revolution?" in *Evangelicals and Catholics in Nineteenth-Century Ireland,* edited by James H. Murphy, 38–54 (Dublin: Four Courts Press, 2005).

17. Andrew Holmes, *The Shaping of Ulster Presbyterian Belief and Practice, 1770–1840* (Oxford: Oxford Univ. Press, 2006), 30–51; Janice Holmes, *Religious Revivals in Britain and Ireland 1859–1905* (Dublin: Irish Academic Press, 2000), xi–xxii; Patrick Griffin, *The People with No Name: Ireland's Ulster Scots, America's Scots Irish, and the Creation of a British Atlantic World, 1689–1714* (Princeton, NJ: Princeton Univ. Press, 2001), 143–59.

18. R. J. Dickson, *Ulster Emigration to Colonial America 1718–1775* (London: Routledge and Kegan Paul, 1966), 1–59. The term *Ulster Scot* is used in the British Isles to describe those Scottish Presbyterians who beginning in the sixteenth century immigrated into Northern Ireland. Some of these migrants eventually left for the American colonies, where in the nineteenth century—after the influx of several million Irish Catholics—they adopted the moniker *Scotch Irish.*

19. Griffin, 115–24.

20. Sydney E. Ahlstrom, *A Religious History of the American People* (New Haven, CT: Yale Univ. Press, 1972), 267–72; James H. Smylie, *A Brief History of the Presbyterians* (Louisville, KY: Geneva Press, 1996), 43–46.

21. Brooke, 93–103.

22. "The Armagh Manifesto" and "Ecumenical Evangelism," *The Revivalist*, Oct. 1965 and Nov. 1965; E. Brooks Holifield, *Theology in America: Christian Thought from the Age of the Puritans to the Civil War* (New Haven, CT: Yale Univ. Press, 2003), 92–101.

23. Westerkamp, 136–213.

24. James G. Leyburn, *The Scotch-Irish: A Social History* (Chapel Hill: Univ. of North Carolina Press, 1989).

25. Smylie, 62–67.

26. George M. Marsden, *The Evangelical Mind and the New School Presbyterian Experience: A Case Study of Thought and Theology in Nineteenth-Century America* (New Haven, CT: Yale Univ. Press, 1970), 6–17.

27. Mark A. Noll, *A History of Christianity in the United States and Canada* (Grand Rapids, MI: Eerdmans, 1992), 167; Schmidt, 59–68.

28. Smylie, 68–73.

29. Richard Carwardine, *Transatlantic Revivalism: Popular Evangelicalism in Britain and America, 1790–1865* (Westport, CT: Greenwood Press, 1978), 3–10; Garth M. Rosell, "Charles G. Finney: His Place in the Stream of American Evangelism," in *The Evangelical Tradition in America*, edited by Leonard I. Sweet, 131–47 (Macon, GA: Mercer Univ. Press, 1980).

30. James F. Findlay Jr., *Dwight L. Moody: American Evangelist 1837–1899* (Chicago: Univ. of Chicago Press, 1969), 28–135.

31. Schmidt, 202–12.

32. New School Presbyterianism modified its Calvinism to deny original sin and add the regenerating work of the Holy Ghost with revivalism, moral reform, and interdenominational cooperation. Charles Grandison Finney was an important New Schooler.

33. Marsden, *The Evangelical Mind*, 48–58.

34. Samuel S. Hill, *Southern Churches in Crisis Revisited* (Tuscaloosa: Univ. of Alabama Press, 1999), 58–79; Marsden, *The Evangelical Mind*, 199–229; Donald G. Matthews, *Religion in the Old South* (Chicago: Univ. of Chicago Press, 1977), 38–52.

35. Carwardine, 3–18; Bradley J. Longfield, *The Presbyterian Controversy: Fundamentalists, Modernists, and Moderates* (Oxford: Oxford Univ. Press, 1991), 132–61.

36. Ahlstrom, 774–79; George M. Marsden, *Understanding Fundamentalism and Evangelicalism* (Grand Rapids, MI: Eerdmans, 1991), 7–36.

37. William R. Hutchinson, *The Modernist Impulse in American Protestantism* (Cambridge, MA: Harvard Univ. Press, 1976), 76–87; Edward J. Larson, *Summer of the Gods: The Scopes Trial and America's Continuing Debate over Science and Religion* (New York:

Basic Books, 1997), 11–30; James R. Moore, *The Post-Darwinian Controversies: A Study of the Protestant Struggle to Come to Terms with Darwin in Great Britain and America 1870–1990* (Cambridge: Cambridge Univ. Press, 1979), 346–51.

38. Ahlstrom, 785–95; Marsden, *Understanding Fundamentalism,* 27–32.

39. Marsden, *The Evangelical Mind,* 82–87, 142–81; Marsden, *Understanding Fundamentalism,* 36–39. The concept of ultra-Calvinism became important to militant fundamentalists such as Paisley and Bob Jones Jr. as their political activities grew. Starting in the 1970s, Paisley and Jones attacked the opponents of their evangelical and political efforts as hyper-Calvinists.

40. Nathan O. Hatch, "Millennialism and Popular Religion in the Early Republic," in Sweet, ed., *The Evangelical Tradition in America,* 113–30; Sandeen, ix–xix, 101–2, 194–351; Timothy P. Weber, "Premillenialism and the Branches of Evangelicalism," in *The Variety of American Evangelicalism,* edited by Donald Dayton and Robert Johnston, 5–21 (Knoxville: Univ. of Tennessee Press, 1991).

41. Paul Boyer, *When Time Shall Be No More: Prophecy Belief in Modern American Culture* (Cambridge, MA: Harvard Univ. Press, 1992), 87–90; Sandeen, 59–80.

42. Boyer, 56–79.

43. Marsden, *Fundamentalism and American Culture,* 49–68; Sandeen, 3–132.

44. Findlay, 339–87.

45. Marsden, *Fundamentalism and American Culture,* 62–63; Marsden, *The Evangelical Mind,* 190–249; see also Sandeen, 132–36.

46. Dale T. Knobel, *America for the Americans: The Nativist Movement in the United States* (New York: Twayne, 1996); Richard Powers, *Not Without Honor: The History of American Anti-communism* (New York: Free Press, 1995).

47. *The Fundamentals: A Testimony to Truth,* 12 vols. (Los Angeles: Bible Institute of Los Angeles, 1917); Louis Gasper, *The Fundamentalist Movement* (The Hague: Mouton, 1963), 1–20; Larson, 11–59; Marsden, *Fundamentalism and American Culture,* 118–30.

48. Longfield, 3–27; Sandeen, 249–50.

49. The Virginia seminary should not be confused with Union Theological Seminary in New York City, also a Presbyterian institution.

50. William Jennings Bryan, *In His Image* (New York: Fleming H. Revell, 1922); Larson, 31–59.

51. Marsden, *Fundamentalism and American Culture*; Joel A. Carpenter, *Revive Us Again: The Reawakening of American Fundamentalism* (Oxford: Oxford Univ. Press, 1997); Larson, *Summer of the Gods.*

52. Within the American Presbyterian Church, fundamentalists lost the following battles: the assembly supported Dr. J. Ross Stevenson's Plan of Organic Union in 1920—Stevenson was president of Princeton Theological Seminary—and voted down seven heresy cases against liberal ministers in 1924. Three battles, which are discussed in chapter 2, were also lost: a vote against the Auburn Affirmation was not affirmed in 1925; the

administration of Princeton Theological Seminary came under liberal control in 1929; and the Presbyterian Board of Foreign Missions, which supported modernist missionaries, was upheld in the 1930s.

53. Carl Douglas Abrams, *Selling the Old-Time Religion: American Fundamentalists and Mass Culture, 1920–1940* (Athens: Univ. of Georgia Press, 2001), 11–39; Carpenter, xii–xiii, 33–56, 237.

54. An additional fundamentalist group—Holiness and Pentecostals—was important to the rise of the modern charismatic movement but is irrelevant to this study.

55. Carpenter, 1–25; Gasper, 1–20.

2. The Twentieth-Century Reformation:
The Gospel of Militant Fundamentalism

1. World Conference on Faith and Order Collection, Special Collections, Univ. of Chicago. After the First World War, the idea of church unity became an international movement. In August 1920, the Faith and Order Preparatory Conference was held in Geneva, Switzerland, and the First World Conference on Faith and Order seven years later in Lausanne. The 1927 conference, initiated by the Episcopal Church General Convention, saw eighty churches from forty nations discuss unity and ecumenism. In Ireland, Protestant clerics and academics formed the United Council of Christian Churches and Religious Communions to discuss social issues (1923) and the Irish Christian Fellowship Conference (1929) to discuss doctrine and to encourage clerics to visit and preach in the churches of other denominations.

2. Marsden, *Understanding Fundamentalism*, 100–109.

3. Livingstone and Wells, 10–30.

4. These modernist concepts included the arguments that the Old Testament messianic predictions were not fulfilled in the gospels and that Moses did not write the Pentateuch—both denying Christ's divinity.

5. New Theology redefined God's nature, morality, and credibility and argued that God manifested his presence through human history and culture. See Charles A. Briggs, *American Presbyterianism: Its Origin and Early History* (New York: Charles Scribner's Sons, 1885); *Biblical Study: Its Principles, Methods, and History* (New York: Charles Scribner's Sons, 1883); *Whither? A Theological Question for the Times* (New York: Charles Scribner's Sons, 1889).

6. Hutchinson, 76–87. The General Assembly still accepted Union Theological graduates for the ministry.

7. Margaret G. Harden, *A Brief History of the Bible Presbyterian Church and Its Agencies* (N.p.: n.p., n.d.), 12–13; Livingstone and Wells, 40–49.

8. Sandeen, xviii. The Five Points constituted Christ's virgin birth, atonement, resurrection, the inerrancy of scripture, and Christ's ability to perform miracles.

9. Longfield, 54–76.

10. Ibid., 77–103.

11. Carpenter, 33–56; Longfield, 77–124.

12. Harden, 19–22.

13. "Sham Orthodoxy versus Real Orthodoxy" and "Why I Applied to the Independent Board," *Independent Bulletin Board,* Feb. 1935 and June 1935; J. Gresham Machen, *Modernism and the Board of Foreign Missions of the Presbyterian Church in the U.S.A., an Argument of J. Gresham Machen in Support of an Overture Introduced in the Presbytery of New Brunswick at Its Meeting on January 24, 1933, and Made the Order of the Day for the Meeting on Apr. 11, 1933* (Philadelphia: Allen, Lane and Scott, 1933).

14. *Digest of Acts and Deliverances of the General Assembly of the Presbyterian Church in the United States of America* (Philadelphia: Divine Word News Service, 1933); Gary K. Clabaugh, *Thunder on the Right: The Protestant Fundamentalists* (Chicago: Nelson-Hall, n.d.), 69–85; John Albert Stroman, "The American Council of Christian Churches: A Study of Its Origin, Leaders, and Characteristic Positions," PhD diss., Boston Univ. School of Theology, 1966, 70–92. Machen's trial and the founding of the Presbyterian Church of America were extensively covered by the media, most notably the *New York Times.*

15. Robert Speer, "Foreign Missions or World-Wide Evangelism," in *The Fundamentals,* 3:229–49.

16. Carl McIntire, *Dr. Robert Speer, the Board of Foreign Missions of the Presbyterian Church in the U.S.A., and Modernism* (Collingswood, NJ: n.p., 1935).

17. Clabaugh, 69–85; Stroman, 70–92.

18. Harden, 34–37.

19. The Presbyterian Synod of Chicago put Buswell on trial and ordered him to stop working with the IBPFM.

20. "Found Guilty," *Christian Beacon,* 5 Mar. 1936; "3 Pastors Ousted by Presbyterians," *New York Times,* 1 July 1936; McIntire, *Dr. Robert E. Speer.*

21. "Criticism of the Kingdom of God," *Princeton Review* (Jan. 1850): 328–32.

22. D. G. Hart and John Muether, *Fighting the Good Fight: A Brief History of the Orthodox Presbyterian Church* (Philadelphia: Orthodox Presbyterian Church, 1995), 41–51; *50 Years . . . Carl McIntire and the Bible Presbyterian Church of Collingswood 1933–1983* (Collingswood: Bible Presbyterian Church of Collingswood, New Jersey, 1983).

23. Hart and Muether, 41–51.

24. Carpenter, 33–56; Sandeen, 250–60. McIntire argued that he was a "martyr" because of his legal and theological battles with the Presbyterian Church in the U.S.A.

25. "Foreign Missions Cause New Revolt" and "Rev Carl McIntire Is Ousted by Court," *New York Times,* 3 June 1937 and 19 Mar. 1938; Abrams, 11–39; Clabaugh, 74–75.

26. Presbyterian Church (U.S.A.), *Book of Order: The Constitution of the Presbyterian Church (U.S.A)* (Louisville, KY: General Assembly of the Presbyterian Church [U.S.A.], 1936).

27. "Quit New Church to Form Another," *New York Times,* 5 June 1937.

28. “Bars Writ to Oust ‘Deposed’ Pastor” and “Rev. Carl M’Intire Is Ousted by Court,” *New York Times,* 7 July 1936 and 19 Mar. 1938; Morris McDonald, *A Brief History of the Bible Presbyterian Church* (Charlotte, NC: Fundamental Presbyterian Publications, 2003), 18–20.

29. “Ousted from Church, 1,200 Meet in a Tent,” *New York Times,* 4 Apr. 1938.

30. Erling Jorstad, *The Politics of Doomsday: Fundamentalists of the Far Right* (Nashville: Abingdon Press, 1970), 34–59; Marsden, *Fundamentalism and American Culture,* 85–93; McIntire, *The Testimony of Separation,* 1–6.

31. Clabaugh, 79–82; McIntire, *The Testimony of Separation,* 7–20.

32. Stroman, 110–33.

33. A corresponding group, the National Association of Evangelicals (made up of evangelicals, conservatives, and fundamentalists), formed in St. Louis, Missouri, in April 1942. McIntire refused to join the new organization. A philosophical approach to fundamentalism split the National Association of Evangelicals and the ACCC: the denominations and independent churches belonging to the former could retain membership in “apostate” organizations such as the Federal Council of Churches, but members of the latter could not. The difference created an irreversible split in the fundamentalist movement (Carpenter, 257–88).

34. J. Oliver Buswell left Wheaton College in 1940 and became president of Shelton College until expelled in 1956 for opposing McIntire’s leadership. Buswell joined the dissident Columbus (Ohio) Synod of the Bible Presbyterian Church.

35. Bob Jones Sr. and supporters within his school—reopened as a university on October 1, 1947, in Greenville, South Carolina—were relatively late converts to militant fundamentalism. Although Jones broke with the Methodist church in the mid-1930s and joined the ACCC in the 1940s, he also was an early member of the National Association of Evangelicals, believing that the evangelical group could bring revival to the United States. In 1951, however, several factors caused Jones to split with the association: the group’s expansion into the Social Gospel and its refusal to hold a convention in Greenville, South Carolina. Denouncing social activism and new evangelicalism, Bob Jones University became a militant fundamentalist institution by the late 1950s. It can be argued that this late conversion to militancy delayed the close fellowship between Paisley and the Joneses until 1962. Mark Taylor Dalhouse, “Bob Jones University and the Shaping of Twentieth-Century Separatism 1926–1990,” PhD diss., Miami Univ., Oxford, OH, 1991; R. K. Johnson, *Builder of Bridges: The Biography of Dr. Bob Jones, Jr.* (Murfreesboro, TN: Sword of the Lord, 1969); Daniel L. Turner, *Standing Without Apology: The History of Bob Jones University* (Greenville, SC: Bob Jones Univ. Press, 1992).

36. Stroman, 111–54.

37. Arnold Foster and Benjamin R. Epstein, *Danger on the Right* (New York: Random House, 1964), 100–115; Carl McIntire, *The Twentieth Century Reformation* (Collingswood, NJ: Christian Beacon Press, 1944); Carl McIntire, *Author of Liberty* (Collingswood, NJ: Christian Beacon Press, 1946).

38. Jorstad, 34–37; George M. Marsden, *Reforming Fundamentalism: Fuller Seminary and the New Evangelism* (Grand Rapids, MI: Eerdmans, 1987), 69–82; McIntire, *The Testimony of Separation,* 1–6 (the source of the ACCC's statement).

39. Quoted in "Churches Demand Test with Russia," *New York Times,* 29 Oct. 1948.

40. "Church Group Backs Use of Atomic Bomb," *New York Times,* 6 Dec. 1950.

41. "Dulles Attacked by Church Council" and "Bible Body Lashes at World Council," *New York Times,* 30 Oct. 1948 and 21 Aug. 1948; "Churchmen Differ on Russian Policy," *Philadelphia Evening Bulletin,* 25 Oct. 1946.

42. "Protestants Join in Assailing Step" and "Clark Says Post Is Up to Congress," *New York Times,* 21 Oct. and 25 Oct. 1951.

43. "500 Clergymen Rally in Capital to Protest Any Envoy to Vatican," *New York Times,* 25 Jan. 1952; Gasper, 55–75.

44. Carl McIntire to J. G. H. Plaus (Steatlerville, South Africa), 4 Apr. 1957, McIntire Collection, Special Collections, Princeton Theological Seminary Libraries, Princeton, NJ; "Church Council Accused: Head of Second Group Says Other Body Is Front for Socialism," *New York Times,* 7 Sept. 1948; Stroman, 215.

45. International Council of Christian Churches (ICCC), *Constitution of the International Council of Christian Churches* (Amsterdam: ICCC, 1948).

46. Jorstad, 49–79; C. Gregg Singer, *The Unholy Alliance* (New Rochelle, NY: Arlington House, 1975), 177–90.

47. Gasper, 55–75. Militants burned the new Bible in North Carolina and Akron, Ohio.

48. Singer, 226. Supporters of the Revised Standard Version insisted that Old Testament passages were retranslated to accurately reflect the textual evidence.

49. Carl McIntire, *The New Bible: Revised Standard Version, Why Christians Should Not Accept It* (Collingswood, NJ: Christian Bacon Press, 1952). The passage "Therefore the Lord himself shall give you a sign, Behold a virgin shall conceive, and bear a son, and shall call his name Immanuel" (King James Version) was changed to "Therefore the Lord himself shall give you a sign, Look the young woman is with child and shall bear a son, and shall name him Immanuel" (Revised Standard Version).

50. "Million-Copy Sale Starts New Bible," *New York Times,* 28 Sept. 1952; McIntire, *The New Bible.*

51. Clabaugh 83–88; Ralph Lord Roy, *Apostles of Discord: A Study of Organized Bigotry and Disruption on the Fringes of Protestantism* (Boston: Beacon Press, 1953), 219–20. The anti-Semitic charges followed a self-serving chain of logic: Jews invented communism; these Communists conspired with modernists to corrupt "true" Bible Protestantism as well as with social activists and integrationists to reconstruct society; thus, Caucasians were corrupted religiously by an apostate Christianity and left to live in a society open to racial integration.

52. In 1934, Winrod had traveled to Germany to meet with pro- Nazi, Christian Germans and to praise Adolf Hitler; during the Second World War, he was arrested three times for sedition.

53. Arnold Forster and Benjamin R. Epstein, *Danger on the Right* (New York: Random House, 1964), 68–86; Roy, 26–58.

54. Quoted in "Mission Parley Split on East Asian Reds" *New York Times,* 4 Dec. 1949; see also "Church Group Is Barred," *New York Times,* 5 Dec. 1949.

55. Quoted in "A World Council President Rejoices in Communist Victor," *Christian Beacon,* 10 Mar. 1949; see also *Who Is Carl McIntire? Testimony to Christ and a Witness for Freedom* (Collingswood, NJ: Twentieth Century Reformation Hour, n.d.), 10–11; Carl McIntire, *The Battle of Bangkok: Second Missionary Journey* (Collingswood, NJ: Christian Beacon Press, 1950).

56. Quoted in "Asia Churches See Red Fight as Basic," *New York Times,* 12 Dec. 1949.

57. Roy, 180–202.

58. Clabaugh, 82–83; Hart and Muether.

59. The connection between McIntire and McCarthy indirectly involved Paisley. The McIntire–McCarthy relationship elevated McIntire's stature among militant fundamentalists in the United States and subsequently in the international community. It also helped his ability to publicly protest Protestant apostasy and the Communist threat to the United States and to present an argument that the entire world, including Northern Ireland, was threatened by a Communist–ecumenical conspiracy. Many of McIntire's associates—Bob Jones Sr., Bob Jones Jr., Harvey Springer, and T. T. Shields, for instance—also argued the same position, and all became important influences on Paisley.

60. See Fred J. Cook, *The Nightmare Decade: The Life and Times of Senator Joe McCarthy* (New York: Random House, 1971); Walter Goodman, *The Committee: The Extraordinary Career of the House Committee on Un-American Activities* (New York: Farrar, Strauss and Giroux, 1964), 3–152; Robert Griffith, *Politics of Fear: Joseph R. McCarthy and the Senate* (Amherst: Univ. of Massachusetts Press, 1987), 30–51.

61. Warren L. Vinz, "Protestant Fundamentalism and McCarthy," *Continuum* 6 (Aug. 1968): 314–25.

62. Quoted in Roy, 308–36.

63. Goodman, 332–45.

64. "Red Infiltration Found in Religion" and "Cleric Repudiates Matthews Charge," *New York Times,* 23 Nov. 1948 and 12 July 1953; Jorstad, 65–69; Roy, 308–36.

65. Griffith, 52–57.

66. Vinz; see also Donald F. Crosby Jr., *God, Church, and Flag: Senator Joseph R. McCarthy and the Catholic Church 1950–1957* (Chapel Hill: Univ. of North Carolina Press, 1978), 40–41.

67. "Moscow-Directed Subversion in the Churches: Address Delivered at the Fifth Plenary Congress of the ICCC by Major Edgar C. Bundy, U.S.A., Aug. 12, 1962," *The Reformation Review,* Oct. 1961 (the ICCC published *The Reformation Review*); Goodman, 24–58.

68. J. B. Matthews, "Reds and Our Churches," *American Mercury* (July 1953): 3–13.

69. Cook, 424–33; Goodman, 24–58, 332–45; Griffith, 221–35. Congressman Kit Clardy of Michigan inserted "Reds and Our Churches" into the *Congressional Record.* Furthermore, in 1958 the Christian Beacon Press published J. B. Matthews's *Communism in Our Churches* (Collingswood, NJ: Christian Beacon Press, 1958).

70. Clabaugh, 86–87; Forster and Epstein, 144–50.

71. "Socialism and the Churches," "The National Council's Program for Revolution," and "High Tide of Black Resistance, 1967," *News and Views,* May 1966, Aug. 1966, and Oct. 1969.

72. Stroman, 239–41.

73. "Captain Bundy, Former News Reporter, Tangles with FC's President Stamm: Harrisburg Hears ICCC–WCC Issue" and "The Battle for Truth by Edgar C. Bundy," *Christian Beacon,* 19 Mar. 1949 and 26 July 1962; Edgar C. Bundy, *Collectivism in the Churches* (New York: Devin-Adair, 1954).

74. John T. Flynn, *The Road Ahead: America's Creeping Revolution* (New York: Devin-Adair, 1949); John T. Flynn, *The Roosevelt Myth* (New York: Devin-Adair, 1948). On Flynn, see Ronald Radosh, *Prophets on the Right: Profiles of Conservative Critics of American Globalism* (New York: Simon and Schuster, 1975), 197–231.

75. "Highlights of Modern Methodism," *Whither Methodism?* Oct. 1965. Oxnam was president of the WCC's Council for North America from 1948 until 1954, the past president of both the FCC and DePauw University, and a member of the American Civil Liberties Union.

76. Carl McIntire, *Russia's Most Effective Fifth Column in America: A Series of Radio Messages by Carl McIntire* (Collingswood, NJ: Christian Beacon Press, 1948); Radosh, 231–73; Roy, 228–50. E. Stanley Jones argued his viewpoint in a series of books, most notably *Christ's Alternative to Communism* (New York: Abingdon Press, 1935).

77. Jorstad, 76–80.

78. "In Memoriam, Dr. Marion Reynolds, Sr.," *The Reformation Review,* Oct. 1970. In 1961, Paisley and Northern Irish militants picketed Jones's visit to Belfast, and Reynolds was one of many American clergymen to visit Paisley's Ravenhill Church after the Ulsterman's imprisonment in 1966.

79. Gasper, 55–75; Stroman, 174–82.

80. "Red Inquiry Group Assails Chairman," *New York Times,* 11 Mar. 1953; Goodman, 332–45.

81. "Women Criticize Inquiry Methods," *New York Times,* 20 Jan. 1954.

82. Gasper, 55–75.

83. ICCC, *Sixth Plenary Congress, Geneva Switzerland Aug. 5–11, 1965* (Amsterdam: ICCC, 1965); ICCC, *The Battle* (Collingswood, NJ: ICCC, 1965); Carl McIntire, *The Russian Baptists: Twenty Years of Soviet Propaganda: The Hammer and Sickle on the Platform of the Baptist World Alliance* (Collingswood, NJ: Twentieth Century Reformation Hour, n.d.). The ICCC report *The Battle* detailed the campaign against the visiting clerics from the Soviet bloc. The quotes are from McIntire, *The Russian Baptists.*

84. Quoted in "Church in Russia Is Found Isolated," *New York Times,* 24 Mar. 1956.

85. "Metropolitan Nikolai Is 'Agent in Secret Police'" and "Senate Committee Hears Agents Control Churches behind Iron Curtain," *Christian Beacon,* 26 Mar. and 21 May 1959; "8 Russian Clerics Arrive for Tour," "Russian Booed at Liberty Bell," and "Churchmen Meet in World Session," *New York Times,* 3 June 1956, 9 June 1956, and 31 July 1957; McIntire, *The Russian Baptists.*

86. Carl McIntire, *The Struggle for South America: First Missionary Journey* (Collingswood, NJ: Christian Beacon Press, 1949).

87. "Reds Appoint Clergy, Polish Exile Asserts at Westmont Rally," *Camden-Courier Post,* 26 July 1954; "Khrushchev Protest Rallies Planned by ACCC," "Washington DC Rally Set for September 14: Groups Co-operating in Protest to Khrushchev's Visit," and "Hromadka Urges WCC's Central Committee to Use Its Power to Get Red China into UN," *Christian Beacon,* 13 Aug. 1959, 27 Aug. 1959, and 1 Sept. 1960; "1,000 Attend Protest Rally," *Philadelphia Evening Bulletin,* 12 Sept. 1959.

88. John Harold Redekop, *The American Far Right: A Case Study of Billy James Hargis and Christian Crusade* (Grand Rapids, MI: Eerdmans, 1968), 1–22.

89. Billy James Hargis, *My Great Mistake* (Green Forest, AR: New Leaf Press, 1985), 61–67.

90. Carl McIntire to Drew Pearson, 19 Sept. 1955, McIntire Collection; Dr. Fernando Penabaz, *"Crusading Preacher from the West": The Story of Billy James Hargis* (Tulsa, OK: Christian Crusade, 1965), 84–149.

91. ICCC, press release, Dec. 1953, McIntire Collection; Evangelist Billy James Hargis, press release, 1958, McIntire Collection. The promoter L. J. White Jr. had previously helped to build the radio empire of Oral Roberts, the Tulsa televangelist and faith healer.

92. Donald Janson and Bernard Eisman, *The Far Right* (New York: McGraw-Hill, 1963), 69–91.

93. *Air Reserve Center Training Manual, Number 45-7550, USAF Reserve Instructor Course, Increment V, Volume 7, Student Text* (Mitchel Air Force Base, NY: Headquarters Continental Air Command, 1960); "Churches to Send Bibles over 'Curtain by Balloon,'" "U.S. Ban on Sending Bibles to Reds by Air Reported," and "Bonn Reported to Halt Bible Balloons to the East," *New York Times,* 26 July 1952, 31 Aug. 1953, and 23 Sept. 1955.

94. In 1961, Hargis was granted an honorary doctorate of law from Bob Jones University. Doctrinal differences precluded the Jones family from granting Hargis a theological degree. Because he was a Disciple of Christ, his religiosity was not Calvinist. The Disciples

are Arminian, and many, such as Hargis, profess premillennial Dispensationalism. However, Hargis viewed American Protestants as God's Elect and ordained to lead the worldwide defense of Bible Protestantism. This sense of exceptionalist predestination enabled him to work with militant fundamentalist Calvinists. Many militants, including the Bob Jones family, supported Hargis's political work while distancing themselves from his theology.

95. Carl McIntire to Billy James Hargis, 15 Oct. 1963, McIntire Collection.

96. "Right-Wing Leaders Shape Secret Fraternity," "Birch Group Labels Some Stores Red," and "Right-Wing Units Pan Federation," *New York Times,* 16 Sept. 1961, 25 Oct. 1962, and 15 Jan. 1962; Morris, 259–314.

97. Billy James Hargis to Carl McIntire, 22 Mar. 1954, McIntire Collection; Carl McIntire to Billy James Hargis, 30 June 1955, McIntire Collection.

98. "Springer Closes Great Campaign," *Christian Beacon,* 17 Feb. 1949; "Democrats List 5 as Extremists," *New York Times,* 17 Sept. 1960; Harvey H. Springer, *Catholicism in America: Our Hope the Bright and Morning Star* (N.p.: n.p., n.d.).

99. Clabaugh, 107–10; Forster and Epstein, 47–67.

3. The Theological and Political Background to Ulster Protestantism

1. "John Knox," *Protestant Telegraph,* 12 Sept. 1970.

2. Ian B. Cowan, *The Scottish Reformation: Church and Society in Sixteenth-Century Scotland* (London: Weidenfeld and Nicolson, 1982), 89–114; J. D. Douglas, *Light in the North: The Story of the Scottish Covenanters* (Grand Rapids, MI: Eerdmans, 1964), 13–21; Richard L. Greaves, *Theology and Revolution in the Scottish Reformation: Studies in the Thought of John Knox* (Grand Rapids, MI: Christian Univ. Press, 1980), 4–67.

3. Ian R. K. Paisley, *John Knox, a Sermon Preached 10th and 17th November 1963 to the Ravenhill Free Presbyterian Church* (N.p.: n.p., n.d.).

4. Jane Dawson, "Calvinism and the Gaidhealtchad in Scotland," in *Calvinism in Europe,* edited by Andrew Pettegree, Alistair Duke, and Gillian Lewis, 231–53 (Cambridge: Cambridge Univ. Press, 1994); Conrad Russell, *The Fall of the British Monarchies, 1637–1642* (Oxford: Clarendon Press, 1991), 38–40; Nicholas Tyacke, *Anti-Calvinists: The Rise of English Arminianism* (Oxford: Oxford Univ. Press, 1987).

5. Douglas, 22–37; Raymond Gillespie, "The Religion of the Protestant Laity in Early Modern Ireland," in *Christianity in Ireland: Revisiting the Story,* edited by Brendan Bradshaw and Daire Keogh, 109–23 (Dublin: Columba Press, 2002); Westerkamp, 15–42.

6. Alan Ford, *The Protestant Reformation in Ireland: Second Impression* (Frankfurt: Peter Lang, 1987), 1–41.

7. Bardon, *A History of Ulster,* 75–147; Ford, 153–92.

8. Bardon, *A History of Ulster,* 115–47; Westerkamp, 15–42.

9. Ford, 193–216; William Alison Phillips, *History of the Church of Ireland from the Earliest Times to the Present Day,* vol. 3: *The Modern Church* (Oxford: Oxford Univ. Press, 1933), 1–58.

10. Bardon, *A History of Ulster,* 115–47; Westerkamp, 43–73.

11. "The Massacre of Irish Protestants 1641," *Protestant Telegraph,* 16 Sept. 1977. In another article published in 1966, Paisley compared the 1641 massacre with the St. Bartholomew's Massacre. He argued that the Roman Catholic Church ordained and promoted the brutal attack on Irish Protestants ("No Surrender," *Protestant Telegraph,* 5 Nov. 1966).

12. Bardon, *A History of Ulster,* 115–47; Brooke, 29–31.

13. Brooke, 37–42.

14. "Oliver Cromwell, a Man of God, a Christian Warrior," *Protestant Telegraph,* 14 Oct. 1967.

15. Bardon, *A History of Ulster,* 115–47; Brooke, 13–42.

16. J. C. Beckett, *Protestant Dissent in Ireland 1687–1780* (London: Faber and Faber, 1948), 27–30; Brooke, 19–53.

17. Phillips, 148–74.

18. "The Siege of Derry, 1689," *Protestant Telegraph,* 5 Aug. 1967.

19. Finlay Holmes, "The Presbyterian Church in Ireland," in Bradshaw and Keogh, eds., *Christianity in Ireland, Revisiting the Story,* 124–33.

20. Griffin, 14–25.

21. Bardon, *A History of Ulster,* 148–71; McBride, *Ulster Presbyterianism,* 22–26.

22. Westerkamp, 15–42.

23. John Brewer and Gareth Higgins, *Anti-Catholicism in Northern Ireland 1600–1998* (London: MacMillan, 1998), 21–28.

24. Bardon, *A History of Ulster,* 171–82.

25. Ibid., 183–239.

26. Alvin Jackson, *Ireland: 1798–1998* (Oxford: Blackwell, 1999), 1–22.

27. McBride, *Ulster Presbyterianism,* 1–13. See also Bardon, *A History of Ulster,* 183–239; Irene Whelan, *The Bible War in Ireland: The "Second Reformation" and the Polarization of Protestant–Catholic Relations, 1800–1840* (Madison: Univ. of Wisconsin Press, 2005), 37–51.

28. McBride, *Ulster Presbyterianism,* 167–224; Myrtle Hill, *The Time of the End: Millennium Beliefs in Ulster* (Belfast: Belfast Society, 2001), 17–36.

29. P. M. H. Bell, *Disestablishment in Ireland and Wales* (London: Society for the Propagation of Christian Knowledge, 1969), 110–57; A. Jackson, *Ireland,* 23–27; Whelan, *The Bible War in Ireland,* 125–31.

30. Sean Farrell, *Rituals and Riots: Sectarian Violence and Political Culture in Ulster, 1784–1886* (Lexington: Univ. Press of Kentucky, 2000), 69–117. The first Orange parades took place on July 12, 1796, in Portadown, Lurgan, and Warington.

31. J. Holmes, *Religious Revivals,* xi–xiii; Irene Whelan, "The Bible Gentry: Evangelical Religion, Aristocracy, and the New Moral Order in Early Nineteenth Century," in Gribben and Holmes, eds., *Protestant Millennialism, Evangelicalism, and Irish Society,* 52–82.

32. Phillips, 325–59.

33. Andrew Boyd, *Montgomery and the Black Man: Religion and Politics in Nineteenth-Century Ulster* (Dublin: Columba Press, 2006), 19–22.

34. Finlay Holmes, *Henry Cooke* (Belfast: Christian Journals, 1981), 31–47; John Jamieson, *The History of the Royal Belfast Academical Institution, 1810–1960* (Belfast: William Mullan and Son, 1959), 1–22; Josias Leslie Porter, *The Life and Times of Henry Cooke, D.D., LL.D., President of Assembly's College, Belfast* (London: John Murray, 1871), 55–71.

35. Tony Gray, *The Orange Order* (London: Bodley Head, 1972), 109–18; McBride, *Ulster Presbyterianism,* 216–24.

36. Catherine Hirst, *Religion, Politics, and Violence in Nineteenth-Century Belfast: The Pound and Sandy Row* (Dublin: Four Courts Press, 2002), 41–51; Janice Holmes, "The Role of Open-Air Preaching in the Belfast Riots of 1857," *Proceedings of the Royal Irish Academy* 102 (2002): 47–66.

37. Andrew Boyd, *Holy War in Belfast* (Tralee, Ireland: Anvil Books, 1969), 10–34; T. Gray, *The Orange Order,* 147–57; J. Holmes, "The Role of Open-Air Preaching"; Mark Doyle, *Fighting Like the Devil for the Sake of God: Protestants, Catholics, and the Origins of Violence in Victorian Belfast* (Manchester, UK: Manchester Univ. Press, 2009), 25–31.

38. Andrew R. Holmes, "Tradition and Enlightenment Conversion and Assurance of Salvation in Ulster Presbyterianism, 1700–1859," in *Converts and Conversion in Ireland, 1650–1850,* edited by Michael Brown, Charles Ivar, and Thomas P. Power, 129–56 (Dublin: Four Courts Press, 2005); Andrew R. Holmes, "Biblical Authority and the Impact of Higher Criticism in Irish Presbyterianism, ca. 1850–1930," *Church History: Studies in Christianity and Culture* 75 (June 2006): 343–73; Victor Maxwell, *Belfast's Halls of Faith and Fame* (Belfast: Ambassador, 1999), 27–46.

39. "Extraordinary Religious Excitement at Ahoghill," *Ballymena Observer,* 26 Mar. 1859; Mark Doyle, "Visible Differences: The 1859 Revival and Sectarianism in Belfast," in *Irish Protestant Identities,* edited by Mervyn Bursteed, Frank Neal, and Jonathan Tonge, 141–54 (Manchester, UK: Manchester Univ. Press, 2008); Andrew R. Holmes, "The Experience and Understanding of Religious Revival in Ulster Protestantism, ca. 1800–1930," *Irish Historical Studies* 34 (Nov. 2005): 361–85; Ian R. K. Paisley, *The '59 Revival: An Authentic History of the Great Ulster Awakening of 1859* (Belfast: Martyr's Memorial Free Presbyterian Church, 1958).

40. Quoted in Boyd, *Holy War in Belfast,* 119–44.

41. "Dr. Henry Cooke," *Protestant Telegraph,* 14 Dec. 1969.

42. "Dr. Henry Cooke," *Protestant Telegraph,* 14 Dec. 1986; S. Farrell, *Rituals and Riots,* 141–50; T. Gray, *The Orange Order,* 159–72; Scott.

43. "Roman Catholic Procession: Disturbance in the City," *Belfast News Letter,* 10 June 1901; John Boyle, "The Belfast Protestant Association and the Independent Orange Order, 1901–1910," *Irish Historical Studies* 13 (1962): 117–52; John Gray, *City in Revolt: James Larkin and the Belfast Dock Strike of 1907* (Belfast: Blackstaff Press, 1985), 44–55.

44. Mitchel, *Evangelicalism and National Identity in Ulster,* 46–79.

45. Ibid., 117.

46. Ibid., 136–55, 173–85.

4. A Fundamental Defense of Ulster Protestantism

1. Bruce, *God Save Ulster!* 15–19; George Marsden, "Fundamentalism as an American Phenomenon: A Comparison with English Evangelicalism," *Church History* 56 (1977): 215–32. Both authors argue that in the early twentieth century Northern Ireland nurtured a semblance of home-grown fundamentalism that arose out of the 1859 Ulster Revival.

2. Stanley Barnes, *All for Jesus: The Life of W. P. Nicholson* (Belfast: Ambassador, 1996), 11–103; Mavis Heaney, *To God Be the Glory: The Personal Memoirs of Reverend William P. Nicholson* (Belfast: Ambassador, 2004), 36–38, 108–11; Mark Sidwell, "W. P. Nicholson and the Rise of Ulster Fundamentalism," *Biblical Viewpoint* 28 (Apr. 1994): 93–104.

3. Sidwell, 93–104. See also Barnes, 60–103; Livingstone and Wells, 107–37.

4. A. Holmes, "Biblical Authority."

5. Reverend John Waddell, *The Life Here and the Life After* (Belfast: Fisherwick Presbyterian Church, n.d.).

6. Reverend J. T. Anderson, *Talks on the Bible to Sunday School Teachers* (N.p.: n.p., n.d.).

7. Steve Bruce, "Nicholson and Paisley," *Evangelical Voice* 8 (1990): 12–13; Sidwell, 93–104.

8. The Reverend F. W. S. O'Neill became the General Assembly moderator in 1936.

9. "An Indictment of the Rev. Professor Davey, Private and Confidential Memo for Members of Belfast Presbytery Only," J. Gresham Machen Archives, Montgomery Library, Westminster Theological Seminary, Philadelphia; James Ernest Davey, *The Changing Vesture of the Faith* (Boston: Pilgrim Press, 1923), 73; James Ernest Davey, *Our Faith in God Through Jesus: Studies in the Origin and Development of Christian Forms of Belief, Institutions, and Observance. Four Apocalyptic Addresses* (New York: George H. Doran, 1922); Austin Fulton, *J. Ernest Davey* (Belfast: Presbyterian Church in Ireland, 1970), 97–125.

10. Beggs, 11–14; W. J. Grier, *The Origin and Witness of the Irish Evangelical Church* (Belfast: Evangelical Book Shop, 1945), 9–37.

11. Grier had by this time become an ordained Presbyterian minister and was superintendent of the Bible Standards League.

12. *Record of the Trial of the Reverend J. E. Davey by the Belfast Presbytery and of the Hearing of Appeals by the General Assembly, 1927* (Belfast: Presbyterian General Assembly, 1927), 4–5.

13. W. J. Grier to J. Gresham Machen, 26 Jan. 1927, and W. J. Grier to J. Gresham Machen, 6 Apr. 1927, J. Gresham Machen Archives.

14. John R. Gillespie to J. Gresham Machen, 21 June 1927, J. Gresham Machen Archives.

15. Grier, *The Origin and Witness,* 33–58; Livingstone and Wells, 60–69; Paisley, *My Father and Mother,* 1–10.

16. Author's phone interview with John Grier, 24 Jan. 2008. John Grier, the son of W. J. Grier, is the proprietor of the Evangelical Book Shop in Belfast, a store that James Hunter founded in 1926.

17. J. Gresham Machen to W. J. Grier, 27 Dec. 1926, 24 Mar. 1927, and 27 Apr. 1927, J. Gresham Machen Archives.

18. W. J. Grier to J. Gresham Machen, 22 June 1937, and "Engagements Billed in Great Britain (1927)," J. Gresham Machen Archives. Machen also spoke to the Manchester Bible Union in Liverpool, to the Bible League of Great Britain in London, at Cambridge University, and to a Bible conference in Wales.

19. Leslie K. Tarr, *Shields of Canada: T. T. Shields (1873–1955)* (Grand Rapids, MI: Baker Book House, 1967).

20. C. A. Rawlyk, *Champions of the Truth: Fundamentalism, Modernism, and the Maritime Baptists* (Montreal: Centre for Canadian Studies, Mount Allison Univ., 1990), 76–98; C. Allyn Russell, "Thomas Todhunter Shields, Canadian Fundamentalist," *Ontario History* 70 (Dec. 1978): 263–80; Bruce L. Shelley, *A History of Conservative Baptists* (Wheaton, IL: Conservative Baptist Press, 1971), 9–17; John Gordon Stackhouse Jr., "Proclaiming the Word of God: Canadian Evangelicalism since World War I," PhD diss., Univ. of Chicago Divinity School, 1987, 13–33. McMaster University is the largest Baptist school in Canada.

21. "Shields of Canada by Ian R. K. Paisley," *Protestant Telegraph,* 11 Nov. 1967.

22. Beggs, 15–24.

23. Paisley, *My Father and Mother;* Ian R. K. Paisley, *The Depths of the Baptist Downgrade: An Exposure of the Infidelity and Unitarianism of the President of the Baptist Union of GT. Britain and Ireland, Dr. Howard Williams* (Belfast: Puritan, 1976).

24. Reformed Presbyterians trace their roots back to the 1640 Covenant, adhere to the theology of John Knox, and have a conservative view of contemporary politics.

25. Moloney, *Paisley,* 14–16; Ian R. K. Paisley, *Life's Four Windows: A Sketch of My Life Story, Two Sermons Preached in the Martyr's Memorial Free Presbyterian Church on the Thirty-Seventh Anniversary of His Ministry* (N.p.: n.p., n.d.), 6–10. We can only speculate as to why Paisley, a staunch Loyalist and Unionist, chose not to enter Britain's war effort; he was old enough to take part in the Second World War's final year. During the 1940s, however, Ulster Protestants did not join the British military in great numbers. There was no conscription in Ulster, and Ulster Protestants, who had suffered extraordinary high casualties in the First World War, felt that they had done enough for the union. Because of Paisley's decision not to enter the military in the mid-1940s, there is no record of his using the Allied victory for theological advantage, and he rarely attacked communism until the late 1950s.

26. Ad for service in Cromkill Orange Hall, *Ballymena Observer,* 3 Sept. 1948; ad for Welcome and C.W.U. Youth Crusade, *Lisburn Herald,* 20 Dec. 1947; Paisley, *Life's Four Windows,* 10–14.

27. Bruce, *God Save Ulster!* 28–38; Moloney and Pollak, 1–29.

28. Bruce, *God Save Ulster!* 28–38; Moloney and Pollak, 1–29.

29. Bruce, *God Save Ulster!* 25–32; Moloney and Pollak, 19–24; Paisley, *Life's Four Windows.*

30. Quoted in Paisley, *Nicholson Centenary, 1876–1976.*

31. Rev. Alan Cairns, "Our Founding Fathers," *Let the Bible Speak,* Jan. 2009.

32. Dennis Cooke, *Persecuting Zeal: A Portrait of Ian Paisley* (Dingle, Ireland: Brandon, 1996), 29–40; Heaney, 139–47; Smyth, *Ian Paisley,* 2–3.

33. "Elder Joins 'Gospel' Pickets in Sunday Protest at County Down Church" and "The New Church of Ulster: Opening Service To-day at Crossgar," *Belfast Telegraph,* 5 Feb. and 17 Mar. 1951; Free Presbyterian Church of Ulster, *The Free Presbyterian Church of Ulster: Crossgar Congregation* (Belfast: Free Presbyterian Church of Ulster, n.d.).

34. Presbyterian Church in Ireland, *The Code: The Book of the Constitution and Government of the Presbyterian Church in Ireland* (Belfast: Presbyterian Church in Ireland, 1945), 47–48. Assembly Rule 254 reads: "No Evangelistic Mission in connection with a congregation of the Church, or in premises belonging to a congregation, shall be conducted by any person other than a minister, a licentiate, or a ruling elder of the Church, or an Agent of the Assembly's Committee on the State of Religion, unless and until such person shall have been expressly authorised to undertake such work by the Presbytery of the bounds."

35. Samuel Rutherford, a Scottish Presbyterian theologian and academic, was also a commissioner to the Westminster Assembly. Rutherford argued that national governments should be Presbyterian, a system he considered biblically ordained.

36. Free Presbyterian Church of Ulster, *The Free Presbyterian Church of Ulster* (short pamphlet), emphasis in original.

37. D. Cooke, *Persecuting Zeal,* 29–40; Moloney and Pollak, 37–41.

38. "Presbytery Ban Led to Split: New Congregation Is Formed in Crossgar," *Belfast Telegraph,* 13 Mar. 1951; Bruce, *Paisley and Politics,* 47–50; Free Presbyterian Church of Ulster, *The Free Presbyterian Church of Ulster.*

39. Cairns, "Our Founding Fathers."

40. Ian Paisley to Carl McIntire, 28 May 1951, McIntire Collection; D. Cooke, *Persecuting Zeal,* 29–40; Moloney and Pollak, 37–41.

41. Alan Cairns, *A Prophet with Honour: The Life and Work of James Wylie, Who Faithfully Served the Lord with Honour, Humour, and Unfeigned Holiness* (Belfast: Presbytery of the Free Presbyterian Church, 1991), 7–11, 46–49; Karen Heggarty, *From Vision to Victory: The History of the Ballymoney Free Presbyterian Church* (N.p.: n.p., n.d.).

42. Moloney and Pollak, 42–51. These authors base their argument on Paisley's willingness to seize on disputes such as the morality of a minister/pastor or congregant. Their argument does not take into consideration that to fundamentalists such as Paisley immorality and ecumenism both break God's commandments and are all part of the same apostasy.

43. Bruce, *God Save Ulster!* 39–62.

44. Ibid., 59–62. The new Free Presbyterian congregations were at Mount Merrion and Sandown Road in East Belfast and at Whiteabbey, Ballyhalbert, Coleraine, Dunmurry, Limavady, and Armagh.

45. Advertisement for Crossgar Free Presbyterian Church, *Belfast Telegraph*, 19 May 1951.

46. Bruce, *God Save Ulster!* 46–50.

47. ICCC, *Minutes of the Second Plenary Congress of the International Council of Christian Churches, Geneva, Switzerland, 16–23 Aug. 1950* (Amsterdam: ICCC, n.d.).

48. Evangelical Protestant Society (EPS), *Introducing the Evangelical Protestant Society* (Belfast: EPS, n.d.); J. Claude Macquigg, *The Minnis Mills Tapestry: 1922–1968 Diaries, Warp and Weft of a Local Church* (Belfast: J. C. Macquigg, 2005), 173–77; Norman Porter, *He Shall Reign for Ever and Ever: A Brief History of the Orangefield Baptist Church* (Belfast: Orangefield Baptist Church, n.d.), 3–9. The EPS was formed out of the Irish branch of the NUP after Paisley won a legal battle, gaining the NUP's Northern Irish assets. Porter and his allies chose to quit the group and drop the NUP name, which Paisley continued to use.

49. Email to author from John Grier, 7 Mar. 2008. W. J. Grier became the chairman of council (moderator) of the Irish Evangelical Church for the 1942–43 and 1977–78 terms, which shows his stature within the denomination. (The Irish Evangelical Church rotated the office of chairman on a yearly basis in the traditional Presbyterian fashion.)

50. A. Warnaar Jr. to Ian Paisley, 11 Dec. 1953, McIntire Collection; ICCC, *Minutes of Proceedings, British Isles Regional Conference of the International Council of Christian Churches, 24–30 July 1952* (Amsterdam: ICCC, n.d.).

51. Program, Third Plenary Congress, ICCC, 3–12 Aug. 1964, Philadelphia, ; "A Special Protestant Rally," flier distributed by the EPS, Mar. 1955; Carl McIntire, *Servants of Apostasy* (Collingswood, NJ: Christian Beacon Press, 1955), 347.

52. Ian Paisley to Carl McIntire, no date (but marked by McIntire as having been received on 28 May 1951), McIntire Collection.

53. Carl McIntire to Ian Paisley, 28 May 1951, and Carl McIntire to Ian Paisley, 9 Nov. 1951, McIntire Collection.

54. Reverend Cecil A. J. MacCausland to Henri F. M. Pol (ICCC, Geneva), 10 Dec. 1951, McIntire Collection; Cairns, 147–53. There is inconclusive evidence, however, that a few issues of *The Revivalist* were printed in 1952.

55. Cairns, 46–49; Moloney and Pollak, 67–76. According to Moloney and Pollak, Lyons initially fled to the home of a Free Presbyterian. But because Paisley was on his

honeymoon in Scotland, the Elim evangelists approached Norman Porter's Catholic Evangelical Fellowship. As Paisley returned home that evening, he quickly ordered his deputy, Wylie, to commandeer the operation.

56. "Maura Lyons Papers to Be Sent to Attorney-General," "Prayer for Maura at Church Service," and "Cases Against Two Clergymen Withdrawn," *Belfast Telegraph,* 11 May, 13 May, and 6 Sept. 1957; Moloney and Pollak, 54–76. The quote can be found in "Maura Lyons' Conversion Vindicated," *The Revivalist,* June 1957. Although there are many accounts of the Maura Lyons affair, Moloney and Pollak show it in its true light. The event was for publicity, and their account is written in a tabloidlike format. In their book *Paisley,* their informative account of the Free Presbyterian preacher, they present an interesting side note. About the same time that Maura Lyons returned to Northern Ireland, another girl at the Star Clothing Company converted to Free Presbyterianism. Kathleen Kelly, however, was Church of Ireland, and so, despite Paisley's efforts, the press declined any interest in a Protestant switching Protestant churches. As Moloney and Pollak point out, Catholic-to-Protestant conversions or vice versa made headlines in Ireland; changing denominations within the same creed did not.

57. "We Were Pilloried for Being Protestants," *Belfast Telegraph,* 7 July 2009.

58. J. H. Whyte, *Church and State in Modern Ireland 1923–1979* (Dublin: Gill and MacMillan, 1998), 322–24.

59. "Belfast Corporation and the Union Jack" and "Unionism and Romanism," *Ulster Protestant,* Jan. 1959 and Dec. 1959; Moloney, Paisley, 53.

60. Examples include: "A Protestant in Spain," *The Irish Evangelical,* Sept. 1957; "Oppression of Protestants in Spain," "Ulster Government Subsidises Romanism," and "Fresh Reports on Colombian Persecutions," *Ulster Protestant,* June 1957, Oct. 1957, Jan. 1960.

61. "The Downgrade Continues! The Irish Presbyterian Church, 1955–56," *The Revivalist,* June 1956.

62. "A Bible Week in Dublin," *Presbyterian Herald,* Apr. 1954; "Conference on Church Unity," *Church of Ireland Gazette,* 2 Jan. 1959; Dennis Cooke, *Peacemaker: The Life and Work of Eric Gallagher* (Peterborough, UK: Methodist Publishing House, 2005), 71–84. The *Annual Report of the General Assembly of the Presbyterian Church in Ireland* had an "Inter-Church Relations" section, and the annual *Minutes of the Methodist Conference* contained a "Co-operation with Other Churches" section throughout the 1950s. In this decade, ecumenical activities within Ireland were restricted to more mundane matters: interdenominational Bible studies and youth groups; interchurch relations; cooperation between Presbyterians and Methodists in rural areas of Ulster and in the Republic of Ireland, where church attendance could not support more than one church; and support for the WCC. Such cooperation was generally limited to the Presbyterian and Methodist churches and included sharing the costs of building new churches and maintaining older ones as well as joint worship services. Irish ecumenism was basically a theological exercise among clerics. For example, in December 1958 a series of informal three-day conferences

began at the Murlough House in Dundrum, outside Dublin, between Church of Ireland, Congregationalist, Methodist, and Presbyterian leaders to discuss church unity.

63. Cairns, 147–53; "Incidents and Demonstrations in Which the Rev Ian R. K. Paisley and Members of the Free Presbyterian Church Were Concerned," Home Secretary File on Paisley Faction, CAB9B/300/1, Public Record Office Northern Ireland (PRONI), Belfast; Presbyterian Church in Ireland, *Minutes of the General Assembly of the Presbyterian Church in Ireland* (Belfast: Presbyterian Church in Ireland, 1955); "Students Threaten to Divide Church" and "Bigger Church Division on the Way He Says: Views of Free Presbyterians," *Belfast Telegraph,* 7 June and 8 June 1955.

64. "Police Take Names of Two Clergymen," *Belfast Telegraph,* 14 Aug. 1957; Moloney, *Paisley,* 79–80.

65. "Dr. Soper Speaks in Belfast Blitz Sq: Stop H-Bomb Production Call," *Belfast Telegraph,* 19 Apr. 1954; Moloney and Pollak, 81–89.

66. Desmond Boal helped to organize the DUP with Paisley in 1971, was an associate of Norman Porter in the EPS (Boal and Paisley first met in the EPS Belfast office), and represented Mrs. Cloney, the Protestant woman involved in the Fethard-on-Sea boycott.

67. "The Dr. Soper Incident—Free Presbyterians Summoned," "Queues for Case Against Free Presbyterians," and "Applause as Paisley Says 'I Won't Pay," *Belfast Telegraph,* 21 Aug., 2 Sept., and 7 Sept. 1959; Bruce, *God Save Ulster!* 71–73; Marrinan, 65–73.

68. Quoted in "Fines Paid for Three Free Presbyterian Clergymen," *Belfast Telegraph,* 8 Sept. 1959.

69. "Free Church Ministers Come under Attack," *Belfast Telegraph,* 2 Nov. 1959.

70. "'Sieg Heils' Greet Rev. Ian Paisley: Uproar at Queen's Univ. Meeting," *Belfast Telegraph,* 8 Mar. 1960.

71. "Iona Community Head Banned in Coleraine: Elders' Fellowship Oppose Visit," *Belfast Telegraph,* 24 Oct. 1960.

72. "Belfast Church Service Picketed by Free Presbyterians" and "Dr. Jones Answers the Free Presbyterians: U.S. Missionary Called Near-Red," *Belfast Telegraph,* 10 Mar. and 10 Apr. 1961.

73. "Paisley Pickets at the Assembly," *Protestant Telegraph,* 7 June 1962; Gallagher and Worrall, 32–33.

74. "Scottish Moderator Sees Pope" and "Coleraine Meeting Is Interrupted by Paisley Protest," *Belfast Telegraph,* 28 Mar. and 4 Oct. 1962; "Moderator Arrives in Rome: Vatican Visit Will Do Good" and "Pope to Meet Moderator at the Vatican," *The Scotsman,* 22 Mar. and 20 Mar. 1962; "Another Betrayer of Protestantism!" *Ulster Protestant,* Mar. 1963.

75. "Romanism and the Romanisers in Church of Ireland Exposed," *The Revivalist,* Dec. 1964; "Royal Visit to Pope: Shocks Protestant Conscience," *Ulster Protestant,* June 1961; Adrian Hastings, *A History of English Christianity 1920–1990* (London: SCM Press, 1991), 193–205, 522–31.

76. Paisley, *The Battle of the Reformation.*

77. "Dr. Fisher Is in Rome for Historic Meeting," *Belfast Telegraph,* 1 Dec. 1960; "Reformers Betrayed" and "The Lambeth Prophet," *Ulster Protestant,* Dec. 1960 and Feb. 1961.

78. "Anglican Observers to Visit Vatican: Rome Council Invitation Is Accepted," "A Very Protestant Plan for a Vatican Visit," "Rev. Ian Paisley Protests at BBC," and "We Have No Connection," *Belfast Telegraph,* 5 July, 23 Aug., 8 Oct. 1962 (last two); Paisley, *For Such a Time as This,* 147–52; "Why True Protestants Cannot Take Part in Unity Meetings with Priests of Rome," *The Revivalist,* May 1965.

79. D. Cooke, *Persecuting Zeal,* 124–26.

80. Marsden, *Reforming Fundamentalism,* 45–93, 157–71. Billy Graham, however, was not heavily involved in social action; his primary focus was to "save" souls.

81. "Crusade Organiser in Belfast," "Dr. Shuler Will Choose Belfast Topic Tonight," and "Billy Graham: 'Negligible Impact'," *Belfast Telegraph,* 1 Apr. 1955, 15 June 1955, and 18 Nov. 1957; "Is Billy Graham Also Amongst the Pro-Romanists?" and "Billy Graham Sends His Converts Back to Rome," *Protestant Telegraph,* 18 June 1966 and 24 June 1967; Dr. Bob Jones, "About Billy Graham's New York Crusade," *The Revivalist,* June 1957; Gasper, v–viii.

82. *Irish Presbyterians, the Downgrade Continues!* (Belfast: Free Presbyterian Church of Ulster, 1955).

83. Ian Paisley to Carl McIntire, 28 June 1951; Carl McIntire to Ian Paisley, 8 Oct. 1951; and Ian Paisley to Carl McIntire, 7 Mar. 1952—all in the McIntire Collection.

84. Carl McIntire to Ian Paisley, 25 May 1951, and Ian Paisley to Carl McIntire, 28 May 1951, McIntire Collection.

85. Carl McIntire to Ian Paisley, 11 Mar. 1952, McIntire Collection.

86. Carl McIntire to Ian Paisley, 8 Apr. 1952, McIntire Collection.

87. W. J. Grier to A. Warnaar Jr. (ICCC, Amsterdam), 4 Feb. 1953, McIntire Collection.

88. J. Kyle Paisley to Carl McIntire, 18 Mar. 1955, McIntire Collection.

89. Ian Paisley to A. Warnaar Jr., n.d. (but with a notation by Warnaar as having received the letter on 1 December 1953), McIntire Collection; A. Warnaar Jr. to the Members of the Credentials Committee of the International Council of Christian Churches (confidential), 6 Mar. 1956, McIntire Collection; and A. Warnaar Jr. to Ian Paisley, 17 June 1956, McIntire Collection.

90. Ian Paisley to Carl McIntire, 23 Aug. 1951; Ian Paisley to Carl McIntire, 7 Mar. 1952; and Carl McIntire to Ian Paisley, 11 Mar. 1952—all in the McIntire Collection.

91. Although there are no letters between McIntire and Paisley about the Soper incident, McIntire's file containing his correspondence with Paisley includes press clippings on various topics of interest. In the folder, McIntire kept a copy of the front page of the 3 September 1959 edition of the *Ballymena Daily Telegraph,* on which the quote given in the text is written. The headline blasted the Free Presbyterian clergymen for their refusal to pay their fines.

92. "Presbyterian Minister in Ireland Publishes New English Bible Review," *Christian Beacon,* 27 Apr. 1961; Ian R. K. Paisley, *The New English Bible: Version or Perversion?* (Belfast: Free Presbyterian Church, 1961).

93. Carl McIntire to Norman Porter, 20 Apr. 1961, McIntire Collection.

94. Carl McIntire to Norman Porter, 14 Mar. 1962, McIntire Collection.

95. W. J. McDowell (Irish Evangelical Church) to A. Warnaar Jr., 9 May 1957, McIntire Collection.

96. Norman Porter to Carl McIntire, 5 Apr. 1961, McIntire Collection; Paisley, *The Depths of the Baptist Downgrade;* and National Union of Protestants, "Strictly Confidential, for Members Only," 1951, McIntire Collection.

97. David P. Gaines, *The World Council of Churches: A Study of Its Background and History* (Peterborough, UK: Richard R. Smith, 1966), 1007–19.

98. Carl McIntire to Ian Paisley, 19 Apr. 1961, and Carl McIntire to Norman Porter, 15 Apr. 1965, McIntire Collection.

99. J. Kyle Paisley to Carl McIntire, 14 Mar. 1962, McIntire Collection.

100. Ian Paisley to Carl McIntire, 25 Sept. 1962, McIntire Collection.

101. Carl McIntire to Ian Paisley, 29 Sept. 1962, McIntire Collection.

102. Carl McIntire to Norman Porter, 2 Oct. 1962, McIntire Collection.

103. Norman Porter to Carl McIntire, 28 Sept. 1962, McIntire Collection.

104. "Norman Porter to Give Devotions at 6th Plenary Session of the ICCC," *Christian Beacon,* 10 June 1965; "Why Bible-Believing Baptists Cannot Join the Ecumenical Movement: Address by Mr. Norman Porter Delivered at the International Baptist Conference, Mulhouse, France, Aug. 4, 1965," *The Gospel Witness,* 25 Nov. 1965. For instance, Porter gave the opening devotion at the ICCC Sixth Plenary Session in August 1965 and was a featured speaker three years later at the Fundamental Baptist Congress of North America in Cincinnati.

105. "Dr. Springer's Engagements in Northern Ireland," "Highlights from Ireland," and "1859 Revival in Ireland," *Western Voice,* 12 Aug., 16 Sept., and 23 Sept. 1965.

106. "Free Presbyterian Church of Ulster Acts in True Protestant Tradition," *Christian Beacon,* 28 Feb. 1963. The article covers Paisley's protests against British prime minister Harold Macmillan's visit to the Vatican.

107. Ian Paisley to Carl McIntire, 28 Nov. 1963 and 1 Feb. 1964, McIntire Collection.

108. "Free Presbyterian Church of Ulster, Ireland Acts in True Protestant Tradition," *Christian Beacon,* 28 Feb. 1963; "Modernist Clerics Assailed at Parley," *New York Times,* 16 Aug. 1962. See also the following correspondence in the McIntire Collection: Ian Paisley to Carl McIntire 8 Sept. 1962; Carl McIntire to Ian Paisley, 29 Sept. 1962; Carl McIntire to Ian Paisley, 4 Dec. 1963; Ian Paisley to Carl McIntire, 2 Feb. 1964; Brian Green and Ian Paisley to Carl McIntire, 4 May 1965; and Carl McIntire to Ian Paisley, 13 May 1965.

109. Ian Paisley to Carl McIntire, 9 Apr. 1963, McIntire Collection.

110. Norman Porter to Carl McIntire, 16 July 1965, and Norman Porter to Carl McIntire, 9 May 1967, McIntire Collection.

111. Carl McIntire to Norman Porter, 12 May 1967, McIntire Collection.

112. "Ecumenical Porter," *Protestant Telegraph,* 29 Aug. 1970; Norman Porter to Carl McIntire, 22 Nov. 1966, McIntire Collection; Evangelical Protestant Society to A. Warnaar Jr./International Council of Churches, 8 May 1967, McIntire Collection; "Bible Conference Speakers," Archives Research Center, Bob Jones Univ., Greenville, SC; N. Porter, *He Shall Reign for Ever and Ever,* 3–9.

5. The Crusade Against O'Neill and Ecumenism

1. During the 1960s, the international ecumenical movement was concerned with three basic concepts: church unity, cooperation among Protestant denominations, and discussions between Protestant churches and the Roman Catholic Church. In the British Isles, ecumenicalism took place in two regional settings—talks among the various English, Irish, and Scottish churches as well as talks between the Church of England and the Catholic Church. Because the Church of England was the established church in England and because the British Constitution required the royal family to remain Protestant, the talks between the Vatican and Canterbury were of great interest to Protestants in Northern Ireland.

2. "Romans Recruit Reds," *Protestant Telegraph,* 7 Mar. 1970; Bruce, *God Save Ulster!* 1–17.

3. "'Civil Rights'—Then Communism," *Belfast Telegraph,* 17 May 1969; "Papal Pattern for World Church Emerges," *Christian Beacon,* 8 July 1965.

4. Bardon, *A History of Ulster,* 479–85.

5. Paul Bew, Peter Gibbon, and Henry Patterson, *Northern Ireland 1921–1994: Political Forces and Special Classes* (London: Serf, 1995), 81–110; M. Farrell, *Northern Ireland.*

6. Dennis Kennedy, *The Widening Gulf: Northern Attitudes to the Independent Irish State, 1919–49* (Belfast: Blackstaff Press, 1983), 150–74; Patrick Murray, *Oracles of God: The Roman Catholic Church and Irish Politics, 1921–1937* (Dublin: Univ. College Press, 2000), 108–69; Whyte, 1–46, 196–238.

7. John Harbinson, *The Ulster Unionist Party 1882–1973: Its Development and Organization* (Belfast: Blackstaff Press, 1973).

8. *Civil Authorities (Special Powers) Act (Northern Ireland), 1922* (Belfast: HMSO, 1922); Kennedy, 34–56.

9. John Biggs-Davison and George Chowdharay-Best, *The Cross of St. Patrick: The Catholic Unionist Tradition in Ireland* (Abbotsbrook, UK: Kensal Press, 1984), 385–94; John A. Oliver, *Working at Stormont* (Dublin: Institute of Public Administration, 1978).

10. Bew, Gibbon, and Patterson, *Northern Ireland 1921–1994,* 81–110; Marc Mulholland, *Northern Ireland at the Crossroads: Ulster Unionism in the O'Neill Years 1960–9* (London: MacMillan, 2000), 12–27.

11. Mulholland, 1–11.

12. Ibid., 38–57.

13. Bardon, *A History of Ulster,* 633; Mulholland, 12–44; Terence O'Neill, *The Autobiography of Terence O'Neill* (London: Granada, 1972), 153.

14. Coogan, *The Troubles,* 60–81. These plans included: *The Matthew Report* (Oct. 1962) to develop a new city, Craigavon, to facilitate industrial development; *The Wilson Plan* (July 1963), a £900 million scheme for new housing, water and sewage infrastructure, education, health services, and new roadways; and *The Lockwood Report* (1964) to establish a second university for Northern Ireland.

15. Bardon, *A History of Ulster,* 631–34; Moloney and Pollak, 115–33; Mulholland, 8–92.

16. Quoted in "I Want Lord Mayor as Witness—Paisley," *Belfast Telegraph,* 25 July 1963.

17. "Summons Against Reverend Ian Paisley" and "I Won't Pay Fine, Says Mr. Paisley," *Belfast Telegraph,* 8 July and 26 July 1963; "Protest March Leads to Court: Minister Fined," *Ulster Protestant,* Aug. 1963; Moloney, *Paisley,* 106–8.

18. Quoted in "Fines Paid, Editor and His Colleagues Not to Go to Prison," *The Revivalist,* Sept. 1963.

19. "Rev. Ian Paisley Tells of Threats," *Belfast Telegraph,* 27 Apr. 1964; Cairns, 60–66; Moloney, *Paisley,* 106–8.

20. This effort had enabled Ulster Protestants to land more than two hundred tons of armaments and twenty-four thousand guns to arm the Ulster Volunteers and to thwart the implementation of Irish Home Rule.

21. "But if not, be it known unto thee, O King that we will not serve thy gods, nor worship the golden image which thou have set up" (King James Version).

22. Ian R. K. Paisley, *Souvenir Booklet: The 50th Anniversary of the Larne Gun-Running. Thanksgiving Service on Sunday, 26th April, 1964, in the Historic Ulster Hall* (Belfast: Puritan, 1964).

23. "Fisherwick Involved in Controversy," *Fisherwick Messenger,* Apr. 1964.

24. "No Tolerance in Protesting, They Say," *Belfast Telegraph,* 10 Feb. 1964; "Fisherwick Session and the Word 'Evangelical'" and "Protestant Councilors Who Went to Mass Attacked," *The Irish Evangelical,* Mar. 1964 and 22 June 1965; "Free Presbyterian Protest Stops R.C. Priests' Inter-Church Meetings" and "Protest March Stops Ecumenical Meeting in Church of Ireland, Carnalea, Bangor," *The Revivalist,* Feb.–Mar. 1964 and May 1965.

25. Ian Paisley to Carl McIntire, 1 Feb. 1954, McIntire Collection.

26. Moloney and Pollak, 114–17; Mulholland, 44–49.

27. *Flags and Emblems (Display) Bill (Northern Ireland), 1954* (Belfast: HMSO, 1954).

28. "Republican Sympathisers Block Road: Scenes in Divis Street," *Belfast Telegraph,* 30 Sept. 1964; Moloney and Pollak, 114–17.

29. "Republican Hint They Will Withdraw Flag" and "Replacement of Flag Blamed for Troubles," *Belfast Telegraph,* 2 Oct. and 8 Oct. 1964; Gerry Adams, *Free Ireland: Towards a Lasting Peace* (Niwot, CO: Roberts Rinehart, 1986), 38–47.

30. *Parliamentary Debates, Parliament of Northern Ireland, House of Commons* (Belfast: HMSO, 1965), 2878.

31. Ibid. (1965), vol. 57, cols. 2845–50.

32. "The Militant Protestant Monthlies," *Focus,* 8 Aug. 1965.

33. *Fisherwick Messenger,* Jan. 1962.

34. Quoted in "Ex-moderator Blames 'Brainless' Protestant for Riots" *Belfast Telegraph,* 21 Nov. 1964.

35. Quoted in "Minister Denounces 'Religious Fascists,'" *Belfast Telegraph,* 4 Jan. 1965.

36. "Churches Unite in Appeal for Peace in City," "Replacement of Flag Blamed for Troubles," *Belfast Telegraph,* 2 Oct. and 8 Oct. 1964; D. Cooke, *Peacemaker,* 113–14; Paisley quoted in "We Are Not Giving Up Our Heritage, Says Mr. Paisley," *Belfast Telegraph,* 5 Oct. 1964.

37. Quoted in "Activities of Mr. Paisley Are Not Commended," *Belfast Telegraph,* 13 Nov. 1964.

38. Bardon, *A History of Ulster,* 630–33; Moloney and Pollak, 18–121.

39. Moloney and Pollak, 118–21.

40. Londonderry is Northern Ireland's second-largest city, but its location in the extreme west of the province and its Catholic majority (approximately 70 percent in 1965) meant that it did not receive as much economic investment proportionally as did Belfast. Because the new university would have been a good economic stimulus as well as a prestigious move, and because Magee College, located within the city, would have provided the core of the new school, a majority of Protestants and Catholics in the city wanted Londonderry to be selected for the new university (Bardon, 630–35).

41. "Paisley's Power Fast Growing—Eire Journal," "Most Back Benchers to Support Capt. O'Neill," and "Unionists Back O'Neill," *Belfast Telegraph,* 5 Nov. 1964, 22 Jan. 1965, and 8 Apr. 1965; "An Open Letter Sent to the Prime Minister When His Secret Meeting with Ulster's Would-Be Destroyer Lemass Was Disclosed," *The Revivalist,* Feb.–Mar. 1965; *Parliamentary Debates, Parliament of Northern Ireland, House of Commons* (1965), vol. 59, cols. 294–97; Mulholland, 80–90.

42. "Mr. Paisley Takes Protest Letter to P.M.," "Mr. Paisley Issues Call for General Election," and "Placard-Bearing Paisley Protesters Miss Premier," *Belfast Telegraph,* 15 Jan., 26 Jan., and 26 Feb. 1965; "The Great Betrayal," *The Revivalist,* Feb.–Mar. 1965.

43. From the *Belfast Telegraph:* "O'Neill in Dublin: Ulster P.M. in Second Talk With Lemass," 9 Feb. 1965; "Extremists Flayed: Premier Attacks 'Flag-Burning Fools,'" 20 Feb. 1965; "Placard-Bearing Paisley Protestors Miss Premier," 26 Feb. 1965; "Unity Will Endure—PM: Packed Unionist Council Meeting Hears Policy Approved," 5 Mar.

1965; "Paisleyism Is Not a New Thing: Liberal," 22 Mar. 1966 (article quotes Reverend A. H. McElroy, president of the Liberal Association of Northern Ireland); and "Paisleyism 'Abhorrent,' Says Mr. Heath in Letter," 10 Oct. 1966. The 26 February 1965 edition of the *Belfast Telegraph* contains the first reference to Paisley's supporters as "Paisleyites"—a tacit recognition that the Reverend Paisley had an organized and substantial following.

44. "The Challenge of 1966," *The Revivalist*, Jan. 1966.

45. Ian R. K. Paisley, *Protestants Remember!* pamphlet (N.p.: n.p., 1966).

46. "The Armagh Manifesto," *The Revivalist*, Oct. 1965.

47. "P.M. to Lead Protestant-Catholic Conference," *Belfast Telegraph*, 5 Apr. 1966; "Orange Call for 1916 Celebrations Ban Rejected by O'Neill: N.I. Government Capitulates to the Rebels," *Protestant Telegraph*, 28 May 1966; "About Turn for I.C.M." and "New Group Will Unite Protestants," *Ulster Protestant*, Feb. and Mar. 1966.

48. *Parliamentary Debates, Parliament of Northern Ireland, House of Commons* (1966), vol. 62, cols. 1542–44.

49. Ibid. (1966), vol. 63, cols. 230–32.

50. Ulster Constitution Defence Committee (UCDC) and Ulster Protestant Volunteers (UPV), *Ulster Constitution Defence Committee and Ulster Protestant Volunteers Constitution and Rules* (N.p.: UCDC and UPV, n.d.); Steve Bruce, *The Edge of the Union: The Loyalist Political Vision* (Oxford: Oxford Univ. Press, 1999), 18–20.

51. "2 Anti-1916 Parades Off: Cancellation Decision Made 'In Interests of Peace" and "'Volunteers' Will Cover All Province, Says Paisley," *Belfast Telegraph*, 9 Apr. 1966 and 11 May 1966; "40,000 Protestants Protest in Belfast," *The Revivalist*, May 1966; Steve Bruce, *The Red Hand: Protestant Paramilitaries in Northern Ireland* (Oxford: Oxford Univ. Press, 1992), 19–22. Steve Bruce estimates the size of Paisley's anti-1916 Rising parade at six thousand. Although the *Belfast Telegraph* made no official estimate on the number of marches, its account stated that five thousand people heard Paisley speak at Carlisle Circus immediately afterward. In part because the Belfast march made its point and in part because of expected trouble, Paisley did cancel marches in Armagh and Newry, two towns with sizeable Catholic populations.

52. Roy Garland, *Gusty Spence* (Belfast: Blackstaff Press, 2001) 48; Bruce, *The Red Hand*, 17.

53. Garland, 44–59; Moloney and Pollak, 136–38.

54. *Parliamentary Debates, Parliament of Northern Ireland, House of Commons* (1966), vol. 64, cols. 820–21; Moloney, *Paisley*, 129–37. O'Neill confirmed Paisley's charges in a speech to Stormont made on June 29, 1966; the prime minister stated that the RUC tape-recorded all of Paisley's public speeches.

55. "Exchange on U.V.F. Closed," *Belfast Telegraph*, 30 June 1966; David Boulton, *The UVF 1966–73: An Anatomy of Loyalist Rebellion* (Dublin: Torc Books, 1973), 54–56; Moloney, *Paisley*, 133–35.

56. "Mac's Rome Visit Protest by Free Presbyterians" and "Free Presbyterian Church of Ulster, Ireland Acts in True Protestant Tradition," *Christian Beacon,* both from 28 Feb. 1963.

57. Quoted in "The Pope Flies over Ulster" and "Paisley Protest over Invitation," *Belfast Telegraph,* 4 Oct. and 13 Oct. 1965.

58. From the *Belfast Telegraph:* "Queen Gets 'Stop Priest' Wire from Mr. Paisley," 14 Jan. 1966; "23 from Ulster to Join Priest Protest," 19 Jan. 1966; "Abbey Protest Was Worthwhile—Paisley: Will Help Arouse the English," 22 Jan. 1966; "Protestants Don't Get Fair Show, Says Mr. Paisley," 3 Jan. 1966. The Paisley quote is from the article dated 22 January 1966.

59. "Paisley Joins in London Protest," *Belfast Telegraph,* 18 Mar. 1966; Jonathan Bardon, *Beyond the Studio: A History of BBC Northern Ireland* (Belfast: Blackstaff Press, 2000), 141–53.

60. Paisley asserted four basic objections to Ramsey's trip: the British Constitution made such a visit illegal; the articles of the Churches of England and Ireland prohibited it; the visit disavowed British history (it was an insult to the *Book of Martyrs*); and it was against biblical teachings (Ian R. K. Paisley, *The Archbishop in the Arms of the Pope of Rome! Protestant Ministers in the Hands of the Police of Rome!* pamphlet [Belfast: Puritan, 1966]). The pamphlet includes a statement from the ICCC written by Carl McIntire on March 22, 1966, denouncing the Vatican police's decision not to admit Paisley and his group, charging that a violation of the United Nations Covenant of Human Rights had occurred. It is interesting that McIntire wanted United Nations policy to be observed—an organization that McIntire and American militant fundamentalists consistently denounced as unbiblical and un-American.

61. "Scenes as Dr. Ramsey Takes Plane to Rome" and "3 Questioned in Rome: Belfast Man Led from Church after Protest," *Belfast Telegraph,* 22 Mar. and 23 Mar. 1966; "Archbishop of Canterbury Publicly to Give Pope Embrace of Peace in Rome" and "Revs. Ian Paisley and John Wylie Deported From Rome," *The Revivalist,* Mar. and Apr. 1966.

62. "Archbishop Ramsey's Tour of U.S.A. to Be Challenged by Mass Meeting in Columbia, S.C.," "McIntire Letter," and "Ian Paisley Protests Ramsey Visit to Rome," *Christian Beacon,* 13 Sept. 1962 and 24 Mar. 1966 (last two).

63. "Ramsey Expresses Two Hopes, Didn't Notice Fundamentalists," *Christian Beacon,* 7 Apr. 1966; "Notes and Comments Column: 'Primate's Path to Rome'" and "The Keynote of the Second Vatican Council," *Evangelical Presbyterian,* Mar. and May 1966.

64. "Minister Won't Curb Paisley Parades" and "Paisleyism Is Not a New Thing: Liberal," *Belfast Telegraph,* 12 May 1965 and 22 Mar. 1966.

65. Some Irish Presbyterian voices, however, disapproved of the Anglican–Catholic dialogue and membership in the WCC. In the *Presbyterian Herald,* Reverend Donald Gillies, minister of Agnes Street Presbyterian Church in Belfast, was given an outlet to

express fundamentalist grievances ("Opposition to W.C.C., by Donald Gillies," *Presbyterian Herald*, July–Aug. 1966). For a better understanding of the theological views of moderate Presbyterians who opposed the ecumenical movement, see Donald Gillies, *Unity in the Dark* (London: Banner of Trust, 1964).

66. Moloney and Pollak, 131–35.

67. "200 Bar Way to Paisley March" and "Rioters Clash with Protest March in Cromac Sq.," *Belfast Telegraph*, both from 7 June 1966.

68. "Right of Assembly," *Presbyterian Herald*, July–Aug. 1966; "R.C.'s Savagely Attack Protestant Parade: General Assembly Wants Government Forces to Suppress Protestant Protests," *Protestant Telegraph*, 18 June 1966.

69. "Demand by Paisley for an Inquiry" and "Parades Debate: Test for MPs," *Belfast Telegraph*, 9 June and 13 June 1966; *Parliamentary Debates, Parliament of Northern Ireland, House of Commons* (1966), vol. 64, cols. 19–24, 135–36, and 394.

70. *Parliamentary Debates, Parliament of Northern Ireland, House of Commons* (1966), vol. 64, cols. 307–11.

71. "Riot 'Provocation' Deplored by 12 Unionists" and "Mr. Paisley's Plan for City Parade," *Belfast Telegraph*, 10 June and 13 June 1966.

72. "McConnell Vows: Never Again" and "Paisley Can Use Hall by 33–1 Vote," *Belfast Telegraph*, 9 June and 1 July 1966; *Parliamentary Debates, Parliament of Northern Ireland, House of Commons* (1966), vol. 64, cols. 20–25, 334–38, and 820–21.

73. "Paisley Wants the Governor as a Witness," *Belfast Telegraph*, 11 July 1966.

74. "Unlawful Assembly Charge Against Paisley" and "Paisley March to Court May Be Banned," *Belfast Telegraph*, 6 July and 7 July 1966.

75. "Government Will Not Ban Paisley Court Parade," "1,000 Locked Out at Paisley Court," and "No Defence Witnesses at Paisley Court," *Belfast Telegraph*, 16 July, 18 July, and 19 July 1966; Moloney and Pollak, 132–35.

76. Quoted in "Paisley Says He Will Be MP at Stormont," *Belfast Telegraph*, 20 July 1966.

77. "The Reasons Why I Chose Jail by Ian R. K. Paisley," *Protestant Telegraph*, 30 July 1966.

78. "Police Hose Crowd: Marchers Defy Order to Halt," *Belfast Telegraph*, 23 July 1966.

79. "Parade Ban Welcomed," *Belfast Telegraph*, 26 July 1966; "Memorandum: Deputation from Ministers of the Free Presbyterian Church Received by the Prime Minister in the Conference Room, Stormont Castle at 11:00 AM on Wednesday, 10th August, 1966," Home Secretary File on Paisley Faction, PRONI.

80. "Cabinet Tackles Unrest: Stronger Security Possible after Week-end Violence," "Fines on Paisley and 2 Others Are Paid," and "Minister to See Paisley Delegates," *Belfast Telegraph*, 25 July, 2 Aug., and 28 July 1966; Ian R. K. Paisley, *An Exposition of the Epistle to the Romans: Prepared in the Prison Cell* (London: Marshall, Morgan and Scott, 1966);

"Messages from the Prison Cell, Prisoner No. 636, HM Prison, Belfast, 1966," McIntire Collection.

81. "The Battle of the Reformation: Why It Must Be Fought Today," *The Gospel Witness,* 8 June 1967; ICCC, *Concerning the Rev. Ian Paisley, Belfast, N.I.* (Cape May, NJ: Bible Presbyterian Church, 1966).

82. "Jail Rally Ban: Released Minister's Proposal Called Defiance," *Belfast Telegraph,* 19 Oct. 1966.

83. Bob Jones Jr., *Cornbread and Caviar* (Greenville, SC: Bob Jones Univ. Press, 1985).

84. "British Delegates Arrive for Second Convocation for Religious Freedom," *Christian Beacon,* 22 Sept. 1966; advertisement for the Second Convocation on Religious Freedom, *Philadelphia Evening Bulletin,* 22 Sept. 1966; "18,000 Attend Harrisburg (U.S.A.) Rally," *Protestant Telegraph,* 8 Oct. 1966.

85. Bob Jones Jr. to Billy James Hargis, 7 Nov. 1966, Fundamentalism File, Bob Jones Univ., Greenville, SC.

86. Ian Paisley to Bob Jones Jr., "Letters and Visits to Prisoners," 16 Aug. 1966, Fundamentalism File; Bob Jones Jr., *Cornbread and Caviar,* 145–51.

87. Bruce, *God Save Ulster!* 81–89; Bruce, *Paisley,* 270.

6. Civil Rights for the Green, the Black, and the Orange

1. Mulholland, 109–14.

2. "CRA = IRA, C.R.A.—Civil Rights Association, I.R.A.—Irish Republican Army," *Protestant Telegraph,* 19 Nov. 1968.

3. David Farber, *The Age of Great Dreams: America in the 1960s* (New York: Hill and Wang, 1994), 263–68.

4. Northern Ireland Civil Rights Association, *"We Shall Overcome": The History of the Struggle for Civil Rights in Northern Ireland, 1968–1978* (Belfast: Northern Ireland Civil Rights Association, 1978), 3–7.

5. Conn McCluskey, *Up Off Their Knees: A Commentary on the Civil Rights Movement in Northern Ireland* (Galway: Self-published, 1989), 1–33.

6. Bob Purdie, *Politics in the Streets: The Origins of the Civil Rights Movement in Northern Ireland* (Belfast: Blackstaff Press, 1990), 92–116.

7. "CRA = IRA, C.R.A.—Civil Right Association, I.R.A.—Irish Republican Army" and "Civil Rights—Then Communism," *Protestant Telegraph,* 19 Nov. 1968 and 15 May 1969; J. Bowyer Bell, *The IRA 1968–2000: Analysis of a Secret Army* (New York: St. Martin's Press), 73–76; Tim Pat Coogan, *The I.R.A.* (Niwot, CO: Roberts Rinehart, 1993), 249–58; Richard English, *Armed Struggle: A History of the IRA* (Oxford: Oxford Univ. Press, 2003). Paisleyites had a point: during the five decades following the 1916 Easter Rising, the Irish labor movement would not promote policies that upset the Roman Catholic Church in Ireland. For instance, at the Annual Conference of the Irish Labour Party (April 1939), Labour removed proposed amendments that called for a workers' republic and attacked

private property because the Catholic hierarchy disliked the proposals. Unlike the Russian revolutionaries of the early twentieth century who were atheists, many Irish leftists retained their Catholic religiosity (W. K. Anderson, *James Connolly and the Irish Left* [Dublin: Irish Academic Press, 1994], 94–96).

8. Bardon, *A History of Ulster,* 652; Northern Ireland Civil Rights Association, *Constitution and Rules* (N.p.: Northern Ireland Civil Rights Association, 1967). Senator Elder walked out of the initial meeting because NICRA denounced capital punishment for the murder of policemen. Robin Cole and the UUP stayed in the civil rights association for a while, but most Liberals and many moderate Unionists joined the Alliance Party after it was formed in April 1970 (W. D. Flackes and Sydney Elliott, *Northern Ireland: A Political Directory 1968–1988* [Belfast: Blackstaff Press, 1989], 203, 278–79).

9. Gerry Adams, *Before the Dawn: An Autobiography* (New York: William Morrow, 1996), 75–91; Brian Dooley, *Black and Green: The Fight for Civil Rights in Northern Ireland and Black America* (London: Pluto Press, 1998), 42–47; M. L. R. Smith, *Fighting for Ireland? The Military Strategy of the Irish Republican Movement* (London: Routledge, 1995), 81–82.

10. "Fenians 'Treason' Marches Throughout Ulster," "Why Does Ulster's Rebel Go Free? Arrest Fenian Fitt and Rout the Republican Clubs," and "Craig Must Go: No Action Against Republicans," *Protestant Telegraph,* 4 Mar. 1967, 1 Apr. 1967, and 13 Apr. 1968; "Fenian Rising Ban Imposed," *Ulster Protestant,* Apr. 1967.

11. "Students' March: Paisley to Protest" and "Students March to Craig's Home," *Belfast Telegraph,* 14 Nov. and 15 Nov. 1967; Paul Arthur, *The People's Democracy 1968–1973* (Belfast: Blackstaff Press, 1974), 21–26; Simon Prince, *Northern Ireland's 68: Civil Rights, Global Revolt, and the Origins of the Troubles* (Dublin: Irish Academic Press, 2007).

12. *Annual Report of the General Assembly of the Presbyterian Church in Ireland* (Dublin: Presbyterian Church in Ireland, 1967).

13. Mulholland, 148–49.

14. *Parliamentary Debates, Parliament of Northern Ireland, House of Commons* (1967), vol. 65, cols. 1763–64, 1811–15, and vol. 66, cols. 145–48, 156–62, and 1049; Vincent E. Feeney, "Westminster and the Early Civil Rights Movement in Northern Ireland," *Eire-Ireland* 11 (1976): 3–13.

15. *Parliamentary Debates, Parliament of Northern Ireland, House of Commons* (1967), vol. 65, col. 1820–21.

16. Farber, 72–74.

17. "Let every soul be subject unto the higher powers: For there is no power but of God: the powers that be are ordained of God" (King James Version).

18. "Civil Disobedience and the Sit-ins," *Christian Beacon,* 19 Feb. 1961; "Guerrilla Warfare in U.S.A.," *Christian Crusade,* Aug.–Sept. 1967; "Integration and the Negro Revolt" and "Communist Use of Negro Agitators in War Against Christianity Not New," *Western Voice,* 12 Aug. 1965 and 24 Aug. 1967.

19. "A Segregationist Advises Rightists," *New York Times,* 30 Jan. 1962; Janson and Eisman, 69–91; Jorstad, 107–11.

20. Quoted in Dooley, 29–30.

21. "Dungannon Women in Housing Protest," *Belfast Telegraph,* 14 May 1963; Catherine B. Shannon, "From Housing Rights to Civil Rights 1963–8," in *The Field Day Anthology of Irish Writing,* vol. 5: *Irish Women's Writing and Traditions,* 379–81 (New York: New York Univ. Press, 2002).

22. Dooley, 43–46; Adams, *Before the Dawn,* 37. See also M. Farrell, *Northern Ireland,* 249; Paddy Devlin, *Straight Left: An Autobiography* (Belfast: Blackstaff Press, 1993), 87. A good example of the articles in the *Belfast Telegraph* is "50 Mile Freedom March on Alabama Resumes," 22 Mar. 1965. In *Black and Green,* Dooley acknowledges the inspiration of the American movement but asserts that Northern Ireland Catholics developed their own strategies, such as squatting in council houses and employing student marches. Very few direct contacts were made between American and Irish civil rights leaders, and almost everything that Northern Irish activists learned about the American movement came from television and newspapers.

23. "Inter-racial Tension in the South" and "Freedom in Alabama," *Irish Christian Advocate,* 27 Jan. and 2 June 1961.

24. "The Theology of Martin Luther King," *Christian Beacon,* 26 Mar. 1964; "Martin Luther King Spokesman for the Enemy," *Weekly Crusader,* 5 May 1967. Militant fundamentalists had a point: the historiography on Martin Luther King Jr. supports the contention that he had contact with socialist and Communist groups and individuals. See, for example, David J. Garrow, *The FBI and Martin Luther King, Jr.: From "Solo" to Memphis* (New York: W. W. Norton, 1981), and Thomas F. Jackson, *From Civil Rights to Human Rights: Martin Luther King, Jr. and the Struggle For Economic Justice* (Philadelphia: Univ. of Pennsylvania Press, 2007).

25. "Martin Luther King," *Protestant Telegraph,* 13 Apr. 1968.

26. "The Theology of Martin Luther King," *Christian Beacon,* 26 Mar. 1964; "Martin Luther King Is Dead" and "Who Is behind the Murder of Martin Luther King?" *The Sword of the Lord,* 26 Apr. and 24 May 1968; "Martin Luther King a Spokesman for the Enemy," *Weekly Crusader,* 5 May 1967; "King and the Communist Front," *Western Voice,* 2 Sept. 1965; "Martin Luther King" and "Violence the Fruit of King's 'Non-violence' Campaign, " *Protestant Telegraph,* 27 Apr. 1968.

27. "Ecumenical News Column," *Church of Ireland Gazette,* 26 Apr. 1968; "The WCC Has Launched a Martin Luther King Memorial Fund," *Presbyterian Herald,* July–Aug. 1968.

28. Although the founding of the Loyal Orange Institution of Ireland (Orange Order) in 1795 and the order's contribution to Irish history has been well documented (I also briefly examine it in chapter 3), the order's historical and political significance is beyond the scope of this study except for the vital years between 1965 and 1968. What is

important, however, is the relationship between the Orange Order and the Reverend Ian Paisley.

29. Geoffrey Bell, *The Protestants of Ulster* (London: Pluto Press, 1976), 15–33; Gary McMichael, *Ulster Voice: In Search of Common Ground in Northern Ireland* (Boulder, CO: Roberts Rinehart, 1999), 4–5.

30. "Church Halls Closed to Rev. Ian Paisley," *Ballymena Observer,* 4 May 1951; Eric P. Kauffman, *The Orange Order: A Contemporary Northern Irish History* (Oxford: Oxford Univ. Press, 2007), 21–48; Moloney, *Paisley,* 46–50.

31. Kauffman, 21–48.

32. "Editorial—Orange Order," *Presbyterian Herald,* July–Aug. 1968; "Turmoil at the Twelfth: Orangemen's No Confidence in O'Neill," *Protestant Telegraph,* 22 July 1967; Moloney and Pollak, 145–47; Mulholland, 120–22.

33. Kauffman, 21–48.

34. "Orangemen Want to Have MP Expelled from Order" and "Orange Order to Take Fresh Look at Its Rules," *Belfast Telegraph,* 16 Feb. 1967 and 8 Feb. 1968; Moloney, *Paisley,* 140–42.

35. Dominic Bryan, *Orange Parades: The Politics of Ritual, Tradition, and Control* (London: Pluto Press, 2000), 52–54.

36. From the *Belfast Telegraph:* "Grand Lodge Glad Bishop Isn't Coming," 3 Feb. 1967; "Orange Order No Right to Dictate to Church of Ireland—Canon," 9 Feb. 1967; "Independent Orangemen Attack Bishop," 11 Feb. 1967; "Orange Services—Bishop Speaks," 10 Feb. 1967. See also "Dr. Alfred Martin Moderator of Irish Presbyterian Church Attacked Orange Institution for Its Stand Against Moorman Visit," *Protestant Telegraph,* 18 Feb. 1967.

37. Quoted in "Views of Anglican Bishop of Primacy, Deacons, and Collegiality," Divine Word News Service, 21 Oct. 1963. This Vatican-run news service issued press releases during the Second Vatican Council.

38. "Pope's Quisling Bishop to Visit Belfast (Unprecedented Protest Planned)," *Protestant Telegraph,* 21 Jan. 1967. Although still a minority opinion within the Anglican community, support for Anglo-Roman unity was increasing among the Anglican ministry and leadership in this period. See A. Hastings, *A History of English Christianity,* 536–80, and Moloney, *Paisley,* 139–40.

39. "Unprecedented Protest Planned: Pope's Quisling Bishop to Visit Belfast," *Belfast Telegraph,* 21 Jan. 1967; Moloney, *Paisley,* 139–40.

40. Quoted in Michael Manktelow, *John Moorman: Anglican, Franciscan, Independent* (Norwich, UK: Canterbury Press, 1999), 72.

41. "Comment," *Church of Ireland Gazette,* 3 Feb. 1967.

42. "Bar on Bishop: Cathedral Permission Is Withdrawn," "Bishop Cancels Visit: Reason Given Is 'Local Opposition,'" and "'No Pressure' Says PM: Reply to MP about Dean's Decision," *Belfast Telegraph,* 30 Jan. and 2 Feb. 1967 (last two); "Bishops Condemn 'Threats of Disturbance,'" *Church of Ireland Gazette,* 17 Feb. 1967.

43. "Great Victory for Ulster Protestants: Bishop's Visit Off," *Protestant Telegraph,* 4 Feb. 1967.

44. From the *Church of Ireland Gazette:* "Bishop of Ripon to Discuss Vatican Council," 8 Aug. 1966; "Church of Ireland Clarifies Its Position in Regards to Others," 23 Sept. 1966; "Dialogue with Roman Churches," 13 Jan. 1967; "Bishops Condemn Threats of Disturbance," 17 Feb. 1967.

45. "Police Cordon as Paisley Stages Parade" and "O'Neill's Pact Foiled: Protest March Banned but General Assembly Picketed," *Belfast Telegraph,* 9 Jan. 1967 and 10 June 1967.

46. Presbyterian Church in Ireland, *Minutes of the General Assembly and Directory of the Presbyterian Church in Ireland, 1968* (Belfast: Presbyterian Church in Ireland, 1968), 20; John M. Barkley, *The Antichrist, a Historical Survey: A Lecture Delivered at the Public Closing of the Presbyterian College, Belfast on 26th May, 1967* (Belfast: Presbyterian Church in Ireland, 1967), 16–21. The Presbyterian Church in Ireland proposed to delete from its confession the reference to the pope as the Antichrist, which was an important tenet of the original Westminster version.

47. "Paisley Pickets in Scene at Assembly," "Paisley Plan for Assembly Protest Is Kept Secret," and "No Charges after Incident at Assembly—RUC," *Belfast Telegraph,* 6 June 1967, 3 June 1968, and 4 June 1968.

48. "O'Neill Welcomes Ulster's Would-Be Destroyer," *Protestant Telegraph,* 23 Dec. 1967.

49. "O'Neill the Dictator," *Belfast Telegraph,* 8 Oct. 1966; see also "Councillor Paisley Stoned by R.C.'s," *Belfast Telegraph,* 30 Sept. 1967.

50. "Free Presbyterian Minister Charged" and "Police Action 'Ridiculous' Says Craig: The Case of Rev. John Douglas," *Belfast Telegraph,* 9 Nov. 1966 and 2 Sept. 1967; Home Secretary File on Paisley Faction, PRONI, passim, but see especially "(Secret) Report on the Paisleyite Faction."

51. "Protest over Royal Visit to Cathedral," "Jeers at Moderator Outside Meeting," and "Protest at Next Year's Assembly," *Glasgow Herald,* 27 Nov. 1967, 6 Apr. 1968, and 25 May 1968; "Pastor Glass Sets Sights on Second Reformation," *Protestant Telegraph,* 3 Feb. 1969.

52. Paisley, *For Such a Time as This,* 142–46.

53. "Theologians Begin 'Unity of Truth' Talks" and "Paisley Leads Church Unity Protest March," *Belfast Telegraph,* 30 Aug. and 2 Sept. 1967; "No Popery Protest at Coventry Cathedral, by Brian Green" and "Traitor Shouts Greet Dr. Ramsey at Unity Service," *Protestant Telegraph,* 5 Aug. 1967 and 24 Jan. 1968. The BCPCC is the British subsidiary of the WCC.

54. Paisley, *For Such a Time as This,* 142–46.

55. "Student Humour Greets Paisley's Charges" and "Paisleyism Rejected in Poll," *Belfast Telegraph,* 24 Nov. and 12 Dec. 1967; "Belfast Telegraph Shocked by Their Own

Rigged Poll: Over Half of Belfast Protestants Support Dr. Paisley" and "Cherwell, the Oxford Univ. Magazine Answered," *Protestant Telegraph*, 23 Dec. and 25 Nov. 1967.

7. Paisley, the Elijah of Ulster

1. "A Report on Religious Persecution in Northern Ireland," *Christian Beacon*, 1 Sept. 1966. Although McIntire did not specifically describe Paisley as a martyr, he made it clear he thought Paisley to be a victim of governmental abuse and compared Paisley's General Assembly protest to the Apostle Paul's arrest in Jerusalem—recorded in Acts 21:27. See also "McIntire Writes Queen," *Christian Beacon*, 1 Sept. 1966; "World Renown Preacher Visits Belfast," *Protestant Telegraph*, 27 Aug. 1966; Bruce, *Paisley and Politics*, 80–90.

2. Carl McIntire to Norman Porter, 15 Apr. 1965, McIntire Collection; Stroman, 141–46. It is interesting that McIntire used the Independent Fundamental Churches of America (IFCA) as an example; an early member of the ACCC, the IFCA withdrew in 1953 over McIntire's dictatorial leadership of the ACCC, his portrayal of the *Christian Beacon* as the official ACCC mouthpiece, and his criticism of the relationships that some IFCA members maintained. IFCA members also disliked McIntire's style of militant fundamentalism ("Shifting Patterns of Theological Affiliations," *The Voice*, Jan. 1968). In 1960, the IFCA had eight hundred affiliated churches; McIntire thus alienated a substantial group.

3. "UPI Report from Belfast," in Bible Presbyterian Church, *Minutes of the Thirtieth General Synod of the Bible Presbyterian Church, Christian Admiral, Cape May, N.J. October 19–25, 1966* (Collingswood, NJ: Bible Presbyterian Church, 1966); ICCC, "Concerning Rev. Ian Paisley," press release, 28 July 1966, McIntire Collection. The UPI report on Paisley's release from prison came during the Thirtieth Bible Presbyterian Synod. It is difficult to ascertain why the Bible Presbyterian Church targeted UPI. Most American and European newspapers used either Associated Press reports ("Militant Pastor Freed from Belfast Jail," *International Herald Tribune*, 20 Oct. 1966) or their own correspondents ("Paisley Released from Belfast Jail," *New York Times*, 20 Oct. 1966), but few relied on reports from UPI.

4. "Associated Press Uses Double Standard in Reporting Religious News from Geneva, Northern Ireland," "The Reasons I Chose Jails," and "Paisley Writes from Belfast Prison," *Christian Beacon*, 4 Aug. (first two) and 25 Aug. 1966.

5. For example, in the foreword to Paisley's *An Exposition of the Epistle to the Romans*, Bob Jones Jr. proclaimed Paisley as a "sent" preacher in the tradition of the Old Testament prophet Jeremiah and the great reformers of the sixteenth century. By "sent," Jones meant a preacher whose ministry to save Elect human souls was preordained by God.

6. "Report on Religious Persecution in Northern Ireland," *Christian Beacon*, 1 Sept. 1966; "Reverend Ian Paisley Writes from Belfast Prison to Dr. Carl McIntire" and "American Presbyterian Church Supports Imprisoned Ministers' Stand," *Protestant Telegraph*, 1 Sept. and 5 Nov. 1966; "Bob Jones, Jr. Defends Irish Patriot," *The Sword of the Lord*, 23 Sept. 1966.

7. "Dr. Carl McIntire Writes Protest to Life on Paisley," *Christian Beacon,* 1 Sept. 1966; Hugh Moffett, "The Unholy War of Preacher Paisley," *Life* magazine, 19 Aug. 1966.

8. "An Innocent Preacher in Prison," *The Gospel Witness,* 18 Aug. 1966; advertisement, *Protestant Telegraph,* 5 Nov. 1966; "Dr. Bob Jones, Jr. Defends Irish Patriot," *The Sword of the Lord,* 23 Sept. 1966. *The Gospel Witness* referred to Paisley as "a modern George Whitefield. Undoubtedly he is God's man for this hour in Northern Ireland" ("Dr. Ian Paisley in Massey Hall," Mar. 1967).

9. "Bible Conference Notes," *Fellowship News,* 15 May 1965.

10. "Bob Jones Univ. Confers D.D. Degree on the Editor," *Protestant Telegraph,* 5 Nov. 1966. On 7 September 1966, the university granted only the fourth honorary degree conferred in its forty-year history and the only one, at the time, given in absentia to a person in jail.

11. Ian Paisley to Bob Jones Jr., 16 Aug. 1966, Fundamentalism File; Jones Jr., *Caviar and Cornbread,* 145–51.

12. Carl McIntire to Norman Porter, 12 May 1967, McIntire Collection.

13. Billy James Hargis to Bob Jones Jr., 17 Nov. 1966, Fundamentalism File.

14. "Ian Paisley to Begin Speaking Tour of U.S.," *Christian Beacon,* 6 Apr. 1967; "Bible Conference Notes," *Fellowship News,* 15 July 1967. The other featured speakers were Dr. H. C. Slade of Jarvis Street Baptist Church, Toronto; evangelist Glen Schunk of Greenville, South Carolina; Dr. Robert T. Ketcham of the General Association of Regular Baptist Churches; and Dr. Charles S. Poling of Phoenix.

15. "Dr. Ian Paisley in Massey Hall, May 5, 8 P.M.," *The Gospel Witness,* 30 Mar. 1967.

16. Advertisement, *Atlanta Constitution,* 1 Apr. 1967; "Restudy Bible, Cleric Urges," *Harrisburg Patriot,* 28 Apr. 1967.

17. Information provided to the author by email from an attendee at Paisley's talk to the Inter-City Baptist Church, Allen Park, Michigan (the home of Dr. William R. Rice), 21 Nov. 2006; Marion H. Reynolds Sr. to Carl McIntire, 21 Apr. 1967, McIntire Collection.

18. Carl McIntire to Norman Porter, 19 Dec. 1966, McIntire Collection; Carl McIntire to Norman Porter, 12 May 1967, McIntire Collection; Bob Jones Jr. to Billy James Hargis, 7 Nov. 1966, Fundamentalism File; Bible Presbyterian Church, *Minutes of the Thirty-First General Assembly of the Bible Presbyterian Church, Christian Admiral, Cape May, NJ, 1967* (Cape May, NJ: Bible Presbyterian Church, 1967); "Episcopal Rector Rectified," *Western Voice,* 20 Apr. 1967.

19. "Paisley to Begin on Short Wave," *Christian Beacon,* 4 July 1968; Heart-to-Heart Hour, Inc., *Dr. Paisley Interviewed on the Heart-to-Heart Hour,* pamphlet (Phoenix: Heart-to-Heart Hour, Inc., 1967). Paisley returned to the airwaves when he began round-the-world broadcasts on McIntire's network in November 1968 ("Dr. Paisley to Broadcast Daily Round the World: Short Wave 'Voice of Protestantism' Programme," *Protestant Telegraph,* 21 Sept. 1968).

20. Paisley, *The Archbishop in the Arms of the Pope of Rome!* 14–15; Paisley, *The Battle of the Reformation.*

21. "10 Reasons Why Romanism Breeds Communism," *Protestant Telegraph,* 16 Nov. 1968.

22. "Rome, Moscow, and Ulster by Councillor R. F. Henderson," *Protestant Telegraph,* 27 Sept. 1969.

23. "Is Loyal Rhodesia Rebellious?" "South Africa and Rhodesia: Report of a Fact-Finding Tour by Dr. Billy James Hargis of Christian Crusade, USA," and "Biafra—Another Vietnam?" *Protestant Telegraph,* 7 Jan. 1967, 13 Apr. 1968, and 19 Apr. 1969; "NCC Leads Vietnam 'Peace' Offensive," *Weekly Crusader,* 3 Feb. 1967; "Churchmen Clash on War in Vietnam," *Christian Beacon,* 8 Feb. 1968; "The Pope and Vietnam," and "Text of Address by Ian Smith," *Christian Crusade,* 3 Feb. 1968 and Apr. 1969.

24. "Rome and the War in Vietnam," *Protestant Telegraph,* 2 Nov. 1968.

25. Twentieth Century Reformation Hour, order form, 1 June 1964, McIntire Collection; Jorstad, 107–11; John Stormer, *None Dare Call It Treason* (Florissant, MO: Liberty Bell Press, 1964).

26. Richard Dudman, *Men of the Far Right* (New York: Pyramid Books, 1962), 52–63.

27. Kent Courtney and Phoebe Courtney, *The Case of General Edwin A. Walker* (New Orleans: Conservative Society of America, 1961), 30–42; Bernard Ledwidge, *DeGaulle* (New York: St. Martin's Press, 1982), 244–58. Walker ran for governor of Texas, but it appears that although he could speak well enough to address religious functions, he was not charismatic enough to inspire purely political audiences.

28. Billy James Hargis, *The Muzzling of General Walker* (Tulsa: Christian Crusade, 1962), 106–8; Stroman, 249–56.

29. "Governor Is Backed by Walker," "General Walker Is Arrested; in Hospital," and "General Walker Held for Mental Exam," *Jackson Clarion Ledger,* 28 Sept., 2 Oct., and 3 Oct. 1962.

30. Billy James Hargis to Bob Jones Jr., 1 Dec. 1961, Fundamentalism File; E. A. Walker to Carl McIntire, 24 May 1967, McIntire Collection; and "Operation: Midnight Ride Rallies!" *Christian Crusade,* Mar. 1963.

31. "Special Centennial Event: Canadian Council of Evangelical Protestant Churches," *The Gospel Witness,* 2 Mar. 1967; "Invocation by Dr. Bob Jones," *Protestant Telegraph,* 10 Aug. 1968.

32. "Address by Senator Strom Thurmond to the 20th Century Reformation Hour Freedom Rally, Robert Lee Gardiner Memorial Auditorium, Cape May, NJ at the Christian Admiral Hotel June 14, 1968 8:00 PM," *Christian Beacon,* 27 June 1968; Nadine Cohodas, *Strom Thurmond and the Politics of Southern Change* (New York: Simon and Schuster, 1993), 268–331. In 1948, as governor of South Carolina, Thurmond became the leading member of the Dixiecrat movement, a group of Southern delegates to the Democratic Party convention who opposed the party's civil rights platform and who

sought to thwart civil rights legislation. Over the next two decades in the US Senate, Thurmond championed segregation. In March 1956, the senator drafted the Southern Manifesto, which outlined southern resistance to integration; he also led the filibuster against the Civil Rights Bill of 1957 and voted against the Civil Rights Act of 1964. Thurmond also sent a telegram to President Kennedy after the Ole Miss riots and, like General Edwin A. Walker, contrasted the federal "invasion" of Mississippi with inaction against Communist Cuba. Thurmond strongly supported General Walker on the Senate floor, making seventeen Senate speeches, orchestrating the wiring of seventeen thousand telegrams to the Armed Forces Committee, and holding thirty-six days of hearings on the Walker affair.

33. Bruce Galphin, *The Riddle of Lester Maddox* (Atlanta: Camelot, 1968), 1–65.

34. Quoted in ibid., 8.

35. Quoted in ibid., 197.

36. "A Message from the Governor," text of remarks prepared for delivery by Governor Lester Maddox at the Calvary Baptist Church, Rittman, Ohio, Sunday, 9 Nov. 1969, 10:30 AM, Lester Maddox Collection, Russell Library for Political Research and Studies, Univ. of Georgia, Athens, GA.

37. "U.S. Needs Revival, Maddox Says," *Atlanta Journal,* 25 Sept. 1967; "Maddox Joins Ranks of Opponents of Church Union" and "Governor Lester Maddox to Join Trenton March," *Christian Beacon,* 3 Apr. and 16 Oct. 1969; Lester Garfield Maddox, *Speaking Out: The Autobiography of Lester Garfield Maddox* (New York: Doubleday, 1975), 167–78.

38. "Governor Maddox Explains His Position," *Christian Beacon,* 23 Oct. 1969.

39. "Governor Maddox of Georgia, U.S.A. Speaks His Mind," *Protestant Telegraph,* 30 Sept. 1967.

40. Quoted in *Fellowship News,* 25 May 1968; see also *Fellowship News,* 29 June 1968, and "Paisley Blasts Church Councils in BJU Talk," *Greenville News,* 7 Apr. 1968.

41. "Bible Conference Notes," *Fellowship News,* 27 Apr. 1968.

42. Matthew 5:13 says: "Ye are the salt of the earth: but if the salt has lost his savour, wherewith shall it be salted? It is thenceforth good for nothing, but to be cast out, and to be trodden under foot of men" (King James Version).

43. "Outline of John Stormer Speech," *Fellowship News,* 25 May 1968. Exact quotations from the Bob Jones Bible Conference are impossible to obtain because the university-published *Fellowship News* employed paraphrased reports from observers.

44. Paisley's first political epiphany occurred in January 1949 and is discussed in chapter 9.

45. "Civil Disobedience and the Sit-Ins" and "The Christian Attitude Towards Race," *Christian Beacon,* 19 Feb. 1961 and 10 Mar. 1966; David L. Chappell, *A Stone of Hope: Prophetic Religion and the Death of Jim Crow* (Chapel Hill: Univ. of North Carolina Press, 2004), 105–24; David L. Chappell, "Disunity and Religious Institutions in the White South," in *Massive Resistance: Southern Opposition to the Second Reconstruction,* edited

by Clive Webb, 136–50 (Oxford: Oxford Univ. Press, 2005); George Lewis, "White South, Red Nation: Massive Resistance and the Cold War," in Webb, ed., *Massive Resistance,* 117–35. Segregationists employed numerous biblical passages and stories to argue against segregation and to show the consequences of miscegenation: the division of Noah's lineage into three racial groups—the white races of Shem and Japheth and the dark races of Ham (Genesis 9:18—10:32); "And the sons of Noah, that went forth of the ark, were Shem, Ham, and Japheth; and Ham is the father of Canaan"; "These are the families of the sins of Noah, after their generations, in their nations: and by these were the nations divided in the earth after the flood"; Ham and his descendants were to become the servant race—"Cursed be Canaan, a servant of servants shall be unto his brethren" (Genesis 9:24–27); in the New Testament, new Christians were ordered not to marry nonbelievers (2 Corinthians 6:14–17); "Be not unequally yoked together with unbelievers: for what fellowship hath righteousness with unrighteousness—and what communion hath light with darkness," so that during the Second Coming all nations in the church triumphant would preserve their cultural and racial distinctiveness (Revelation 22:24); "And the nations of them which are saved shall walk in the light of it: and the Kings of the earth do bring their glory and honour into it." Militant fundamentalists insisted, then, that divinely ordered segregation was part of God's plan. (All Bible quotes are from the King James Version.)

46. Bible Presbyterian Church, *Minutes of the Twenty-Ninth General Synod of the Bible Presbyterian Church, Christian Admiral, Cape May, NJ, Oct. 19–25, 1965* (Cape May, NJ: Bible Presbyterian Church, 1965); *Segregation and God's Word* (Decatur, IL: Voice of Liberty, n.d.); Billy James Hargis, *The Truth about Segregation* (N.p.: n.p., n.d.).

47. "From the President of Bob Jones University," *Fellowship News,* 9 Oct. 1965.

48. Bob Jones Sr., *Is Segregation Scriptural?* (Greenville, SC: Bob Jones Univ. Press, 1960).

49. "Bob Jones University, New Curricula for Bigotry," *The Nation,* 29 Mar. 1965.

50. *Bob Jones University Handbook 1982–1983,* 20, Archives Research Center, Bob Jones Univ.; "Bob Jones University's Position on Interracial Marriage," 1982; Jones Jr., *Cornbread and Caviar*; Turner, 223–30.

8. Christian Disobedience in Ulster

1. *Disturbances in Northern Ireland: Report of the Cameron Commission Appointed by the Governor of Northern Ireland (Cameron Report)* (Belfast: HMSO, 1969).

2. "Right Group Protest at Caledon" and "Currie Squats in House," *Belfast Telegraph,* 19 June and 20 June 1968; Purdie, 135–37.

3. "Dungannon March Just the Beginning," *Belfast Telegraph,* 26 Aug. 1968; *Parliamentary Debates, Parliament of Northern Ireland, House of Commons* (1968), vol. 64, col. 1091; Max Hastings, *Barricades in Belfast: The Fight for Civil Rights in Northern Ireland* (New York: Taplinger, 1970), 43–45; Niall O'Dochartaigh, *From Civil Rights to Armalites: Derry and the Birth of the Irish Troubles* (Cork: Cork Univ. Press, 1977), 12–26.

4. "Fitt, Currie, and the I.R.A." and "No Surrender," *Protestant Telegraph*, 7 Sept. 1968 and 5 Nov. 1966.

5. Moloney, *Paisley*, 150; Purdie, 135.

6. Ian McBride, *The Siege of Derry in Ulster Protestant Mythology* (Dublin: Four Courts Press, 1997), 9–15.

7. N. O'Dochartaigh, *From Civil Rights to Armalites*, 19–25.

8. "Nationalists to Shelve Civil Disobedience, Currie Proposal Lost" and "Paisley's Maghera Parade Goes Without Incident," *Belfast Telegraph*, 24 June and 9 Sept. 1968; "Fitt, Currie, and the I.R.A.: Provocation by Rebel Mob," *Protestant Telegraph*, 7 Sept. 1968; M. Hastings, *Barricades in Belfast*, 50–52; Eamonn McCann, *War and an Irish Town*, 2nd ed. (London: Pluto Press, 1993), 69; Fionnbarra O'Dochartaigh, *Ulster's White Negroes* (Edinburgh: AK Press, 1974), 39–74.

9. McCann, 37–40. Prior to 5 October 1968, no Catholic parade or procession had been allowed inside Londonderry's city walls. Thus, Protestants dubbed the town the "maiden city": its walls had never been violated. The reference also alludes to the siege of Derry.

10. Coogan, *The Troubles*, 179–90.

11. Ronald Bunting, a former British army officer and one-time socialist supporter of Gerald Fitt, founded the Loyal Citizens of Ulster. After being saved by Paisley's evangelism, Bunting formed small Paisleyite groups that often counterdemonstrated against civil rights marches—for instance, in Armagh in November 1968 and against the Long March in January 1969.

12. Boulton, 71–88; N. O'Dochartaigh, *From Civil Rights to Armalites*, 19–25.

13. Moloney and Pollak, 153–60.

14. Quoted in O'Dochartaigh, *From Civil Rights to Armalites*, 42–43.

15. "2 Derry Rallies: Civil Rights Demonstrators Face Opposition," "We'll Not Change Route Marchers Tell Craig," and "8,000 Marchers Halted Near Paisley Crowd," *Belfast Telegraph*, 18 Oct., 14 Nov., and 30 Nov. 1968; "10,000 Loyalists Demonstrate at Londonderry," *Protestant Telegraph*, 11 Nov. 1968; Michael Farrell, *Civil Rights Twenty Years On: A Personal View* (Dingle, Ireland: Brandon, 1988), 54–74.

16. Purdie, 139–44; Barry White, *John Hume: Statesman of the Troubles* (Belfast: Blackstaff Press, 1984), 40–51.

17. "Wilson Blackmails Ulster," *Protestant Telegraph*, 16 Nov. 1968; Tony Benn, *Office Without Power: Diaries 1968–1972*, vol. 2 (London: Hutchinson, 1987), 101; Richard Crossman, *The Diaries of a Cabinet Minister*, vol. 3: *Secretary of State for Social Services* (London: Hamish Hamilton and Jonathan Cape, 1972), 478; Eric Gallagher and Stanley Worrall, *Christians in Ulster, 1968–1980* (Oxford: Oxford Univ. Press, 1982), 42–45.

18. "Civil Rights—Then Communism," *Protestant Telegraph*, 17 May 1969.

19. "Missiles Thrown as Rival Factions Clash in Dungannon," *Belfast Telegraph*, 5 Dec. 1968; O'Neill, *Autobiography*, 145–49.

20. "1,000 Stage Sit-Down: Chanting Students 'Squat' in Street after Route Switch," *Belfast Telegraph,* 9 Oct. 1968; People's Democracy, *Why PD?* (N.p.: People's Democracy, n.d.); People's Democracy, "A People's Democracy: A Discussion on Strategy," *New Left Review* 55 (1969), 31–33.

21. M. Farrell, *Northern Ireland,* 242–45; McCann, 214.

22. "75 Taken to Hospital in Day of Ambushes," *Belfast Telegraph,* 4 Jan. 1968; Egan Bowes and Vincent McCormick, *Burntollet* (London: LSR, 1969); Bernadette Devlin, *The Price of My Soul* (New York: Knopf, 1969), 126; "'Civil Rights March' Smokescreen for Outlawed Republican Clubs," *Protestant Telegraph,* 11 Jan. 1969.

23. Quoted in Moloney and Pollak, 167.

24. Purdie, 210–18.

25. J. Bowyer Bell, *The Irish Troubles: A Generation of Violence 1967–1992* (New York: St. Martin's Press, 1992), 88–92.

26. Arthur, 56–58; Harbinson, 43–46; Terence O'Neill, *Ulster at the Crossroads* (London: Faber and Faber, 1969), 172.

27. "IRA Plots Unfolds: The Second Phase: Civil Disobedience," *Protestant Telegraph,* 22 Mar. 1969.

28. Brian Faulkner, *Memoirs of a Statesman,* edited by John Houston (London: Weidenfeld and Nicolson, 1978), 56.

29. Moloney, *Paisley,* 165–88.

30. Bardon, *A History of Ulster,* 672–79; Coogan, *The Troubles,* 60–81.

31. "W.C.C. Uppsala Sweden: A Report from Scotland by Rev. Jack Glass" and "What Really Happened at the W.C.C. at Uppsala," *Protestant Telegraph,* 27 July and 24 Aug. 1968; "Free Presbyterians Protest at W.C.C. Assembly," *The Revivalist,* July–Aug. 1968.

32. "Paisley Caught Up in Police Net at St. Paul's," *Belfast Telegraph,* 23 Jan. 1969.

33. Quoted in "Paisley Hits Back at Soper," *Belfast Telegraph,* 4 Dec. 1968.

34. *Parliamentary Debates, House of Lords* (London: HMSO, 1968), vol. 278, col. 1859; D. Cooke, *Peacemaker,* 152–53.

35. Presbyterian Church in Ireland, *Minutes of the General Assembly of the Presbyterian Church in Ireland, 1969* (Belfast: Presbyterian Church in Ireland, 1969).

36. "Civil Rights for Protestants," *Church of Ireland Gazette,* 20 Apr. 1969.

37. "Paisley in Court Row at Armagh," "Paisley Out Again: Leaves Jail After Signing Bail Bond," and "Paisley, Bunting Appeal Sentences," *Belfast Telegraph,* 27 Jan., 30 Jan., and 25 Mar. 1969.

38. "Ian Paisley—Ecumenical Power," *Christian Beacon,* 3 Apr. 1969; "11,000 Mar. in Support of Paisley," *Western Voice,* 3 Mar. 1969.

39. "Ian Paisley Shares Platform with His U.S. Mentor," *The Glasgow Herald,* 17 Feb. 1969; "Bob Jones III to Visit Ulster," *Protestant Telegraph,* 14 June 1969.

40. "Bible Conference Notes," *Fellowship News,* 24 May 1969.

41. "Paisley Arrested, Sentenced to Prison," "Ian Paisley—Ecumenical Prisoner," and "Paisley Released from Prison," *Christian Beacon,* 6 Feb., 10 Apr., and 8 May 1969; "IRA Plot Unfolds: The Second Phase of Civil Disobedience," *Protestant Telegraph,* 22 Mar. 1969; "Bible Conference Notes," *Fellowship News,* 24 May 1969; "11,000 March in Support of Paisley" and "A.C.C.C. Commends Paisley," *Western Voice,* 13 Mar. and 29 May 1969.

42. "Churches Awake to World Problems of To-Day," "Paisley Plans to Defy Swiss Ban," and "Paisley Protest in Bangor," *Belfast Telegraph,* 22 July 1968, 2 June 1969, and 9 June 1969; "Great Protest inside Geneva: An Eyewitness Account," *Protestant Telegraph,* 28 May 1969.

9. The Genesis of Ulster Amilitant Politics

1. "Mr Protestant, Nelson Gonzalez Talks to the Rev Ian Paisley MP MEP," *Third Way* 19 (Nov. 1996): 13–17. *"Big House" Unionism* is a derisive term that working-class Protestants use to refer to the UUP leadership, who are mostly middle and upper class.

2. Ibid.

3. Bardon, *A History of Ulster,* 588–91; Moloney and Pollak, 28–29.

4. Bruce, *God Save Ulster!* 64–68; Moloney, *Paisley,* 24–27.

5. "West Belfast Victor," *Derry Standard,* 27 Feb. 1950; Moloney and Pollak, 35–37; Smyth, *Ian Paisley,* 4–6.

6. Moloney, *Paisley,* 19–24.

7. "National Union of Protestants Organise Petition Creed and Hospitals," *Belfast Telegraph,* 20 Jan. 1950; *Intoxicating Liquor and Licencing Bill (Northern Ireland)* (Belfast: HMSO, 1958); Moloney, *Paisley,* 28–31.

8. "Drinking Blamed on Television," *Belfast Telegraph,* 19 May 1960; "I.F.A. and the Sunday Matches," "Protestantism in Bangor: Is it Declining?" and "Limavady and the Lord's Day," *Ulster Protestant,* July 1958, Apr. 1959, and Feb. 1960.

9. Moloney, *Paisley,* 19–45.

10. Ibid.; Moloney and Pollak, 33–51. In the spring of 1954, London forced Porter to split with Paisley a £400 endowment left to the NUP. Porter and his supporters resigned from the group afterward and formed the EPS.

11. "Little 'Twelfth' at Shipyards," *Belfast Telegraph,* 10 July 1959; *Parliamentary Debates, Parliament of Northern Ireland, House of Commons* (1957), vol. 41, cols. 1993–95, and (1958), vol. 42, cols. 1987–2016.

12. Moloney, *Paisley,* 92–99.

13. "National Union of Protestants," *Belfast Telegraph,* 24 Jan. 1952; Macquigg, 176–177; Smyth, *Ian Paisley,* 6–9.

14. Moloney and Pollak, 98–102.

15. "The Urban Council Elections," *Northern Constitution,* 24 May 1958.

16. Cairns, 60–64; Moloney, *Paisley,* 92–99.

17. Moloney, *Paisley,* 80–84.

18. Quoted in "Paisley Says He'll Be MP at Stormont," *Belfast Telegraph,* 20 July 1966; "Paisley Wants to Become Northern Ireland MP," *Daily Telegraph,* 21 July 1966.

19. Moloney, *Paisley,* 122–25. Paisley and the PUP helped to defeat Kilfedder by making it known that the Unionist had attended Fine Gael meetings as a student at Trinity College Dublin. Fine Gael is a major political party in the Republic of Ireland.

20. Moloney, *Paisley,* 148–49. Paisley won approximately 39 percent of the vote; Terence O'Neill took 47 percent; and Michael Farrell of People's Democracy received the other 14 percent. The PUP's populist economic policy was laid out in the *Protestant Telegraph* for 22 February 1969: "Complete parity with the United Kingdom, both in services and taxation; Reorganisation of local government with reform of its taxation system to ensure that every elector obtains his full democratic rights and equable financial treatment; Crash programme on housing, with particular reference to the improvement of existing houses and twilight zones and the speed-up of slum clearances and redevelopment; Reduction of the rate of employment to at least one third of its present level, that is to the United Kingdom limit or below, by the gearing of the whole Government machinery to this end; Full employment must be the final goal of government; Improvement of household incomes by 25 percent to bring them to the United Kingdom standard by the immediate introduction of modern management techniques and production methods; Raising of education, health, and welfare standards to the levels reached in the progressive regions of Great Britain; and a new deal in agriculture with a firm future for the small farmer ensured." For the next thirty-five years, the PUP and the DUP followed a similar platform.

21. O'Neill, however, kept his Stormont seat.

22. "Requiem for O'Neill," *Protestant Telegraph,* 3 May 1969; Moloney, *Paisley,* 81–192.

23. *Report of the Advisory Committee on Police in Northern Ireland (Hunt Report)* (Belfast: HMSO, 1969).

24. K. Bloomfield, *A Tragedy of Errors,* 30–49; Michael Cunningham, *British Government Policy in Northern Ireland, 1969–2000* (Manchester, UK: Manchester Univ. Press, 2001), 5–11; English, 134–47.

25. Bardon, *A History of Ulster,* 672–703; Ed Moloney, *A Secret History of the IRA* (New York: W. W. Norton, 2002), 84–118.

26. "Paisley to Come to U.S.; Bernadette Faces Opposition," *Christian Beacon,* 4 Sept. 1969; "Rev. Paisley Arrives in Phila. to Counter Miss Devlin's Drive," *Philadelphia Inquirer,* 7 Sept. 1969; "Ireland Becomes 'Test Case' for World Domination by Rome," *Western Voice,* 4 Sept. 1969. In fall 1969, the Twentieth Century Reformation Hour also published the eight-page pamphlet *Report on Ulster.*

27. "Northern Ireland 'Truth Squad' Hits Castro in Miniskirt," *Western Voice,* 25 Sept. 1969.

28. "Bias Against Protestants, Says Paisley" and "RC Church Nearer to Communism—Paisley," *Belfast Telegraph,* 10 Sept. and 11 Sept. 1969; "Hymn-Singers, McIntire Welcome Rev. Paisley to Phila," *Christian Beacon,* 11 Sept. 1969; Ian R. K. Paisley, *Northern Ireland: Message Delivered at Bob Jones University, September 12, 1969* (N.p.: n.p., n.d.), 5–22.

29. "Surrender by Installments—Faulkner Policy of Appeasement" and "Action—Now?" *Protestant Telegraph,* 3 July and 4 Sept. 1971.

30. Boulton, 104–11; Faulkner, 50–51.

31. "ICR Launches Campaign to Help Afflicted Protestants in Ulster" and "ICR Receiving Funds for Ulster Protestants," *Christian Beacon,* 4 Sept. and 11 Sept. 1969; "Dr. Bob Jones in Ireland Revival," *Sword of the Lord,* 14 Nov. 1969.

10. The Second Coming: Paisley and the "Civil" Religion of Democratic Unionism

1. For the rest of this study (from January 1970 onward), the name "Irish Republican Army" refers to the Provisional IRA; other Republican paramilitaries, such as the Official IRA and the Irish National Liberation Army, although important to the military and political histories of the "Troubles," are peripheral to this work.

2. "Paisley Party to Fight 2 Seats" and "Protestant Unionists Triumph in Woodvale," *Belfast Telegraph,* 19 Jan. and 5 Feb. 1970; "Protestant Unionists Win in Woodvale," *Protestant Telegraph,* 21 Feb. 1970. The PUP contested and won the two seats from the Woodvale Ward of Belfast.

3. "Double Paisleyite Victory Stunning Blow to Unionists," *Belfast Telegraph,* 17 Apr. 1970.

4. Quoted in "Paisley's Only Seeking Publicity Voters Told: Bannside Would Be Left to Rot," *Protestant Telegraph,* 11 Apr. 1970.

5. "Paisleyites at London R.C. March" and "Double Paisleyite Victory Stunning Blow for Unionists," *Belfast Telegraph,* 26 Jan. and 17 Apr. 1970; "Ulster Needs Deliverance," *Protestant Telegraph,* 13 June 1970.

6. "Articles of Faith of FPCU," *The Revivalist,* Nov.–Dec. 1969.

7. Email to author from Patrick Robbins, director of the Fundamentalism File, Bob Jones Univ., undated.

8. "Protestant Unionists in the Battle," *Protestant Telegraph,* 22 Feb. 1969.

9. Moloney, *Paisley,* 227–32; Walker, 190–97.

10. Smyth, *Ian Paisley,* 28–34.

11. Bardon, *A History of Ulster,* 672–89.

12. Faulkner, 139–59.

13. "Internment: Dr. Paisley's Comments," "Whitelaw—Political Pope," and "Whitelaw's Plan—Blueprint for United Ireland," *Protestant Telegraph,* 4 Sept. 1971, 21 Apr. 1972, and 4 Nov. 1972; Kerr, 9–34, 117–37; Ian R. K. Paisley, *Union with Great Britain, Speech by Reverend Ian R. K. Paisley MP (Leader of the Opposition) Delivered in the Northern Ireland House*

of Commons on Wednesday, 22 March 1972 (N.p.: n.p., n.d.); Ian R. K. Paisley, *No to a United Ireland, Speech by Reverend Dr. Ian R. K. Paisley MP Delivered in the Northern Ireland House of Commons on Tuesday, 8th February 1972* (N.p.: n.p., n.d.).

14. Oliver Gibson, *We Are Not Divided* (Omagh, Northern Ireland: Omagh Democratic Unionist Association, 1972); Kauffman, 83–87; Ian R. K. Paisley, *The Ulster Problem Spring 1972: A Discussion of the True Situation in Northern Ireland* (Greenville, SC: Bob Jones Univ. Press, 1972).

15. Flackes and Elliott, 138–41.

16. Thomas Hennessey, *The Northern Ireland Peace Process: Ending the Troubles?* (New York: Palgrave, 2001), 6–18; MacGinty and Darby, 16–20.

17. "Total Integration" and "Outline of Some Proposals of the Ulster Democratic Unionist Party for the Consideration of Her Majesty's Government," *Protestant Telegraph,* 22 Apr. and 4 Nov. 1972; Brian Barton, "The Historical Background to the Belfast Agreement," in Barton and Roche, eds., *The Northern Ireland Question,* 12–37.

18. Ulster Democratic Unionist Party (DUP), *Ulster Democratic Unionist Party Election Manifesto* (Belfast: Ulster DUP, 1973).

19. Bew, Gibbon, and Patterson, *Northern Ireland 1921–1994,* 145–91; Faulkner, 239–50.

20. *Northern Ireland Constitution Act (1973)* (London: HMSO, 1973); Hennessey, 10–18.

21. "Vote for the Loyalist Coalition" and "Why I Chose to Serve," *Protestant Telegraph,* 6 July and 18 Aug. 1973; Hennessey, 10–18. The Vanguard Unionist Progressive Party, also known as the Vanguard Movement, began as an outlet for Unionists and Loyalists who wanted more violent efforts than the UUP and DUP would publicly condone. But many right-wing Unionists, such as the Reverend Martyn Smith and James Molyneaux, would not join Vanguard because of Craig's pro-independence stance and association with paramilitary groups. Although Vanguard did not gain wide electoral popularity, it did cause some UUP branches around Belfast to close temporarily. However, at times the UUP and the DUP would work with Craig and Vanguard when a unified Unionist political front was deemed necessary to thwart British policy—for instance, during the 1974 British general election and the Ulster Worker's Council Strike.

22. "Pitt-Faulkner Regime Forced on Ulster at the End of a Bayonet," *Protestant Telegraph,* 8 Feb. 1974.

23. "Loyalist Results" and "United Ulster Unionist Council," *Protestant Telegraph,* 9 Mar. and 11 May 1974; Walker, 212–21; Faulkner, 248–49.

24. Moloney, *Paisley,* 255–66.

25. Ibid., 266–81.

26. "Craig and the SDLP: The Facts about the Voluntary Coalition," *Protestant Telegraph,* 15 Nov. 1975.

27. Hennessey, 10–18; Walker, 212–21.

28. "The Halting of the Strike," *Protestant Telegraph,* 4 June 1977.

29. "Great Victories," *Protestant Telegraph,* July 1979; Walker, 225–28. Paisley sat in the European Parliament until 2004 despite his belief that the European Economic Community (and subsequently the European Union) was one of the ten horns of the Beast, as revealed in Revelation. To Paisley, the European Economic Community was founded by the Treaty of Rome, a majority of the countries comprising the community were Catholic, and the organization backed the reunification of Ireland. Although Paisley and the DUP opposed Britain's entry into the Common Market, Paisley felt that Irish Protestantism needed a voice in Strasbourg.

30. "Third Force Recruiting Begins," *Protestant Telegraph,* 6 Sept. 1974. The "Third Force" had also been proposed in the mid-1970s.

31. "Ulster's Day of Action," *Protestant Telegraph,* 21 Nov. 1981; Kauffman, 99–105; Walker, 228–33.

32. Liam Clarke, *Broadening the Battlefield: The H-Blocks and the Rise of Sinn Fein* (Dublin: Gill and MacMillan, 1987), 221–27; Hennessey, 19–27.

33. "The D.U.P's Response to the Prior Initiative" and "D.U.P. Gain Top Posts," *The Voice of Ulster,* June and July 1982.

34. "D.U.P. Will Fight Irish Dimension and Power-Sharing in Prior's Plan," *Protestant Telegraph,* Apr. 1982; Kerr, 9–34; O'Donnell, 22–24.

35. Bruce, *Paisley,* 210–19; Arwell Ellis Owen, *The Anglo-Irish Agreement: The First Three Years* (Cardiff: Univ. of Wales Press, 1994), 12–34; Patterson and Kauffman, 219–23.

36. Fergal Cochrane, *Unionist Politics and the Politics of Unionism since the Anglo-Irish Agreement* (Cork: Cork Univ. Press, 1997), 133–39; Hennessey, 38–48.

37. *An End to Drift: The Task Force Report Presented to Mr. Molyneaux and Dr. Paisley* (N.p.: n.p., 16 June 1987); *Common Sense: Northern Ireland—an Agreed Process* (Belfast: Ulster Political Research Group, 1987); Arthur Aughey, *Under Siege: Ulster Unionism and the Anglo-Irish Agreement* (London: Hurst, 1989), 176–82; Henry McDonald and Jim Cusack, *UDA: Inside the Heart of Loyalist Terror* (Dublin: Penguin, 2004), 103–10.

38. David Bloomfield, *Political Dialogue in Northern Ireland: The Brooke Initiative 1989–92* (London: MacMillan Press, 1998), 2–8, 40–55, 66–200; Cunningham, 78–80; Hennessey, 54–88. Thomas Hennessey, however, argues that the Anglo-Irish Agreement forced Unionists to begin a dialogue with the SDLP.

39. "Paisley Warns: Shutters Come Down If Conference Restarts," *Protestant Telegraph,* Nov. 1992; D. Bloomfield, *Political Dialogue,* 55–112; Cochrane, 273–82. During the opening of the Mayhew talks, Paisley went to Greenville, South Carolina, for the annual Bob Jones Bible Conference.

40. Bew, Gibbon, and Patterson, *Northern Ireland 1921–1994,* 228; David Bloomfield, *Developing Dialogue in Northern Ireland: The Mayhew Talks, 1992* (Houndmills, UK: Palgrave, 2001), 113–39; Hennessey, 88–99. The Downing Street Declaration stated: "The situation in Northern Ireland should never be changed by violence or the threat of

violence; any political settlement must depend on consent freely given in the absence of force or intimidation; there can be no talks between the two governments and those who use, threaten, or support political violence; there can be no secret agreements or understandings between government and organisations supporting violence 'as a price for its cessation'; those claiming a serious interest in advancing peace in Ireland should renounce for good the use or support for violence; if and when a renunciation of violence has been made and sufficiently demonstrated, 'new doors could open' and both governments would wish to respond 'imaginatively' to the new situation which would then arise."

41. Aughey, *The Politics of Northern Ireland,* 54–59; MacGinty and Darby, 29–32.

42. Steve Bruce, "Fundamentalism and Political Violence: The Case of Paisley and Ulster Evangelicals," *Religion* 31 (2001): 387–405; Dominic Bryan, "Drumcree: Marching Towards Peace in Northern Ireland," in *Peace at Last: The Impact of the Good Friday Agreement on Northern Ireland?* edited by Jorg Neuheiser and Steffan Wolff, 94–110 (New York: Berghahn Books, 2002); George J. Mitchell, *Making Peace* (New York: Knopf, 1999), 46–70; Chris Ryder and Vincent Kearney, *Drumcree: The Orange Order's Last Stand* (London: Methuen, 2001), 111–16.

43. Kerr, 9–34; MacGinty and Darby, 42–49; Mitchell, 46–70; Stefan Wolff, "Introduction: From Sunningdale to Belfast, 1973–98," in Neuheiser and Wolff, eds., *Peace at Last,* 1–24; Peter Shirlow, "Sinn Fein: Beyond and within Containment," in Neuheiser and Wolff, eds., *Peace at Last,* 60–75.

44. Hennessey, 188–220; Kauffman, 226–27; Walker, 257–62.

45. Kerr, 62–79; Chris Ryder, *The Fateful Split: Catholics and the Royal Ulster Constabulary* (London: Methuen, 2004), 247–79.

46. "Paisleyites at London R. C. March," *Belfast Telegraph,* 26 Jan. 1970; "Third Coast-to-Coast Tour of U.S.A.," *Protestant Telegraph,* 6 Dec. 1969; Ian R. K. Paisley, *God's Ultimatum to the Nation* (N.p.: n.p., n.d.).

47. "Paisley Disrupts House of Commons Catholic Mass," *Baptist Bible Tribune,* 21 July 1978; "Denial of Paisley's Visa a Disgrace," *The Reformation Reader,* Jan.–Mar. 1982; "State Department Denies Freedom of Speech: Government Bows to Roman Catholic Pressure," *The Evangelical Methodist,* Feb. 1982.

48. "Bible Conference Speakers," Archives Research Center, Bob Jones Univ.

49. "U.S. Is Said to Be Reviewing Issuance of a Visa to Paisley," *New York Times,* 15 Dec. 1981; "Paisley, Banned from U.S., Travels to Canada," *Philadelphia Inquirer,* 16 Jan. 1982; Ronald Cooke, *Ian Paisley: Protestant Protagonist par Excellence* (Hollidaysburg, PA: Manahath Press, 1984).

50. Rod Bell Sr., *The Mantle of the Mountain Man* (Greenville, SC: Bob Jones Univ. Press, 1999), 177–91; email from Rod Bell Sr. to the author, 8 Jan. 2008.

51. "Reports from America," *The Revivalist,* Feb. 1973; email from the Reverend Alan Cairns to the author, 20 June 2008.

52. Paisley, *God's Ultimatum to the Nation.*

53. Ibid.; "Ulster Needs Deliverance," *Protestant Telegraph,* 13 June 1970.

54. "Heath's Talks with Pope—Illegal" and "An Audience for Maggie," *Protestant Telegraph,* 7 Oct. 1972 and 19 Aug. 1977; "Archbishop of Canterbury Confronted with His Treachery" and "Dr Paisley Hits Out at 'Quislings,'" *The Revivalist,* May 1973 and Feb. 1975.

55. "The Proposed Visit of the Pope to Ulster," "Independent Orange Grand Master Speaks Out," and "Our Protest in Rome," *The Revivalist,* June–Aug., Sept., and Oct. 1989.

56. Advertisement, *News Letter,* 8 Nov. 1985; Paisley, *God's Ultimatum to the Nation.*

57. "Save Ulster from Sodomy Campaign," "DUP Leads Sex Shop Opposition," and "Around the Councils: Johnston Slams Abortion Act," *The Voice of Ulster,* June, Sept., and Nov. 1982.

58. "Ulster Triumphs—but Protestors Not Won Over," *Belfast Telegraph,* 12 Jan. 2004; "My Protest at Strasbourg: A Personal Account by Ian R. K. Paisley," *The Revivalist,* Jan. 1987; Bruce, *Paisley and Politics,* 163–66.

59. Carl McIntire to Norman Porter, 14 Nov. 1960, McIntire Collection.

60. "Kennedy Administration Cracks Down on Fundamental Churches: Income Tax Used to Harass Churches That Leave NC" and "ACCC Launches Campaign to Abolish Federal Income Tax: Authorities Provide Evidence of Abuse and Discrimination Against Independent Bible-Believing Churches," *Christian Beacon,* 19 Sept. and 8 Nov. 1962.

61. Billy James Hargis to Bob Jones Jr., 25 Oct. 1966, Fundamentalism Files; "Right-Wing Group Loses Tax Status," "Tax Status Is Lost by Hargis Crusade," and "Free Rebuttals on Radio Upheld," *New York Times,* 17 Nov. 1964, 22 Oct. 1966, and 14 June 1967. The IRS specifically cited the Christian Crusade's support for the Becker Amendment, an initiative to amend the Constitution to allow prayer and Bible reading in public schools.

62. "Station Accused of Rightist Stand" and "Fairness Rules for Reply to Radio or TV Attack Upheld by Supreme Court," *New York Times,* 15 Oct. 1967 and 10 June 1969; "Liberty Bell Rings, WXUR Leaves Air," *Philadelphia Evening Bulletin,* 6 July 1973; Clabaugh, 91–93; Morris, 259–314.

63. "Church Council Drops McIntire," *Christian Beacon,* 6 Nov. 1969; "McIntire Splits with Church Group He Founded, Charges 'Softness,'" *New York Times,* 1 Nov. 1969; "Dr. McIntire Denies Misusing Council Funds," *Philadelphia Evening Bulletin,* 15 Apr. 1971; ACCC news release, Nov. 1970; Morris, 212–13. The other groups voted out of the ACCC were: the United Christian Church, the Methodist Protestant Church, the South Carolina Baptist Fellowship, and the Independent Baptist Bible Mission.

64. The award—"For the Defense of the Scripture"—posthumously honored Bob Jones Sr. On 3 October 1971, Paisley became the fifth recipient of the honorarium in a ceremony at Martyrs Memorial Free Presbyterian Church. Bob Jones Jr. cited Paisley's book *Christian Foundations* as the basis for the award ("Dr. Paisley Honoured by Bob Jones University," *Protestant Telegraph,* 16 Oct. 1971).

65. Bible Presbyterian Church, *Minutes of the Thirtieth General Synod of the Bible Presbyterian Church; The Millennial Road* (Collingswood, NJ: Bible Presbyterian Church, 1966).

66. "The World Congress of Fundamentalists," *The Revivalist,* Aug. 1976; Ian Paisley to Carl McIntire, 20 Aug. 1977, McIntire Collection; Ian Paisley to J. C. Maris, General Secretary, ICCC, Amsterdam, 20 Aug. 1977, Fundamentalism File; Bob Jones Jr. to Ian Paisley, 11 Aug. 1978, Fundamentalism File; and Ian R. K. Paisley, "The Faith, the Fire, and Fight of a Fundamentalist," in *Word of Their Testimony: Sermons Delivered at the World Congress of Fundamentalists, Edinburgh, Scotland June 15–22, 1976,* 1–16 (Greenville, SC: Bob Jones Univ. Press, 1976). The McIntire quote can be found in Carl McIntire to Ian Paisley, 29 Sept. 1977, Fundamentalism File.

67. Carl McIntire to Ian Paisley, 29 Sept. 1977, Fundamentalism File.

68. Paisley, "The Faith, the Fire, and Fight of a Fundamentalist."

69. "Regarding Northern Ireland," World Congress of Fundamentalists Resolution, 1999, Fundamentalism File; Ian R. K. Paisley, *The Fundamentalist and His State* (Greenville, SC: Bob Jones Univ. Press, 1976); Oran Smith, *The Rise of Baptist Republicanism* (New York: New York Univ. Press, 1997), 113–24. Beginning with the 1964 Goldwater presidential campaign, the faculty, staff, and alumni of Bob Jones University made their own excursions into Republican politics. In 1976, a caucus of South Carolina Republicans associated with Bob Jones University took control of the Greenville Republican Party in order to back Ronald Reagan's presidential aspirations. After a successful effort, Bob Jones University became an important part of Republican politics in South Carolina. Since the late 1970s, conservative Republicans in South Carolina have accordingly pandered to the Bob Jones vote. It must be noted, however, that although political involvement by faculty, staff, and alumni was not official university policy, it existed with the school's tacit approval.

Bob Jones University also took an interest in Northern Ireland politics. In a letter to Representative Joseph J. DioGuardi (R–NY), dated 18 August 1988, Bob Jones III denounced the Congressman's "One Ireland Resolution," which aimed to raise money in order to press the British government into ending the partition of Ireland. Jones wrote: "Your blatant pro-Catholic bigotry makes me sick. Your pious protestations that your interest in a United Ireland is simply a matter of concern for the poor and the oppressed is a blatant mockery. You are a puppet on the Pope's string. The majority in Northern Ireland live in their little country because they want to be free of that Catholic Church tyranny which enslaves the south of Ireland. Why do you seek to deny that right? If the Catholics of Northern Ireland don't like what is there, they can move to the South. If not, they can remain where they are as a minority. The majority in Northern Ireland want nothing to do with the Pope. What business is it of yours, as an elected official in the U.S. Congress, to meddle in their affairs and raise money to overthrow the government?" (Robert Muldrow Cooper Library, Special Collections, Clemson Univ., Clemson, SC).

70. ICCC, "Open Letter to President Ronald Reagan," 26 Jan. 1982, McIntire Collection.

71. Jones Jr., *Cornbread and Caviar,* 189–94.

72. "Pastor Glass to Protest Against His Former Ally," *The Scotsman,* 15 June 1976; Jones Jr., *Cornbread and Caviar,* 179–88.

73. "Mr Jack Glass Ordained," *Protestant Telegraph,* 8 June 1968.

74. "Right Wing Legacy of Hargis and McIntire Remembered by Prominent Pastor in Texas, by Don Wilkey," *Baptists Today,* 20 Nov. 1967; "Statement from Billy James Hargis" and "Concerning American Christian College and the Summit by Billy James Hargis," *Christian Crusade Weekly,* 12 Oct. 1975 and 21 Mar. 1976; "Billy James Hargis, 79, Pastor and Anticommunist Crusader, Dies," *New York Times,* 29 Nov. 2004; "Evangelist Accused," *Oakland Tribune,* 10 Jan. 1976; "The Sins of Billy James Hargis," *Time* magazine, 16 Feb. 1976.

75. Clifford Smyth, "The DUP as a Politico-Religious Organisation," *Irish Political Studies* 1 (1986): 33–43.

76. Aughey, *Under Siege,* 176–82.

77. Cochrane, 40–58; "The H-Block Issue," *The Revivalist,* Nov. 1980–.

78. Bruce, *Paisley,* 138–47; Neil Southern, "The Democratic Unionist Party and the Politics of Religious Fundamentalism," PhD diss., Queen's Univ., Belfast, 2000, 189–225; Neil Southern, "Ian Paisley and Evangelical Democratic Unionists: An Analysis of the Role of Evangelical Protestantism within the Democratic Unionist Party," *Irish Political Studies* 20 (June 2005): 127–45.

79. For example, the DUP opposed increased charges for water usage in Northern Ireland. In September 1999, the UUP backed the renaming of the RUC as the "Police Services of Northern Ireland" and a recruitment drive to enlist more Catholic officers (a move to placate Catholics and the British government), but the DUP was hostile to these changes (Moloney, *Paisley,* 356–59).

80. Democratic Unionist Party (DUP), *DUP Manifesto 2005* (Belfast: DUP, 2005); DUP, *Getting It Right* (Belfast: DUP, 2007); Bruce, *Paisley and Politics,* 113–30.

81. William Brown, *An Army with Banners: The Real Face of Orangeism* (Belfast: Beyond the Pale, 2009); Kauffman and Patterson, 226–37; Jonathan Tonge and James W. McAuley, "The Contemporary Orange Order in Northern Ireland," in Bursteed, Neal, and Tonge, eds., *Irish Protestant Identities,* 289–302. Donaldson was the Westminster MP for Lagan Valley and a member of the UUP team that negotiated the Belfast Agreement.

82. Moloney, *Paisley,* 412–41.

83. Quoted in "Paisley Brazenly Rewrites His Own History to Take Credit for the Deal," *London Times,* Sunday, 15 Oct. 2006; Moloney, *Paisley,* 461–65.

84. "Paisley Talks Peace with Ireland's Leading Catholic," *London Times,* 10 Oct. 2006.

85. Moloney, *Paisley,* 499–511.

86. David Calvert, "A Short History of the D.U.P.," *Protestant Telegraph,* 9 Sept. 1981; Ganiel, "Ulster Says Maybe"; Smyth, "The DUP as a Politico-Religious Organisation"; Spencer, 29–39.

87. "Whither Free Presbyterian?" *The Burning Bush,* July 2007. Ivan Foster left the DUP in 1989.

88. "Presbytery Statement of Rededication Following the Election of a New Moderator," *The Burning Bush,* Feb. 2008; Moloney, *Paisley,* 499–511; "The Attack on God-Appointed, God-Anointed Leadership," *The Revivalist,* May 2007.

89. Bruce, *Paisley: Religion and Politics,* 163–66; Gladys Ganiel and Paul Dixon, "Religion, Pragmatic Fundamentalism, and the Transformation of the Northern Ireland Conflict," *Journal of Peace Research* 45 (2008): 419–36.

90. Email statement from Ivan Foster, 19 Mar. 2008; Moloney, *Paisley,* 225–27, 435–41.

91. "A Statement from Rev Ivan Foster on the Stepping Down of Dr. Ian Paisley as First Minister and Leader of the DUP," *The Burning Bush,* 4 Mar. 2008.

92. Moloney, *Paisley,* 513–16.

93. Mitchel, "Unionism"; see also Andrew R. Holmes, "The Evolution of Ian Paisley and the Movement He Led," 2009, a review of Steve Bruce's *For God and Ulster,* at http://www.christianitytoday.com/bc/2009/marapr/20.28.html.

94. Ganiel, *Evangelicalism and Conflict in Northern Ireland,* 120–52.

95. *"None Dare Call It Treason": Sermon Delivered to Martyrs Memorial Free Presbyterian Church by Ian R K Paisley,* pamphlet (N.p.: n.p., 22 Oct. 2000).

96. "The Northern Ireland Situation," *Canadian Revivalist,* Jan.–Feb. 2007; Bruce, *Paisley,* 163–66. In North America, Free Presbyterianism is a growing denomination with fourteen US and ten Canadian congregations in 2009.

97. Email to the author from the Free Presbyterian Church of North America, June 2008.

Works Cited

Primary Sources

Collections

Archives Research Center. Bob Jones Univ., Greenville, SC.

Fundamentalism File. Bob Jones Univ., Greenville, SC.

J. Gresham Machen Archives. Montgomery Library, Westminster Theological Seminary, Philadelphia.

Lester Maddox Collection. Russell Library for Political Research and Studies, Univ. of Georgia, Athens, GA.

McIntire Collection. Special Collections, Princeton Theological Seminary Libraries, Princeton, NJ.

Robert Muldrow Cooper Library. Special Collections, Clemson Univ., Clemson, SC.

World Conference of Faith and Order Collection. Special Collections, Univ. of Chicago.

Government Documents

Air Reserve Center Training Manual, Number 45-7550, USAF Reserve Instructor Course, Increment V, Volume 7, Student Text. Mitchel Air Force Base, NY: Headquarters Continental Air Command, 1960.

Civil Authorities (Special Powers) Act (Northern Ireland), 1922. Belfast: HMSO, 1922.

Disturbances in Northern Ireland: Report of the Cameron Commission Appointed by the Governor of Northern Ireland (Cameron Report). Belfast: HMSO, 1969.

Flags and Emblems (Display) Bill (Northern Ireland), 1954. Belfast: HMSO, 1954.

Home Secretary File on Paisley Faction. Public Record Office Northern Ireland (PRONI), Belfast.

Intoxicating Liquor and Licencing Bill (Northern Ireland). Belfast: HMSO, 1958.

Northern Ireland Constitution Act (1973). London: HMSO, 1973.

Parliamentary Debates, House of Lords. London: HMSO, 1968.

Parliamentary Debates, Parliament of Northern Ireland, House of Commons. Belfast: HMSO, 1957–67.

Report of the Advisory Committee on Police in Northern Ireland (Hunt Report). Belfast: HMSO, 1969.

Institutional Publications

50 Years . . . Carl McIntire and the Bible Presbyterian Church of Collingswood 1933–1983. Collingswood: Bible Presbyterian Church of Collingswood, New Jersey, 1983.

Bible Presbyterian Church. *Minutes of the Thirtieth General Synod of the Bible Presbyterian Church, Christian Admiral, Cape May, N.J. October 19–25, 1966.* Cape May, NJ: Bible Presbyterian Church, 1966.

———. *Minutes of the Thirty-First General Assembly of the Bible Presbyterian Church, Cape May, N.J., 1967.* Cape May, NJ: Bible Presbyterian Church, 1967.

———. *Minutes of the Twenty-Ninth General Synod of the Bible Presbyterian Church, Christian Admiral, Cape May, N.J., October 19–25, 1965.* Cape May, NJ: Bible Presbyterian Church, 1965.

Democratic Unionist Party (DUP). *DUP Manifesto 2005.* Belfast: DUP, 2005.

———. *Getting It Right.* Belfast: DUP, 2007.

Digest of Acts and Deliverances of the General Assembly of the Presbyterian Church in the United States of America. Philadelphia: Divine Word News Service, 1933.

An End to Drift: The Task Force Report Presented to Mr. Molyneaux and Dr. Paisley. N.p.: n.p., 16 June 1987.

Evangelical Protestant Society (EPS). *Introducing the Evangelical Protestant Society.* Belfast: EPS, n.d.

Free Presbyterian Church of Ulster. *The Free Presbyterian Church of Ulster: Crossgar Congregation.* Belfast: Free Presbyterian Church of Ulster, n.d.

Heart-to-Heart Hour, Inc. *Dr. Paisley Interviewed on the Heart-to-Heart Hour.* Pamphlet. Phoenix: Heart-to-Heart Hour, 1967.

International Council of Christian Churches (ICCC). *The Battle.* Collingswood, NJ: ICCC, 1965.

———. *Concerning Rev. Ian Paisley, Belfast, N.I.* Cape May, NJ: Bible Presbyterian Church, 1966.

———. *Constitution of the International Council of Christian Churches.* Amsterdam: ICCC, 1948.

———. *Minutes of Proceedings, British Isles Regional Conference of the International Council of Christian Churches, 24–30 July 1952.* N.p.: ICCC, n.d.

———. *Minutes of the Second Plenary Congress of the International Council of Christian Churches, Geneva, Switzerland, 16–23 Aug. 1950.* N.p.: ICCC, n.d.

———. *Sixth Plenary Congress, Geneva Switzerland, August 5–11, 1965.* Amsterdam: ICCC, 1965.

Irish Presbyterians, the Downgrade Continues! Belfast: Free Presbyterian Church of Ulster, 1955.

The Millennial Road. Collingswood, NJ: Bible Presbyterian Church, 1966.

Northern Ireland Civil Rights Association. *Constitution and Rules.* Belfast: Northern Ireland Civil Rights Association, 1967.

People's Democracy. *Why PD?* N.p.: People's Democracy, n.d.

Presbyterian Church in Ireland. *Annual Report of the General Assembly of the Presbyterian Church in Ireland.* Dublin: Presbyterian Church in Ireland, 1950–68.

———. *The Code: The Book of the Constitution and Government of the Presbyterian Church in Ireland.* Belfast: Presbyterian Church in Ireland, 1945.

———. *Minutes of the General Assembly and Directory of the Presbyterian Church in Ireland, 1968.* Belfast: Presbyterian Church in Ireland, 1968.

———. *Minutes of the General Assembly of the Presbyterian Church in Ireland.* Belfast: Presbyterian Church in Ireland, 1955–69.

Presbyterian Church (U.S.A.). *Book of Order: The Constitution of the Presbyterian Church (U.S.A).* Louisville, KY: General Assembly of the Presbyterian Church (U.S.A.), 1936.

Record of the Trial of the Reverend J. E. Davey by the Belfast Presbytery and of the Hearing of Appeals by the General Assembly, 1927. Belfast: Presbyterian General Assembly, 1927.

Segregation and God's Word. Decatur, IL: Voice of Liberty, n.d.

Ulster Constitution Defence Committee (UCDC) and Ulster Protestant Volunteers (UPV). *Ulster Constitution Defence Committee and Ulster Protestant Volunteer Constitution and Rules.* N.p.: UCDC and UPV, n.d.

Ulster Democratic Unionist Party (DUP). *Ulster Democratic Unionist Party Election Manifesto.* Belfast: Ulster DUP, 1973.

Ulster Political Research Group. *Common Sense: Northern Ireland—an Agreed Process.* Belfast: Ulster Political Research Group, 1987.

Who Is Carl McIntire? Testimony to Christ and a Witness for Freedom. Collingswood, NJ: Twentieth Century Reformation Hour, n.d.

Religious-Political Commentaries and Biographical Materials

Adams, Gerry. *Before the Dawn: An Autobiography.* New York: William Morrow, 1996.

———. *Free Ireland: Towards a Lasting Peace.* Niwot, CO: Roberts Rinehart, 1986.

Anderson, Reverend J. T. *Talks on the Bible to Sunday School Teachers.* N.p.: n.p., n.d.

Barkley, John M. *The Antichrist, a Historical Survey: A Lecture Delivered at the Public Closing of the Presbyterian College, Belfast on 26th May, 1967.* Belfast: Presbyterian Church in Ireland, 1967.

Bell, Rod, Sr. *The Mantle of the Mountain Man.* Greenville, SC: Bob Jones Univ. Press, 1999.

Benn, Tony. *Office Without Power: Diaries 1968–1972.* Vol. 2. London: Hutchinson, 1987.

Briggs, Charles A. *American Presbyterianism: Its Origin and Early History.* New York: Charles Scribner's Sons, 1885.

———. *Biblical Study: Its Principles, Methods, and History.* New York: Charles Scribner's Sons, 1883.

———. *Whither? A Theological Question for the Times.* New York: Charles Scribner's Sons, 1889.

Bryan, William Jennings. *In His Image.* New York: Fleming H. Revell, 1922.

Bundy, Edgar C. *Collectivism in the Churches.* New York: Devin-Adair, 1954.

Cairns, Alan. *A Prophet with Honour: The Life and Work of John Wylie, Who Faithfully Served the Lord with Honour, Humour, and Unfeigned Holiness.* Belfast: Presbytery of the Free Presbyterian Church, 1991.

"Criticism of the Kingdom of God," *Princeton Review* (Jan. 1850): 328–32.

Crossman, Richard. *The Diaries of a Cabinet Minister.* Vol. 3, *Secretary of State for Social Services.* London: Hamish Hamilton and Jonathan Cape, 1972.

Davey, James Ernest. *The Changing Vesture of the Faith.* Boston: Pilgrim Press, 1923.

———. *Our Faith in God Through Jesus: Studies in the Origin and Development of Christian Forms of Belief, Institutions, and Observance. Four Apocalyptic Addresses.* New York: George H. Doran, 1922.

Devlin, Bernadette. *The Price of My Soul.* New York: Knopf, 1969.

Devlin, Paddy. *Straight Left: An Autobiography.* Belfast: Blackstaff Press, 1993.

Faulkner, Brian. *Memoirs of a Statesman.* Edited by John Houston. London: Weidenfeld and Nicolson, 1978.

Flynn, John T. *The Road Ahead: America's Creeping Revolution.* New York: Devin-Adair, 1949.

———. *The Roosevelt Myth.* New York: Devin-Adair, 1948.

The Fundamentals: A Testimony to Truth. 12 vols. Los Angeles: Bible Institute of Los Angeles, 1917.

Gibson, Oliver. *We Are Not Divided.* Omagh, Northern Ireland: Omagh Democratic Unionist Association, 1972.

Gillies, Donald. *Unity in the Dark.* London: Banner of Trust, 1964.

Grier, W. J. *The Momentous Event: A Discussion of Scripture Teaching on the Second Advent.* Edinburgh: Banner of Truth Trust, 1976.

———. *The Origin and Witness of the Irish Evangelical Church.* Belfast: Evangelical Book Shop, 1945.

Hargis, Billy James. *The Muzzling of General Walker.* Tulsa: Christian Crusade, 1962.

———. *My Great Mistake.* Green Forest, AR: New Leaf Press, 1985.

———. *The Truth about Segregation.* N.p.: n.p., n.d.

Jones, Bob, Jr. *Cornbread and Caviar.* Greenville, SC: Bob Jones Univ. Press, 1985.

———. *Fundamentals of Faith: A Series of Chapel Messages on the Bob Jones University Creed.* Greenville, SC: Bob Jones Univ. Press, 1964.

Jones, Bob, Sr. *Is Segregation Scriptural?* Greenville, SC: Bob Jones Univ. Press, 1960.

Jones, E. Stanley. *Christ's Alternative to Communism.* New York: Abingdon Press, 1935.

Machen, J. Gresham. *Modernism and the Board of Foreign Missions of the Presbyterian Church in the U.S.A., an Argument of J. Gresham Machen in Support of an Overture Introduced in the Presbytery of New Brunswick at Its Meeting on January 24, 1933, and Made the Order of the Day for the Meeting on April 11, 1933.* Philadelphia: Allen, Lane and Scott, 1933.

Maddox, Lester Garfield. *Speaking Out: The Autobiography of Lester Garfield Maddox.* New York: Doubleday, 1975.

Matthews, J. B. *Communism in Our Churches.* Collingswood, NJ: Christian Beacon Press, 1958.

———. "Reds and Our Churches." *American Mercury* (July 1953): 3–13.

McCann, Eamonn. *War and an Irish Town.* 2nd ed. London: Pluto Press, 1993.

McCluskey, Conn. *Up off Their Knees: A Commentary on the Civil Rights Movement in Northern Ireland.* Galway: Self-published, 1989.

McIntire, Carl. *Author of Liberty.* Collingswood, NJ: Christian Beacon Press, 1946.

———. *The Battle of Bangkok: Second Missionary Journey.* Collingswood, NJ: Christian Beacon Press, 1950.

———. *Dr. Robert Speer, the Board of Foreign Missions of the Presbyterian Church in the U.S.A., and Modernism.* Collingswood, NJ: n.p., 1935.

———. *The New Bible: Revised Standard Version, Why Christians Should Not Accept It.* Collingswood, NJ: Christian Beacon Press, 1952.

———. *The Russian Baptists: Twenty Years of Soviet Propaganda: The Hammer and Sickle on the Platform of the Baptist World Alliance.* Collingswood, NJ: Twentieth Century Reformation Hour, n.d.

———. *Russia's Most Effective Fifth Column in America: A Series of Radio Messages by Carl McIntire.* Collingswood, NJ: Christian Beacon Press, 1948.

———. *Servants of Apostasy.* Collingswood, NJ: Christian Beacon Press, 1955.

———. *The Struggle for South America: First Missionary Journey.* Collingswood, NJ: Christian Beacon Press, 1949.

———. *The Testimony of Separation.* Collingswood, NJ: Christian Beacon Press, 1952.

———. *The Twentieth Century Reformation.* Collingswood, NJ: Christian Beacon Press, 1944.

McMichael, Gary. *Ulster Voice: In Search of Common Ground in Northern Ireland.* Boulder, CO: Roberts Rinehart, 1999.

Northern Ireland Civil Rights Association. *"We Shall Overcome": The History of the Struggle for Civil Rights in Northern Ireland, 1968–1978.* Belfast: Northern Ireland Civil Rights Association, 1978.

Oliver, John A. *Working at Stormont.* Dublin: Institute of Public Administration, 1978.

O'Neill, Terence. *The Autobiography of Terence O'Neill.* London: Granada, 1972.

———. *Ulster at the Crossroads.* London: Faber and Faber, 1969.

Paisley, Ian R. K. *The '59 Revival: An Authentic History of the Great Ulster Awakening of 1859.* Belfast: Martyr's Memorial Free Presbyterian Church, 1958.

———. *The Archbishop in the Arms of the Pope of Rome! Protestant Ministers in the Hands of the Police of Rome!* Pamphlet. Belfast: Puritan, 1966.

———. *The Battle of the Reformation: Why It Must Be Fought Today.* Belfast: Puritan, 1967.

———. *Christian Foundations.* Greenville, SC: Bob Jones Univ. Press, 1971.

———. *The Depths of the Baptist Downgrade: An Exposure of the Infidelity and Unitarianism of the President of the Baptist Union of GT. Britain and Ireland, Dr. Howard Williams.* Belfast: Puritan, 1976.

———. *An Exposition of the Epistle to the Romans: Prepared in the Prison Cell.* London: Marshall, Morgan and Scott, 1966.

———. "The Faith, the Fire, and Fight of a Fundamentalist." In *Word of Their Testimony: Sermons Delivered at the World Congress of Fundamentalists, Edinburgh, Scotland, June 15–22, 1976*, 1–16. Greenville, SC: Bob Jones Univ. Press, 1976.

———. *For Such a Time as This: Recollections, Reflections, Recognitions.* Belfast: Ambassador, 1999.

———. *The Fundamentalist and His State.* Greenville, SC: Bob Jones Univ. Press, 1976.

———. *God's Ultimatum to the Nation.* N.p.: n.p., n.d.

———. *John Knox, a Sermon Preached 10th and 17th November 1963 to the Ravenhill Free Presbyterian Church.* N.p.: n.p., n.d.

———. *Life's Four Windows: A Sketch of My Life Story, Two Sermons Preached in the Martyr's Memorial Free Presbyterian Church on the Thirty-Seventh Anniversary of His Ministry.* N.p.: n.p., n.d.

———. *My Father and Mother: A Loving Tribute by Their Younger Son.* Belfast: Martyrs Memorial, 1976.

———. *The New English Bible: Version or Perversion?* Belfast: Free Presbyterian Church, 1961.

———. *Nicholson Centenary, 1876–1976: From Civil War to Revival Victory.* Belfast: Martyr's Memorial, 1976.

———. *"None Dare Call It Treason": Sermon Delivered to Martyrs Memorial Free Presbyterian Church by Ian R K Paisley.* Pamphlet. N.p.: n.p., 22 Oct. 2000.

———. *Northern Ireland: Message Delivered at Bob Jones University, September 12, 1969.* N.p.: n.p., n.d.

———. *No to a United Ireland, Speech by Reverend Dr. Ian R. K. Paisley MP Delivered in the Northern Ireland House of Commons on Tuesday, 8th February 1972.* N.p.: n.p., n.d.

———. *Protestants Remember!* Pamphlet. N.p.: n.p., 1966.

———. *Souvenir Booklet: The 50th Anniversary of the Larne Gun-Running. Thanksgiving Service on Sunday, 26th April, 1964, in the Historic Ulster Hall.* Belfast: Puritan, 1964.

———. *The Ulster Problem Spring 1972: A Discussion of the True Situation in Northern Ireland.* Greenville, SC: Bob Jones Univ. Press, 1972.

———. *Union with Great Britain, Speech by Reverend Ian R. K. Paisley MP (Leader of the Opposition) Delivered in the Northern Ireland House of Commons on Wednesday, 22 March 1972.* N.p.: n.p., n.d.

People's Democracy. "A People's Democracy: A Discussion on Strategy." *New Left Review* 55 (1969): 31–45.

Porter, Norman. *He Shall Reign for Ever and Ever: A Brief History of the Orangefield Baptist Church.* Belfast: Orangefield Baptist Church, n.d.

Springer, Harvey H. *Catholicism in America: Our Hope the Bright and Morning Star.* N.p.: n.p., n.d.

Stormer, John. *None Dare Call It Treason.* Florissant, MO: Liberty Bell Press, 1964.

Waddell, Reverend John. *The Life Here and the Life After.* Belfast: Fisherwick Presbyterian Church, n.d.

Christian Periodicals

Baptist Bible Tribune, 1978.

Baptists Today, 1967.

The Burning Bush, 2007–2008.

Canadian Revivalist, 2007.

Christian Beacon, 1936–69.

Christian Crusade/Christian Crusade Weekly, 1963–98.

Church of Ireland Gazette, 1959–69.

The Evangelical Methodist, 1982.

Evangelical Presbyterian, 1966.

Fellowship News, 1968–70.

Fisherwick Messenger, 1962–64.

The Gospel Witness, 1965-68.

Independent Bulletin Board, 1935.

Irish Christian Advocate, 1961.

The Irish Evangelical, 1957–65.

Let the Bible Speak, 2009.

News and Views, 1966–69.

Presbyterian Herald, 1954–68.

Princeton Review, 1850.

Protestant Telegraph, 1966–86.

Reformation Reader, 1982.

The Reformation Review, 1961–70.

The Revivalist, 1956–89.
The Sword of the Lord, 1966–69.
Third Way, 1996.
Ulster Protestant, 1957–67.
The Voice, 1968.
Weekly Crusader, 1967.
Western Voice, 1965–69.
Whither Methodism? 1965.

Secular Newspapers

Atlanta Constitution, 1967.
Atlanta Journal, 1967.
Ballymena Observer, 1948-51.
Belfast News Letter, 1901.
Belfast Telegraph, 1950–2009.
Camden-Courier Post, 1954.
Daily Telegraph, 1966.
Derry Standard, 1950.
Focus, 1965.
Glasgow Herald, 1967–68.
Greenville News, 1968.
Harrisburg Patriot, 1967.
International Herald Tribune, 1966.
Jackson Clarion Ledger, 1962.
Life magazine, 1966
Lisburn Herald, 1947.
London Times, 2006.
The Nation, 1965.
New York Times, 1935–81.
News Letter, 1976.
Northern Constitution, 1958.
Oakland Tribune, 1976.
Philadelphia Evening Bulletin, 1946–71.
Philadelphia Inquirer, 1969, 1982.
The Scotsman, 1962–76.
Time magazine, 1976.
The Voice of Ulster, 1982.

Secondary Sources

Books

Abrams, Carl Douglas. *Selling the Old-Time Religion: American Fundamentalists and Mass Culture, 1920–1940*. Athens: Univ. of Georgia Press, 2001.

Ahlstrom, Sydney E. *A Religious History of the American People*. New Haven, CT: Yale Univ. Press, 1972.

Anderson, W. K. *James Connolly and the Irish Left*. Dublin: Irish Academic Press, 1994.

Arthur, Paul. *The People's Democracy 1968–1973*. Belfast: Blackstaff Press, 1974.

Aughey, Arthur. *The Politics of Northern Ireland: Beyond the Belfast Agreement*. New York: Routledge, 2005.

———. *Under Siege: Ulster Unionism and the Anglo-Irish Agreement*. London: Hurst, 1989.

Bardon, Jonathan. *Beyond the Studio: A History of BBC Northern Ireland*. Belfast: Blackstaff Press, 2000.

———. *A History of Ulster*. Belfast: Blackstaff Press, 1992.

Barnes, Stanley. *All for Jesus: The Life of W. P. Nicholson*. Belfast: Ambassador, 1996.

Barton, Brian, and Patrick J. Roche, eds. *The Northern Ireland Question: The Peace Process and the Belfast Agreement*. Houndmills, UK: Palgrave Mac-Millan, 2009.

Beckett, J. C. *Protestant Dissent in Ireland 1687–1780*. London: Faber and Faber, 1948.

Beggs, Reverend R. J. *Great Is Thy Faithfulness: An Account of the Ministry of Pastor James Kyle Paisley and a History of the Separatist Testimony in Ballymena*. Ballymena, Northern Ireland: Ballymena Free Presbyterian Church, n.d.

Bell, Geoffrey. *The Protestants of Ulster*. London: Pluto Press, 1976.

Bell, J. Bowyer. *The IRA 1968–2000: Analysis of a Secret Army*. New York: St. Martin's Press, 2000.

———. *The Irish Troubles: A Generation of Violence 1967–1992*. New York: St. Martin's Press, 1992.

Bell, P. M. H. *Disestablishment in Ireland and Wales*. London: Society for the Propagation of Christian Knowledge, 1969.

Bew, Paul, Peter Gibbon, and Henry Patterson. *Northern Ireland 1921–1994: Political Forces and Special Classes*. London: Serf, 1995.

———. *The State in Northern Ireland, 1921–72: Political Forces and Social Class.* Manchester, UK: Manchester Univ. Press, 1979.

Biggs-Davison, John, and George Chowdharay-Best. *The Cross of St. Patrick: The Catholic Unionist Tradition in Ireland.* Abbotsbrook, UK: Kensal Press, 1984.

Birrell, Derek. *Direct Rule and the Government of Northern Ireland.* Manchester, UK: Manchester Univ. Press, 2009.

Bloomfield, David. *Developing Dialogue in Northern Ireland: The Mayhew Talks, 1992.* Houndmills, UK: Palgrave, 2001.

———. *Political Dialogue in Northern Ireland: The Brooke Initiative 1989–92.* London: MacMillan Press, 1998.

Bloomfield, Kenneth. *A Tragedy of Errors: The Government and Misgovernment of Northern Ireland.* Liverpool: Liverpool Univ. Press, 2007.

Boulton, David. *The UVF 1966–73: An Anatomy of Loyalist Rebellion.* Dublin: Torc Books, 1973.

Bowes, Egan, and Vincent McCormick. *Burntollet.* London: LSR, 1969.

Boyd, Andrew. *Holy War in Belfast.* Tralee, Ireland: Anvil Books, 1969.

———. *Montgomery and the Black Man: Religion and Politics in Nineteenth-Century Ulster.* Dublin: Columba Press, 2006.

Boyer, Paul. *When Time Shall Be No More: Prophecy Belief in Modern American Culture.* Cambridge, MA: Harvard Univ. Press, 1992.

Brewer, John, and Gareth Higgins. *Anti-Catholicism in Northern Ireland 1600–1998.* London: MacMillan, 1998.

Brooke, Peter. *Ulster Presbyterianism: The Historical Perspective 1619–1970.* New York: St. Martin's Press, 1987.

Brown, William. *An Army with Banners: The Real Face of Orangeism.* Belfast: Beyond the Pale, 2009.

Bruce, Steve. *The Edge of the Union: The Loyalist Political Vision.* Oxford: Oxford Univ. Press, 1999.

———. *God Save Ulster! The Religion and Politics of Paisleyism.* Oxford: Oxford Univ. Press, 1989.

———. *No Pope of Rome! Anti-Catholicism in Modern Scotland.* Edinburgh: Mainstream, 1985.

———. *Paisley: Religion and Politics in Northern Ireland.* Oxford: Oxford Univ. Press, 2007.

———. *The Red Hand: Protestant Paramilitaries in Northern Ireland.* Oxford: Oxford Univ. Press, 1992.

Bursteed, Mervyn, Frank Neal, and Jonathan Tonge, eds. *Irish Protestant Identities.* Manchester, UK: Manchester Univ. Press, 2008.

Bryan, Dominic. *Orange Parades: The Politics of Ritual, Tradition, and Control.* London: Pluto Press, 2000.

Carpenter, Joel A. *Revive Us Again: The Reawakening of American Fundamentalism.* Oxford: Oxford Univ. Press, 1997.

Carwardine, Richard. *Transatlantic Revivalism: Popular Evangelicalism in Britain and America, 1790–1865.* Westport, CT: Greenwood Press, 1978.

Chappell, David L. *A Stone of Hope: Prophetic Religion and the Death of Jim Crow.* Chapel Hill: Univ. of North Carolina Press, 2004.

Clabaugh, Gary K. *Thunder on the Right: The Protestant Fundamentalists.* Chicago: Nelson-Hall, n.d.

Clarke, Liam. *Broadening the Battlefield: The H-Blocks and the Rise of Sinn Fein.* Dublin: Gill and MacMillan, 1987.

Clouse, Robert G., ed. *The Meaning of the Millennium: Four Views.* Downers Grove, IL: InterVarsity Press, 1977.

Cochrane, Fergal. *Unionist Politics and the Politics of Unionism since the Anglo-Irish Agreement.* Cork: Cork Univ. Press, 1997.

Cohodas, Nadine. *Strom Thurmond and the Politics of Southern Change.* New York: Simon and Schuster, 1993.

Coogan, Tim Pat. *The I.R.A.* Niwot, CO: Roberts Rinehart, 1993.

———. *The Troubles: Ireland's Ordeal, 1966–1995, and the Search for Peace.* London: Hutchinson, 1995.

Cook, Fred J. *The Nightmare Decade: The Life and Times of Senator Joe McCarthy.* New York: Random House, 1971.

Cooke, Dennis. *Peacemaker: The Life and Work of Eric Gallagher.* Peterborough, UK: Methodist Publishing House, 2005.

———. *Persecuting Zeal: A Portrait of Ian Paisley.* Dingle, Ireland: Brandon, 1996.

Cooke, Ronald. *Ian Paisley: Protestant Protagonist par Excellence.* Hollidaysburg, PA: Manahath Press, 1984.

Coulter, Colin, and Michael Murray, eds. *Northern Ireland after the Troubles: A Society in Transition.* Manchester, UK: Manchester Univ. Press, 2008.

Courtney, Kent, and Phoebe Courtney. *The Case of General Edwin A. Walker.* New Orleans: Conservative Society of America, 1961.

Cowan, Ian B. *The Scottish Reformation: Church and Society in Sixteenth-Century Scotland.* London: Weidenfeld and Nicolson, 1982.

Crosby, Donald F., Jr. *God, Church, and Flag: Senator Joseph R. McCarthy and the Catholic Church 1950–1957.* Chapel Hill: Univ. of North Carolina Press, 1978.

Cunningham, Michael. *British Government Policy in Northern Ireland, 1969–2000.* Manchester, UK: Manchester Univ. Press, 2001.

Darby, John. *Conflict in Northern Ireland: The Development of a Polarised Community.* Dublin: Gill and MacMillan Books, 1976.

Dickson, R. J. *Ulster Emigration to Colonial America 1718–1775.* London: Routledge and Kegan Paul, 1966.

Dixon, Paul. *Northern Ireland: The Politics of Peace and War.* Houndmills, UK: Palgrave, 2001.

Dooley, Brian. *Black and Green: The Fight for Civil Rights in Northern Ireland and Black America.* London: Pluto Press, 1998.

Douglas, J. D. *Light in the North: The Story of the Scottish Covenanters.* Grand Rapids, MI: Eerdmans, 1964.

Doyle, Mark. *Fighting Like the Devil for the Sake of God: Protestants, Catholics, and the Origins of Violence in Victorian Belfast.* Manchester, UK: Manchester Univ. Press, 2009.

Dudman, Richard. *Men of the Far Right.* New York: Pyramid Books, 1962.

Edwards, Owen Dudley. *The Sins of Our Fathers: The Roots of Conflict in Northern Ireland.* Dublin: Gill and MacMillan, 1970.

English, Richard. *Armed Struggle: A History of the IRA.* Oxford: Oxford Univ. Press, 2003.

Farber, David. *The Age of Great Dreams: America in the 1960s.* New York: Hill and Wang, 1994.

Farrell, Michael. *Civil Rights Twenty Years On: A Personal View.* Dingle, Ireland: Brandon, 1988.

———. *Northern Ireland: The Orange State.* London: Pluto Press, 1976.

Farrell, Sean. *Rituals and Riots: Sectarian Violence and Political Culture in Ulster, 1784–1886.* Lexington: Univ. Press of Kentucky, 2000.

Farrington, Christopher. *Ulster Unionism and the Peace Process in Northern Ireland.* Houndmills, UK: Palgrave MacMillan, 2006.

Findlay, James F., Jr. *Dwight L. Moody: American Evangelist 1837–1899.* Chicago: Univ. of Chicago Press, 1969.

Flackes, W. D., and Sydney Elliott. *Northern Ireland: A Political Directory 1968–1988.* Belfast: Blackstaff Press, 1989.

Ford, Alan. *The Protestant Reformation in Ireland, 1590–1641: Second Impression.* Frankfurt: Peter Lang, 1987.

Forster, Arnold, and Benjamin R. Epstein. *Danger on the Right.* New York: Random House, 1964.

Fulton, Austin. *J. Ernest Davey.* Belfast: Presbyterian Church in Ireland, 1970.

Gaines, David P. *The World Council of Churches: A Study of Its Background and History.* Peterborough, UK: Richard R. Smith, 1966.

Gallagher, Eric, and Stanley Worrall. *Christians in Ulster, 1968–1980.* Oxford: Oxford Univ. Press, 1982.

Gallaher, Carolyn. *After the Peace: Paramilitaries in Post-accord Northern Ireland.* Ithaca, NY: Cornell Univ. Press, 2007.

Galphin, Bruce. *The Riddle of Lester Maddox.* Atlanta: Camelot, 1968.

Ganiel, Gladys. *Evangelicalism and Conflict in Northern Ireland.* Houndmills, UK: Palgrave, 2008.

Garland, Roy. *Gusty Spence.* Belfast: Blackstaff Press, 2001.

Garrow, David J. *The FBI and Martin Luther King, Jr.: From "Solo" to Memphis.* New York: W. W. Norton, 1981.

Gasper, Louis. *The Fundamentalist Movement.* The Hague: Mouton, 1963.

Goodman, Walter. *The Committee: The Extraordinary Career of the House Committee on Un-American Activities.* New York: Farrar, Strauss and Giroux, 1964.

Gordon, David. *The O'Neill Years: Unionist Politics, 1963–1969.* Cork, Ireland: Athol Books, 1969.

Gray, John. *City in Revolt: James Larkin and the Belfast Dock Strike of 1907.* Belfast: Blackstaff Press, 1985.

Gray, Tony. *The Orange Order.* London: Bodley Head, 1972.

Greaves, Richard L. *Theology and Revolution in the Scottish Reformation: Studies in the Thought of John Knox.* Grand Rapids, MI: Christian Univ. Press, 1980.

Gribben, Crawford, and Andrew R. Holmes, eds. *Protestant Millennialism, Evangelicalism, and Irish Society, 1790–2005.* Houndmills, UK: Palgrave, 2006.

Griffin, Patrick. *The People with No Name: Ireland's Ulster Scots, America's Scots Irish, and the Creation of a British Atlantic World, 1689–1714.* Princeton, NJ: Princeton Univ. Press, 2001.

Griffith, Robert. *Politics of Fear: Joseph R. McCarthy and the Senate.* Amherst: Univ. of Massachusetts Press, 1987.

Harbinson, John. *The Ulster Unionist Party 1882–1973: Its Development and Organization.* Belfast: Blackstaff Press, 1973.

Harden, Margaret G. *A Brief History of the Bible Presbyterian Church and Its Agencies.* N.p.: n.p., n.d.

Hart, D. G., and John Muether. *Fighting the Good Fight: A Brief History of the Orthodox Presbyterian Church*. Philadelphia: Orthodox Presbyterian Church, 1995.

Hastings, Adrian. *A History of English Christianity 1920–1990*. London: SCM Press, 1991.

Hastings, Max. *Barricades in Belfast: The Fight for Civil Rights in Northern Ireland*. New York: Taplinger, 1970.

Heaney, Mavis. *To God Be the Glory: The Personal Memoirs of Reverend William P. Nicholson*. Belfast: Ambassador, 2004.

Heggarty, Karen. *From Vision to Victory: The History of the Ballymoney Free Presbyterian Church*. N.p.: n.p., n.d.

Hennessey, Thomas. *The Northern Ireland Peace Process: Ending the Troubles?* New York: Palgrave, 2001.

Hill, Myrtle. *The Time of the End: Millennium Beliefs in Ulster*. Belfast: Belfast Society, 2001.

Hill, Samuel S. *Southern Churches in Crisis Revisited*. Tuscaloosa: Univ. of Alabama Press, 1999.

Hirst, Catherine. *Religion, Politics, and Violence in Nineteenth- Century Belfast: The Pound and Sandy Row*. Dublin: Four Courts Press, 2002.

Holifield, E. Brooks. *Theology in America: Christian Thought from the Age of the Puritans to the Civil War*. New Haven, CT: Yale Univ. Press, 2003.

Holmes, Andrew. *The Shaping of Ulster Presbyterian Belief and Practice, 1770–1840*. Oxford: Oxford Univ. Press, 2006.

Holmes, Finlay. *Henry Cooke*. Belfast: Christian Journals, 1981.

Holmes, Janice. *Religious Revivals in Britain and Ireland 1859–1905*. Dublin: Irish Academic Press, 2000.

Holmes, R. F. G. *Our Irish Presbyterian Heritage*. Belfast: Presbyterian Church in Ireland, 1985.

Hutchinson, William R. *The Modernist Impulse in American Protestantism*. Cambridge, MA: Harvard Univ. Press, 1976.

Jackson, Alvin. *Ireland: 1798–1998*. Oxford: Blackwell, 1999.

Jackson, Thomas F. *From Civil Rights to Human Rights: Martin Luther King, Jr. and the Struggle For Economic Justice*. Philadelphia: Univ. of Pennsylvania Press, 2007.

Jamieson, John. *The History of the Royal Belfast Academical Institution, 1810–1960*. Belfast: William Mullan and Son, 1959.

Janson, Donald, and Bernard Eisman. *The Far Right.* New York: McGraw-Hill, 1963.

Johnson, R. K. *Builder of Bridges: The Biography of Dr. Bob Jones, Jr.* Murfreesboro, TN: Sword of the Lord, 1969.

Jorstad, Erling. *The Politics of Doomsday: Fundamentalists of the Far Right.* Nashville: Abingdon Press, 1970.

Kauffman, Eric P. *The Orange Order: A Contemporary Northern Irish History.* Oxford: Oxford Univ. Press, 2007.

Kennedy, Dennis. *The Widening Gulf: Northern Attitudes to the Independent Irish State, 1919–49.* Belfast: Blackstaff Press, 1983.

Kerr, Michael. *Transforming Unionism: David Trimble and the 2005 General Election.* Dublin: Irish Academic Press, 2006.

Knobel, Dale T. *America for the Americans: The Nativist Movement in the United States.* New York: Twayne, 1996.

Larson, Edward J. *Summer of the Gods: The Scopes Trial and America's Continuing Debate over Science and Religion.* New York: Basic Books, 1997.

Ledwidge, Bernard. *DeGaulle.* New York: St. Martin's Press, 1982.

Leyburn, James G. *The Scotch-Irish: A Social History.* Chapel Hill: Univ. of North Carolina Press, 1989.

Livingstone, David N., and Ronald A. Wells. *Ulster-American Religion: Episodes in the History of a Cultural Connection.* Notre Dame, IN: Univ. of Notre Dame Press, 1999.

Longfield, Bradley J. *The Presbyterian Controversy: Fundamentalists, Modernists, and Moderates.* Oxford: Oxford Univ. Press, 1991.

MacGinty, Roger, and John Darby. *Guns and Government: The Management of the Northern Ireland Peace Process.* Houndmills, UK: Palgrave, 2002.

Macquigg, J. Claude. *The Minnis Mills Tapestry: 1922–1968 Diaries, Warp and Weft of a Local Church.* Belfast: J. C. Macquigg, 2005.

Manktelow, Michael. *John Moorman: Anglican, Franciscan, Independent.* Norwich, UK: Canterbury Press, 1999.

Marrinan, Patrick. *Paisley: Man of Wrath.* Dublin: Anvil Books, 1973.

Marsden, George M. *The Evangelical Mind and the New School Presbyterian Experience: A Case Study of Thought and Theology in Nineteenth-Century America.* New Haven, CT: Yale Univ. Press, 1970.

———. *Fundamentalism and American Culture: The Shaping of Twentieth Century Evangelicalism: 1870–1925.* Oxford: Oxford Univ. Press, 1980.

———. *Reforming Fundamentalism: Fuller Seminary and the New Evangelism.* Grand Rapids, MI: Eerdmans, 1987.

———. *Understanding Fundamentalism and Evangelicalism.* Grand Rapids, MI: Eerdmans, 1991.

Matthews, Donald G. *Religion in the Old South.* Chicago: Univ. of Chicago Press, 1977.

Maxwell, Victor. *Belfast's Halls of Faith and Fame.* Belfast: Ambassador, 1999.

McBride, Ian. *The Siege of Derry in Ulster Protestant Mythology.* Dublin: Four Courts Press, 1997.

———. *Ulster Presbyterianism and Irish Radicalism in the Late Eighteenth Century.* Oxford: Clarendon Press, 1998.

McDonald, Henry, and Jim Cusack. *UDA: Inside the Heart of Loyalist Terror.* Dublin: Penguin, 2004.

McDonald, Morris. *A Brief History of the Bible Presbyterian Church.* Charlotte, NC: Fundamental Presbyterian, 2003.

Mitchel, Patrick. *Evangelicalism and National Identity in Ulster 1921–1998.* Oxford: Oxford Univ. Press, 2003.

Mitchell, George J. *Making Peace.* New York: Knopf, 1999.

Moloney, Ed. *Paisley: From Demagogue to Democrat?* Dublin: Poolbeg, 2008.

———. *A Secret History of the IRA.* New York: W. W. Norton, 2002.

Moloney, Ed, and Andy Pollak. *Paisley.* Dublin: Poolbeg Press, 1986.

Moore, James R. *The Post-Darwinian Controversies: A Study of the Protestant Struggle to Come to Terms with Darwin in Great Britain and America 1870–1900.* Cambridge: Cambridge Univ. Press, 1979.

Morris, James. *The Preachers.* New York: St. Martin's Press, 1973.

Mulholland, Marc. *Northern Ireland at the Crossroads: Ulster Unionism in the O'Neill Years 1960–9.* London: MacMillan, 2000.

Murray, Ian H. *Spurgeon v. Hyper-Calvinism: The Battle for Gospel Preaching.* Carlisle, PA: Banner of Truth Trust, 1951.

Murray, Patrick. *Oracles of God: The Roman Catholic Church and Irish Politics, 1921–1937.* Dublin: Univ. College Press, 2000.

Neuheiser, Jorg, and Steffan Wolff, eds. *Peace at Last: The Impact of the Good Friday Agreement on Northern Ireland?* New York: Berghahn Books, 2002.

Noll, Mark A. *A History of Christianity in the United States and Canada.* Grand Rapids, MI: Eerdmans, 1992.

O'Dochartaigh, Fionnbarra. *Ulster's White Negroes.* Edinburgh: AK Press, 1974.

O'Dochartaigh, Niall. *From Civil Rights to Armalites: Derry and the Birth of the Irish Troubles.* Cork: Cork Univ. Press, 1977.

O'Donnell, Catherine. *Fianna Fail, Irish Republicanism, and the Northern Ireland Troubles, 1968–2005.* Dublin: Irish Academic Press, 2007.

O'Duffy, Brendan. *British–Irish Relations and Northern Ireland: From Violent Politics to Conflict Regulation.* Dublin: Irish Academic Press, 2007.

Owen, Arwell Allis. *The Anglo-Irish Agreement: The First Three Years.* Cardiff: Univ. of Wales Press, 1994.

Paor, Liam. *Divided Ulster.* Hardmondsworth, UK: Penguin, 1970.

Patterson, Henry, and Eric Kaufmann. *Unionism and Orangeism in Northern Ireland since 1945.* Manchester, UK: Manchester Univ. Press, 2007.

Penabaz, Dr. Fernando. *"Crusading Preacher from the West": The Story of Billy James Hargis.* Tulsa: Christian Crusade, 1965.

Pettegree, Andrew, Alistair Duke, and Gillian Lewis, eds. *Calvinism in Europe.* Cambridge, UK: Cambridge Univ. Press, 1994.

Phillips, William Alison. *History of the Church of Ireland from the Earliest Times to the Present Day.* Vol. 3, *The Modern Church.* Oxford: Oxford Univ. Press, 1933.

Porter, Josias Leslie. *The Life and Times of Henry Cooke, D.D., LL.D., President of Assembly's College, Belfast.* London: John Murray, 1871.

Powers, Richard. *Not Without Honor: The History of American Anticommunism.* New York: Free Press, 1995.

Prince, Simon. *Northern Ireland's '68: Civil Rights, Global Revolt, and the Origins of the Troubles.* Dublin: Irish Academic Press, 2007.

Purdie, Bob. *Politics in the Streets: The Origins of the Civil Rights Movement in Northern Ireland.* Belfast: Blackstaff Press, 1990.

Radosh, Ronald. *Prophets on the Right: Profiles of Conservative Critics of American Globalism.* New York: Simon and Schuster, 1975.

Rawlyk, C. A. *Champions of the Truth: Fundamentalism, Modernism, and the Maritime Baptists.* Montreal: Centre for Canadian Studies, Mount Allison Univ., 1990.

Redekop, John Harold. *The American Far Right: A Case Study of Billy James Hargis and Christian Crusade.* Grand Rapids, MI: Eerdmans, 1968.

Roy, Ralph Lord. *Apostles of Discord: A Study of Organized Bigotry and Disruption on the Fringes of Protestantism.* Boston: Beacon Press, 1953.

Russell, Conrad. *The Fall of the British Monarchies, 1637–1642.* Oxford: Clarendon Press, 1991.

Ryder, Chris. *The Fateful Split: Catholics and the Royal Ulster Constabulary.* London: Methuen, 2004.

Ryder, Chris, and Vincent Kearney. *Drumcree: The Orange Order's Last Stand.* London: Methuen, 2001.

Sandeen, Ernest R. *The Roots of Fundamentalism: British and American Millenarianism 1800–1930.* Chicago: Univ. of Chicago Press, 1970.

Schmidt, Leigh Eric. *Holy Fairs: Scotland and the Making of American Revivalism.* Grand Rapids, MI: Eerdmans, 2001.

Shelley, Bruce L. *A History of Conservative Baptists.* Wheaton, IL: Conservative Baptist Press, 1971.

Singer, C. Gregg. *The Unholy Alliance.* New Rochelle, NY: Arlington House, 1975.

Skinner, Craig. *Spurgeon and Son: The Forgotten Story of Thomas Spurgeon and His Famous Father, Charles Haddon Spurgeon.* Grand Rapids, MI: Kregel, 1999.

Smith, M. L. R. *Fighting for Ireland? The Military Strategy of the Irish Republican Movement.* London: Routledge, 1995.

Smith, Oran. *The Rise of Baptist Republicanism.* New York: New York Univ. Press, 1997.

Smylie, James H. *A Brief History of the Presbyterians.* Louisville, KY: Geneva Press, 1996.

Smyth, Clifford. *Ian Paisley: Voice of Protestant Ulster.* Edinburgh: Scottish Academic Press, 1987.

Spencer, Graham. *The State of Loyalism in Northern Ireland.* Houndmills, UK: Palgrave, 2008.

Stewart, A. T. Q. *The Narrow Ground: Aspects of Ulster, 1609–1969.* London: Faber and Faber, 1977.

Tarr, Leslie K. *Shields of Canada: T. T. Shields (1873–1955).* Grand Rapids, MI: Baker Book House, 1967.

Thompson, Joshua. *Century of Grace: The Baptist Union of Ireland, a Short History 1895–1995.* Belfast: Baptist Union of Ireland, 1995.

Turner, Daniel L. *Standing Without Apology: The History of Bob Jones University.* Greenville, SC: Bob Jones Univ. Press, 1992.

Tyacke, Nicholas. *Anti-Calvinists: The Rise of English Arminianism.* Oxford: Oxford Univ. Press, 1987.

Walker, Graham. *A History of the Ulster Unionist Party: Protest, Pragmatism, and Pessimism.* Manchester, UK: Manchester Univ. Press, 2004.

Webb, Clive, ed. *Massive Resistance: Southern Opposition to the Second Reconstruction.* Oxford: Oxford Univ. Press, 2005.

Westerkamp, Marilyn J. *The Triumph of the Laity: Scots-Irish Piety and the Great Awakening, 1625–1760.* Oxford: Oxford Univ. Press, 1988.

Whelan, Irene. *The Bible War in Ireland: The "Second Reformation" and the Polarization of Protestant–Catholic Relations, 1800–1840.* Madison: Univ. of Wisconsin Press, 2005.

White, Barry. *John Hume: Statesman of the Troubles.* Belfast: Blackstaff Press, 1984.

Whyte, J. H. *Church and State in Modern Ireland 1923–1979.* Dublin: Gill and MacMillan, 1998.

Wood, Ian S. *Crimes of Loyalty: A History of the UDA.* Edinburgh: Edinburgh Univ. Press, 2006.

Articles and Chapters

Abbott, Don. "Ian Paisley: Evangelism and Confrontation in Northern Ireland." *Today's Speech* (Fall 1973): 49–55.

Archer, J. R. "The Unionist Tradition in Ireland." *Eire-Ireland* 15 (1980): 47–53.

Aunger, E. A. "Religion and Occupational Class in Northern Ireland." *Economic and Social Review* 7 (1975): 1–18.

Barton, Brian. "The Historical Background to the Belfast Agreement." In *The Northern Ireland Question: The Peace Process and the Belfast Agreement,* edited by Brian Barton and Patrick J. Roche, 12–37. Houndmills, UK: Palgrave MacMillan, 2009.

Birrell, Derek. "Relative Depravation as a Factor in Conflict in Northern Ireland." *Sociological Review* 20 (1972): 321–25.

Boserup, Anders. "Contradictions and Struggles in Northern Ireland." *Socialist Register* (1972): 157–92.

Boyle, John. "The Belfast Protestant Association and the Independent Orange Order, 1901–1910." *Irish Historical Studies* 13 (1962): 117–52.

Bruce, Steve. "Fundamentalism and Political Violence: The Case of Paisley and Ulster Evangelicals." *Religion* 31 (2001): 387–405.

———. "Nicholson and Paisley." *Evangelical Voice* 8 (1990): 12–13.

Bryan, Dominic. "Drumcree: Marching Towards Peace in Northern Ireland." In *Peace at Last: The Impact of the Good Friday Agreement on Northern Ireland?* edited by Jorg Neuheiser and Steffan Wolff, 94–110. New York: Berghahn Books, 2002.

Chappell, David L. "Disunity and Religious Institutions in the White South." In *Massive Resistance: Southern Opposition to the Second Reconstruction,* edited by Clive Webb, 136–50. Oxford: Oxford Univ. Press, 2005.

Dawson, Jane. "Calvinism and the Gaidhealtchad in Scotland." In *Calvinism in Europe,* edited by Andrew Pettegree, Alistair Duke, and Gillian Lewis, 231–53. Cambridge: Cambridge Univ. Press, 1994.

Doyle, Mark. "Visible Differences: The 1859 Revival and Sectarianism in Belfast." In *Irish Protestant Identities,* edited by Mervyn Bursteed, Frank Neal, and Jonathan Tonge, 141–54. Manchester, UK: Manchester Univ. Press, 2008.

Feeney, Vincent E. "Westminster and the Early Civil Rights Movement in Northern Ireland." *Eire-Ireland* 11 (1976): 3–13.

Ganiel, Gladys. "Ulster Says Maybe: The Restructuring of Evangelical Politics in Northern Ireland." *Irish Political Studies* 21 (June 2006): 137–55.

Ganiel, Gladys, and Paul Dixon. "Religion, Pragmatic Fundamentalism, and the Transformation of the Northern Ireland Conflict." *Journal of Peace Research* 45 (2008): 419–36.

Gillespie, Raymond. "The Religion of the Protestant Laity in Early Modern Ireland." In *Christianity in Ireland: Revisiting the Story,* edited by Brendan Bradshaw and Daire Keogh, 109–23. Dublin: Columba Press, 2002.

Hatch, Nathan O. "Millennialism and Popular Religion in the Early Republic." In *The Evangelical Tradition in America,* edited by Leonard I. Sweet, 113–30. Macon, GA: Mercer Univ. Press, 1980.

Holmes, Andrew R. "Biblical Authority and the Impact of Higher Criticism in Irish Presbyterianism, ca. 1850–1930." *Church History: Studies in Christianity and Culture* 75 (June 2006): 343–73.

———. "The Evolution of Ian Paisley and the Movement He Led." 2009. Review of Steve Bruce's *For God and Ulster.* At http://www.christianitytoday.com/bc/2009/marapr/20.28.html.

———. "The Experience and Understanding of Religious Revival in Ulster Protestantism, ca. 1800–1930." *Irish Historical Studies* 34 (Nov. 2005): 361–85.

———. "Tradition and Enlightenment Conversion and Assurance of Salvation in Ulster Presbyterianism, 1700–1859." In *Converts and Conversion in Ireland, 1650–1850,* edited by Michael Brown, Charles Ivar, and Thomas P. Power, 129–56. Dublin: Four Courts Press, 2005.

Holmes, Finley. "The Presbyterian Church in Ireland." In *Christianity in Ireland: Revisiting the Story,* edited by Brendan Bradshaw and Daire Keogh, 124–33. Dublin: Columba Press, 2002.

Holmes, Janice. "The Role of Open-Air Preaching in the Belfast Riots of 1857." *Proceedings of the Royal Irish Academy* 102 (2002): 47–66.

Lewis, George. "White South, Red Nation: Massive Resistance and the Cold War." In *Massive Resistance: Southern Opposition to the Second Reconstruction,* edited by Clive Webb, 117–35. Oxford: Oxford Univ. Press, 2005.

Lijphart, Arend. "The Northern Ireland Problem: Cases, Theories, and Solutions." *British Journal of Political Science* 5 (1975): 92–94.

MacIver, Martha Abele. "Ian Paisley and the Reformed Tradition." *Political Studies* 35 (Sept. 1987): 359–79.

Marsden, George. "Fundamentalism as an American Phenomenon: A Comparison with English Evangelicalism." *Church History* 56 (1977): 215–32.

Miller, David. "Did Ulster Presbyterians Have a Devotional Revolution?" In *Evangelicals and Catholics in Nineteenth-Century Ireland,* edited by James H. Murphy, 38–54. Dublin: Four Courts Press, 2005.

———. "Religious Commotions in the Scottish Diaspora: A Transatlantic Perspective on 'Evangelicalism' in a Mainline Denomination." In *Ulster Presbyterians in the Atlantic World: Religion, Politics, and Identity,* edited by David A. Wilson and Mark G. Spencer, 22–38. Dublin: Four Courts Press, 2006.

Mitchel, Patrick. "Unionism and the Eschatological 'Fate' of Ulster." In *Protestant Millennialism, Evangelicalism, and Irish Society, 1790–2005,* edited by Crawford Gribben and Andrew R. Holmes, 202–27. Houndmills, UK: Palgrave, 2006.

Rosell, Garth M. "Charles G. Finney: His Place in the Stream of American Evangelism." In *The Evangelical Tradition in America,* edited by Leonard I. Sweet, 131–47. Macon, GA: Mercer Univ. Press, 1980.

Russell, C. Allyn. "Thomas Todhunter Shields, Canadian Fundamentalist." *Ontario History* 70 (Dec. 1978): 263–80.

Scott, F. Eugene. "The Political Preaching Tradition in Ulster: Prelude to Paisley." *Western Speech Communications* (Fall 1976): 249—59.

Shannon, Catherine B. "From Housing Rights to Civil Rights 1963–8." In *The Field Day Anthology of Irish Writing,* vol. 5: *Irish Women's Writing and Traditions,* 379–81. New York: New York Univ. Press, 2002.

Shirlow, Peter. "Sinn Fein: Beyond and within Containment." In *Peace at Last: The Impact of the Good Friday Agreement on Northern Ireland?* edited by Jorg Neuheiser and Steffan Wolff, 60–75. New York: Berghahn Books, 2002.

Sidwell, Mark. "W. P. Nicholson and the Rise of Ulster Fundamentalism." *Biblical Viewpoint* 28 (Apr. 1994): 93–104.

Smyth, Clifford. "The DUP as a Politico-Religious Organisation." *Irish Political Studies* 1 (1986): 33–43.

Southern, Neil. "Ian Paisley and Evangelical Democratic Unionists: An Analysis of the Role of Evangelical Protestantism within the Democratic Unionist Party." *Irish Political Studies* 20 (June 2005): 127–45.

Tonge, Jonathan, and James W. McAuley. "The Contemporary Orange Order in Northern Ireland." In *Irish Protestant Identities,* edited by Mervyn Bursteed, Frank Neal, and Jonathan Tonge, 289–302. Manchester, UK: Manchester Univ. Press, 2008.

Vinz, Warren L. "Protestant Fundamentalism and McCarthy." *Continuum* 6 (Aug. 1968): 314–25.

Weber, Timothy P. "Premillenialism and the Branches of Evangelicalism." In *The Variety of American Evangelicalism,* edited by Donald Dayton and Robert Johnston, 5–21. Knoxville: Univ. of Tennessee Press, 1991.

Whelan, Irene. "The Bible Gentry: Evangelical Religion, Aristocracy, and the New Moral Order in Early Nineteenth Century." In *Protestant Millennialism, Evangelicalism, and Irish Society, 1790–2005,* edited by Crawford Gribben and Andrew R. Holmes, 52–82. Houndmills, UK: Palgrave, 2006.

Wolff, Stefan. "Introduction: From Sunningdale to Belfast, 1973–98." In *Peace at Last: The Impact of the Good Friday Agreement on Northern Ireland?* edited by Jorg Neuheiser and Steffan Wolff, 1–24. New York: Berghahn Books, 2002.

Dissertations

Dalhouse, Mark Taylor. "Bob Jones University and the Shaping of Twentieth-Century Separatism 1926–1990," PhD diss., Miami Univ., Oxford, OH, 1991.

MacIver, Martha Abele. "Militant Protestant Political Ideology: Ian Paisley and the Reformation Tradition." Ph.D. diss., Univ. Of Michigan, 1984.

Southern, Neil. "The Democratic Unionist Party and the Politics of Religious Fundamentalism." PhD diss., Queen's Univ., Belfast, 2000.

Stackhouse, John Gordon, Jr. "Proclaiming the Word of God: Canadian Evangelicalism since World War I." PhD diss., Univ. of Chicago Divinity School, 1987.

Stroman, John Albert. "The American Council of Christian Churches: A Study of Its Origin, Leaders, and Characteristic Positions." PhD diss., Boston Univ. School of Theology, 1966.

Index